NT AND STONE IN THE NEOLITHIC PERIOD

AL

The Univers

This volume in the Neolithic Studies Group Seminar Papers series is dedicated to

Frances Healy

in recognition of her career-long contribution to Neolithic artefact studies in the UK

Flint and Stone in the Neolithic Period

Neolithic Studies Group Seminar Papers 11

Edited by

Alan Saville

Oxbow Books
Oxford and Oakville

Neolithic Studies Group Seminar Papers
Series Editor: Timothy Darvill

Published by
Oxbow Books, Oxford, UK

© Oxbow Books and the authors, 2011

ISBN 978-1-84217-420-3

This book is available direct from:

Oxbow Books, Oxford, UK
(Phone: 01865-241249; Fax: 01865-794449)

and

The David Brown Book Company
PO Box 511, Oakville, CT 06779, USA
(Phone: 860-945-9329; Fax: 860-945-9468)

or from our website

www.oxbowbooks.com

A CIP record for this book is available from the British Library

Library of Congress Cataloging-in-Publication Data

Flint and stone in the neolithic period / edited by Alan Saville.
  p. cm. -- (Neolithic studies group seminar papers 11)
Includes bibliographical references.
ISBN 978-1-84217-420-3
1. Neolithic period--Great Britain. 2. Tools, Prehistoric--Great Britain. 3. Stone implements--Great
Britain. 4. Flint implements--Great Britain. 5. Great Britain--Antiquities. I. Saville, Alan.
GN776.22.G7F57 2012
936.1--dc23

2011031282

Cover image: Unpolished Neolithic flint axehead dredged from the seabed in outer Loch Indaal, off Islay, Inner Hebrides, in 2001. The axehead is of Antrim flint, now densely stained from its seabed context, and with one face retaining traces of marine life, including keel-worm casts. (Photo: Trustees of the National Museums of Scotland)

Printed in Great Britain by
Hobbs the Printer, Totton, Hampshire

Foreword

This book presents the proceedings of a seminar organized by the Neolithic Studies Group (NSG), working in association with the Lithic Studies Society, and forms part of an ongoing series of NSG seminar papers. The NSG is an informal organization comprising archaeologists with an interest in Neolithic archaeology. It was established in 1984 and has a large membership based mainly in the UK and Ireland, but also including workers from the nations of the Atlantic seaboard. The annual programme includes two or three meetings spread throughout the year and includes seminars held in London and field meetings at various locations in north-west Europe.

Membership is open to anyone with an active interest in the Neolithic in Europe. The present membership includes academic staff and students, museums staff, archaeologists from government institutions, units, trusts and amateur organizations. There is no membership procedure or application forms and members are those on the current mailing list. Anyone can be added to the mailing list at any time, the only membership rule being that names of those who do not attend any of four consecutive meetings are removed from the list (in the absence of apologies for absence or requests to remain on the list).

The Group relies on the enthusiasm of its members to organize its annual meetings and the two co-ordinators to maintain mailing lists and finances. Financial support for the group is drawn from a small fee payable for attendance of each meeting.

Anyone wishing to contact the Group and obtain information about forthcoming meetings should contact the co-ordinators at the following addresses:

TIMOTHY DARVILL
School of Applied Sciences
Bournemouth University
Poole
Dorset BH12 5BB

KENNETH BROPHY
Department of Archaeology
University of Glasgow
Glasgow
G12 8QQ

Alternatively visit the NSG website: http://www.neolithic.org.uk/

Contents

Preface and acknowledgements

This volume arises from the autumn meeting of the Neolithic Studies Group, held at the British Museum in London on Monday 7 November 2005. The conference, entitled 'Flint and Stone in the Neolithic Period', was arranged in association with the Lithic Studies Society, and was designed to reflect some of the range and high quality of studies currently being focused on the lithic artefacts of this period and their analysis and interpretation.

Not all of the speakers on the day have been able to submit papers, some have submitted papers on different topics than those on which they spoke, and other papers have been solicited to expand the volume. My concern that the theme of the meeting might be too specialist for engagement by the wider Neolithic community was thankfully allayed by the size and enthusiasm of the audience at the British Museum.

The specific 'manifesto' which accompanied the initial call for papers read as follows:

Artefacts of flint and stone have tended to play second fiddle to ceramics as soon as the latter appear in the archaeological record. Yet it is abundantly clear that, both in terms of everyday practical use and also in ritual and symbolic mode, lithic artefacts were just as vital a part of Neolithic life. Neolithic people had the knowledge to locate and exploit all kinds of lithic raw materials, and the craft-skill to work those materials to create functional tools and objects of great beauty. Consideration of struck lithic artefacts is often dominated by rich flint assemblages from classic zones such as Wessex in southern Britain, but to what extent do these provide a blueprint for areas where the Neolithic is less well documented, particularly those regions where flint is not the dominant raw material? And how does the British and Irish evidence for the use of flint and stone compare with that in other parts of western and northern Europe? This meeting offers the opportunity to take stock of the current state of knowledge, to consider case studies on particular implement types and raw materials, and to have progress reports on current work and new discoveries.

The success of the meeting can now be judged on the basis of this volume which represents its permanent outcome. I am very grateful to all the speakers and contributors for their papers, and (especially in some cases) for their very considerable patience and forbearance while the volume was in its long preparation, though it must be stressed that the opportunity has been taken by all authors to update their papers prior to publication. Tim Darvill and Kenny Brophy administered and publicized the meeting on behalf of the Neolithic Studies Group and Caroline Wells publicized the meeting via the Lithic Studies Society. Gill Varndell very kindly organized all the arrangements for holding the meeting at the British Museum. At Oxbow I thank Clare Litt for her guilt-inducing reminders and her and her colleagues, especially Sam McLeod, for seeing the volume so successfully through the press.

Alan Saville
Edinburgh
April 2010

List of Contributors

TORBEN BJARKE BALLIN
Lithic Research, Banknock Cottage
Denny, Stirlingshire, FK6 5NA
Scotland, UK
email: lithicresearch@btinternet.com

NIGEL BLACKAMORE
Brecknock Museum
Captain's Walk, Brecon
Powys, LD3 7DW
Wales, UK
email: nigel.blackamore@powys.gov.uk

CLIVE JONATHON BOND
Department of Archaeology
Faculty of Humanities & Social Sciences
University of Winchester, West Hill
Winchester, Hampshire, SO22 6HY
England, UK
email: clivejbond@aol.com

MEGAN BRICKLEY
Faculty of Social Sciences
McMaster University, 1280 Main Street West
Hamilton, Ontario, L8S4L8
Canada
email: brickley@mcmaster.ca

STEVE BURROW
Department of Archaeology & Numismatics
Amgueddfa Cymru – National Museum Wales
Cathays Park, Cardiff, CF10 3NP
Wales, UK
email: steve.burrow@museumwales.ac.uk

BENJAMIN TUN-YEE CHAN
Department of Archaeology
University of Sheffield, Northgate House
West Street, Sheffield, S1 4ET
England, UK
email: b.chan@sheffield.ac.uk

DIANA COLES
2 Tompion House, Percival Street
London, EC1 0HU
England, UK
email: dianacoles@bevars.co.uk

DAVID FIELD
English Heritage, Kemble Drive
Swindon, Wiltshire, SN2 2GZ
England, UK
email: david.field@english-heritage.org.uk

FRANÇOIS GILIGNY
Université Paris 1 Panthéon-Sorbonne
UFR d'Histoire de l'art et d'archéologie
3 rue Michelet, 75006 Paris
France
email: francois.giligny@univ-paris1.fr

ELIZABETH HEALEY
School of Arts, Histories and Cultures
Mansfield Cooper Building
University of Manchester
Oxford Road, Manchester, M13 9PL
England, UK
elizabeth.healey@manchester.ac.uk

HEATHER JACKSON
Department of Geology
Amgueddfa Cymru – National Museum Wales
Cathays Park, Cardiff, CF10 3NP
Wales, UK
email: heather.jackson@museumwales.ac.uk

STEPHANY LEACH
Centre for Forensic Science
School of Applied Sciences
Bournemouth University, Fern Barrow
Poole, Dorset, BH12 5BB
England, UK
email: sleach@bmth.ac.uk

ROY LOVEDAY
School of Archaeology and Ancient History
University of Leicester, University Road
Leicester, LE1 7RH
England, UK
email: royloveday@spinneylodge.fsnet.co.uk

AMELIA PANNETT
Archaeology Wales Ltd, Pen-y-Parc Cottage
Malthouse Lane, Llantarnam
Cwmbran, NP44 3EE
Wales, UK
email: amelia@arch-wales.co.uk

ALAN SAVILLE
Archaeology Department
National Museums Scotland
Chambers Street, Edinburgh, EH1 1JF
Scotland, UK
email: a.saville@nms.ac.uk

MARTIN SMITH
Centre for Forensic Science
School of Applied Sciences
Bournemouth University, Fern Barrow, Poole
Dorset, BH12 5BB
England, UK
email: mjsmith@bmth.ac.uk

PETER TOPPING
English Heritage
Bessie Surtees House, 41-44 Sandhill
Newcastle upon Tyne, NE1 3JF
England, UK
email: Pete.Topping@english-heritage.org.uk

CHRISTINA TSORAKI
Department of Archaeology
University of Sheffield
Northgate House, West Street
Sheffield, S1 4ET
England, UK
email: Christina.Tsoraki@sheffield.ac.uk

PAUL WHEELER
8 Damask Close
Tring
Hertfordshire, HP23 5UA
England, UK
email: pabs42@hotmail.com

Chapter 1

Neolithic lithic studies: what do we know, what do we want to know?

Alan Saville

INTRODUCTION

Both in terms of everyday practical use and in ritual/symbolic mode we deduce that lithic artefacts were an intrinsic part of Neolithic life. As archaeologists and prehistorians studying the Neolithic period we are obliged to take due cognizance of this, and accordingly we strive to maximize relevant data recovery and subsequently to exploit the available data to the full. Fulfilling these ambitions requires specialist input, which not only comes from lithic analysts themselves, but also draws on a wide range of expertise from across archaeology and other disciplines and practices. The chapters in this volume demonstrate some of the diverse approaches and applications, both direct and theoretical, which are contributing towards our ultimate goal of allowing increased understanding of stone tools to reveal more about Neolithic life.

In this introductory chapter I review aspects of the past and present state of Neolithic lithic studies in the UK, looking at how we got to where we are and offering some thoughts on where we might be going, or want to go, in the near future. Inevitably this will be a selective overview of what is now a wide field of study with its own considerable body of literature, often obscurely published, but it may provide an appropriate *amuse-bouche* or *hors-d'oeuvre* for the chapters to follow. If nothing else, the deliberately extensive bibliography attached to this chapter will showcase the amount of work which has been achieved and will furnish a useful literature quarry for neophyte lithic analysts.

THE BACKGROUND TO WHAT WE KNOW NOW

Any look back over the field of lithic studies in the UK will inevitably begin with John Evans's masterwork, *The Ancient Stone Implements, Weapons and Ornaments, of Great Britain*, first published in 1872 and then definitively in an expanded second edition in 1897. Evans was not the first to consider Neolithic stone tools in Britain and Ireland (that distinction probably rests with Wilde and his Irish catalogue of 1857), but Evans was the first to systematically group and comprehensively describe them – with exquisite woodcut illustrations – in such a way that his volumes are still used today as an initial reference point for many implement categories (see Roberts and Barton 2008). At around the same time in Scotland one could point to the work of Joseph Anderson (e.g. 1886; Anderson and Black 1892; see Clarke

2002) and in Ireland to that of W. G. Knowles (e.g. 1893; 1898; 1903; see Woodman *et al.* 2006) as important developmental planks in the study of Neolithic stone tools; and the later 19th and early 20th centuries did indeed witness a plethora of lithic artefact notes and papers in magazines and journals, especially in the *Proceedings of the Prehistoric Society of East Anglia* (the Society was founded in 1908).

In the period between the two World Wars significant attention was focused on particular tool types, for example by Reginald Smith (1927) on arrowheads and most significantly by Grahame Clark on discoidal knives (1929), 'sickle blades' (1932), and transverse arrowheads (1934). Many authors were also already using stone tools as a major component in accounts of regional prehistory (e.g. Curwen 1937a; Elgee 1930; Hawkes 1939; Oakley *et al.* 1939). In strictly Neolithic terms, however, the use of stone tools as an integral part of constructing the archaeological story of the period came of age in Britain, and in a sense reached its apogee, with Stuart Piggott's *Neolithic Cultures* of 1954. As well as the lithic tool-kit being one of the defining elements of the Windmill Hill Culture, lithic artefacts were crucial in the definition of Piggott's Secondary Neolithic. One feels that Piggott was not particularly interested in stone tool technology as such, but utilized typology and association to great effect in seeing lithic artefacts as cultural markers or packages to underpin his reconstruction of this phase of prehistory.

The modern modes of lithic assemblage analysis and presentation for the British Neolithic began to emerge soon after Piggott's volume. The Hurst Fen, Suffolk, report (Clark and Higgs 1960) – although extending the typological work summarized by Piggott – demonstrated a new interest in assemblage analysis, in raw material quantification, and in the statistical analysis of metrical criteria. The latter aspect, undertaken by Eric Higgs on the large sample of scrapers available from Hurst Fen, took the form of a simple length and breadth analysis to show the preferred size. The length and breadth profiles of the Hurst Fen scrapers were then compared with those taken from samples of other Early/Middle Neolithic scrapers from Abingdon and Windmill Hill and Early Bronze Age scrapers from Peacock's Farm and Plantation Farm. The fact that the Neolithic scrapers were all comparable in size range, and distinctly larger in the main than the Early Bronze Age scrapers, led to the conclusion that this denoted 'cultural bias' and that size alone could be used to differentiate between quite small samples of this tool type from sites in the East Anglian Fens and probably further afield. This was a critical moment. The Hurst Fen report is silent on why it was decided to apply metrical analysis in this way; perhaps it derived from Higgs's experience of working with Charles McBurney on Palaeolithic assemblages (and Angela Mace (1959) had published length and breadth flake data from her Hengistbury Head Upper Palaeolithic site in the previous issue of *PPS*), or perhaps there was influence from the work of Bohmers with Neolithic material on the Continent (e.g. Bohmers 1956; Bohmers and Bruijn 1959).

Clark and Higgs were acknowledged for advising the Ozannes on the reporting of the Arreton Down Late Neolithic flint assemblage, which also used measurement data (Ozanne and Ozanne 1960), though it was definitely Bohmers whom Isobel Smith (1965, 89) credited as the source for her use of metrical analysis applied to flint industries in the *Windmill Hill and Avebury* monograph. Smith's seminal work which – along with the Hurst Fen report – was to become the standard reference point for lithic analysts in the UK until well into the 1980s and beyond, is still extensively quarried. Smith extended and refined the basic lithic typology for the Neolithic – then as now known primarily from Wessex – and further developed the statistical approach, applying length:breadth ratios to unretouched, utilized, and serrated flakes and applying new measures of thickness and angle of retouch to scrapers. By contrasting the unretouched flake dimensions from Windmill Hill with those of the Late Neolithic assemblage from the West Kennet Avenue, Smith (1965, 89) pointed to a marked shift towards broad, squat flakes in the latter, betokening a change of knapping technique. The scrapers from Windmill Hill and West Kennet Avenue could not be separated by length and breadth, but could by thickness and scraping angle (the latter being thinner and more steeply angled), though not so clearly as to allow sorting of the more than 1000 unstratified scrapers from Windmill Hill into earlier or later groups (Smith 1965, 95–96). As with the Early Bronze Age scrapers studied in the Hurst Fen report, however, Smith found that the Beaker-associated scrapers from Windmill Hill were markedly different by all measures because of their preferred small size, reflecting a distinctive flint-working tradition and specialized use adaptation (Smith 1965, 107). It has to be admitted, however, that thus far the ubiquitous Neolithic scraper has otherwise proved stubbornly resistant to the isolation of chronologically meaningful sub-types (Pollard 1999, 335–336; Riley 1990).

Another noteworthy aspect of the Windmill Hill report was the careful attention paid to the non-flint lithic finds, including stone implements, querns, rubbers, and carved chalk. In this chapter I am focusing on flaked stone, but in passing it is important to note some of the advances which have been made over the years in the study of Neolithic perforated stone tools, so-called 'coarse stone tools', and other related types of stone artefacts. Sian Rees's (1986) report on the stone tools from the Scord of Brouster site on Shetland gave a Neolithic context to some of the tool types – such as ard-points – which she had previously studied generically (Rees 1979); and Ann Clarke, the author of numerous specialist reports, has recently published an overview of the range of Neolithic coarse stone tools found in the far north of Britain (Clarke 2006). The late Dorothy Marshall's (1977; 1983) study of Scotland's carved stone balls has not been superseded, though there is now a pressing need for an updated inventory. Gillian Varndell (1991) has produced a comprehensive account of the worked chalk (Neolithic and Bronze Age) from Grimes Graves. Perforated stone tools have been studied particularly by Fiona Roe (1968; 1979; Roe and Radley 1968) and the late Derek Simpson (1998; 1989; 1996; Simpson and Ransom 1992). For Neolithic querns the classic study remains that of Curwen (1937b; 1941), but recent detailed considerations can be found in Buckley and Ingle (2001) and Roe (2008; 2009), while the concept of funerary querns has been considered in Ireland (McQuillan and Logue 2008). Roe (2008, 638) also considers axehead-polishers (*polissoirs*) in light of the portable example from Hambledon Hill, Dorset; and one could add the early discoveries of an example together with a stone axehead at Stoneykirk, Dumfries and Galloway (Wilson 1881, 253, fig. 1), and another associated with six axeheads at Culbane in the north of Ireland (Knowles 1912, 219; Raftery 1951, fig. 72). Woodward *et al.* (2006) have published a preliminary paper on their project to study stone 'archer's' bracers from Britain.

Stone implement studies, in the sense of petrological classifications of rock types and the identification of 'axe-factories', were among the early triumphs of lithic analysis in the UK, as has conveniently been summarized by Grimes (1979), and they came of age with the first *Stone Axe Studies* volume (Clough and Cummins 1979). Capitalizing on and consolidating initial successes has not been so easy. The second *Stone Axe Studies* volume

(Clough and Cummins 1988) now seems to have represented an intermediate peak beyond which the informal collegiate infrastructure supporting such studies in Britain has found it difficult to climb (see Edmonds 1989; Kinnes 1989). Individual targeted research in this field has proved much more successful (e.g. Bradley and Edmonds 1993; Bradley and Suthren 1990; Edmonds *et al.* 1992; Ixer *et al.* 2004; and see especially Fenton 1984; 1988, albeit on Bronze Age stone implements), but doubts have lingered about aspects of the scientific and interpretative underpinnings (Berridge 1994; Briggs 1989; 1990; Williams-Thorpe *et al.*1999, 235–237). As new techniques and equipment for raw material characterization have developed (e.g. Curran *et al.* 2001; Jones and Williams-Thorpe 2001; Mandal 1997; Mandal and Cooney 1997; Shackley 2008; Williams-Thorpe *et al.* 2003) an Irish project (Cooney and Mandal 1998) and now various Continental ones (e.g. Pétrequin *et al.* 2006; 2008) have rather changed the rules of the game and UK workers have yet to fully catch up. Typological studies of axeheads have progressed to a certain extent (e.g. Chappell 1987; Howell 1981; Pailler and Sheridan 2009, 44–46; Pétrequin *et al.* 2008; Pitts 1996; Sheridan *et al.* 1992), but would definitely benefit from the availability of more corpora of UK axehead finds (e.g. Adkins and Jackson 1978; Field and Woolley 1984; Tyler 1976; Williams 1970).

In many ways typological and technological studies of flaked Neolithic lithic artefacts in Britain did not advance rapidly beyond those in the Windmill Hill monograph in terms of the way most flint assemblages were reported. Isobel Smith's approach very much underlay my own work in the 1970s and 1980s on the large Neolithic collections from Carn Brea, Grimes Graves, and Hambledon Hill (Saville 1981a; 1981b; 2008a) and this can be seen in many other reports of the period (e.g. Bradley, Richard 1970; Wainwright 1972; cf. Brown 1995a). Nevertheless, several variations on the method of data presentation were introduced, for example Martin Bell's (1977) use of a scatter diagram for length/breadth analysis and pie-charts for depicting assemblage compositions.

On the technological front Mike Pitts, in a series of influential papers (Pitts 1978a; 1978b; Pitts and Jacobi 1979), applied multivariate analysis to the metrics of Smith and others and developed a general model for a chronological trend through the Neolithic towards broader flakes and, as he saw it, less structured core preparation and reduction. Perhaps because of lack of expertise and computer access/software at the time, or perhaps because it was felt the point had been made, few other lithic analysts in the UK pursued multivariate analyses (Burton 1980 and Green 1980 were two of the exceptions), but they did continue amassing the basic length:breadth statistics (e.g. Bamford 1985; Healey and Green 1984; Healey and Robertson-Mackay 1983; 1987) as well as bringing in other elements of quantified characterization such as butt type and hinge fracturing (e.g. Healy 1993a, fig. 33). On the whole, however, over the years curiously little attention has been paid to specific technological aspects of Neolithic flintworking in Britain since the papers by Burton (1980) and Gingell and Harding (1981). Perhaps a return in this regard is marked by the recent work of Jon Humble (2006), who has applied an extended list of attributes during analysis of the fieldwalked assemblages from the Raunds Area Project. Whether this is actually appropriate or helpful for the type of fieldwalked material involved, and indeed whether the analysis can in due course be correlated with the excavated assemblages from the same project, remains to be seen and evaluated.

Flint arrowheads are one of the few individual categories of Neolithic lithic artefacts subjected to detailed scrutiny in recent times. Stephen Aldhouse-Green's PhD thesis, subsequently published as a two-volume monograph and also in handy summary form in *Lithics* (Green 1980; 1984), has yet to be emulated, though there have been some valuable local corpora (e.g. Richardson *et al.* 2002) and several other considerations of Neolithic arrowheads from other perspectives (e.g. Devaney 2005; Edmonds and Thomas 1987; Woodman *et al.* 2006). One of the many useful innovations stemming from Aldhouse-Green's study was the development, clarification, and simplification of Clark's (1934) *petit tranchet* derivative arrowheads into the chisel and oblique types, although it is interesting that recently several analysts have chosen to revert to the Clark typology on the grounds that Green's was over simplified (e.g. Humble 2006). Knowledge of Later Neolithic flintwork, of which the chisel and oblique arrowheads were a diagnostic type, had been advanced by the reports on assemblages from Clacton (Longworth *et al.* 1971), Durrington Walls (Wainwright and Longworth 1971), Mount Pleasant (Wainwright 1979), and elsewhere, and by Terry Manby's (1974) monograph on lithic artefacts associated with Grooved Ware in northern England. These have been followed by the description and discussion of Later Neolithic assemblages from Newgrange in Ireland, with its oblique arrowheads and discoidal knives (Lahane 1983), and particularly from East Anglia by Frances Healy (1985; 1988; 1993a; 1993b), in which she used novel methods of presentation (e.g. Healy 1985, fig. 15) and incorporated the concept of a glossary defining the terms she was using in describing lithic material (e.g. Healy 1985, 201–203; 1993a, 39). The latter probably reflected the fact that Healy, along with other analysts in the Lithic Studies Society, had for many years been working on the compilation of a comprehensive glossary for postglacial lithic artefacts in Britain, something which regrettably never came to fruition and has now been abandoned (see Saville 2010). The aim of that project, to go beyond the then existing flintwork vade-mecums such as those by Pierpoint (1981), Pitts (1980), and Watson (1968), has not been met entirely by any subsequent publications, although Chris Butler's book (2005) goes some way towards filling the gap (cf. Saville 2005a).

Whenever excavation on Neolithic sites is undertaken, appropriate lithic artefact reports are normally included in the resulting final reports as standard practice (for a selection of examples in addition to those mentioned elsewhere in this chapter see Beadsmoore 2006; Bellamy 1997; Bellamy and Montague 2009; Bradley, P. 1999a; 1999b; Cotton 2008; Cramp 2007; Edmonds and Bellamy 1991; Garton 2009; Harding 1990a; 1995; Healey 2001; Middleton 1998; 2005; Pollard 1999; Saville 1990a; 2008a). Some archaeologists have felt that the traditional method of presenting specialist lithic artefact reports as separate and arguably relatively unintegrated parts of excavation reports is inadequate, and have experimented with various levels of integration (e.g. Barclay and Halpin 1999; Richards 2005). Problems arise, however, when the desire to assimilate lithic artefacts into the 'story' told by an excavation report leads to the exclusion of the basic data on which lithic analysts rely for inter-site assemblage comparison or individual artefact studies (e.g. Harding and Healy 2007; Lelong and MacGregor 2007). Directing researchers to the 'archive' (often locationally unspecified) is not an adequate publication strategy, and one wonders if the current trend for putting specialist reports on CDs/DVDs at the back of books is sensible; will these CDs shortly become as technologically redundant as the unlamented microfiche?

Apart from typology and excavated assemblage analysis, many other avenues for Neolithic lithic studies have opened up. One which became very popular in England in the late 1970s and 1980s (e.g. Field *et al.* 1987; Ford 1987a; Hall 1985; Holgate 1988; Richards

1990; Schofield 1987; 1991a; Shennan 1981; 1985; Tingle 1987; Woodward 1978a; 1978b) and is now a well-established and developed part of the archaeological tool-kit (e.g. Bradley, P. 1999b; Edmonds *et al.* 1999; Parry 2006; Passmore and Waddington 2009; cf. Bond this volume), is surface collection via fieldwalking. Surface prospection for lithic concentrations on arable land or at chance exposures elsewhere is a key method of site discovery and has in many cases led on to excavation. Exactly what lithic scatters mean for Neolithic activity and settlement, and how to deal with them in archaeological and heritage management terms, are nevertheless continuing conundrums (English Heritage 2000; Healy 1983; Schofield 1991b; 1994; Smith 2005; and see papers in the special lithic-scatters issue 19 of *Lithics* 1998; cf. Schofield 2000). Steve Ford's (1987b) approach to deciphering the chronological and functional status of field survey assemblages was aspirational and for a while very influential, but in retrospect was insufficiently objective in its criteria to provide a universal solution for temporal subdivision within the Neolithic beyond the trends already known (see above) or for identifying 'settlement' type. Similarly, optimism about the potential for use-wear of artefacts from surface collection has not entirely been fulfilled (Brown 1989; 1996).

Small samples of lithic artefacts recovered during evaluation have debatable value (Bradley, P. 1998), but large-scale lithic-scatter projects have enabled the specialists concerned to undertake more insightful studies (e.g. Clay 2002; Edmonds *et al.* 1999; Schofield 1991; cf. Chan this volume). And it is to be hoped that the accumulated residues from previous decades of fieldwalking surveys preserved in museums and private collections may one day get appropriate specialist attention, as well as appropriate long-term curation (Holgate 1994). Clearly it is impracticable for lithic specialists always to be involved directly in fieldwalking projects while they are taking place – and anyway such surveys are often non-period specific. However, unless an area of land is about to be destroyed by open-cast mining or some such large-scale development, 'non-pick-up' survey is becoming more common, which demands classification in the field and precludes subsequent analysis – a worrying trend.

Linked to the study of lithic scatters is the question of the value and usability of older collections of lithic material in museums or remaining in private hands, which have generally not been collected during organized field survey (Gardiner 1984; 1987a; 2001). The potential for these collections to make a contribution is limited by lack of available information on their actual existence, let alone their nature, especially when attached provenance details are sketchy. But when sympathetically analysed or catalogued and published (e.g. Burrow 2003; Healy 1996; Middleton 1990; 1992; Murray 2005; Saville 1973; Woodman *et al.* 2006), particularly when well illustrated, these collections provide valuable reference data and can be the starting point for further research. As more museums in the UK start to make their collection databases available publically on-line then it will at least be possible to discover more easily where assemblages are housed, but without specialist description it would not normally be feasible to determine their relevance for Neolithic studies without inspection in person.

Raw material analysis has already been mentioned in the context of stone axeheads, but it is a key aspect of struck lithic studies as well. The application of such analysis has been far more successful on the European mainland (e.g. Bostyn 1997; Högberg and Olausson 2007; Hughes *et al.* 2010; Ihuel 2004; cf. Giligny and Tsoraki this volume), and indeed on other continents, than it has been in Britain, despite investigation by techniques such as micropalaeontology (Brooks 1989; Harding *et al.* 2004). This is largely because of two main factors: non-diagnosticity and redeposition. In most of Britain, flaked lithic artefacts are dominated by those made of Cretaceous flint. On the one hand this flint is sufficiently uniform that it has for the most part resisted totally-reliable macroscopic discrimination and has thwarted detailed, localized scientific characterization, even when specific extraction locations are known (see discussion in Newberry 2002; Tingle 1998); on the other hand the geological history of Britain since the flint was formed has caused it to be widespread in secondary contexts, thus confusing potential source analyses (Bush and Sieveking 1987; Cowell and Bowman 1985; Ferguson 1980; Griffiths and Woodman 1987; cf. Healy 1989, 187–189). There are exceptions to this (e.g. Henson 1985; 1989), but they tend to prove the rule, such as when artefacts found in south-west Scotland and on Arran can be recognized as being of Antrim flint from north-east Ireland, since the additional attribute of size makes it clear they are not made from local coastal pebble flint (Saville 1999a).

Raw material studies have been more successful when applied to the few rarer, locationally specific types of flakeable stone (Healey this volume). Arran pitchstone is probably the best example so far of this application in the UK (Ballin 2009; cf. Coles this volume); its macroscopic distinctiveness has allowed its dispersal from Arran to be tracked as far as Ireland and Orkney. But pitchstone in the Neolithic was not an everyday, multi-purpose raw material like flint (at least not outside of Arran itself). In contrast to pitchstone, which still seems to have its origins on the Isle of Arran alone, Portland chert is no longer considered to have been exclusively derived from the Isle of Portland (Sharples 1991, 254). Rather, it is now seen to have had a wider distribution in pebble form and, on the evidence of some assemblages, to have been 'collected, brought to living sites, and worked together with local flint' (Healy 1997, 296). Although this may undermine the notion of Maiden Castle as a redistribution centre for Portland chert in the Neolithic (Care 1982, 282), it does not necessarily exclude the possibility that this chert sometimes had a value or significance as an exotic, perhaps particularly when used for arrowheads (Saville 2008a, 652, 696). A very different type of raw material, quartz, was used both as an everyday item in flaked form (e.g. at Scord of Brouster, Shetland; Ballin 2005) and in pebble form apparently for aesthetic purposes (e.g. Darvill 2002). Quartz and quartz artefacts have recently become the focus for increased attention in recognition of the fact that in certain areas it was in common usage (e.g. Ballin 2008; Bradley, Richard 1995; Driscoll and Warren 2007).

Refitting has now begun to be routinely considered when struck lithic assemblages are being investigated. Apart from being an obvious guide to whether or not a deposit is *in situ* and represents on-site knapping, refitting is a multi-faceted tool for investigating reduction methodology and other technological detail, raw material usage, and spatial intra-site and activity analysis. The value has long been recognized in Palaeolithic archaeology, but on any scale is a relatively new technique for the British Neolithic (see e.g. Beadsmore 2006; Bradley, P. 1999b; Brown 1991; Harding 1990b; 1990c; 1991; Saville 1990a; 2008a).

Use-wear and residue analysis have been relatively little exploited in the UK with respect to Neolithic tools. One of the earliest considerations was by Martin Bell (1977) in his report on the flint assemblage from a pit at Bishopstone, Sussex. Using low-power magnification he focused in particular on observing the edge-gloss on serrated-edge flakes – now recognized as a key tool-type for the British early/middle Neolithic – with accompanying artefact illustrations by Lysbeth Drewett on which the use-traces were shown by symbols. An early proponent of more fully-fledged microwear analysis was Rosemary Bradley (1981). In a subsequent study she examined 86 flints from Earlier Neolithic pits at Spong Hill (Bradley 1988). Bradley found that 11 had traces of use; seven of these were unretouched pieces, and only four of the eight retouched pieces had been used. Five pieces, including two scrapers, were interpreted as having been used to work wood; three for meat or fresh hide processing (including one scraper); one for cutting damp vegetable matter; and the remaining two had unknown use. Combined into Frances Healy's (1988) Spong Hill monograph, the results were presented in exemplary fashion with annotated drawings and photo-micrographs of the relevant microwear pieces. The same is true of Bradley's (1993) other major report on the flints from Tattershall Thorpe. Her report was written in 1982 (Bradley *et al.* 1993, xi), although not published until 1993, long after she had ceased working in this field and before the major crisis in confidence which beset British microwear studies (Donahue 1994; see also Grace 1996; Ibáñez and González 2003, 163; Van Gijn 2008a, 193).

Randy Donahue's (1994) overview of microwear research failed to reveal any other examples applied in Britain at that stage except his own work on a small sample of artefacts from Dragonby, the details of which were never fully published (May *et al.* 1996). In a subsequent review (Donahue and Burroni 2004), however, Donahue was able to report on a microwear analysis of 114 Middle and Late Neolithic flint artefacts from a site in Wales (Donahue 1999). This latter study is one of the more comprehensive to date on British Neolithic flints, but, apart from the fact that, as at Spong Hill, relatively few artefacts evidenced interpretable tool-use, it suffered from the fact that the location of the microwear traces was not indicated on the accompanying illustrations. Morris (1984) in a study (not mentioned by Donahue) of 26 flakes from the Sweet Track in the Somerset Levels was more successful in depicting the presence and location of use-traces on artefacts identified as wood-working and reed-cutting tools. This work further reinforced the message that it is unretouched artefacts which often functioned as tools, although Finlayson's (1999) analysis was able to conclude that the unretouched flakes contained within a cache of Neolithic flints found in south-west Scotland were largely unused. Linda Hurcombe (2008) has recently re-examined the Sweet Track flints for traces of basketry and cordage production and, in another example, Hurcombe (2001) undertook a detailed microwear study of the three blades from a presumptively Late Neolithic (burial?) pit at the centre of ring-ditch M at the Springfield cursus. All three showed signs of use and two had been hafted. More recently Bamforth (2006; Bamforth and Woodman 2004) has looked at Irish scrapers, including hollow scrapers on which the concave edges seem almost exclusively to be used for woodworking.

Donahue's most recently published report concerns a few artefacts from Willington, Derbyshire, and – given the very small number of other works which he and his co-author are able to reference – it is difficult to agree with their statement that '[l]ithic microwear analyses of artefacts from British Neolithic sites are no longer rare' (Donahue and Evans 2009, 114). I have elsewhere referred to use-wear analysis as '… an especially arcane pursuit, which suffers in particular from the difficulty of characterising use-wear effects in words in such a way as to enable general understanding and comparability between studies by different analysts' (Saville 2003a, 186–187). This was perhaps overcritical, and I return to this topic in a more positive manner below.

Experimental and replication studies relevant to Neolithic British and Irish lithic artefacts are best known in the case of axeheads (Coles 1979; Harding, P. 1987; Harding, A. and Young 1979; Mandal *et al.* 2004), although there is clearly potential and need for this to be done with all implement forms, especially in parallel with use-wear analyses. The efficacy of Neolithic flint and stone axeheads in working wood has of course been amply demonstrated by the tool-marked timbers recovered from the Somerset Levels and elsewhere (e.g. Coles and Orme 1985; Coles and Coles 1986; Taylor and Bradley 2007), and identification of woodworking is often the outcome of use-wear studies of other types of flaked stone artefact.

Studies of hoarding or caching of Neolithic stone artefacts have suffered from the fact that these are normally casual finds and have rarely been found in the course of archaeological excavation (the excavated cache from the Culbane stone circle is one exception: Yates 1985). Consequently the accounts of exactly what was found and of the contexts of the finds are often inadequate and confused, and the finds sometimes dispersed if not lost altogether (e.g. Robins 2002). The famous York hoard discovered in 1868 is a classic example where considerable doubt over its size and integrity remain (Clarke *et al.* 1985, 252–253 & fig. 5.9; Pitts 1996, 367; Radley 1967). Armstrong's (1918) and Smith's (1921) seminal papers on axehead hoards have been superseded for Britain at least by Pitts's (1996) summary and catalogue, in which he stresses the importance of being able to consider associated types, but much remains to be done on co-ordinating the many scattered accounts and unpublished discoveries (see Varndell 2004 for the important Great Baddow, Essex, hoard of axeheads associated with a discoidal knife; and Saville 1999a for the Auchenhoan, Kintyre, hoard of axeheads associated with numerous flake artefacts). Non-axehead hoards of lithic artefacts seem common in the flint-rich north of Ireland (Bamforth and Woodman 2004; Flanagan 1966; 1970; Woodman *et al.* 2006, 201–218), and the occurrence of two such hoards in south-west Scotland is likely to be a culturally related phenomenon (Saville 1999a). The rare examples of hoards known from the Scottish northeast (Callander 1917) and from Thetford, Norfolk (Robins 2002), may be connected with the proximity of those findspots to locations where large-scale Neolithic flint extraction was taking place.

Much of the work I have described thus far could be characterized as of a descriptive, analytical, investigative, or typological nature, but another important, interpretative strand of lithic studies began to emerge in the 1980s, along with the growth of theoretical developments in Neolithic studies in general (Bradley and Gardiner 1984a). The first major indication of this in Britain came with the volumes of papers edited by Bradley and Gardiner (1984b) and by Brown and Edmonds (1987), and the books by Robin Torrence (1986; 1989). In part the new approach can be characterized by Richard Bradley's statement that '[t]here can be little doubt that the study of lithic technology has moved from a descriptive phase to a greater concern with explanation' (Bradley 1987, 181). This development was received enthusiastically (e.g. Finlayson 1989; Schofield 1995) or more circumspectly (e.g. Saville 1987a; 1991) depending perhaps on one's position relative to post-processual trends in archaeology. In a sense this strand, which strives to locate lithic artefact data in a social context, reached a culmination with a series of volumes and papers by Mark Edmonds and colleagues in the 1990s (e.g. Bradley and Edmonds 1993; Brown 1991; 1995; Edmonds 1990; 1993a; 1993b; 1995; 1999; Edmonds and Richards 1998), which have defined much of the interpretative thinking about British Neolithic flint and stone tools up to the present.

Aspects such as movement and exchange of materials and objects, discard and deposition, ethnographic analogy, and specialist, gender and childhood/apprentice issues relating to tool manufacture and use continue to be explored, often taking inspiration from theoretical positions developed elsewhere in the social sciences. Surprisingly, given its popularity in interpretations of later prehistoric activity, votive deposition of lithic artefacts in the Neolithic period has rarely been broached (for an exception see Clare *et al.* 2002).

One of the – unfortunately relatively rare – occasions when the interests of everyone concerned with the British Neolithic coincide with those of specialists working on flint artefacts arises in the case of flint mines. The physical evidence for these remarkable industrial survivals from the 4th–3rd millennia cal BC has recently been comprehensively reviewed (Barber *et al.* 1999), and this has reinforced their key place in Neolithic studies. Inevitably, Grimes Graves, Norfolk, continues to loom largest in any consideration of flint mining and summaries of the long back-history of investigations at the site have been given by several workers, including Piggott (1954, 36–45), Mercer (1981, 1–8), and Sieveking (1979). The sheer volume of knapped debris recovered from any archaeological intervention at Grimes Graves provides an enormous challenge for lithic analysts, but a series of recent studies has been able to shift the focus in the perception of this and other Neolithic flint extraction sites as simply 'axe-factories' to centres of production for other types of implement such as discoidal knives and oblique arrowheads (Gardiner 2001; 2008; Healy 1991; 1998; Hearne 1991; Lech and Longworth 2000; 2006; Saville 1981b; 2005b; 2006a; 2008b). Archaeologists have also been looking into the ways in which the extraction and production activities at Grimes Graves and other extraction sites can be seen to have a much wider social significance than the crude economic models which previously prevailed (e.g. Field 1997; Topping 1997; 2004; 2005; and this volume).

Finally in this section it is interesting to consider the extent to which lithic studies impact on works of synthesis for the Neolithic period. Strictly speaking there has been no subsequent equivalent to Piggott's *Neolithic Cultures* (1954), but obviously all texts on British prehistory feature the Neolithic period to a lesser or greater degree. Textbooks in the 1970s were still much influenced by and indebted to Piggott's work, for example the chapters by Smith (1974) and Simpson (1979a; 1979b), of which only Simpson's carried any illustrations of Neolithic stone tools (and these were reproduced from *Neolithic Cultures*). Tim Darvill's (1987) book of a decade later also jumped a decade in taking as the source of his comparable illustrations Smith's *Windmill Hill*. It is unfair to criticize these and other general overviews for not including much detail, if any, about Neolithic stone tools, when there is so much else to describe in the way of monuments before considering portable material culture, and it should not surprise that it is axeheads and their origin and distribution which tend to dominate when stone tools are mentioned (e.g. Bradley, Richard 1978; 2007; Dyer 1990; Longworth *et al.* 1986; Parker Pearson 1993; Whittle 1999; 2009). In the main the conclusion must be that when writing these syntheses the authors either felt that stone tools were a minor aspect of the Neolithic story or, although recognizing their place within the contemporary material culture, they were unable to explain how and why they mattered.

Julian Thomas, though avowedly not writing a textbook (1999, xi) and albeit that his focus was primarily on Wessex rather than Britain as whole, did take some cognizance of lithic artefacts and he dealt with the question of lithic scatters and their implications

(Thomas 1991, 18; 1999, 18). But syntheses of the Neolithic period in various separate parts of the UK have also generally not featured lithic artefacts to any extent. Apart from considering axeheads, Grimes (1965) largely avoided stone tools from Wales, and more recently Frances Lynch (2000a, 54–59; 2000b, 110–111) has taken only a slightly broader view, and surprisingly commented that '[f]lint implements ... of the earlier Neolithic in Wales are neither common nor distinctive' (Lynch 2000a, 59). This conflicts somewhat with the stance taken by Savory (1980) in an earlier paper, where he attempted to plot the distribution of selected implement types including leaf-arrowheads; and even with Lynch's own study of Anglesey in which lithic artefacts featured prominently, and indeed with her Brenig report (Lynch 1993), which included a useful consideration of Neolithic flintwork by Elizabeth Healey (1993). A much more positive recognition of the importance of lithic finds was given by Peterson and Pollard (2004) from the perspective of Gwent, and Steve Burrow (2003) has now provided more comprehensive data for the whole of Wales which future synthesisers will be unable to ignore.

For Scotland, Atkinson (1962) featured lithic artefacts quite extensively and perceptively, for example when discussing polished flint knives, whereas, relatively speaking, Ashmore (1996) and Barclay (1997) paid them less attention, though acknowledging that Henshall's (1963; 1972) volumes already provided a comprehensive catalogue of lithic artefacts from Scottish Neolithic tombs. I have twice surveyed Scottish lithic artefact evidence in general, including that from the Neolithic period (Saville 1994; 2003b), but rather superficially so in the absence of much needed corpora for the non-tomb material (cf. Kinnes 1985, 24–25).

Piggott's *Neolithic Cultures* included Ireland but, because the text was essentially written by 1951 (Mercer 1998, 434), he does not mention Raftery's synthesis, which included the comment that '[a]part from the flints, relics of the period [Early Neolithic] are slight' (Raftery 1951, 70). Subsequent overviews of Irish prehistory have been able to contradict this, but have nevertheless given due consideration to stone tools (e.g. Herity and Eogan 1977; Mallory and McNeill 1991; O'Kelly 1989; Waddell 1998), though no lithic artefacts were figured by Harbison (1988) apart from the Knowth macehead and basin. Michael Ryan (1991) took a different approach and included a separate section on lithic artefacts in Irish prehistory (Anderson 1991), as well as having mention of stone tools in the specifically Neolithic sections of the volume. Given its range and perspective, Cooney and Grogan's (1994) prehistory found little space for stone tools, but in his more focused Neolithic volume Gabriel Cooney (2000) deliberately chose to concentrate on axeheads to the exclusion of other stone tools. Now perhaps, with the availability of works specifically on stone tools (Nelis 2004; Woodman *et al.* 2006), it will be much easier for authors of syntheses to expand their coverage.

WHAT DO WE WANT TO KNOW?

To say we want to know everything there is to know about, or that can be understood from, stone tools is the obvious answer to this question, and all I can hope to do here is point to what may be current areas of debate and perhaps fruitful ways forward in some areas of research. As an initial guide for this there is the research frameworks document prepared by the Lithic Studies Society (2004), which took the form of a series of questions about the lithic artefact resource. Those questions most specifically relevant to the Neolithic period could be summarized as concerning the following aspects: deposition, occupation events, residential composition, chronology, regionalization, visibility, specialization, recovery, usewear, residue analysis, mobility, sourcing, extraction sites, raw materials, curation and record, and education, and I will attempt to touch on at least some of these in this section.

Deposition has attracted most interest in the sense of investigating the evidence for and against 'structured deposition' of lithic artefacts. This topic has rather polarized analysts' opinions, between the proponents who see intentional structure in the positioning of most artefacts recovered from pits, ditches, bogs, rivers, etc, and the sceptics who are more inclined towards residuality and serendipity as explanations, except in obviously ritualized contexts such as burials. The structured deposition view, in terms of the British Neolithic, received its main initial boost from a paper discussing the distribution of all finds at the Durrington Walls henge monument in Wiltshire (Richards and Thomas 1984), and was further developed by others including Andy Brown (e.g. 1986; 1991). More recently the notion has been restated and expanded upon by many workers including Philippa Bradley (2004), Jan Harding (2006), and Hugo Lamdin-Whymark (2008). I have taken the contrary, or at least agnostic, view with regard to the lithic finds from causewayed enclosures (Saville 2002a), and feel strongly that the desire to see structured deposition has led archaeologists to push interpretation too far beyond the capacity of the data capture on most Neolithic sites. Just to make one observation – when arguing the case for structured deposition it is surely not enough simply to take at face value the reported contents of a particular feature or context without examining the condition and contemporaneity of the items involved (e.g. Garrow 2007). With the lithic contents of Neolithic pits, for example, such attributes as cortication, burning, raw material, refitting, technology, and micro-context of the artefacts, as well as their typology, should ideally be considered before drawing conclusions about their role in the infill formation process(es) or making comparisons with other pit contents. This would allow such factors as the differential biographies and residuality of lithic artefacts to be properly considered before incorporating them in over-arching explanations of Neolithic practice.

The same reservations need to be made, I believe, with regard to occupation events and residential composition, since the key to elucidating these factors lies in the quality of the information recovered during excavation and post-excavation. Can lithic artefacts help us to understand what happens where or when, can they indicate specific events and activity zones, and can these be pinpointed in time? Lithic artefacts can and should play a part in the higher-resolution appreciation of Neolithic settlement activity, but this will only be achieved with much improved recovery standards than currently apply in most excavations of Neolithic sites. If the same level of information is required of Neolithic lithic artefacts as for those of earlier periods, then they will have to be excavated with the same degree of attention as those on Palaeolithic and Mesolithic sites. This will apply to all spatial details of on-site recovery and post-excavation processing, with the metre-square as the minimum horizontal control, and including very close consideration of the formation processes involved in those contexts which encompass flint artefacts. In other words, if prehistorians want to use lithic artefact data to support high-level interpretation of various kinds of behavioural and social activity, including structured deposition, then the data will need to be acquired through high-definition, high-resolution archaeology (Gowlett 1997; and see other papers in the 29.2 (1997) issue of *World Archaeology*).

Currently one of the best examples of high-resolution archaeology permitting lithic artefact distributional data to play a key role in inferring a Neolithic event in the UK is the 'battle of Crickley Hill', where the concentrated distribution of leaf-shaped arrowheads at the entrances to this enclosure on the Cotswold scarp-edge in Gloucestershire has been seen as providing a credible story of attack and defence (Dixon 1988; Saville 2002a). Lithic distributional data could be equally valuable in relation to the definition of activity areas within and around house structures and domestic settlements; the problem here is that the archaeological evidence is usually only determined in terms of negative features in subsoil or bedrock after all superficial levels have been removed. If this removal was achieved by machine, as is often the case, then most of the potential lithic evidence in this regard will have been lost. Similarly, the full benefits of refitting can only be gained if there has been locational control over recovery in the field.

Other events – cases where lithic artefact evidence brings us close up with Neolithic individuals – are instanced by the examples of human skeletal remains which either retain actual implements lodged in the bones, or traces of wounds which lithic artefacts have inflicted (Smith *et al.* this volume), or other signs of tool-use affecting human bones (e.g. Smith and Brickley 2004). This is also the case with funerary evidence where individuals are buried with stone items as grave goods, perhaps the most evocative example of which in the British Neolithic record is the 'flintknapper' burial in the Hazleton North chambered long cairn in Gloucestershire (Saville 1990b, 263).

The contribution of lithic studies to Neolithic chronology, or indeed vice-versa, has been limited. I have discussed some aspects of this in more detail elsewhere and have highlighted the various difficulties which make it hard to pinpoint specific artefact types or technologies with any precise chronological parameters *within* the British Neolithic (Saville 2006b; 2008a, 733–735). In the absence of the kind of stratified sequences of Neolithic deposits available elsewhere in Europe (e.g. Perrin 2003), critical to progress in this regard will be the accumulation of lithic evidence throughout Britain from individual meaningful contexts with associated radiocarbon dates. There may actually be a number of relevant associations and dates already, but significant research input would be required to discover them from the literature (both the 'black-and-white' and the 'grey' kinds) and to correlate their implications; this is a priority. The problem may still remain that lithic technology during the Neolithic period in Britain appears in many respects remarkably conservative and homogenous, both temporally and spatially (Smith 1974, 105), but it should at least be possible to define some traits more closely than can be done at present. For example, when (and where) in the UK did transverse arrowheads become established? Even in the case of implement types such as polished stone axeheads and discoidal flint knives most of our chronological assumptions are based on very limited and debatable foundations (Gardiner 2008; Smith 1979; Varndell 2004), which currently are subject to re-evaluation with every newly dated example (e.g. the very early 4th millennium cal BC age for porcellanite axeheads in Ireland: Cooney 2008, 208). One way forward in this regard will be for in-depth studies of individual artefact types. The fashion for such studies has largely passed but, as the constant reference in flint reports to Grahame Clark's (1929; 1932; 1934) early publications shows, this type of work is an essential bedrock. Andy Brown's (1995b, 82–83) comments on laurel leaves, Frances Healy's (1982) on single-piece sickles, and Joshua Pollard's (1994) review of edge-polished blade knives are rare recent instances of focusing on a specific flint implement type, as is David Field's study of Seamer axeheads (this volume). Equally valuable is research which considers particular aspects of implement types, such as Daryl Garton's (1988) review of axehead reworking. That some of these studies are only local in scope, as in the case of Garton (1988), is a limitation, but they are of generic applicability and deserve emulation elsewhere.

Of real concern is the 'visibility' and retrievability of information on lithic artefacts and assemblages, and not just because of the 'grey' literature factor. Some sites known primarily for their pre- or post-Neolithic phases may also have produced significant Neolithic lithic assemblages, the reports on which tend to become forgotten because of the prominence of the main phases (e.g. Gardiner 1987b; Pieksma and Gardiner 1990; Saville 1987b; Young and Bevan 2000). Similarly many large-scale multi-phase archaeological projects may accumulate potentially important Neolithic artefact assemblages and/or associations, the account of which is given only summary treatment in the published report, is dispersed throughout a large report in such a way that it becomes difficult to get an overview, or is simply 'below the radar' for most archaeologists interested in stone tools (e.g. Cramp 2006; Durden 1999; Engl 2008; Guinan and Nolan 2007). Detailed regional syntheses will be required for the existence and value of such reports to emerge.

On the question of homogeneity, is it really correct to assume that the British Neolithic exhibits little in the way of regional lithic disparity? Convincing contrasts have been drawn between the lithic inventories in Yorkshire and southern England, especially for the Later Neolithic in terms of types which are special to, or more common in, the North (Durden 1995; 1996; Manby 1974; 1988; Manby *et al.* 2003; Pierpoint 1980). But Yorkshire Neolithic sites do have large lithic assemblages which can readily be compared and contrasted with those from southern England. The situation in other parts of Britain is generally one of much smaller assemblages, which complicates cross-comparison, although some analysts challenge this (Cooper 2009, 113). As for Scotland, the main contrast with the rest of the UK in terms of flaked stone seems to be the paucity of lithic artefacts found in Neolithic contexts, particularly on the mainland (Ballin 2006; Donnelly 2002; Sheridan and Sharples 1992, 7–8; Warren 2006; 2009); and sometimes this is in circumstances very hard to explain, as with the only seven lithic artefacts from the excavation of the large Neolithic structure at Claish, Stirling (Saville 2002b), or the 33 artefacts from the enclosure and pit site at Bannockburn, Stirling (Clarke 1997). This is not the case in the Northern Isles, where contrastingly large assemblages have been recovered from Neolithic sites on Orkney (Finlayson 2007) and Shetland (Ballin 2005), and so is not simply a question of access to raw material.

Given the widespread distribution of most Neolithic flint implement types, it still seems remarkable that Ireland has distinctive indigenous forms – such as the hollow scraper and the polished 'javelin-head' (Collins 1981; Herity 1987; Nelis 2004; Woodman 1992; 1994; Woodman *et al.* 2006) – which are not found elsewhere despite the contacts with the British mainland manifest in other aspects of material culture (e.g. Cooney 2000b, fig. 4). Looking at Neolithic stone tools as a whole, two of the most striking indications of regionality within the British mainland are provided by the polished stone knives of Shetland, which are found nowhere else (Ritchie 1968; cf. Ballin this volume); and by the carved stone balls predominantly from north-east Scotland (Marshall 1977), surely a sign of significant cultural difference and one which would not be apparent from the basic, and otherwise largely unexceptional, flaked lithic inventory (arrowheads etc.) in that area.

Regionality has become a topic of particular interest of late because of the archaeological resource assessment and research agenda exercises being undertaken across much of Britain. These almost uniformly point to the wealth of lithic evidence which has accumulated in museums, private collections, and the stores of commercial units, and bemoan the absence of analysis and synthesis which prevents exploitation of its potential. For example:

> *Lithic assemblages are widespread and, importantly, often recovered from lowland areas. Important collections are held in most local museums. Development-driven archaeology has also led to the collection of new assemblages. Both museum collections and more recently collected assemblages are poorly understood and require critical analysis and publication.* (Petts and Gerrard 2006, 127)

One laudable attempt to do this in the West Midlands discovered systemic problems in that research on what assemblages are available is handicapped by the inadequate data in county Sites and Monuments Records/Historic Environment Records (Barfield 2007). Inadequacy of information on lithic findspots or lithic finds from interventions of any kind is a difficulty for the national record databases, and is certainly a UK-wide problem for SMRs/HERs. The CARN database in Wales (http://carn.rcahmw.org.uk/), which has integrated numerous individual databases, including that of the National Museums of Wales, has marked a huge step forward in this regard, but comparable linkages for the whole of the UK and Ireland seem a long way off.

The late Lawrence Barfield's (2007, 106–107) ambitious proposals for the future research needed on lithic artefacts in the West Midlands bear repeating for their general relevance:

1. Detailed and consistent examination of existing collections. This should take into account multiple criteria, including manufacturing technology, raw material, and other aspects reviewed here, to enable a comparative review to be made.
2. Seminars for flint collectors, both amateur and professional, would be helpful as a way of explaining the purpose and potential of flint artefact studies, and to give encouragement and advice to non-professional collectors.
3. The study of raw materials using criteria such as colour, texture and cortex type may offer a means of sourcing lithic artefacts, and differentiating artefact categories and assemblage types more finely, in both typological and chronological terms. An archive of colour photographs of flint varieties and representative artefacts could be established, and disseminated digitally on the web or by CD, as part of this process.
4. Studies of *un-worked* flint in collection areas should be made in order to locate flint sources.
5. More systematic and extensive field collection is necessary in order to produce more meaningful distribution patterns, perhaps either parish-based or related to specific geological and/or geomorphological contexts.
6. Targeted excavation of flint artefact scatters at several spatial scales to establish more clearly the nature, spatial contexts and date of activities and forms of occupation represented in this kind of evidence.

As mentioned in the previous section, for various reasons use-wear studies in Britain – which anyway were focused more on periods earlier than the Neolithic – have not become a fully established part of the lithic analysis of Neolithic assemblages. This needs to change. Although it may never become routine – for example because assemblages are in an unsuitable condition, because their contexts are unsatisfactory, or on grounds of cost-benefit considerations – nevertheless it is clear from the advances made elsewhere in Europe that use-wear should be applied more widely. One only need reference the impressive body of work of Annelou van Gijn and her colleagues at Leiden on flaked artefacts (Van Gijn 1990; 1998; 2008a; 2008b; 2010; Van Gijn *et al.* 2001; 2006) and recently that of Caroline Hamon on macrolithic items (Hamon 2006; 2008) to demonstrate how British archaeology has fallen behind in use-wear analysis and to hope that existing initiatives (e.g. Evans and Donahue 2005; 2008) and facilities can be developed and resourced (e.g. www.brad.ac.uk/archenvi/research/microwear/; www.ucl.ac.uk/archaeology/facilities/laboratories/lithics.htm). As for experiment and replication, there are interesting signs in England of a developing popularization of 'knapping', which is no longer the sole preserve of the master knappers such as Phil Harding and John Lord (Bond 2002; 2003; Lord 1993), although so far this is on nowhere near the scale of knapping activity in France or the USA (Whittaker 2004).

Although residue analysis has progressed by leaps and bounds in recent years when applied to Neolithic ceramics, there are very few instances of its successful application to British Neolithic lithic artefacts (Cattaneo *et al.* 1994; Morris 1984; cf. Grace 1996, 213–216). As has recently been concluded:

> *stone artefacts, such as lithics, have yielded generally disappointing results from organic residues, except in cases where surface deposits are evident. The fundamental problem is the lack of protection offered to organic residues by non-porous minerals … [although] querns, grinding stones and other stone containers may be worthy of further consideration.* (Evershed 2008, 915)

Also perhaps this technique, whether to detect blood traces or other indicators, has not been considered to have much potential in the relatively harsh contextual conditions from which most UK Neolithic tools are recovered. However, the application of protein residue analysis in combination with use-wear study of a sample of Early Neolithic flint artefacts from a site in southern Sweden, which concluded that the tools were intended to process fish (Högberg *et al.* 2009), does suggest that residue analysis could in future become a very valuable part of the lithic studies tool-kit.

Typology and terminology, descriptive definition and rigorous classification; these have tended to slip from the forefront of concerns for lithic analysts in recent years. Yet, as Torben Ballin (2000) has shown, without a basically common language and methodology, lithic description and analysis are in danger of descending into a state of anarchy in which all lithic reports are *sui generis* and mostly incompatible (cf. Garton 1989). Andrefsky (2005, 245–251) has usefully summarized some of the problems involved and distinguishes between 'description' and 'analysis' (cf. Healy 1994), making the point that not all lithic assemblages will be capable of yielding relevant information or contributing to interesting archaeological questions. Without a readily comprehensible presentation of the basic 'facts' of an assemblage, however, other analysts or archaeologists are unable to assess the assemblage's significance and potential for further study. This also applies to illustration, the good quality of which is a *sine qua non* of adequate lithic reporting (Martingell and Saville 1988). Most of the same points I have made with regard to the value of illustration for Mesolithic artefacts apply equally to Neolithic finds (Saville 2009). But it is not just the technical, academic aspect of lithic illustration which demands close attention. As the *Symbols of Power* catalogue demonstrated so strikingly (Clarke *et al.* 1985; cf. Beuker 2010; Sheridan 2007), skilful colour photography can bring out the character and beauty of the lithic items we study in a way which can be appreciated by all and which serves to promote the case for lithic studies in general, as well as making us think about the relevance of colour and variegation in stone for Neolithic people (Cooney 2002; Saville 1999b).

Above all, the challenge for lithic studies in a Neolithic context is for them to become less niche, less ghetto-ized, and for them to be fully integrated in all aspects of archaeological thinking about the Neolithic. By this I am thinking not so much of the recognition of the wider conceptual relevance of stone in a generic sense for Neolithic society (e.g. Cooney 2008), but rather of lithic artefacts in their more prosaic role as items of everyday practical application for Neolithic people. Thus we need a return to the way in which authorities such as the late Stuart Piggott incorporated lithic artefacts, along with all other elements of material culture, so centrally within their concepts of the British Neolithic. To achieve this it is important that lithic analysts, alongside the inevitable detail of their reporting and the specialist vocabulary of their literature, also make the effort to synthesize and to offer their own views on the role which all aspects of activity involving lithic materials had within Neolithic society (cf. Kinnes 1994, 93).

BIBLIOGRAPHY

Adkins, R. and Jackson, R., 1978, *Neolithic Stone and Flint Axes from the River Thames*. London: British Museum.

Anderson, E., 1991, Flint and stone tools. In M. Ryan, *The Illustrated Archaeology of Ireland*, 35–38. Dublin: Country House.

Anderson, J., 1886, *Scotland in Pagan Times: The Bronze and Stone Ages*. Edinburgh: David Douglas.

Anderson, J. and Black, G. [published anonymously], 1892, *Catalogue of the National Museum of Antiquities of Scotland*. Edinburgh: Society of Antiquaries of Scotland.

Andrefsky, W. Jr., 2005, *Lithics: Macroscopic Approaches to Analysis*. Second edition. Cambridge: Cambridge University Press (Cambridge Manuals in Archaeology).

Armstrong, E. C. R., 1918, Associated finds of Irish Neolithic celts. *Proceedings of the Royal Irish Academy* 34 C, 81–95.

Ashmore, P. J., 1996, *Neolithic and Bronze Age Scotland*. London: Batsford / Historic Scotland.

Atkinson, R. J. C., 1962, Fishermen and farmers. In S. Piggott (ed.), *The Prehistoric Peoples of Scotland*, 1–38. London: Routledge and Kegan Paul.

Ballin, T. B., 2000, Classification and description of lithic artefacts: a discussion of the basic lithic terminology. *Lithics* 21, 9–15.

Ballin, T. B., 2005, *Re-examination of the Quartz Artefacts from Scord of Brouster: A Lithic Assemblage from Shetland and its Neolithic Context*. Scottish Archaeological Internet Reports 17 [http://www.sair.org.uk/sair17].

Ballin, T. B., 2006, Re-examination of the Early Neolithic pitchstone-bearing assemblage from Auchategan, Argyll, Scotland. *Lithics* 27, 12–32.

Ballin, T. B., 2008, *Quartz Technology in Scottish Prehistory*. Scottish Archaeological Internet Reports 26 [http://www.sair.org.uk/sair26].

Ballin, T. B., 2009, *Archaeological Pitchstone in Northern Britain: Characterization and Interpretation of an Important Prehistoric Source*. Oxford: British Archaeological Reports (British Series 476).

Bamford, H. M., 1985, The worked flints. In H. M. Bamford, *Briar Hill, Excavation 1974–1978*, 60–91. Northampton: Northampton Development Corporation (Archaeological Monograph No. 3).

Bamforth, D. B., 2006, A microwear analysis of selected artefacts. In P. Woodman, N. Finlay and E. Anderson, 2006. *The Archaeology of a Collection: The Keiller–Knowles Collection of the National Museum of Ireland*, 221–238. Bray: Wordwell.

Bamforth, D. B. and Woodman, P. C., 2004, Tool hoards and Neolithic use of the landscape in north-eastern Ireland. *Oxford Journal of Archaeology* 23(1), 21–44.

Barber, M., Field, D. and Topping, P., 1999, *The Neolithic Flint Mines of England*. Swindon: English Heritage.

Barclay, A. and Halpin, C., 1999, *Excavations at Barrow Hills, Radley, Oxfordshire. Vol. 1. The Neolithic and Bronze Age Monument Complex*. Oxford: Oxford Archaeological Unit (Thames Valley Landscapes Volume 11).

Barclay, G. J., 1997, The Neolithic. In K. J. Edwards and I. B. M. Ralston (eds), *Scotland: Environment and Archaeology, 8000 BC–AD 1000*, 127–149.

Barfield, L., 2007, Later lithics in the West Midlands counties. In P. Garwood (ed.), *The Undiscovered Country. The Earlier Prehistory of the West Midlands*, 97–108. Oxford: Oxbow Books.

Beadsmoore, E., 2006, Earlier Neolithic flint. In D. Garrow, S. Lucy and D. Gibson, *Excavations at Kilverstone, Norfolk: an Episodic Landscape History. Neolithic Pits, Later Prehistoric, Roman and Anglo-Saxon Occupation, and Later Activity*, 53–70, 215–228. Cambridge: Cambridge Archaeological Unit (East Anglian Archaeology Report No. 113).

Bell, M., 1977, Excavations at Bishopstone. *Sussex Archaeological Collections* 115, 1–299.

Bellamy, P., 1997, Flaked stone assemblages. In R. J. C. Smith, F. Healy, M. J. Allen, E. L. Morris, I. Barnes and P. J. Woodward, *Excavations Along the Route of the Dorchester By-pass, Dorset, 1986–8*, 136–154. Salisbury: Wessex Archaeology (Report No. 11).

Bellamy, P. S. and Montague, R., 2009, The flaked stone. In L. Ladle and A. Woodward, *Excavations at Bestwell Quarry, Wareham 1992–2005. Volume 1. The Prehistoric Landscape*: 154–199. Dorchester: Dorset Natural History and Archaeological Society (Monograph 19).

Berridge, P., 1994, Cornish axe factories: fact or fiction? In N. Ashton and A. David (eds), *Stories in Stone: Proceedings of Anniversary Conference at St Hilda's College, Oxford, April 1993*: 45–56. London: Lithic Studies Society (Occasional Paper No. 4).

Beuker, J., 2010, *Vuurstenen Werktuigen: Technologie op het Scherp van de Snede*. Leiden: Sidestone Press.

Bohmers, A., 1956, Statistics and graphs in the study of flint assemblages. *Palaeohistoria* 5, 1–5.

Bohmers, A. and Bruijn, A., 1959, Statistische und graphische Methoden zur Untersuchung von Flintkomplexen. IV. Das lithische Material aus den bandkeramischen Siedlungen in den Niederlanden. *Palaeohistoria* 6–7 (1958–59), 183–212.

Bond, C. J., 2002, Knapping techniques, manufacture and replication reconsidered. *Lithics* 23, 71–73.

Bond, C. J., 2003, Working stone in the past and the present. A report on the conference: Knapping Techniques, Manufacture and Replication Reconsidered. *Lithics* 24, 91–99.

Bostyn, F., 1997, Characterization of flint production and distribution of the tabular Bartonian flint during the Early Neolithic (Villeneuve-Saint-Germain period) in France. In R. Schild and Z. Sulgostowska (eds), *Man and Flint: Proceedings of the VIIth International Flint Symposium Warszawa – Ostrowiec Świętokrzyski, September 1995*, 171–183. Warszawa: Institute of Archaeology and Ethnology, Polish Academy of Sciences.

Bradley, P., 1998, Lithics from evaluations – help or hindrance? *Lithics* 19, 87–92.

Bradley, P., 1999a, Worked flint. In A. Barclay and C. Halpin, *Excavations at Barrow Hills, Radley, Oxfordshire. Vol. 1. The Neolithic and Bronze Age Monument Complex*: 211–228. Oxford: Oxford Archaeological Unit (Thames Valley Landscapes Volume 11).

Bradley, P., 1999b, The worked flint from the Dunn collection and the excavations. In A. Gibson, *The Walton Basin Project: Excavation and Survey in a Prehistoric Landscape 1993–7*, 49–80. York: Council for British Archaeology (Research Report 118).

Bradley, P., 2004, Causewayed enclosures: monumentality, architecture, and spatial distribution of artefacts – the evidence from Staines, Surrey. In J. Cotton and D. Field (eds), *Towards a New Stone Age: Aspects of the Neolithic in South-East England*, 115–123. York: Council for British Archaeology (Research Report 137).

Bradley, Richard, 1970, The excavation of a Beaker settlement at Belle Tout, East Sussex, England. *Proceedings of the Prehistoric Society* 36, 312–379.

Bradley, Richard, 1978, *The Prehistoric Settlement of Britain*. London: Routledge & Kegan Paul.

Bradley, Richard, 1995, Fieldwalking without flints: worked quartz as a clue to the character of prehistoric settlement. *Oxford Journal of Archaeology* 14(1), 13–22.

Bradley, Richard, 2007, *The Prehistory of Britain and Ireland*. Cambridge: Cambridge University Press.

Bradley, Richard and Edmonds, M., 1993, *Interpreting the Axe Trade: Production and Exchange in Neolithic Britain*. Cambridge: Cambridge University Press.

Bradley, Richard and Gardiner, J., 1984a, Introduction: closing doors and opening windows. In R. Bradley and J. Gardiner (eds), *Neolithic Studies: a Review of Some Current Research*, 1–3. Oxford: British Archaeological Reports (British Series 133).

Bradley, Richard and Gardiner, J. (eds), 1984b, *Neolithic Studies: a Review of Some Current Research*. Oxford: British Archaeological Reports (British Series 133).

Bradley, Richard and Suthren, R., 1990, Petrographic analysis of hammerstones from the Neolithic quarries at Great Langdale. *Proceedings of the Prehistoric Society* 56, 117–122.

Bradley, Rosemary, 1981, The low-power microwear analysis of the flaked stone pieces. In N. M. Sharples, The excavation of a chambered cairn, the Ord North, at Lairg, Sutherland by J X W P Corcoran. *Proceedings of the Society of Antiquaries of Scotland* 111, 45–47.

Bradley, Rosemary, 1988, Microwear analysis of struck flint from pits 3080, 3083, and 3087. In F. Healy, *The Anglo-Saxon Cemetery at Spong Hill, North Elmham, Part VI: Occupation during the Seventh to Second Millennia BC*, 36–39 and microfiche 2:B.2–C.13. Gressenhall: Norfolk Archaeological Unit (East Anglian Archaeology Report No. 39).

Bradley, Rosemary, 1993, The microwear analysis. In R. Bradley, P. Chowne, R. M. J. Cleal, F. Healy and I. Kinnes, *Excavations on Redgate Hill, Hunstanton, Norfolk, and at Tattershall Thorpe, Linclonshire*, 106–110. Gressenhall/Sleaford: East Anglian Archaeology Report No. 57.

Bradley, Rosemary, Chowne, P., Cleal, R. M. J., Healy, F. and Kinnes, I., 1993, *Excavations on Redgate Hill, Hunstanton, Norfolk, and at Tattershall Thorpe, Linclonshire*. Gressenhall/Sleaford: East Anglian Archaeology Report No. 57.

Briggs, C. S., 1989, Axe-making traditions in Cumbrian stone. *Archaeological Journal* 146, 1–43 and microfiche M1/01–09.

Briggs, C. S., 1990, Stone resources and implements in prehistoric Ireland: a review. *Ulster Journal of Archaeology* 51, 5–20.

Brooks, I. P., 1989, Debugging the system: the characterization of flint by micropalaeontology. In I. Brooks and P. Phillips (eds), *Breaking the Stony Silence: Papers from the Sheffield Lithics Conference 1988*, 53–71. Oxford: British Archaeological Reports (British Series 213).

Brown, A. G., 1986, Flint and chert small finds from the Somerset Levels: part 1, the Brue Valley. *Somerset Levels Papers* 12, 12–27.

Brown, A. [G.], 1989, Use-wear analysis of surface material – can it really be done? *Lithics* 10, 33–36.

Brown, A. [G.], 1991, Structured deposition and technological change among the flaked stone artefacts from Cranborne Chase. In J. Barrett, R. Bradley and M. Hall (eds), *Papers on the Prehistoric Archaeology of Cranborne Chase*, 101–133. Oxford: Oxbow Books (Monograph 11).

Brown, A. G., 1995a, Beyond Stone Age economics: a strategy for a contextual lithic analysis. In A. J. Schofield (ed.), *Lithics in Context: Suggestions for the Future Direction of Lithic Studies*, 27–36. London: Lithic Studies Society (Occasional Paper 5).

Brown, A. [G.], 1995b, The Mesolithic and later flint artefacts. In T. G. Allen, *Lithics and Landscape: Archaeological Discoveries on the Thames Water Pipeline at Gatehampton Farm, Goring, Oxfordshire 1985–92*, 65–84. Oxford: Oxford University Committee for Archaeology (Oxford Archaeological Unit Thames Valley Landscapes Monograph No. 7).

Brown, A. [G.], 1996, Appendix 3: use and non-use: aspects of the prehistoric exploitation of the fen-edge at Isleham. In D. Hall, *The Fenland Project, Number 10: Cambridgeshire Survey, The Isle of Ely and Wisbech*: 202–212. Cambridge: East Anglian Archaeology Report No. 79.

Brown, A. G. and Edmonds, M. R. (eds), 1987, *Lithic Analysis and Later British Prehistory: Some Problems and Approaches*. Oxford: British Archaeological Reports (British Series 162).

Buckley, D. G. and Ingle, C. J., 2001, The saddle querns from Flag Fen. In F. Pryor, *The Flag Fen Basin: Archaeology and Environment of a Fenland Landscape*, 322–328. Swindon: English Heritage.

Burrow, S., 2003, *Catalogue of the Mesolithic and Neolithic Collections in the National Museums & Galleries of Wales*. Cardiff: National Museums and Galleries of Wales.

Burton, J., 1980, Making sense of waste flakes: new methods for investigating the technology and economics behind chipped stone assemblages. *Journal of Archaeological Science* 7, 131–148.

Bush, P. R. and Sieveking, G. de G., 1987, Geochemistry and the provenance of flint axes. In G. de G. Sieveking and M. B. Hart (eds), *The Scientific Study of Flint and Chert. Proceedings of the International Flint Symposium Held at Brighton Polytechnic 10–15 April 1983*: 133–140. Cambridge: Cambridge University Press.

Butler, C., 2005, *Prehistoric Flintwork*. Stroud: Tempus.

Callander, J. G., 1917, A flint workshop on the Hill of Skares, Aberdeenshire. *Proceedings of the Society of Antiquaries of Scotland* 51 (1916–17), 117–127.

Care, V., 1982, The collection and distribution of lithic materials during the Mesolithic and Neolithic periods in southern England. *Oxford Journal of Archaeology* 1(3), 269–285.

Cattaneo, C., Gelsthorpe, K., Dixon, P., Gale, J, Phillips, P. and Sokal, R. J., 1994, Erratic survival: blood on stones. In N. Ashton and A. David (eds), *Stories in Stone: Proceedings of Anniversary Conference at St Hilda's College, Oxford, April 1993*: 24–27. London: Lithic Studies Society (Occasional Paper No. 4).

Chappell, S., 1987, *Stone Axe Morphology and Distribution in Neolithic Britain*. Oxford: British Archaeological Reports (British Series 177).

Clare, T., Clapham, A. J., Wilkinson, D. M. and Taylor, J. J., 2002, The context of the stone axes found at Portinscale and in the vicinity of the Castlerigg stone circle. Neolithic settlement sites or a case of votive offerings? *Archaeological Journal* 159, 242–265.

Clark, J. G. D., 1929, Discoidal polished flint knives – their typology and distribution. *Proceedings of the Prehistoric Society of East Anglia* 6, 40–54.

Clark, J. G. D., 1932, The curved flint sickle blades of Britain. *Proceedings of the Prehistoric Society of East Anglia* 7, 67–81.

Clark, J. G. D., 1934, Derivative forms of the *petit tranchet* in Britain. *Archaeological Journal* 91, 32–58.

Clark, J. G. D. and Higgs, E. S., 1960, Flint industry. In J. G. D. Clark, E. S. Higgs and I. H. Longworth, Excavations at the Neolithic site at Hurst Fen, Mildenhall, Suffolk (1954, 1957 and 1958). *Proceedings of the Prehistoric Society* 26, 214–226.

Clarke, A., 1997, Stone artefacts. In J. S. Rideout, Excavation of Neolithic enclosures at Cowie Road, Bannockburn, Stirling, 1984–5. *Proceedings of the Society of Antiquaries of Scotland* 127, 48–51.

Clarke, A., 2006, *Stone Tools and the Prehistory of the Northern Isles*. Oxford: British Archaeological Reports (British Series 406).

Clarke, D. V., 2002, 'The foremost figure in all matters relating to Scottish archaeology': aspects of the work of Joseph Anderson (1832–1916). *Proceedings of the Society of Antiquaries of Scotland* 132, 1–18.

Clarke, D. V., Cowie, T. G. Cowie and Foxon, A. 1985, *Symbols of Power at the Time of Stonehenge.* Edinburgh: HMSO.

Clay, P., 2002, *The Prehistory of the East Midlands Claylands: Aspects of Settlement and Land-Use from the Mesolithic to the Iron Age in Central England.* School of Archaeology and Ancient History, University of Leicester (Leicester Archaeology Monographs No. 9).

Clough, T. H. McK. and Cummins, W. A., 1979, *Stone Axe Studies. Archaeological, Petrological, Experimental and Ethnographic.* London: Council for British Archaeology (Research Report 23).

Clough, T. H. McK. and Cummins, W. A., 1988, *Stone Axe Studies. Volume 2. The Petrology of Prehistoric Stone Implements from the British Isles.* London: Council for British Archaeology (Research Report 67).

Coles, B. [J.] and Coles, J. [M.], 1986, *Sweet Track to Glastonbury: The Somerset Levels in Prehistory.* London: Thames and Hudson.

Coles, J. [M.], 1979, An experiment with stone axes. In T. H. McK. Clough and W. A. Cummins (eds), *Stone Axe Studies. Archaeological, Petrological, Experimental and Ethnographic*: 106–107. London: Council for British Archaeology (Research Report 23).

Coles, J. M. and Orme, B. J., 1985, Prehistoric woodworking from the Somerset Levels: 3. roundwood. *Somerset Levels Papers* 11, 25–50.

Collins, A. E. P., 1981, The flint javelin heads of Ireland. In D. Ó Corráin (ed.), Irish *Antiquity. Essays and Studies Presented to Professor M. J. O'Kelly*, 111–133. Cork: Tower Books.

Cooney, G., 2000a, *Landscapes of Neolithic Ireland.* London: Routledge.

Cooney, G., 2000b, Recognising regionality in the Irish Neolithic. In A. Desmond, G. Johnson, M. McCarthy, J. Sheehan and E. Shee Twohig (eds), *New Agendas in Irish Prehistory: Papers in Commemoration of Liz Anderson*, 49–65. Bray: Wordwell.

Cooney, G., 2002, So many shades of rock: colour symbolism and Irish stone axeheads. In A. Jones and G. MacGregor (eds), *Colouring the Past: the Significance of Colour in Archaeological Research*, 93–107. Oxford: Berg.

Cooney, G., 2008, Engaging with stone: making the Neolithic in Ireland and Western Britain. In H. Fokkens, B. J. Coles, A. L. Van Gijn, J. P. Kleijne, H. H. Ponjee and C. G. Slappendel (eds), *Between Foraging and Farming: An Extended Broad Spectrum of Papers Presented to Leendert Louwe Kooijmans*: 203–214. Leiden: Leiden University (*Analecta Praehistorica Leidensia* 40).

Cooney, G. and Grogan, E., 1994, *Irish Prehistory: A Social Perspective.* Bray: Wordwell.

Cooney, G. and Mandal, S., 1998, *The Irish Stone Axe Project: Monograph 1.* Bray: Wordwell.

Cooper, L., 2009, The lithics. In M. G. Beamish, Island visits: Neolithic and Bronze Age activity on the Trent Valley floor. Excavations at Egginton and Willington, Derbyshire, 1998–1999. *Derbyshire Archaeological Journal* 129, 107–113.

Cotton, J., 2008, The struck and burnt flint. In P. Jones, *A Neolithic Ring Ditch and Later Prehistoric Features at Staines Road Farm, Shepperton*, 37–54. Woking: Spoilheap Publications (Monograph 1).

Cowell, M. R. and Bowman, S. G. E., 1985, Provenancing and dating of flint. In P. Phillips (ed.), *The Archaeologist and the Laboratory*, 36–40. London: Council for British Archaeology (Research Report 58).

Cramp, K., 2006, Flint. In L. Brown, J. Lewis and A. Smith (eds), *Landscape Evolution in the Middle Thames Valley. Heathrow Terminal 5 Excavations: Volume 1, Perry Oaks*, CD section 3. Oxford / Salisbury: Framework Archaeology (Monograph No. 1).

Cramp, K., 2007, The flint. In D. Benson and A. Whittle (eds), *Building Memories: the Neolithic Cotswold Long Barrow at Ascott-under-Wychwood*, Oxfordshire, 289–314. Oxford: Oxbow Books.

Curran, J. M., Meighan, I. G., Simpson, D. D. A., Rogers, G. and Fallick, A. E., 2001, ^{87}Sr/^{86}Sr: a new discriminant for provenancing Neolithic porcellanite artifacts from Ireland. *Journal of Archaeological Science* 28, 713–720.

Curwen, E. C., 1937a, *The Archaeology of Sussex*. London: Methuen.

Curwen, E. C., 1937b, Querns. *Antiquity* 11, 133–151.

Curwen, E. C., 1941, More about querns. *Antiquity* 15, 15–32.

Darvill, T., 1987, *Prehistoric Britain*. London: Batsford.

Darvill, T., 2002, White on blonde: quartz pebbles and the use of quartz at Neolithic monuments in the Isle of Man and beyond. In A. Jones and G. MacGregor (eds), *Colouring the Past: the Significance of Colour in Archaeological Research*, 73–91. Oxford: Berg.

Devaney, R., 2005, Ceremonial and domestic flint arrowheads. *Lithics* 26, 9–22.

Dixon, P., 1988, The Neolithic settlements on Crickley Hill. In C. Burgess, P. Topping, C. Mordant and M. Maddison (eds), *Enclosures and Defences in the Neolithic of Western Europe*, 75–87. Oxford: British Archaeological Reports (International Series 403i).

Donahue, R. E., 1994, The current state of lithic microwear research. In N. Ashton and A. David (eds), *Stories in Stone: Proceedings of Anniversary Conference at St Hilda's College, Oxford, April 1993*, 156–168. London: Lithic Studies Society (Occasional Paper No. 4).

Donahue, R. E., 1999, Microwear analysis of the flint artefacts from Upper Ninepence. In A. Gibson, *The Walton Basin Project: Excavation and Survey in a Prehistoric Landscape 1993–7*, 100–112. York: Council for British Archaeology (Research Report 118).

Donahue, R. E. and Burroni, D. B., 2004, Lithic microwear analysis and the formation of archaeological assemblages. In E. A. Walker, F. Wenban-Smith and F. Healy (eds), *Lithics in Action: Papers from the Conference Lithic Studies in the Year 2000*, 140–148. Oxford: Oxbow Books (Lithic Studies Society Occasional Paper No. 8).

Donahue, R. E. and Evans, A. A., 2009, Microwear analysis of lithic artefacts. In M. G. Beamish, Island visits: Neolithic and Bronze Age activity on the Trent Valley floor. Excavations at Egginton and Willington, Derbyshire, 1998–1999. *Derbyshire Archaeological Journal* 129, 113–115.

Donnelly, M., 2002, Struck stone. In J. A. Atkinson, Excavation of a Neolithic occupation site at Chapelfield, Cowie, Stirling. *Proceedings of the Society of Antiquaries of Scotland* 132, 169–173.

Driscoll, K. and Warren, G. M., 2007, Dealing with the 'quartz problem' in Irish lithic research. *Lithics* 28, 4–14.

Durden, T., 1995, The production of specialised flintwork in the later Neolithic: a case study from the Yorkshire Wolds. *Proceedings of the Prehistoric Society* 61, 409–432.

Durden, T., 1996, Lithics in the north of England: production and consumption on the Yorkshire Wolds. In P. Frodsham (ed.), *Neolithic Studies in No-Man's Land: Papers on the Neolithic of Northern England from the Trent to the Tweed*, 79–86. Newcastle: Northumberland Archaeological Group (= *Northern Archaeology* 13/14 Special Edition).

Durden, T., 1999, The struck flint. In A. Mudd, R. J. Williams and A. Lupton, *Excavations Alongside Roman Ermin Street, Gloucestershire and Wiltshire. The Archaeology of the A419/A417 Swindon to Gloucester Road Scheme. Volume 2: Medieval and Post-Medieval Activity, Finds and Environmental Evidence*, 307–315. Oxford: Oxford Archaeological Unit.

Dyer, J., 1990, *Ancient Britain*. London: Batsford.

Edmonds, M., 1989, Review of T. H. McK. Clough and W. A. Cummins, *Stone Axe Studies. Volume 2. The Petrology of Prehistoric Stone Implements from the British Isles. Antiquity* 63(240), 633–634.

Edmonds, M., 1990, Description, understanding and the *chaîne opératoire*. *Archaeological Review from Cambridge* 9(1), 55–70.

Edmonds, M., 1993a, Interpreting causewayed enclosures in the past and the present. In C. Tilley (ed.), *Interpretative Archaeology*, 99–142. Oxford: Berg.

Edmonds, M., 1993b, Towards a context for production and exchange: the polished stone axe in earlier Neolithic Britain. In C. Scare and F. Healy (eds), *Trade and Exchange in Prehistoric Europe*, 69–86. Oxford: Oxbow Books (Oxbow Monograph 33).

Edmonds, M., 1995, *Stone Tools and Society: Working Stone in Neolithic and Bronze Age Britain*. London: Batsford.

Edmonds, M., 1999, *Ancestral Geographies of the Neolithic: Landscapes, Monuments and Memory*. London: Routledge.

Edmonds, M. and Bellamy, P., 1991, The flaked stone. In N. M. Sharples, *Maiden Castle: Excavations and Field Survey 1985–6*, 214–229. London: English Heritage.

Edmonds, M. and Richards, C. (eds), 1998, *Understanding the Neolithic of North-Western Europe*. Glasgow: Cruithne Press.

Edmonds, M. and Thomas, J., 1987, The archers: an everyday story of country folk. In A. G. Brown and M. R. Edmonds (eds), *Lithic Analysis and Later British Prehistory: Some Problems and Approaches*, 187–199. Oxford: British Archaeological Reports (British Series 162).

Edmonds, M., Evans, C. and Gibson, D., 1999, Assembly and collection – lithic complexes in the Cambridgeshire Fenlands. *Proceedings of the Prehistoric Society* 65, 47–82.

Edmonds, M., Sheridan, A. and Tipping, R., 1992, Survey and excavation at Creag na Caillich, Killin, Perthshire. *Proceedings of the Society of Antiquaries of Scotland* 122, 77–112 and microfiche 1:A5–11.

Elgee, F., 1930, *Early Man in North-East Yorkshire*. Gloucester: John Bellows.

Engl, R., 2008, Chipped stone. In M. Cook and L. Dunbar, *Rituals, Roundhouses and Romans: Excavations at Kintore, Aberdeenshire 2000–2006. Volume I: Forest Road*, 226–238. Edinburgh: Scottish Trust for Archaeological Research (Monograph 8).

English Heritage, 2000, *Managing Lithic Scatters: Archaeological Guidance for Planning Authorities and Developers*. London: English Heritage.

Evans, A. A. and Donahue, R. E., 2005, The elemental chemistry of lithic microwear: an experiment. *Journal of Archaeological Science* 32, 1733–1740.

Evans, A. A. and Donahue, R. E., 2008, Laser scanning confocal microscopy: a potential technique for the study of lithic microwear. *Journal of Archaeological Science* 35, 2223–2230.

Evans, J., 1872, *The Ancient Stone Implements, Weapons, and Ornaments, of Great Britain*. London: Longmans, Green, Reader, and Dyer.

Evans, J., 1897, *The Ancient Stone Implements, Weapons, and Ornaments, of Great Britain* (second edition, revised). London: Longmans, Green & Co.

Evershed, R. P., 2008, Organic residue analysis in archaeology: the archaeological biomarker revolution. *Archaeometry* 50(6), 895–924.

Fenton, M. B., 1984, The nature of the source and the manufacture of Scottish battle-axes and axe-hammers. *Proceedings of the Prehistoric Society* 50, 217–243.

Fenton, M. B., 1988, The petrological identification of stone battle-axes and axe-hammers from Scotland. In T. H. McK. Clough and W. A. Cummins, *Stone Axe Studies. Volume 2. The Petrology of Prehistoric Stone Implements from the British Isles*, 92–132. London: Council for British Archaeology (Research Report 67).

Ferguson, J., 1980, Application of data coding to the differentiation of British flint mine sites. *Journal of Archaeological Science* 7, 277–286.

Field, D., 1997, The landscape of extraction: aspects of the procurement of raw material in the Neolithic. In P. Topping (ed.), *Neolithic Landscapes*, 55–67. Oxford: Oxbow Books (Neolithic Studies Group Seminar Papers 2 / Oxbow Monograph 86).

Field, D., Graham, D., Thomas, S. N. H. and Winser, K., 1987, Fieldwalking in Surrey: surveys in Waverley and at Paddington Farm, Abinger. *Surrey Archaeological Collections* 78, 79–102.

Field, D. and Woolley, A. R., 1984, Neolithic and Bronze Age ground stone implements from Surrey: morphology, petrology and distribution. *Surrey Archaeological Collections* 75, 85–109.

Finlayson, B., 1989, Review of R. Torrence (ed.), *Time, Energy and Stone Tools*. *Lithics* 10, 54–58.

Finlayson, B., 1999, Use wear study of the Auchenhoan cache. In A. Saville, A cache of flint axeheads and other flint artefacts from Auchenhoan, near Campbeltown, Kintyre, Scotland. *Proceedings of the Prehistoric Society* 65, 114–117.

Finlayson, B., 2007, Flint. In J. Hunter, *Investigations in Sanday, Orkney. Vol.1: Excavations at Pool, Sanday. A Multi-Period Settlement from Neolithic to Late Norse Times*, 389–403. Kirkwall: The Orcadian.

Flanagan, L. N. W., 1965, Flint hollow scrapers and the Irish Neolithic. In Union International des Sciences Préhistoriques et Protohistoriques, *Atti del VI Congresso Internazionale delle Scienze Preistoriche e Protostoriche, Roma, 1962, Vol.II*, 323–328. Florence: G. C. Sansoni Editore.

Flanagan, L. N. W., 1966, An unpublished flint hoard from the Braid valley, Co. Antrim. *Ulster Journal of Archaeology* 29, 82–90.

Flanagan, L. N. W., 1970, A flint hoard from Ballyclare, Co. Antrim. *Ulster Journal of Archaeology* 33, 15–22.

Ford, S., 1987a, Flint scatters and prehistoric settlement patterns in south Oxfordshire and east Berkshire. In A. G. Brown and M. R. Edmonds (eds), *Lithic Analysis and Later British Prehistory: Some Problems and Approaches*, 101–135. Oxford: British Archaeological Reports (British Series 162).

Ford, S., 1987b, Chronological and functional aspects of flint assemblages. In A. G. Brown and M. R. Edmonds (eds), *Lithic Analysis and Later British Prehistory: Some Problems and Approaches*, 67–85. Oxford: British Archaeological Reports (British Series 162).

Gardiner, J., 1984, Lithic distribution and Neolithic settlement patterns in central southern England. In R. Bradley and J. Gardiner (eds), *Neolithic Studies: a Review of Some Current Research,* 15–40. Oxford: British Archaeological Reports (British Series 133).

Gardiner, J., 1987a, Tales of the unexpected: approaches to the assessment and interpretation of museum flint collections. In A. G. Brown and M. R. Edmonds (eds), *Lithic Analysis and Later British Prehistory: Some Problems and Approaches*, 49–65. Oxford: British Archaeological Reports (British Series 162).

Gardiner, J., 1987b, The Late Neolithic flint assemblage. In B. Cunliffe, *Hengistbury Head, Dorset. Volume 1: The Prehistoric and Roman Settlement, 3500 BC–AD 500*, 24–38. Oxford: Oxford University Committee for Archaeology (Monograph No. 13).

Gardiner, J., 2001, Catalogue of surviving flintwork from the Worthing group of mines. In M. Russell (ed.), *Rough Quarries, Rocks and Hills: John Pull and the Neolithic Flint Mines of Sussex*, 202–223. Oxford: Oxbow Books (Bournemouth University School of Conservation Sciences Occasional Paper 6).

Gardiner, J., 2008, On the production of discoidal flint knives and changing patterns of specialist flint procurement in the Neolithic on the South Downs, England. In H. Fokkens, B. J. Coles, A. L. Van Gijn, J. P. Kleijne, H. H. Ponjee and C. G. Slappendel (eds), *Between Foraging and Farming: An Extended Broad Spectrum of Papers Presented to Leendert Louwe Kooijmans*, 235–246. Leiden: Leiden University (*Analecta Praehistorica Leidensia* 40).

Garrow, D., 2007, Placing pits: landscape occupation and depositional practice during the Neolithic in East Anglia. *Proceedings of the Prehistoric Society* 73, 1–24.

Garton, D., 1988, A study of used and re-worked stone axes from Derbyshire. *Derbyshire Archaeological Journal* 108, 38–47.

Garton, D., 1989, The flintwork definitions. In P. Phillips (ed.), *Archaeology and Landscape Studies in North Lincolnshire. Part ii. Aerial and Surface Survey on the Lincolnshire Wolds and Excavation at Newton Cliffs, North Lincolnshire*, 174–175. Oxford: British Archaeological Reports (British Series 208ii).

Garton, D., 2009, Flintwork. In G. Guilbert, *Great Briggs: Excavation of a Neolithic Ring-Ditch on the Trent Gravels at Holme Pierrepont, Nottinghamshire*: 114–131. Oxford: British Archaeological Reports (British Series 489).

Gingell, C. and Harding, P., 1981, A method of analysing the technology of flaking in Neolithic and Bronze Age flint assemblages. *Staringia* 6, 73–76. (=Proceedings of the Third International Symposium on Flint, Maastricht, 24–27 May 1979.)

Gowlett, J., 1997, High definition archaeology: ideas and evaluation. *World Archaeology* 29(2), 152–171.

Grace, R., 1996, Use-wear analysis: the state of the art. *Archaeometry* 38(2), 209–229.

Green, H. S., 1980, *The Flint Arrowheads of the British Isles*. Oxford: British Archaeological Reports (British Series 75).

Green, H. S., 1984, Flint arrowheads: typology and interpretation. *Lithics* 5, 19–39.

Griffiths, D. and Woodman, P. C., 1987, Cretaceous chert sourcing in north east Ireland: preliminary results. In G. de G. Sieveking and M. H. Newcomer (eds), *The Human Uses of Flint and Chert. Proceedings of the Fourth International Flint Symposium held at Brighton Polytechnic 10–15 April 1983*: 249–252. Cambridge: Cambridge University Press.

Grimes, W. F., 1965, Neolithic Wales. In I. Ll. Foster and G. Daniel (eds), *Prehistoric and Early Wales*, 35–69. London: Routledge and Kegan Paul.

Grimes, W. F., 1979, The history of implement petrology in Britain. In T. H. McK. Clough and W. A. Cummins (eds), *Stone Axe Studies Archaeological. Petrological, Experimental and Ethnographic*: 1–4. London: Council for British Archaeology (Research Report 23).

Guinan, B. and Nolan, J., 2007, Lithics analysis [Magheraboy causewayed enclosure]. In E. Danaher, *Monumental Beginnings: The Archaeology of the N4 Sligo Inner Relief Road*, on CD. Dublin: National Roads Authority (NRA Scheme Monographs 1).

Hall, D., 1985, Survey work in eastern England. In S. Macready and F. H. Thompson, *Archaeological Field Survey in Britain and Abroad*, 25–44. London: Society of Antiquaries of London

Hamon, C., 2006, *Broyage et Abrasion au Néolithique Ancien. Caractérisation Fonctionnelle de l'Outillage en Grès du Bassin Parisien*. Oxford: British Archaeological Reports (International Series 1551).

Hamon, C., 2008, Functional analysis of stone grinding and polishing tools from the earliest Neolithic of north-western Europe. *Journal of Archaeological Science* 35, 1502–1520.

Harbison, P., 1988, *Pre-Christian Ireland. From the First Settlers to the Early Celts*. London: Thames and Hudson.

Harding, A. and Young, R., 1979, Reconstruction of the hafting methods and function of stone implements. In T. H. McK. Clough and W. A. Cummins (eds), *Stone Axe Studies. Archaeological, Petrological, Experimental and Ethnographic*, 102–105. London: Council for British Archaeology (Research Report 23).

Harding, I. C., Trippier, D. and Steele, J., 2004, The provenancing of flint artefacts using palynological techniques. In E. A. Walker, F. Wenban-Smith and F. Healy (eds), *Lithics in Action: Papers from the Conference Lithic Studies in the Year 2000*, 78–88. Oxford: Oxbow Books (Lithic Studies Society Occasional Paper No. 8).

Harding, J. and Healy, F., 2007, *The Raunds Area Project: a Neolithic and Bronze Age Landscape in Northamptonshire*. Swindon: English Heritage.

Harding, P., 1987, An experiment to produce a ground flint axe. In G. de G. Sieveking and M. H. Newcomer (eds), *The Human Uses of Flint and Chert. Proceedings of the Fourth International Flint Symposium held at Brighton Polytechnic 10–15 April 1983*, 37–42. Cambridge: Cambridge University Press.

Harding, P., 1990a, The comparative analysis of four stratified flint assemblages and a knapping cluster. In J. Richards, *The Stonehenge Environs Project*, 213–225. London: English Heritage (Archaeological Report No. 16).

Harding, P., 1990b, The analysis of a sealed knapping deposit from the phase 1 ditch. In J. Richards, *The Stonehenge Environs Project*, 99–104. London: English Heritage (Archaeological Report No. 16).

Harding, P., 1990c, Sealed flint assemblages [from Wilsford Down]. In J. Richards, *The Stonehenge Environs Project*, 164–169. London: English Heritage (Archaeological Report No. 16).

Harding, P., 1991, The worked stone. In P. J. Woodward, *The South Dorset Ridgeway: Survey and Excavations 1977–84*, 73–87. Dorchester: Dorset Natural History and Archaeological Society (Monograph No. 8).

Harding, P., 1995, Flint. In R. M. J. Cleal, K. E. Walker and R. Montague, *Stonehenge in its Landscape: Twentieth-Century Excavations*, 368–375. London: English Heritage (Archaeological Report 10).

Hawkes, J., 1939, *The Archaeology of the Channel Islands. Vol.II: The Bailiwick of Jersey*. Jersey: Société Jersiaise.

Healey, E., 1993, The Neolithic and Bronze Age flintwork. In F. Lynch, *Excavations in the Brenig Valley: a Mesolithic and Bronze Age Landscape in North Wales*, 187–195 and microfiche. Bangor: Cambrian Archaeological Association (Cambrian Archaeological Monographs No. 5).

Healey, E., 2001, Lithic material. In D. Buckley, J. D. Hedges and N. Brown, Excavations at a Neolithic cursus, Springfield, Essex, 1979–85. *Proceedings of the Prehistoric Society* 67, 135–143.

Healey, E. and Green, H. S., 1984, The lithic industries. In W. J. Britnell and H. N. Savory, *Gwernvale and Penywyrlod: Two Neolithic Long Cairns in the Black Mountains of Brecknock*, 113–132. Cardiff: Cambrian Archaeological Association (Monograph 2).

Healey, E. and Robertson-Mackay, R., 1983, The lithic industries from Staines causewayed enclosure and their relationship to other earlier Neolithic industries in southern Britain. *Lithics* 4, 1–27.

Healey, E. and Robertson-Mackay, R., 1987, The flint industry. In R. Robertson-Mackay, The Neolithic causewayed enclosure at Staines, Surrey: excavations 1961–63. *Proceedings of the Prehistoric Society* 53, 95–118.

Healy, F., 1982, Single-piece flint sickles in Britain. *Antiquity* 56(218), 214–215.

Healy, F., 1983, Are first impressions only topsoil deep? The evidence from Tattershall Thorpe, Lincolnshire. *Lithics* 4, 28–33.

Healy, F., 1985, The struck flint. In S. J. Shennan, F. Healy and I. F. Smith, The excavation of a ring-ditch at Tye Field, Lawford, Essex. *Archaeological Journal* 142, 177–207.

Healy, F., 1988, *The Anglo-Saxon Cemetery at Spong Hill, North Elmham, Part VI: Occupation during the Seventh to Second Millennia BC*. Gressenhall: Norfolk Archaeological Unit (East Anglian Archaeology Report no.39).

Healy, F., 1989, Afterthoughts. In I. Brooks and P. Phillips (eds), *Breaking the Stony Silence: Papers from the Sheffield Lithics Conference 1988*, 187–198. Oxford: British Archaeological Reports (British Series 213).

Healy, F., 1991, The hunting of the floorstone. In A. J. Scofield (ed.), *Interpreting Artefact Scatters: Contributions to Ploughzone Archaeology*, 29–37. Oxford: Oxbow Books.

Healy, F., 1993a, Lithic material. In R. Bradley, P. Chowne, R. M. J. Cleal, F. Healy and I. Kinnes, *Excavations on Redgate Hill, Hunstanton, Norfolk, and at Tattershall Thorpe, Lincolnshire*, 28–39. Gressenhall/Sleaford: East Anglian Archaeology Report No. 57.

Healy, F., 1993b, The struck flint. In R. Bradley, P. Chowne, R. M. J. Cleal, F. Healy and I. Kinnes, *Excavations on Redgate Hill, Hunstanton, Norfolk, and at Tattershall Thorpe, Linclonshire*, 93–105. Gressenhall/Sleaford: East Anglian Archaeology Report No. 57.

Healy, F., 1994, Typology: the maker's or the analyst's? In N. Ashton and A. David (eds), *Stories in Stone: Proceedings of Anniversary Conference at St Hilda's College, Oxford, April 1993*, 179–181. London: Lithic Studies Society (Occasional Paper 4).

Healy, F., 1996, *The Fenland Project, Number 11: The Wissey Embayment: Evidence for Pre-Iron Age Occupation Accumulated Prior to the Fenland Project*. Gressenhall. Norfolk Museums Service (East Anglian Archaeology Report No. 78).

Healy, F., 1997, Settlement: Neolithic and Bronze Age. In R. J. C. Smith, F. Healy, M. J. Allen, E. L. Morris, I. Barnes and P. J. Woodward, *Excavations Along the Route of the Dorchester By-pass, Dorset, 1986–8*, 295–299. Salisbury: Wessex Archaeology (Report No. 11).

Healy, F., 1998, The surface of the Breckland. In N. Ashton, F. Healy and P. Pettitt (eds), *Stone Age Archaeology: Essays in Honour of John Wymer*, 225–235. Oxford: Oxbow Books (Lithic Studies Society Occasional Paper 6).

Henshall, A. S., 1963, *The Chambered Tombs of Scotland, Volume 1*. Edinburgh: Edinburgh University Press.

Henshall, A. S., 1972, *The Chambered Tombs of Scotland, Volume 2*. Edinburgh: Edinburgh University Press.

Henson, D., 1985, The flint resources of Yorkshire and the East Midlands. *Lithics* 6, 2–9.

Henson, D., 1989, The raw materials. In P. Phillips (ed.), *Archaeology and Landscape Studies in North Lincolnshire. Part ii. Aerial and Surface Survey on the Lincolnshire Wolds and Excavation at Newton Cliffs, North Lincolnshire*, 173. Oxford: British Archaeological Reports (British Series 208ii).

Herity, M., 1987, The finds from Irish court tombs. *Proceedings of the Royal Irish Academy* 87 C, 103–281.

Herity, M. and Eogan, G., 1977, *Ireland in Prehistory*. London: Routledge and Kegan Paul

Herne, A., 1991, The flint assemblage. In I. Longworth, A. Herne, G. Varndell and S. Needham, *Excavations at Grimes Graves, Norfolk, 1972–1976. Fascicule 3: Shaft X: Bronze Age Flint, Chalk and Metal Working*, 21–74. London: British Museum Press.

Högberg, A. and Olausson, D., 2007, *Scandinavian Flint – An Archaeological Perspective*. Aarhus: Aarhus University Press.

Högberg, A., Puseman, K. and Yost, C., 2009, Integration of use-wear with protein residue analysis – a study of tool use and function in the south Scandinavian Early Neolithic. *Journal of Archaeological Science* 36, 1725–1737.

Holgate, R., 1988, *Neolithic Settlement of the Thames Basin*. Oxford: British Archaeological Reports (British Series 194).

Holgate, R., 1994, Binford's hyperbole: the cuartion of flintwork. In N. Ashton and A. David (eds), *Stories in Stone: Proceedings of Anniversary Conference at St Hilda's College, Oxford, April 1993*, 99–103. London: Lithic Studies Society (Occasional Paper No. 4).

Howell, J. M., 1981, The typology of Scottish stone axes. In J. Kenworthy (ed.), *Early Technology in North Britain*, 15–24. Edinburgh: Edinburgh University Press (Scottish Archaeological Forum 11).

Hughes, R. E., Högberg, A. and Olausson, D., 2010, Sourcing flint from Sweden and Denmark: a pilot study employing non-destructive energy dispersive X-ray fluorescence spectrometry. *Journal of Nordic Archaeological Science* 17, 15–25.

Humble, J., 2006, Flint and stone artefacts. In S. Parry, *Raunds Area Survey. An Archaeological Study of the Landscape of Raunds, Northamptonshire 1985–94*, 46–60. Oxford: Oxbow Books

Hurcombe, L., 2001, Microwear on flints from 8004. In D. Buckley, J. D. Hedges and N. Brown, Excavations at a Neolithic cursus, Springfield, Essex, 1979–85. *Proceedings of the Prehistoric Society* 67, 143–146.

Hurcombe, L., 2008, Looking for prehistoric basketry and cordage using inorganic remains: the evidence from stone tools. In L. Longo and N. Skakun, *'Prehistoric Technology' 40 Years Later: Functional Studies and the Russian Legacy*, 205–216. Oxford: Archaeopress (British Archaeological Reports International Series 1783).

Ibáñez, J. J. and González, J. E., 2003, Use-wear in the 1990s in Western Europe: potential and limitations of a method. In N. Moloney and M. J. Shott (eds), *Lithic Analysis at the Millennium*, 163–172. London: Institute of Archaeology, University College London.

Ihuel, E., 2004, *La diffusion du silex du Grand-Pressigny dans le Massif Armoricain au Néolithique*. Joué-lès-Tours: Editions la Simarre.

Ixer, R. A., Williams-Thorpe, O., Bevins, R. E. and Chambers, A. D., 2004, A comparison between 'total petrography' and geochemistry using portable X-ray fluorescence as provenancing tools for some Midlands axeheads. In E. A. Walker, F. Wenban-Smith and F. Healy (eds), *Lithics in Action: Papers from the Conference Lithic Studies in the Year 2000*, 105–115. Oxford: Oxbow Books (Lithic Studies Society Occasional Paper No. 8).

Jones, M. C. and Williams-Thorpe, O., 2001, An illustration of the use of an atypicality index in provenancing British stone axes. *Archaeometry* 43(1), 1–18.

Kinnes, I., 1985, Circumstance not context: the Neolithic of Scotland as seen from outside. *Proceedings of the Society of Antiquaries of Scotland* 115, 15–57.

Kinnes, I., 1989, Review of T. H. McK. Clough and W. A. Cummins (eds), *Stone Axe Studies Volume 2. Archaeological Journal* 146, 597–598.

Kinnes, I., 1994, The Neolithic in Britain. In B. Vyner (ed.), *Building on the Past: Papers Celebrating 150 Years of the Royal Archaeological Institute*, 90–102. London: Royal Archaeological Institute.

Knowles, W. J., 1893, Irish stone axes and chisels. *Journal of the Royal Society of Antiquaries of Ireland* 23, 140–163.

Knowles, W. J., 1898, Irish flint scrapers. *Journal of the Royal Society of Antiquaries of Ireland* 28, 367–391.

Knowles, W. J., 1903, Irish flint arrow- and spear-heads. *Journal of the Royal Anthropological Institute* 33, 44–56.

Knowles, W. J., 1912, Prehistoric stone implements from the River Bann and Lough Neagh. *Proceedings of the Royal Irish Academy* 30 C, 195–222.

Lahane, D., 1983, The flint work. In M. J. O'Kelly, R. M. Cleary and D. Lahane, *Newgrange, Co. Meath, Ireland: The Late Neolithic/Beaker Period Settlement*, 118–167. Oxford: British Archaeological Reports (International Series 190).

Lamdin-Whymark, H., 2008, *The Residue of Ritualised Action: Neolithic Deposition Practices in the Middle Thames Valley*. Oxford: British Archaeological Reports (British Series 466).

Lech, J. and Longworth, I., 2000, Kopalnia krzemienia Grimes Graves w świetle nowych badań. *Przegląd Archeologiczny* 48, 19–73.

Lech, J. and Longworth, I., 2006, The Grimes Graves flint mine site in the light of two Late Neolithic workshop assemblages: a second approach. In G. Körlin and G. Weisgerber (eds), *Stone Age – Mining Age*, 413–422. Bochum: Deutsches Bergbau-Museum (=*Der Anschnitt* 19).

Lelong, O. and MacGregor, G., 2007, *The Lands of Ancient Lothian: Interpreting the Archaeology of the A1*. Edinburgh: Society of Antiquaries of Scotland.

Lithic Studies Society, 2004, *Research Frameworks for Holocene Lithics in Britain*. Salisbury: Lithic Studies Society.

Longworth, I. H., Wainwright, G. J. and Wilson, K. E., 1971, The Grooved Ware site at Lion Point, Clacton. In G. de G. Sieveking (ed.), *Prehistoric and Roman Studies: Commemorating the Opening of the Department of Prehistoric and Romano-British Antiquities*, 93–124. London: Trustees of the British Museum.

Longworth, I., Ashton, N. and Rigby, V., 1986, Prehistoric Britain. In I. Longworth and J. Cherry (eds), *Archaeology in Britain Since 1945: New Directions*, 12–72. London: British Museum Publications.

Lord, J. W., 1993, *The Nature and Subsequent Uses of Flint. Volume 1. The Basics of Lithic Technology*. Privately published.

Lynch, F., 1970, *Prehistoric Anglesey: the Archaeology of the Island to the Roman Conquest*. Llangefni: Anglesey Antiquarian Society.

Lynch, F., 1993, *Excavations in the Brenig Valley: a Mesolithic and Bronze Age Landscape in North Wales*. Bangor: Cambrian Archaeological Association (Cambrian Archaeological Monographs No 5).

Lynch, F., 2000a, The earlier Neolithic. In F. Lynch, S. Aldhouse-Green and J. L. Davies, *Prehistoric Wales*, 42–78. Thrupp: Sutton Publishing.

Lynch, F., 2000b, The later Neolithic and earlier Bronze Age. In F. Lynch, S. Aldhouse-Green and J. L. Davies, *Prehistoric Wales*, 79–138. Thrupp: Sutton Publishing.

McQuillan, L. and Logue, P., 2008, Funerary querns: rethinking the role of the basin in Irish passage tombs. *Ulster Journal of Archaeology* 67, 14–21.

Mace, A., 1959, An Upper Palaeolithic open-site at Hengistbury Head, Christchurch, Hants. *Proceedings of the Prehistoric Society* 25, 233–259.

Mallory, J. P. and McNeill, T. E., 1991, *The Archaeology of Ulster from Colonization to Plantation*. Belfast: Institute of Irish Studies, Queen's University Belfast.

Mandal, S., O'Sullivan, A., Byrnes, E., Weddle, D. and Weddle, J., 2004, Archaeological experiments in the production of stone axeheads. In E. A. Walker, F. Wenban-Smith and F. Healy (eds), *Lithics in Action: Papers from the Conference Lithic Studies in the Year 2000*, 116–123. Oxford: Oxbow Books (Lithic Studies Society Occasional Paper No. 8).

Manby, T. G., 1974, *Grooved Ware Sites in the North of England*. Oxford: British Archaeological Reports (British Series 9).

Manby, T. G., 1988, The Neolithic period in eastern Yorkshire. In T. G. Manby (ed.), *Archaeology in Eastern Yorkshire: Essays in Honour of T. C. M. Brewster*, 35–88. Sheffield: Department of Archaeology and Prehistory, University of Sheffield.

Manby, T. G., King, A. and Vyner, B. E., 2003, The Neolithic and Bronze Ages: a time of early agriculture. In T. G. Manby, S. Moorhouse and P. Ottaway (eds), *The Archaeology of Yorkshire: An Assessment at the Beginning of the 21st Century*, 35–116. Leeds: Yorkshire Archaeological Society (Occasional Paper No. 3).

Mandal, S., 1997, Striking the balance: the roles of petrography and geochemistry in stone axe studies in Ireland. *Archaeometry* 39(2), 289–308.

Mandal, S. and Cooney, G., 1997, Using geochemistry to interpret porcellanite stone axe production in Ireland. *Journal of Archaeological Science* 24, 757–763.

Marshall, D. N., 1977, Carved stone balls. *Proceedings of the Society of Antiquaries of Scotland* 108 (1976–77), 40–72.

Marshall, D. N., 1983, Further notes on carved stone balls. *Proceedings of the Society of Antiquaries of Scotland* 113, 628–630.

Martingell, H. and Saville, A., 1988, *The Illustration of Lithic Artefacts: A Guide to Drawing Stone Tools for Specialist Reports*. Northampton: Association of Archaeological Illustrators and Surveyors (Technical Paper 9) and the Lithic Studies Society (Occasional Paper 3).

May, J., Elsdon, S. M., Phillips, P., Guirr, H. and Donahue, R., 1996, Earlier Neolithic artifacts from pits and hollow. In J. May, *Dragonby: Report on Excavations at an Iron Age and Romano-British Settlement in North Lincolnshire*, 38–40. Oxford: Oxbow Monograph 61.

Mercer, R. J., 1981, *Grimes Graves, Norfolk, Excavations 1971–72: Volume I*. London: HMSO (Department of the Environment Archaeological Reports No 11).

Mercer, R. J., 1998, Stuart Piggott 1910–1996. *Proceedings of the British Academy* 97, 412–442.

Middleton, [H.] R., 1990, The Walker Collection: a quantitative analysis of lithic material from the March/Manea area of the Cambridgeshire Fens. *Proceedings of the Cambridge Antiquarian Society* 79, 13–38.

Middleton, [H.] R., 1992, The Walker Collection. In D. Hall, *The Fenland Project, Number 6: The South-Western Cambridgeshire Fenlands*: 106–108. Cambridge: East Anglian Archaeology Report No.56.

Middleton, H. R., 1998, Flint and chert artefacts. In F. Pryor, *Etton: Excavations at a Neolithic Causewayed Enclosure near Maxey, Cambridgeshire, 1982–7*, 215–255. London: English Heritage (Archaeological Report 18).

Middleton, H. R., 2005, The Barnhouse lithic assemblage. In C. Richards (ed.), *Dwelling Among the Monuments. The Neolithic Village of Barnhouse, Maeshowe Passage Grave and Surrounding Monuments at Stenness, Orkney*, 293–321. Cambridge: McDonald Institute Monographs.

Morris, G., 1984, Microwear and organic residue studies on Sweet Track flints. *Somerset Levels Papers* 10, 97–106.

Murray, J., 2005, The William McDowall Selby collection. *Transactions of the Dumfriesshire and Galloway Natural History and Antiquarian Society* 79, 147–171.

Nelis, E., 2004, Neolithic flint-work from the north of Ireland: some thoughts on prominent tool types and their production. In A. Gibson and A. Sheridan (eds), *From Sickles to Circles: Britain and Ireland at the Time of Stonehenge*, 155–175. Stroud: Tempus.

Newberry, J., 2002, Inland flint in prehistoric Devon: sources, tool-making quality and use. *Proceedings of the Devon Archaeological Society* 60, 1–36.

Oakley, K. P., Rankine, W. F., Lowther, A. W. G., Keiller, A. and Piggott, S., 1939, *A Survey of the Prehistory of the Farnham District (Surrey)*. Guildford: Surrey Archaeological Society.

O'Kelly, M. J., 1989, *Early Ireland: An Introduction to Irish Prehistory*. Cambridge: Cambridge University Press.

Ozanne, P. C. and Ozanne, A., 1960, The flint industry. In J. Alexander, P. C. Ozanne and A. Ozanne, Report on the investigation of a round barrow on Arreton Down, Isle of Wight. *Proceedings of the Prehistoric Society* 26, 284–296.

Pailler, Y. and Sheridan, A., 2009, Everything you always wanted to know about … *la néolithisation de la Grande-Bretagne et de l'Irlande. Bulletin de la Société préhistorique française* 106(1), 25–56.

Parker Pearson, M., 1993, *Bronze Age Britain*. London: Batsford/English Heritage.

Parry, S., 2006, *Raunds Area Survey. An Archaeological Study of the Landscape of Raunds, Northamptonshire 1985–94*. Oxford: Oxbow Books

Passmore, D. G. and Waddington, C., 2009, *Managing Archaeological Landscapes in Northumberland: Till-Tweed Studies Volume 1*. Oxford: Oxbow Books.

Perrin, T., 2003, Evolution des industries lithiques du Centre-Est de la France du VIᵉ au IIIᵉ millénaire av. J.-C. *Germania* 81, 385–400.

Peterson, R. and Pollard, J., 2004, The Neolithic: the first farming societies. In M. Aldhouse-Green and R. Howell (eds), *The Gwent County History. Vol.1: Gwent in Prehistory and Early History*, 56–83. Cardiff: University of Wales Press.

Pétrequin, P., Errera, M., Pétrequin, A.-M. and Allard, P., 2006, The Neolithic quarries of Mont Viso, Piedmont, Italy: initial radiocarbon dates. *European Journal of Archaeology* 9(1), 7–30.

Pétrequin, P., Sheridan, A., Cassen, S., Errera, M., Gauthier, E., Klassen, L., Le Maux, N. and Pailler, Y., 2008, Neolithic Alpine axeheads, from the Continent to Great Britain, the Isle of Man and Ireland. In H. Fokkens, B. J. Coles, A. L. Van Gijn, J. P. Kleijne, H. H. Ponjee and C. G. Slappendel (eds), *Between Foraging and Farming: An Extended Broad Spectrum of Papers Presented to Leendert Louwe Kooijmans*, 261–279. Leiden: Leiden University (*Analecta Praehistorica Leidensia* 40).

Petts, D. and Gerrard, C., 2006, *Shared Visions: The North-East Regional Research Framework for the Historic Environment*. Durham: Durham County Council.

Pieksma, E. J. and Gardiner, J., 1990, The prehistoric flint and stone assemblage. In S. West, *West Stow, Suffolk: The Prehistoric and Romano-British Occupations*, 46–59. Bury St Edmunds: Suffolk County Planning Department (East Anglian Archaeology Report No. 48).

Pierpoint, S., 1980, *Social Patterns in Yorkshire Prehistory 3500–750 BC*. Oxford: British Archaeological Reports (British Series 74).

Pierpoint, S., 1981, *Prehistoric Flintwork in Britain*. Highworth: Vorda Archaeological and Historical Publications.

Piggott, S., 1954, *The Neolithic Cultures of the British Isles*. Cambridge: Cambridge University Press.

Pitts, M. W., 1978a, On the shape of waste flakes as an index of technological change in lithic industries. *Journal of Archaeological Science* 5, 17–37.

Pitts, M. W., 1978b, Towards an understanding of flint industries in Post-glacial England. *Bulletin of the University of London Institute of Archaeology* 15, 179–197.

Pitts, M. W., 1980, *Later Stone Implements*. Princes Risborough: Shire Publications.

Pitts, M. [W.], 1996, The stone axe in Neolithic Britain. *Proceedings of the Prehistoric Society* 62, 311–371.

Pitts, M. W. and Jacobi, R. M., 1979, Some aspects of change in flaked stone industries of the Mesolithic and Neolithic in southern Britain. *Journal of Archaeological Science* 6, 163–177.

Pollard, J., 1994, Appendix 2. Dating, associations and contexts of flint polished-edge blade knives. In A. Whittle, Excavations at Millbarrow Neolithic chambered tomb, Winterbourne Monkton, North Wiltshire. *Wiltshire Archaeological Magazine* 87, 51–52.

Pollard, J., 1999, Flint. In A. Whittle, J. Pollard and C. Grigson, *The Harmony of Symbols: The Windmill Hill Causewayed Enclosure, Wiltshire*, 318–337. Oxford: Oxbow Books.

Radley, J., 1967, The York hoard of flint tools, 1868. *Yorkshire Archaeological Journal* 42(1), 131–132.

Raftery, J., 1951, *Prehistoric Ireland*. London: Batsford.

Rees, S., 1979, *Agricultural Implements in Prehistoric and Roman Britain*. Oxford: British Archaeological Reports (British Series 69).

Rees, S., 1986, Stone implements and artefacts. In A. Whittle, M. Keith-Lucas, A. Milles, B. Noddle, S. Rees and J. C. C. Romans, *Scord of Brouster: An Early Agricultural Settlement on Shetland, Excavations 1977–1979*, 75–91. Oxford: Oxford University Committee for Archaeology (Monograph 9).

Richards, C. (ed.), 2005, *Dwelling Among the Monuments. The Neolithic Village of Barnhouse, Maeshowe Passage Grave and Surrounding Monuments at Stenness, Orkney*. Cambridge: McDonald Institute Monographs.

Richards, C. and Thomas, J., 1984, Ritual activity and structured deposition in later Neolithic Wessex. In R. Bradley and J. Gardiner (eds), *Neolithic Studies: A Review of Some Current Research*, 189–218. Oxford: British Archaeological Reports (British Series 133).

Richards, J., 1990, *The Stonehenge Environs Project*. London: English Heritage (Archaeological Report No. 16).

Richardson, R. S., Richardson, J. A. and Thorp, J. A., 2002, Lithic arrowheads of the Craven area. *Yorkshire Archaeological Journal* 74, 1–28.

Riley, H., 1990, The scraper assemblages and petit tranchet derivative arrowheads. In J. Richards, *The Stonehenge Environs Project*, 225–228. London: English Heritage (Archaeological Report No. 16).

Ritchie, P. R., 1968, The stone implement trade in third-millennium Scotland. In J. M. Coles and D. D. A. Simpson (eds), *Studies in Ancient Europe: Essays Presented to Stuart Piggott*, 117–136. Leicester: Leicester University Press.

Roberts, A. and Barton, N., 2008, Reading the unwritten history: Evans and *Ancient Stone Implements*. In A. MacGregor (ed.), *Sir John Evans 1823–1908: Antiquity, Commerce and Natural Science in the Age of Darwin*, 95–115. Oxford: Ashmolean Museum.

Robins, P., 2002, A Late Neolithic flint hoard at Two Mile Bottom, near Thetford, Norfolk. *Lithics* 23, 29–32.

Roe, F. E. S., 1968, Stone maceheads and the latest Neolithic cultures of the British Isles. In J. M. Coles and D. D. A. Simpson (eds), *Studies in Ancient Europe: Essays Presented to Stuart Piggott*, 145–172. Leicester: Leicester University Press.

Roe, F. E. S., 1979, Typology of stone implements with shaft holes. In T. H. McK. Clough and W. A. Cummins (eds), *Stone Axe Studies*, 23–48. London: Council for British Archaeology (Research Report 23).

Roe, F. E. S., 2008, Worked stone other than axes. In R. Mercer and F. Healy, *Hambledon Hill, Dorset, England. Excavation and Survey of a Neolithic Monument Complex and its Surrounding Landscape*, 632–640. Swindon: English Heritage.

Roe, F. E. S., 2009, Corn grinding in southern England: what can the querns tell us? In K. Brophy and G. Barclay (eds), *Defining a Regional Neolithic: the Evidence from Britain and Ireland*, 26–34. Oxford: Oxbow Books (Neolithic Studies Group Seminar Papers 9).

Roe, F. E. S. and Radley, J., 1968, Pebble mace-heads with hour-glass perforations from Yorkshire, Nottinghamshire and Derbyshire. *Yorkshire Archaeological Journal* 42, 169–177.

Ryan, M. (ed.), 1991, *The Illustrated Archaeology of Ireland*. Dublin: Country House.

Savory, H. N., 1980, The Neolithic in Wales. In J. A. Taylor (ed.), *Culture and Environment in Prehistoric Wales*, 207–241. Oxford: British Archaeological Reports (British Series 76).

Saville, A., 1973, A reconsideration of the prehistoric flint assemblage from Bourne Pool, Aldridge, Staffs. *Transactions of the South Staffordshire Archaeological and Historical Society* 14 (1972–1973), 6–28.

Saville, A., 1981a, The flint and chert artefacts. In R. J. Mercer, Excavations at Carn Brea, Illogan, Cornwall, 1970–73: a Neolithic fortified complex of the third millennium bc. *Cornish Archaeology* 20, 101–152.

Saville, A., 1981b, *Grimes Graves, Norfolk, Excavations 1971–72: Volume II: The Flint Assemblage.* London: HMSO (Department of the Environment Archaeological Reports No 11).

Saville, A., 1987a, Review of A. G. Brown and M. R. Edmonds (eds), *Lithic Analysis and Later British Prehistory: Some Problems and Approaches. Lithics* 8, 38–41.

Saville, A., 1987b, The flint artefacts. In C. S. Green, *Excavations at Poundbury. Volume I: The Settlements,* 99, 102–103, & microfiche 2,D11–E3. Dorchester: Dorset Natural History and Archaeological Society (Monograph No. 7).

Saville, A., 1990a, Flint and chert artefacts. In A. Saville, *Hazleton North: the Excavation of a Neolithic Long Cairn of the Cotswold-Severn Group,* 153–175. London: English Heritage.

Saville, A., 1990b, *Hazleton North: the Excavation of a Neolithic Long Cairn of the Cotswold-Severn Group.* London: English Heritage.

Saville, A., 1991, Review of R. Torrence (ed.), *Time, Energy and Stone Tools. Proceedings of the Prehistoric Society* 57(2), 215–216.

Saville, A., 1994, Exploitation of lithic resources for stone tools in earlier prehistoric Scotland. In N. Ashton and A. David (eds), *Stories in Stone: Proceedings of Anniversary Conference at St Hilda's College, Oxford, April 1993,* 57–70. London: Lithic Studies Society (Occasional Paper 4).

Saville, A., 1999a, A cache of flint axeheads and other flint artefacts from Auchenhoan, near Campbeltown, Kintyre, Scotland. *Proceedings of the Prehistoric Society* 65, 83–123.

Saville, A., 1999b, An exceptional polished flint axe-head from Bolshan Hill, near Montrose, Angus. *Tayside and Fife Archaeological Journal* 5, 1–6.

Saville, A., 2002a, Lithic artefacts from Neolithic causewayed enclosures: character and meaning. In G. Varndell and P. Topping (eds), *Enclosures in Neolithic Europe: Essays on Causewayed and Non-Causewayed Sites,* 91–105. Oxford: Oxbow Books.

Saville, A., 2002b, Struck lithic artefacts. In G. J. Barclay, K. Brophy and G. MacGregor, Claish, Stirling: an early Neolithic structure in its context. *Proceedings of the Society of Antiquaries of Scotland* 132, 88–90.

Saville, A., 2003a, Review of E. A. Walker, F. Wenban-Smith and F. Healy (eds), *Lithics in Action: Papers from the Conference Lithic Studies in the Year 2000. Scottish Archaeological Journal* 25(2), 185–188.

Saville, A., 2003b, Lithic resource exploitation for artefacts in prehistoric and early historic Scotland. In T. Stöllner, G. Körlin, G. Steffens and J. Cierny (eds), *Man and Mining – Mensch und Bergbau: Studies in Honour of Gerd Weisgerber on Occasion of his 65th Birthday,* 405–413. Bochum: Bergbau-Museum Bochum.

Saville, A., 2005a, Review of C. Butler, *Prehistoric Flintwork.* www.ucl.ac.uk/prehistoric/reviews/05_09_butler.htm

Saville, A., 2005b, Prehistoric quarrying of a secondary flint source: evidence from north-east Scotland. In P. Topping and M. Lynott (eds), *The Cultural Landscape of Prehistoric Mines,* 1–13. Oxford: Oxbow Books.

Saville, A., 2006a, Flint technology and production associated with extraction sites in north-east Scotland. In G. Körlin and G. Weisgerber (eds), *Stone Age – Mining Age,* 449–454. Bochum: Deutsches Bergbau-Museum (=*Der Anschnitt* 19).

Saville, A., 2006b, The early Neolithic lithic assemblage in Britain: some chronological considerations. In P. Allard, F. Bostyn and A. Zimmermann (eds), *Contribution des matériaux lithiques dans la chronologie du Néolithique ancien et moyen en France et dans les régions limitrophes,* 1–14. Oxford: Archaeopress, British Archaeological Reports (International Series 1494).

Saville, A., 2008a, The flint and chert artefacts. In R. Mercer and F. Healy, *Hambledon Hill, Dorset, England. Excavation and Survey of a Neolithic Monument Complex and its Surrounding Landscape*, 648–743. Swindon: English Heritage.

Saville, A., 2008b, Flint extraction and processing from secondary flint deposits in the north-east of Scotland in the Neolithic period. In P. Allard, F. Bostyn, F. Giligny and J. Lech (eds), *Flint Mining in Prehistoric Europe: Interpreting the Archaeological Records*, 1–10. Oxford: British Archaeological Reports (International Series 1891).

Saville, A., 2009, The illustration of Mesolithic artefacts and its contribution to the understanding of Mesolithic technology. In S. McCartan, R. Schulting, G. Warren and P. Woodman (eds), *Mesolithic Horizons: Papers Presented at the Seventh International Conference on the Mesolithic in Europe, Belfast 2005. Vol. II*, 745–753. Oxford: Oxbow Books.

Saville, A., 2010, The origins and first 30 years of the Lithic Studies Society. *Lithics* 31, 78–87.

Schofield, A. J., 1987, Putting lithics to the test: non-site analysis and the Neolithic settlement of southern England. *Oxford Journal of Archaeology* 6(3), 269–286.

Schofield, A. J., 1991a, Lithic distributions in the Upper Meon Valley: behavioural response and human adaptation on the Hampshire chalklands. *Proceedings of the Prehistoric Society* 57(2), 159–178.

Schofield, A. J., 1991b, Artefact distributions as activity areas: examples from south-east Hampshire. In A. J. Scofield (ed.), *Interpreting Artefact Scatters: Contributions to Ploughzone Archaeology*, 117–128. Oxford: Oxbow Books.

Schofield, A. J., 1994, Looking back with regret; looking forward with optimism: making more of surface lithic scatter sites. In N. Ashton and A. David (eds), *Stories in Stone: Proceedings of Anniversary Conference at St Hilda's College, Oxford, April 1993*, 90–98. London: Lithic Studies Society (Occasional Paper 4).

Schofield, A. J., 1995, Artefacts mean nothing. In A. J. Schofield (ed.), *Lithics in Context: Suggestions for the Future Direction of Lithic Studies*, 3–8. London: Lithic Studies Society (Occasional Paper No.5).

Schofield, A. J., 2000, Reflections on the future for surface lithic artefact study in England. In J. L. Bintliff, M. Kuna and N. Venclová (eds), *The Future of Surface Artefact Survey in Europe*, 45–55. Sheffield: Sheffield Academic Press.

Shackley, M. S., 2008, Archaeological petrology and the archaeometry of lithic materials. *Archaeometry* 50(2), 194–215.

Sharples, N. M., 1991, The early prehistoric activity. In N. M. Sharples, *Maiden Castle: Excavations and Field Survey 1985–6*, 253–257. London: English Heritage.

Shennan, S. J., 1981, Settlement history in east Hampshire. In S. J. Shennan and R. T. Schadla-Hall (eds), *The Archaeology of Hampshire from the Palaeolithic to the Industrial Revolution*, 106–121. Farnborough: Hampshire Field Club and Archaeological Society (Monograph 1).

Shennan, S. J., 1985, *Experiments in the Collection and Analysis of Archaeological Survey Data: The East Hampshire Survey*. Sheffield: Department of Archaeology, University of Sheffield.

Sheridan, A., 2007, Green treasures from the magic mountains. *British Archaeology* 96 (Sept–Oct), 22–27.

Sheridan, A. and Sharples, N., 1992, Introduction: the state of Neolithic studies in Scotland. In N. Sharples and A. Sheridan (eds), *Vessels for the Ancestors. Essays on the Neolithic of Britain and Ireland in Honour of Audrey Henshall*, 1–10. Edinburgh: Edinburgh University Press.

Sheridan, A., Cooney, G. and Grogan, E., 1992, Stone axe studies in Ireland. *Proceedings of the Prehistoric Society* 58, 389–416.

Sieveking, G. de G., 1979, Grime's Graves and prehistoric European flint mining. In H. Crawford (ed.), *Subterranean Britain: Aspects of Underground Archaeology*, 1–43. London: John Baker.

Simpson, D. D. A., 1979a, The first agricultural communities (*c.* 3,500–2,5000 bc). In J. V. S. Megaw and D. D. A. Simpson (eds), *Introduction to British Prehistory from the Arrival of* Homo Sapiens *to the Claudian Invasion*, 78–129. Leicester: Leicester University Press.

Simpson, D. D. A., 1979b, The later Neolithic (*c.* 2,500–1,700 bc). In J. V. S. Megaw and D. D. A. Simpson (eds), *Introduction to British Prehistory from the Arrival of* Homo Sapiens *to the Claudian Invasion*, 130–177. Leicester: Leicester University Press.

Simpson, D. D. A., 1988, The stone maceheads of Ireland. *Journal of the Royal Society of Antiquaries of Ireland* 118, 27–52.

Simpson, D. D. A., 1989, The stone maceheads of Ireland: part 2. *Journal of the Royal Society of Antiquaries of Ireland* 119, 113–126.

Simpson, D. D. A., 1996, Irish perforated stone implements in context. *Journal of Irish Archaeology* 7, 65–76.

Simpson, D. D. A. and Ransom, R., 1992, Maceheads and the Orcadian Neolithic. In N. Sharples and A. Sheridan (eds), *Vessels for the Ancestors. Essays on the Neolithic of Britain and Ireland in Honour of Audrey Henshall*, 221–243. Edinburgh: Edinburgh University Press.

Smith, G. H., 2005, The north-west Wales lithic scatters project. *Lithics* 26, 38–56.

Smith, I. F., 1965, *Windmill Hill and Avebury: Excavations by Alexander Keiller 1925–1939*. Oxford: Oxford University Press.

Smith, I. F., 1974, The Neolithic. In C. Renfrew (ed.), *British Prehistory: a New Outline*, 100–136. London: Duckworth.

Smith, I. F., 1979, The chronology of British stone implements. In T. H. McK. Clough and W. A. Cummins (eds), *Stone Axe Studies Archaeological. Petrological, Experimental and Ethnographic*, 13–22. London: Council for British Archaeology (Research Report 23).

Smith, M. J. and Brickley, M. B., 2004, Analysis and interpretation of flint toolmarks found on bones from West Tump long barrow, Gloucestershire. *International Journal of Osteoarchaeology* 14, 18–33.

Smith, R. A., 1921, Hoards of Neolithic celts. *Archaeologia* 71(1920–21), 113–124.

Smith, R. A., 1927, Flint arrowheads in Britain. *Archaeologia* 76, 81–106.

Taylor, M. and Bradley, P., 2007, Woodworking at the long barrow. In J. Harding and F. Healy, *The Raunds Area Project: a Neolithic and Bronze Age Landscape in Northamptonshire*, 80–81. Swindon: English Heritage.

Thomas, J., 1991, *Rethinking the Neolithic*. Cambridge: Cambridge University Press.

Thomas, T., 1999, *Understanding the Neolithic*. London: Routledge.

Tingle, M., 1987, Inferential limits and surface scatters: the case of the Maddle Farm and Vale of the White Horse fieldwalking survey. In A. G. Brown and M. R. Edmonds (eds), *Lithic Analysis and Later British Prehistory: Some Problems and Approaches*, 87–99. Oxford: British Archaeological Reports (British Series 162).

Tingle, M., 1998, *The Prehistory of Beer Head: Field Survey and Excavations at an Isolated Flint Source on the South Devon Coast*. Oxford: British Archaeological Reports (British Series 270).

Topping, P., 1997, Structured deposition, symbolism and the English flint mines. In R. Schild and Z. Sulgostowska (eds), *Man and Flint: Proceedings of the VIIth International Flint Symposium Warszawa – Ostrowiec Świętokrzyski, September 1995*, 127–132. Warsaw: Polish Academy of Sciences, Institute of Archaeology and Ethnology.

Topping, P., 2004, The South Downs flint mines: towards an ethnography of prehistoric flint extraction. In J. Cotton and D. Field (eds), *Towards a New Stone Age: Aspects of the Neolithic in South-East England*, 177–190. York: Council for British Archaeology (Research Report 137).

Topping, P., 2005, Shaft 27 revisited: an ethnography. In P. Topping and M. Lynott (eds), *The Cultural Landscape of Prehistoric Mines*, 63–93. Oxford: Oxbow Books.

Torrence, R., 1986, *Production and Exchange of Stone Tools*. Cambridge: Cambridge University Press.

Torrence, R. (ed.), 1989, *Time, Energy and Stone Tools*. Cambridge: Cambridge University Press.

Tyler, A., 1976, *Neolithic Flint Axes from the Cotswold Hills*. Oxford: British Archaeological Reports (British Series 25).

Van Gijn, A. L., 1990, *The Wear and Tear of Flint. Principles of Functional Analysis Applied to Dutch Neolithic Assemblages*. Leiden: Leiden University (*Analecta Praehistorica Leidensia* 22).

Van Gijn, A. L., 1998, Craft activities in the Dutch Neolithic: a lithic viewpoint. In M. Edmonds and C. Richards (eds), *Understanding the Neolithic of North-Western Europe*, 328–350. Glasgow: Cruithne Press.

Van Gijn, A. L., 2008a, Exotic flint and the negotiation of a new identity in the 'margins' of the agricultural world: the case of the Rhine-Meuse delta. In H. Fokkens, B. J. Coles, A. L. Van Gijn, J. P. Kleijne, H. H. Ponjee and C. G. Slappendel (eds), *Between Foraging and Farming: An Extended Broad Spectrum of Papers Presented to Leendert Louwe Kooijmans*, 193–202. Leiden: Leiden University (*Analecta Praehistorica Leidensia* 40).

Van Gijn, A. L., 2008b, Toolkits and technological choices at the Middle Neolithic site of Schipluiden, The Netherlands. In L. Longo and N. Skakun, *'Prehistoric Technology' 40 Years Later: Functional Studies and the Russian Legacy*, 217–225. Oxford: Archaeopress, British Archaeological Reports (International Series 1783).

Van Gijn, A. L., 2010, *Flint in Focus: Lithic Biographies in the Neolithic and Bronze Age*. Leiden: Sidestone Press.

Van Gijn, A. L., Lammers-Keijsers, Y and Houkes, R., 2001, Vuursteen. In L. P. Louwe Kooijmans (ed.), *Hardinxveld-Giessendam De Bruin, een woonplaats uit het laat-mesolithicum en de vroege Swifterbantcultuur in de Rijn/Maasdelta, 5500–4450 v. Chr*, 153–191. Amersfoort: Rapportage Archeologische Monumentenzorg 88.

Van Gijn, A. L., Van Betuw, V., Verbaas, A. and Wentink, K., 2006, Flint, procurement and use. In L. P. Louwe Kooijmans and P. F .B. Jongste (eds), *Schipluden, a Neolithic Settlement on the Dutch North Sea Coast c. 3500 Cal BC*, 129–166. Leiden: Leiden University (*Analecta Praehistorica Leidensia* 37/38).

Varndell, G., 1991, The worked chalk. In I. Longworth, A. Herne, G. Varndell and S. Needham, *Excavations at Grimes Graves, Norfolk, 1972–1976. Fascicule 3: Shaft X: Bronze Age Flint, Chalk and Metal Working*, 94–153. London: British Museum Press.

Varndell, G., 2004, The Great Baddow hoard and discoidal knives: more questions than answers. In A. Gibson and A. Sheridan (eds), *From Sickles to Circles: Britain and Ireland at the Time of Stonehenge*, 116–122. Stroud: Tempus.

Waddle, J., 1998, *The Prehistoric Archaeology of Ireland*. Galway: Galway University Press.

Wainwright, G. J., 1972, The excavation of a Neolithic settlement on Broome Heath, Ditchingham, Norfolk, England. *Proceedings of the Prehistoric Society* 38, 1–97.

Wainwright, G. J., 1979, *Mount Pleasant, Dorset: Excavations 1970–1971*. London: Society of Antiquaries of London (Research Report 37).

Wainwright, G. J. and Longworth, I. H., 1971, *Durrington Walls: Excavations 1966–1968*. London: Society of Antiquaries of London (Research Report 29).

Warren, G., 2006, Chipped stone tool industries of the earlier Neolithic in eastern Scotland. *Scottish Archaeological Journal* 28(1), 27–47.

Warren, G., 2009, Stone tools. In H. K. Murray, J. C. Murray and S. M. Fraser, *A Tale of the Unknown Unknowns: A Mesolithic Pit Alignment and a Neolithic Timber Hall at Warren Field, Crathes, Aberdeenshire*, 97–107. Oxford: Oxbow Books.

Watson, W., 1968, *Flint Implements: An Account of Stone Age Techniques and Cultures* (third edition). London. British Museum.

Whittle, A., 1999, The Neolithic period, *c*. 4000–2500/2200 BC: changing the world. In J. Hunter and I. Ralston (eds), *The Archaeology of Britain: An Introduction from the Upper Palaeolithic to the Industrial Revolution*, 58–76. London: Routledge.

Whittle, A., 2009, The Neolithic period, *c*. 4000–2400 cal BC: a changing world. In J. Hunter and I. Ralston (eds), *The Archaeology of Britain: An Introduction from Earliest Times to the Twenty-First Century* (second edition), 78–102. London: Routledge.

Whittaker, J. C., 2004, *American Flintknappers: Stone Age Art in the Age of Computers*. Austin: University of Texas Press.

Wilde, W., 1857, *A Descriptive Catalogue of the Antiquities of Stone, Earthen and Vegetable Materials in the Museum of the Royal Irish Academy*. Dublin.

Williams, J., 1970, Neolithic axes in Dumfries and Galloway. *Transactions of the Dumfriesshire and Galloway Natural History and Antiquarian Society* 47, 111–122.

Williams-Thorpe, O., Aldiss, D., Rigby, I. J. and Thorpe, R. S., 1999, Geochemical provenancing of igneous glacial erratics from southern Britain, and implications for prehistoric stone implement distributions. *Geoarchaeology* 14(3), 209–246.

Williams-Thorpe, O., Webb, P. C. and Jones, M. C., 2003, Non-destructive geochemical and magnetic characterisation of Group XVIII dolerite stone axes and shaft-hole implements from England. *Journal of Archaeological Science* 30, 1237–1267.

Wilson, G., 1881, Notes on a collection of implements and ornaments of stone, bronze, &c from Glenluce, Wigtownshire. *Proceedings of the Society of Antiquaries of Scotland* 15 (1880–1881), 262–276.

Woodman, P., 1992, Excavations at Mad Mans Window, Glenarm, Co. Antrim: problems of flint exploitation in east Antrim. *Proceedings of the Prehistoric Society* 58, 77–106.

Woodman, P., 1994, Towards a definition of Irish early Neolithic lithic assemblages. In N. Ashton and A. David (eds), *Stories in Stone: Proceedings of Anniversary Conference at St Hilda's College, Oxford, April 1993*, 213–218. London: Lithic Studies Society (Occasional Paper No. 4).

Woodman, P., Finlay, N. and Anderson, E., 2006, *The Archaeology of a Collection: The Keiller–Knowles Collection of the National Museum of Ireland*. Bray: Wordwell.

Woodward, A., Hunter, J., Ixer, R., Roe, F., Potts, P., Webb, P. C., Watson, J. and Jones, M. C., 2006, Beaker age bracers in England: sources, function and use. *Antiquity* 80, 530–543.

Woodward, P. J., 1978a, Flint distribution, ring ditches and Bronze Age settlement patterns in the Great Ouse Valley. *Archaeological Journal* 135, 32–56.

Woodward, P. J., 1978b, A problem-oriented approach to the recovery of knapped flint debris: a field walking strategy for answering questions posed by site distributions and excavation. In J. F. Cherry, C. Gamble and S. Shennan (eds), *Sampling in Contemporary British Archaeology*, 121–127. Oxford: British Archaeological Reports (British Series 50).

Yates, M. J., 1985, Restoration of the Cuilbane stone circle, Garvagh, County Londonderry, and the discovery of a cache of flints. *Ulster Journal of Archaeology* 48, 41–50.

Young, R. and Bevan, L., 2000, The flint. In G. Hughes, *The Lockington Gold Hoard: an Early Bronze Age Barrow Cemetery at Lockington, Leicestershire*, 62–75. Oxford: Oxbow Books.

Chapter 2

The Levallois-like approach of Late Neolithic Britain: a discussion based on finds from the Stoneyhill Project, Aberdeenshire

Torben Bjarke Ballin

An attempt is made at defining the Late Neolithic Levallois-like reduction method by characterization and quantification of cores and blanks from one chronologically unmixed assemblage (Stoneyhill in Aberdeenshire), supplemented by examples from the archaeological literature. The exact date of the distinctive Levallois-like cores is discussed, and these cores are compared with classic Levalloisian cores from the Middle Palaeolithic period. It is also attempted to precisely characterize the Late Neolithic blanks with finely faceted platform remnants, to allow these to be distinguished from ordinarily faceted blanks from other prehistoric periods. It is hoped that this chapter will add to the understanding of this specific Late Neolithic industry by addressing the question of why an approach usually associated with the Middle Palaeolithic period was reintroduced in British later prehistory.

INTRODUCTION

Through the second half of the twentieth century, increasing numbers of 'tortoise' or 'Levallois-like' cores were reported from British Late Neolithic sites. Initially, these cores were perceived as residual Middle Palaeolithic artefacts, but with the mounting evidence for a Late Neolithic link (e.g. the publication of the finds from Beacon Hill in Yorkshire; Moore 1964), this direction of research was soon abandoned. With Manby's (1974) synthetic work on the Grooved Ware settlements of Yorkshire, the case for a Late Neolithic link strengthened further, as Levallois-like cores were found to form part of most larger Late Neolithic assemblages. He also identified a specific type of flake with a faceted platform remnant as the characteristic product of Late Neolithic blank production on Levallois-like cores (Manby 1974, 83).

Since the publication of Manby's work, these cores and their products have been reported from Late Neolithic sites throughout Britain, and they were discussed by Saville (1981, 44–48) in connection with his examination of the Late Neolithic and Middle Bronze Age assemblages from the flint mines at Grimes Graves in Norfolk. Recently, Levallois-like cores have been recovered from Late Neolithic settlement sites in East Anglia (e.g. Healy 1993; 1995), with further supplements from Yorkshire (e.g. Durden 1995). They have also been encountered on Late Neolithic sites in Aberdeenshire, where they were retrieved from extraction sites (e.g. Den of Boddam and Skelmuir Hill; Saville 2005; 2006) as well as settlement sites (e.g. Stoneyhill; Ballin 2004b).

However, no attempts were made at defining this lithic industry in detail, leaving a number of important questions unanswered. The more significant ones are:

- What is the exact chronology of the later (i.e. post-Palaeolithic) Levallois-like cores?
- Is it possible to distinguish between Levallois-like cores from the British Late Neolithic period and true Levallois cores from the Late Acheulean and Mousterian periods (e.g. by comparison of dimensions, degree of regularity, or presence/absence of specific attributes)?
- Faceted platforms are produced in many industries when partial core tablets are detached, and the larger the platform remnant, the larger the likelihood of that area being faceted. Is it possible to define the faceting of Late Neolithic platform remnants (on flakes from Levallois-like cores) more precisely, allowing this attribute to become truly diagnostic?
- Is the production of blanks on Levallois-like cores the only Late Neolithic reduction method, or were more than one approach applied (e.g. standard platform or bipolar reduction)? If more reduction methods were in use simultaneously, do they form sequential parts of one phased operational schema (e.g. blade core ⇒ flake core ⇒ bipolar core; cf. Ballin forthcoming b; Ballin and Johnson 2005), or do they represent parallel, independent operational schemas?

It is the aim of the present chapter to characterize and discuss the operational schema of one chronologically unmixed Late Neolithic assemblage, supported by examples from the archaeological literature. As part of this presentation, the above four questions are addressed. The assemblage from the recently excavated site Stoneyhill Area 1/Grid J in Aberdeenshire (Ballin 2004b) was selected for this purpose. This collection of 850 lithic artefacts is not only thought to be chronologically 'clean', but the size and composition of the assemblage (Table 2.1) also suggest that it may be statistically representative of its parent industry. Apart from including acceptable numbers of faceted blanks and Levallois-like cores, it also embraces typical Late Neolithic tools, such as, chisel-shaped arrowheads and finely serrated pieces. As a prelude to the definition of the site's operational schema, the available raw material, as well as the recovered blanks, preparation flakes and cores, are presented. The attribute analysis of the blanks follows the approach previously put forward elsewhere by the author (Ballin 2002; 2004a).

The following terminology is adhered to:

- 'Levalloisian' is not a culture or a period, but a reduction technique (Roe 1981, 78–89): '*This technique is important in the later part of the Lower Palaeolithic and throughout the Middle Palaeolithic in various parts of the Old World; closely related techniques occur sporadically in the Upper Palaeolithic too, and survive or are reborn later still, in the post-Pleistocene period*' (*ibid.*, 78).
- The term 'tortoise' is limited to the description of core rough-outs of tortoise-shape, that is, rough-outs for Levallois or Levallois-like cores (Figure 2.1.I–III). The reason for this stricter use of the terminology is the fact that the clearly tortoise-shaped rough-outs loose their domed appearance when reduced, and in Ballin (2004b) the reduced Levallois-like cores were referred to simply as 'flat cores'. As pointed out by Moore (1964, 192),

these bifacial pieces may be confused with the 'small, unpolished celts' (i.e. rough-outs for flint axeheads) associated with this period.

- The term 'Levallois cores' is used to refer to cores produced in the Levallois technique (Figure 2.1.IV), but of a Palaeolithic date, whereas the term 'Levallois-like cores' is used to refer to similar cores of post-Palaeolithic dates. The reason for this distinction is the anticipation of subtle differences between the original, or 'true', Levalloisian technique and its later adaptations (see discussion, below), possibly resulting in minor, but observable, differences between early and late cores produced in this manner.

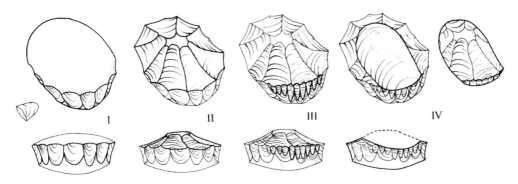

Figure 2.1. The operational schema of the Late Acheulean/Mousterian Levalloisian (from Roe 1981, fig. 3:9; drawn by the late M. H. R. Cook): I. basic shaping of nodule; II. preparation of domed dorsal surface; III. preparation of faceted striking platform on core; IV. the flake and the struck core, with their characteristic features.

THE STONEYHILL PROJECT AND AREA 1/GRID J – A BRIEF RESEARCH HISTORY

During 2002 and 2003, CFA Archaeology Ltd. carried out fieldwork at Stoneyhill Landfill Site near Peterhead, Aberdeenshire (Figure 2.2). The work was undertaken in response to planned expansion of the landfill site and involved a survey of the upstanding remains, evaluative excavation, trial trenching, gridded test-pit excavation, and actual excavation of the more promising sites (for a more detailed overview of the project area, see maps and plans in Suddaby 2002; 2003a–c).

The archaeological investigation was organized in the form of two consecutive sub-projects, COSL 2 and COSL 3, with the former focusing on a relatively small area east of the existing landfill site, surrounding and including a number of recorded cairns, whereas the latter was a much larger area north, west and southwest of the old landfill site, surrounding and including recorded cairns, a possible battle site, earthworks, and quarry remains (Suddaby 2002; 2003a; Suddaby and Ballin 2011).

As a consequence of the fieldwork, many of the recorded remains had to be re-interpreted. Only two of the known cairns were prehistoric, whereas all other cairns were associated with later field clearance. In terms of lithic yield (Table 2.1), the author

Figure 2.2. The location of the Stoneyhill site, Peterhead, Aberdeenshire.

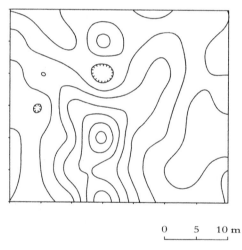

0   5   10 m

Figure 2.3. Distribution of flint across Test Pit Grid J. North is at the top; each grid unit is 5 × 5m. Contour intervals: 3 / minimum: 3. Area 1 was not explored by the excavation of systematically spaced test-pits, thus disallowing the production of a contour map of the flint distribution of that part of the site.

sub-divided the project area into 11 more substantial sites and assemblages (Ballin 2004b), one of which is Area 1/Grid J.

This area was located west of the existing landfill site. It was initially probed by the excavation of Trenches 44 and 48. The former was orientated approximately north-south, and the latter east-west, with the southern end of Trench 44 and the western end of Trench 48 almost meeting (Suddaby 2003b, 18). As lithic artefacts were recovered from the adjacent parts of the two trenches, it was decided to investigate the surrounding area by the excavation of a series of test pits. This exploratory system was labelled Grid J, and it contained 60 evenly spaced 0.5 × 0.5m test pits within an approximate square of 35 × 30m. The adjacent, and partly overlapping area, Area 1, was located east of Grid J, and it was examined by removing the topsoil by machine and subsequently excavating the appearing features by hand. Approximately 70 pits were investigated in Area 1 and the adjacent parts of Grid J (Suddaby 2003c; Suddaby and Ballin 2011).

The contour map (Figure 2.3) shows that, in Grid J, the finds are concentrated roughly along the central north-south going axis. There are three 5–7m long concentrations and, as the southernmost concentration is truncated by the margin of the grid, it must be assumed that the flint distribution continued in this direction. In Area 1, east of Grid J, lithic finds were primarily found in Feature 18 (27 lithic artefacts) and its neighbouring features, as well as in Feature 15 (eight lithic artefacts) and its surroundings, again forming a north-south going line of concentrations. The character of the finds, as well as their distribution, suggest that Area 1/Grid J may represent a Late Neolithic settlement site, and the finds recovered from Area 1's pottery-dated Bronze Age features are therefore likely to represent later intrusion. As the site has been ploughed, it is quite possible that shallow postholes may have been removed and, with them, any traces of Late Neolithic dwellings.

THE ASSEMBLAGE FROM AREA 1/GRID J – ITS COMPONENTS AND PROBABLE DATE

From Area 1/Grid J, a total of 850 lithic artefacts were retrieved (Table 2.1), including 688 pieces of debitage, 46 cores, and 116 tools. The evaluation of the Stoneyhill lithic assemblage is founded upon a detailed catalogue of the finds, and the artefacts in this report are referred to by their number (CAT no.) in this catalogue.

DEBITAGE	
Chips	51
Flakes	536
Blades	35
Microblades	6
Indeterminate pieces	45
Crested pieces	11
Platform rejuvenation flakes	4
Total debitage	*688*
CORES	
Split/flaked pebbles	1
Tortoise core rough-outs	1
'Flat cores' – remains of Levallois-like cores	25
Single-platform cores	7
Opposed-platform cores	2
Cores w two platforms at an angle	1
Irregular cores	2
Bipolar cores	1
Core fragments	6
Total cores	*46*
TOOLS	
Scalene microliths	1
Chisel-shaped arrowheads	2
Bifacial implements	2
Short end-scrapers	20
Blade-scrapers	1
Double-scrapers	2
Side-scrapers	1
Truncated pieces	1
Notches	12
Serrated pieces and saws	2
Pieces with invasive retouch	2
Pieces with edge-retouch	67
Hammerstones and anvils	3
Total tools	*116*
TOTAL	850

Table 2.1. General artefact list.

Apart from one flake and a hammerstone in quartz, a hammerstone in sandstone, and a hammerstone/anvil in quartzite, all finds are of flint. As the site is located in the Buchan Ridge Gravel zone (Kesel and Gemmell 1981), all flint from Area 1/Grid J derives from this secondary flint resource. Although the raw material is somewhat flawed, with frequent impurities and cracks, its local abundance made it relevant to the later prehistoric people in the Buchan area, and the flint was 'mined' in the later Neolithic period and possibly into the Early Bronze Age (Saville 2003; 2005; 2006).

The *debitage* includes 51 chips, 536 flakes, 35 blades, six microblades, 45 indeterminate pieces, 11 crested pieces, and four platform rejuvenation flakes. The 46 *cores* include one split pebble, one tortoise-shaped core-rough-out, 25 remains of Levallois-like cores (with one, two or three platforms), seven single-platform cores, two opposed-platform cores, one core with two platforms at an angle, two irregular cores, one bipolar core, and six core fragments. The 116 *tools* include one microlith (probably a fragmented scalene triangle), two chisel-shaped arrowheads (Types C and D; Clark 1934, 34–5), two bifacial implements, 24 scrapers, one truncated piece, 12 notched pieces, two finely serrated pieces, two fragments with bifacial/invasive retouch, 67 pieces with edge-retouch, and three hammerstones. The three largest tool groups are scrapers (21%), notched pieces (10%) and pieces with edge-retouch (59%).

Below, the technologically most significant elements – the cores, core preparation flakes and blanks – are characterized in detail. For a more detailed discussion of the tools and the assemblage as a whole, see Ballin (2004b; Suddaby and Ballin 2011).

The assemblage from Area 1/Grid J includes few strictly diagnostic types, but in terms of technological approach it appears homogeneous. The bulk of the lithic artefacts is likely to be contemporary and, though the finds were not necessarily deposited during the same occupation of the site, they were most likely abandoned in the area during one prehistoric period. The narrow microlith is thought to be a solitary stray find, and may have been lost during a Late Mesolithic hunting episode.

A chisel-shaped arrowhead [CAT 890] (Figure 2.4), and the probable fragment of another [CAT 881], suggest a general Late Neolithic date for the assemblage (Clark 1934; Green 1980; Manby 1974). This date is supported by the distinctive operational schema adhered to by the knappers of Area 1/Grid J, including the reduction of tortoise-shaped rough-outs into characteristic 'flat cores' and, not least, the application of fine faceting of the platform and abrasion of the platform-edge (see below). This particular technological approach has frequently been referred to in the archaeological literature as 'Levallois-like', and tortoise cores or rough-outs and 'Levallois-like' cores have been reported from Late Neolithic contexts throughout Britain (e.g. Durden 1995; Healy 1993; Manby 1974; Moore 1964; Saville 1981; 2005; 2006). These objects are, for unknown reasons, especially common in Yorkshire (e.g. Moore 1964), and their affinity with Late Neolithic settlement sites was noticed by Manby (1974) in his volume on the Grooved Ware sites of that county.

Manby (1974, 83) also defines a typical Late Neolithic lithic tool kit, which combines the above-mentioned cores with chisel-shaped/oblique arrowheads, discoidal flint knives, various forms of edge-ground tools, plano-convex knives on blades (where the Bronze Age variant would be on flakes), finely serrated flakes and blades (Figures 2.5–6), and robust, well-executed scrapers. Several of these implements are relatively uncommon on settlement sites, such as discoidal and plano-convex knives, but with its characteristic cores, chisel-shaped points, finely serrated pieces and robust scrapers (several of which are on abandoned Levallois-like cores) the assemblage from Area 1/Grid J presents itself as typically Late Neolithic.

The two bifacial pieces [CAT 764, 768] are unquestionably post-Mesolithic, but their shapes are too indistinct to allow precise classification and thereby dating. They both appear to have lost a pointed end and may be rough-outs for Early Neolithic leaf-shaped points, but CAT 764 could also be a rough-out for a discoidal knife. It is estimated that probably approximately 95% of the present assemblage is Late Neolithic, supplemented by a small number of mainly earlier pieces.

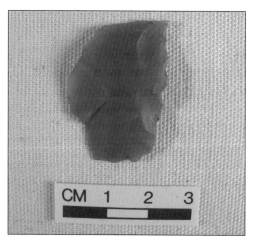

Figure 2.4. Chisel-shaped arrowhead.

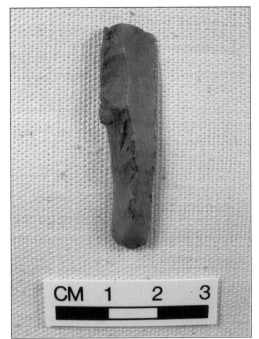

Figure 2.5. A finely serrated blade – full size.

Figure 2.6. Enlarged section of the finely serrated blade shown in Figure 2.5.

RAW MATERIAL AND RAW MATERIAL PROCUREMENT

Virtually all finds from the Stoneyhill Project are in flint (2,756 of 2,788 pieces, or approximately 99%), supplemented by 32 pieces in other types of raw material (*c.* 1%). As the colour of the flint artefacts apparently co-varies with general flint quality and flaking-properties, the colours of the preparation flakes, cores and tools were classified according to a detailed colour scheme. It was possible to group the many flint colours and qualities in the following three main categories: 1) flint of red/orange/honey-brown colours (following the terminology of the author's report on the flint artefacts from the Carmelite Friary in Aberdeen (Ballin forthcoming a), this flint is referred to as flint of the orange group); 2) grey flint; and 3) flint of other colours (due to the dominance of light olive-green hues, this flint is referred to as flint of the light olive-green group). It was possible to further subdivide the flint of the orange group into two varieties, namely I) fine-grained, homogeneous, relatively pure flint, frequently associated with a superficial sheen, and II) somewhat coarser flint characterized by the same level of impurities and weaknesses as flint of the light olive-green group, and with a fresh appearance (i.e. no sheen); grey flint is generally fresh, fine- to medium-grained and relatively homogeneous; and flint of the light olive-green group is mostly fine- to coarse-grained, fresh and with abundant impurities and weaknesses (chalk balls, fossils, frost cracks and planes of weakness).

Within the Stoneyhill project area in general (for overview see Suddaby 2002; 2003a–c), grey flint was practically only found in Pit 7183 beneath Cairn 7/17, with the odd grey piece of debitage in Cairn 7/17's general fill. In Table 2.2 (based on the cores and tools of the Stoneyhill collection), grey flint makes up 72% of the finds from Pit 7183, but the debitage from this feature is almost exclusively in flint of this colour. Flint of the orange group's variety I tends to be associated with early prehistoric material (e.g. Site 14), and flint of the light olive-green group (e.g. Area 1/Grid J), as well as orange flint of Variety II (e.g. Cairn 7/6/Trench 9 Ext.), with later prehistoric material (a distinction is made between earlier prehistoric – Mesolithic and Early Neolithic – and later prehistoric – Late Neolithic and Bronze Age – based on technological differences. The former period embraces microblade and blade industries, and the latter mainly flake-based industries (Pitts and Jacobi 1979)). The grey assemblage from Cairn 7/17 is thought to date to the later part of the Late Neolithic period, or the earliest part of the Early Bronze Age period.

It is difficult to unequivocally determine the provenance of the three flint types. As indicated by Saville's work at the Den of Boddam and Skelmuir Hill (Bridgland *et al.* 1997, 46; Saville 1995, 360), the colour of the flint in the local Buchan Ridge Gravels varies from brownish hues to a grey colour, possibly depending on ultra-local differences in matrix composition; a higher content of kaolin in the matrix seems to result in greyer colour tones. This experience is confirmed by the author's work at Nørholm in northern Jutland, Denmark, where the same type of flint differed in colour from yellow-orange-brown (boggy areas), over grey (the chalk-rich hill area), to pitch-black (the sulphur-rich tidal zone), with flint colour clearly being dependent on ultra-local chemical factors. It is quite possible that the project's red, orange and honey-coloured flint derives from watercourses and bog areas (iron-rich environments), with grey and light olive-green flints deriving from drier environments at higher elevations.

However, with flint colours also co-varying with flint grain-sizes and the level of impurities, the picture is probably somewhat more complex. Two scenarios are possible:

- *either* the relatively fine-grained flints of the orange and grey groups were imported into the area, for example from coastal areas, with the light olive-green and coarser orange varieties being local flint forms,
- *or* all three flint types are locally available but represent different procurement strategies, with early prehistoric knappers being more selective and being willing to invest more time in selecting finer-grained flint nodules with better flaking-properties.

The fact that the presently available evidence (Saville 1995, 365) suggests that extensive exploitation (e.g. in the form of pit extraction) of the Buchan Ridge flint deposits is a mainly late prehistoric activity supports the first option. It is, however, difficult to imagine that early prehistoric people of the Stoneyhill area lived their lives on top of a huge deposit of flint gravels without exploiting this, and it is possible that they made use of more superficial sources of local flint, for example exposed in local streams (explaining the 'orangey' colours). If the grey flint, which may be of a Late Neolithic date (see below), was not procured from a local source, it may represent importation from more southern parts of Britain, such as Yorkshire. As noted by Saville (2003, 407), many Late Neolithic arrowheads found in Scotland are in exotic dark grey flint that probably derives from sources in northern England.

The lithic assemblage from Area 1/Grid J is composed primarily of flint of the light olive-green variety (66%), with the remainder mainly belonging to the orange group's category II, that is, the coarser form of this colour variety. The flint is generally heavily affected by cracks and fissures and, due to the combined effects of frost shattering, plough impacts, and prehistoric knapping of weakened nodules, much of the flint found on the site is in the process of disintegration. It is thought that many of the indistinct nodule fragments (i.e. pieces entirely defined by natural surfaces) in the area were created when the Late Neolithic settlers attempted to reduce weakened pebbles and cobbles. This, however, is not immediately clear from the composition of the assemblage (Table 2.1), as all fragments without distinct man-made attributes were discarded.

The material from this assemblage is obviously local gravel flint, rather than coastal flint or imported southern flint (for a detailed description of the Buchan Ridge flint, see Bridgland *et al.* 1997; Saville 1995). The fact that the flint preference of the Stoneyhill settlers has 'switched' from fine-grained orange flint to coarser, largely light olive-green flint suggests a change to a local procurement pattern, and it is thought that the flint recovered from Area 1/Grid J may have been 'mined' rather than collected. The earliest dates for the extractive operations in the area are Late Neolithic, based partly on radiocarbon dating of buried soils and peat (*terminus post quem* of *c.* 3500–3000 cal BC/*terminus ante quem* of *c.* 2500–2000 cal BC; Saville 1995, 366), and partly on the find of a Late Neolithic chisel-shaped arrowhead (*ibid.* 365). The latter makes the assemblages from the Buchan Ridge quarries roughly contemporary with the present assemblage (two chisel-shaped arrowheads). For a discussion of the actual mining operations, and the associated features, see Saville (1995; 2005).

THE BLANKS, PREPARATION FLAKES AND CORES

Debitage

The debitage includes 51 chips, 536 flakes, 35 blades, six microblades, 45 indeterminate pieces, 11 crested pieces, and four platform rejuvenation flakes. Attribute analysis of a random selection of flakes and blades showed that this industry is based entirely on hard-hammer platform technique, with the blanks having average dimensions of 31.8 × 23.5 × 8.0mm. The aim of the industry was clearly to produce elongated flakes and short blades, though blades from the first production series (particularly from the removal of crests) occasionally turned out long and slender. In the discussion section (below), this industry is compared with two other late prehistoric industries, and an attempt is made at distinguishing between the blanks of apparently similar late prehistoric material cultures. The operational schema of the present material culture is obviously similar to that of Late Neolithic assemblages throughout Britain (see references above), for which reason the characterization of the industry has been given some priority.

Preparation flakes

Eleven intact or fragmented crested blades [CAT 747, 799, 818, 819, 837, 842, 850, 856, 888, 903, 909] are relatively slender pieces (Figure 2.7). Three intact pieces have average dimensions of 32 × 15 × 10mm (L:W ratio = 2.1), but the dimensions of the fragmented specimens suggest

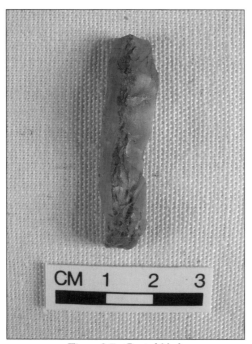

that, on this site, crested blades frequently had L:W ratios of 3 or more, and CAT 850 has a L:W ratio of 4. In comparison, the standard flakes of this industry have an average L:W ratio of 1.4. The platform remnants of intact and proximal pieces show how the crests frequently met the platform-edge at a distinct angle [e.g., CAT 799, 837]. Four pieces have been classified as platform rejuvenation flakes [CAT 742, 771, 836, 862], as they are short irregular flakes (mean dimensions: 23 × 23 × 7mm) with fine modification of the platform remnants. However, where this would usually characterize a traditional core tablet, with the fine modification being surviving trimming, this modification may be the fine platform-faceting recognized on many ordinary Late Neolithic flakes (see discussion section, below). Or in other words, these 'platform rejuvenation flakes' may be irregular, shorter-than-intended, ordinary flakes, rather than preparation flakes.

Figure 2.7. Crested blade.

Cores

The cores form an exceedingly homogeneous group, with almost 60% of all cores representing different stages of the same core type. The core group includes one split pebble, one tortoise core rough-out, 25 Levallois-like cores (with varying numbers of platforms), seven single-platform cores, two opposed-platform cores, one core with two platforms at an angle, two irregular cores, one bipolar core, and six core fragments (Table 2.1). The average dimensions of the Levallois-like cores are 52 × 44 × 23mm, and the average L:W and W:Th ratios are 1.21 and 1.95 (Figures 2.8–9). This indicates that, at the time of abandonment, these cores were generally slightly longer than their width, and almost twice as broad as they were thick, explaining why these pieces were preliminarily defined as 'flat cores' in the database's sub-type field, prior to their correct identification as Levallois-like cores.

Most likely, the first step of this operational schema (Figure 2.1) was to produce thick discoidal, or tortoise-shaped, rough-outs, such as CAT 798 (68 × 59 × 39mm) (Figure 2.10). This rough-out was probably discarded as a result of the creation of several deep step-fractures. Contrary to CAT 798, which has been almost completely decorticated, most rough-outs would have had fully cortex-covered, domed 'under-sides' and slightly arched, decorticated 'top-sides' (the prospective flaking-fronts). Mostly, flakes and blades were only detached from one face of the parent piece (at Beacon Hill in Yorkshire, 'single-sided tortoise cores' and 'double-sided tortoise cores' are present at a ratio of *c.* 3:1; Moore 1964,

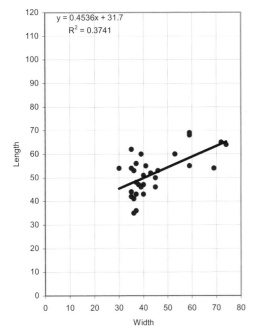

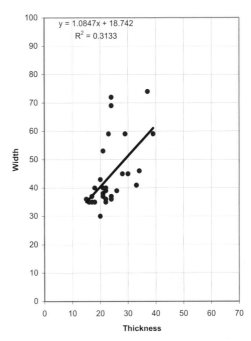

Figure 2.8. Length: width of all Levallois-like cores.

Figure. 2.9. Width: thickness of all Levallois-like cores.

194; from Area 1/Grid J, only one core had been worked in a double-sided fashion [CAT 885], seemingly in an attempt to exhaust the core completely).

As best indicated by CAT 738 (which was discarded shortly after commencement of production), these special cores were prepared by first detaching small flakes around the entire circumference, at a perpendicular angle to the flaking-front (Figure 2.1 and Figures 2.11–12). Then one end was transformed into a faceted platform, which would be faceted more finely before the first flakes or blades were struck off (basically, this corresponds to horizontal trimming). Occasionally, the cores were trimmed in the traditional manner (vertical trimming) and in many cases the trimming, or the fine faceting, was combined with abrasion of the platform-edge (see Table 2.2). A crest flanked either side of the flaking-front, from platform to apex.

The morphology of the Levallois-like cores reveals some of the weaknesses of this approach, the main one being the tendency of blanks to become rather broad due to the flatness of the flaking-fronts (Figure 2.13). The longest blanks are the crested pieces (the first blanks of the production process proper), which were detached from the distinctly ridged edges of the cores. Blanks from the central part of the cores frequently removed the core apexes by plunging. The tendency of many flakes to terminate in step- or hinge-factures reflects the properties of the flint, as well as the approach (i.e. the application of insufficient force). In a number of cases, it was attempted to revive the cores by adding a secondary (opposed-platform cores) or tertiary platform (irregular cores) (see Table 2.1).

Table 2.2. The attributes of the Levallois-like cores from Area 1 / Grid J (Surv. lat. prep. = surviving lateral preparation, or partial lateral crests).

CAT NO	CORE TYPE	PROVENANCE	L	W	TH	L:W	W:TH	L:TH	PLATFORMS PLAIN	FACETED	FINELY FACETED	PLATFORM-EDGE UN-TRIMMED	TRIMMED	ABRADED	PLUNGED APEX	SURV. LAT. PREP.
798	Tortoise' core (rough-out)	Area 1 / Test Pit Grid J	68	59	39	1.15	1.51	1.74		NA			x			x
738	Single-platform core	Area 1 / Test Pit Grid J	69	59	29	1.17	2.03	2.38		x		x				x
739	Single-platform core	Area 1 / Test Pit Grid J	54	35	16	1.54	2.19	3.38		x		x			x	
745	Single-platform core	Area 1 / Test Pit Grid J	41	36	22	1.14	1.64	1.86			x	x				x
775	Single-platform core	Area 1 / Test Pit Grid J	51	40	21	1.28	1.90	2.43			x	x		x		
780	Single-platform core	Area 1 / Test Pit Grid J	35	36	15	0.97	2.40	2.33			x		x		x	x
789	Single-platform core	Area 1 / Test Pit Grid J	46	39	26	1.18	1.50	1.77		x			x	x		
795	Single-platform core	Area 1 / Test Pit Grid J	54	30	20	1.80	1.50	2.70		x			x			
800	Single-platform core	Area 1 / Test Pit Grid J	47	40	18	1.18	2.22	2.61	x				x		x	x
803	Single-platform core	Area 1 / Test Pit Grid J	52	43	20	1.21	2.15	2.60	x				x		x	
814	Single-platform core	Area 1 / Test Pit Grid J	36	37	17	0.97	2.18	2.12			x		x	x	x	
816	Single-platform core	Area 1 / Test Pit Grid J	42	35	17	1.20	2.06	2.47			x		x			x
825	Single-platform core	Area 1 / Test Pit Grid J	43	40	22	1.08	1.82	1.95	x				x			x
849	Single-platform core	Area 1 / Test Pit Grid J	55	41	33	1.34	1.24	1.67		x		x				
894	Single-platform core	Area 1 / Test Pit Grid J	54	69	24	0.78	2.88	2.25		x			x			
902	Single-platform core	Area 1 / Test Pit Grid J	46	45	28	1.02	1.61	1.64		x		x			x	
905	Single-platform core	Area 1 / Test Pit Grid J	48	37	24	1.30	1.54	2.00		x			x			
790	Opposed-platform core	Area 1 / Test Pit Grid J	62	35	22	1.77	1.59	2.82	xx				xx			
793	Opposed-platform core	Area 1 / Test Pit Grid J	64	74	37	0.86	2.00	1.73		x	x	x	x			
797	Opposed-platform core	Area 1 / Test Pit Grid J	65	72	24	0.90	3.00	2.71		xx		xx				
812	Opposed-platform core	Area 1 / Test Pit Grid J	60	39	22	1.54	1.77	2.73	x		x	x	x			x
813	Opposed-platform core	Area 1 / Test Pit Grid J	53	36	24	1.47	1.50	2.21	x		x	x	x			
839	Opposed-platform core	Area 1 / Test Pit Grid J	44	35	18	1.26	1.94	2.44		x	x	xx				
883	Opposed-platform core	Area 1 / Test Pit Grid J	60	53	21	1.13	2.52	2.86		x	x	xx				x
885	Irregular core	Area 1 / Test Pit Grid J	50	45	30	1.11	1.50	1.67	x		xx	xxx				
886	Irregular core	Area 1 / Test Pit Grid J	56	37	17	1.51	2.18	3.29			x	x				

Figure 2.10. Tortoise-shaped core rough-out.

Figure 2.11. Early-stage Levallois-like core, from above.

Figure 2. 12. Early-stage Levallois-like core, from the platform / right lateral side.

Figure 2.13. Late-stage Levallois-like core ('flat core').

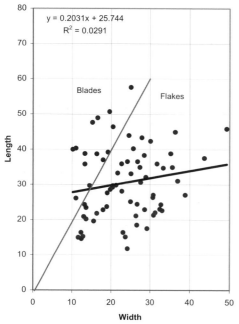

Figure 2.14. *Length:width of selected blanks from Area 1/Grid J.*

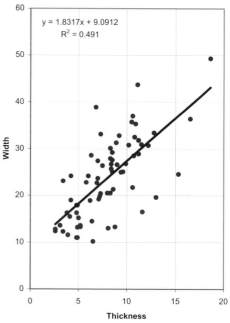

Figure 2.15. *Width:thickness of selected blanks from Area 1/Grid J.*

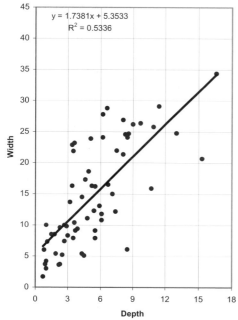

Figure 2.16. *Width:depth (platform remnant) of selected blanks from Area 1/Grid J.*

Seven more traditional single-platform cores do not fit the general characteristics of the Levallois-like cores presented above. CAT 765 and 827 are core-sides of conventional single-platform cores (mean dimensions: 43 × 38 × 19mm), and they probably broke off their parent pieces due to the presence of planes of weakness or frost cracks. CAT 860 is a small rolled single-platform core (32 × 25 × 16mm) which may pre-date the bulk of the Area 1/Grid J assemblage. The remaining four single-platform cores [CAT 736, 757, 794, 815] are considerably bulkier than the flat Levallois-like cores, but they also share attributes with this category, such as faceting/fine faceting of the platforms. The latter suggests that the Levallois-like cores and these four single-platform cores are parts of the same technological tradition. CAT 736 and 794 are relatively long, traditional single-platform cores (mean dimensions: 54 × 42 × 38mm), whereas CAT 757 and 815 are fairly short specimens (31 × 40 × 38mm), which may be re-shaped/re-cycled Levallois-like cores.

Traditional opposed-platform cores are few, with one [CAT 792] being a stocky, relatively irregular specimen (53 × 44 × 32mm). It has massive step-fractures at one end, which probably caused it to be abandoned. CAT 910 is somewhat thicker than most 'flat cores' (53 × 46 × 34mm), but its general shape (in particular its flat corticated 'under-side') suggests that it may be an 'outsider' of the Levallois-like core group. One core with two platforms at an angle [CAT 744] (58 × 35 × 27 mm) is probably a Levallois-like single-platform core which split due to an unexpected plane of weakness. After having split along its long axis, a secondary platform was created perpendicular to the original one. Two relatively cubic irregular cores have three or more platforms or flaking axes; one [CAT 767] is relatively small (49 × 29 × 28mm), and one [CAT 748] considerably larger (56 × 56 × 48mm). A bipolar core [CAT 851] is a Levallois-like core (55 × 42 × 25mm), which was exhausted completely by the application of hammer-and-anvil technique, whereas a split pebble [CAT 907] is an oval pebble from which one flake was removed by the use of bipolar technique (68 × 51 × 38mm). It was not possible to classify six core fragments [CAT 843, 848, 868, 869, 877, 879] more precisely. They are all from Grid J, and they all disintegrated due to either frost cracks / planes of weakness or exposure to fire (mean dimensions: 50 × 39 × 27mm).

TECHNOLOGICAL PROFILE OF THE INDUSTRY

As shown in Table 2.3, the 70-piece blank sample from this site consists predominantly of flint of the light olive-green group, which was procured from the local gravel deposits. The blanks are mainly elongated flakes (L:W ratio 1.4), and in Figures 2.14–16 the main dimensions of these pieces are shown. The assemblage includes several high-quality blades, most of which are crested pieces. Figure 2.17 illustrates the widths of the blanks, and the almost bell-shaped curve of the diagram indicates that the sample is likely to be chronologically unmixed (cf. Ballin and Johnson 2005); the small secondary peak is probably largely a result

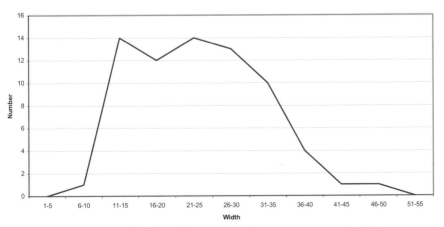

Figure 2.17. The widths of selected blanks from Area 1/Grid J.

of the small sample size (n=70). As stated in Ballin (2002), samples of at least 100 pieces are preferable, as smaller sample sizes may result in random statistical fluctuations. However, it is also possible that the two peaks are the results of the intentional and simultaneous production of two different types of blanks – slender blades and broad flakes.

The operational schema of this industry is obviously phased, with the first stage representing careful core preparation. Basically, the shaping of the core rough-out follows the steps described by Roe (1981, fig. 3:9; this report Figure 2.1) in his discussion of the Late Acheulean/Mousterian Levalloisian, resulting first in the production of a thick discoid (a 'tortoise' core), with a relatively flat flaking-front and a more domed 'under-side' (Roe 1981, fig. 3.9: Steps I–II). Only one such core was recovered from Area 1/Grid J [CAT 798]. Though most Late Neolithic 'tortoise' cores would have had an almost fully corticated 'under-side' (as demonstrated by the many discarded Levallois-like cores from this site), CAT 798 has been almost completely decorticated (for a detailed description of the site's Levallois-like cores, see Table 2.3).

In contrast to Palaeolithic Levalloisian cores (Figure 2.1), the core rough-outs of Area 1/Grid J were provided not only with a finely faceted striking-platform (Roe 1981, fig. 3.9: Step III), but also with two regular lateral crests along either side of the flaking-front. Scrutiny of the platform remnants of the site's crested blades shows that the slightly curved lateral crests met the platform at almost right or obtuse angles. When the core rough-out was fully formed, the first blade/flake series was initiated by detaching the crests (Figure 2.18). These blanks were long, elegant blades (not uncommonly with L:W ratios of 4 or more), due to the well-defined dorsal guide ridges. As blanks were detached further and further towards the centre of the flat, or slightly domed, flaking-front, these blanks grew increasingly shorter and broader. Due to the flat flaking-fronts, the broad central flakes frequently removed the cores' apex by plunging. Considering this 'design flaw', it is puzzling why it was chosen to introduce a 'Levallois-like' approach into the British Late Neolithic. It is possible that this particular technique was perceived as beneficial, as it allowed the production of long blades for, for example, serrated pieces [e.g. CAT 741, 874] and broad flakes for chisel-shaped arrowheads [e.g. CAT 881, 890] within the same operational schema?

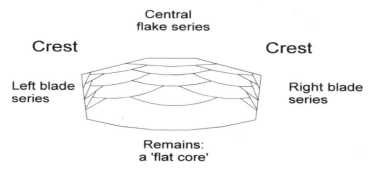

Figure 2.18. The Levallois-like reduction sequence: first, a number of crested blades and ordinary blades are detached from the core's flanks, near the two lateral guide ridges; then, a series of flakes are detached from the relatively flat central flaking front.

	EARLY LN (?)	LATE LN (?)	LBA (?)	LBA
	AREA 1/TP GRID J	CAIRN 7/17 (PIT 7183)	CAIRN 7/6 / TRENCH 9 EXT.	RAUNDS
POPULATION	N=70	N=80	N=96	3 SAMPLES
Grey flint	1%	100%	0%	NA
Flint of the orange group	4%	0%	77%	NA
Flint of the light olive-green group	95%	0%	23%	NA
Primary material	4.3%	7.5%	15.6%	10-12%
Secondary material	42.8%	55.0%	46.9%	50-65%
Tertiary material	52.9%	37.5%	37.5%	25-38%
Av. length	31.8 mm	24.6 mm	24.1 / 24.6 mm (2)	19-21 mm
Av. width	23.5 mm	20.5 mm	21.6 / 17.0 mm (2)	18-20 mm
Av. thickness	8.0 mm	6.3 mm	5.9 / 6.0 mm (2)	6-7 mm
Av. platform remnant width	14.6 mm	11.4 mm	13.5 mm (1)	11-13 mm
Av. platform remnant depth	5.3 mm	4.0 mm	4.2 mm (1)	4-5 mm
Av. flaking-angle	100.8°	106.1°	106.5° (1)	109-113°
Av. no. of parallel dorsal ridges	1.10	0.89	0.60	Almost none
LW ratio	1.4	1.2	1.1 / 1.5 (2)	1.0-1.1
WTh ratio	2.9	3.3	3.7 / 2.8 (2)	Not calc.
WD ratio	2.8	2.6	3.2 (1)	2.7-2.8
Platform : bipolar technique	100:00	100:00	35:65	100:00
Pronounced bulbs	80.9%	81.3%	73.5% (1)	72-83%
Multiple bulbs	25.0%	16.3%	8.8% (1)	13-16%
Platform collapse	2.9%	8.8%	1.0%	1.9%
Split bulbs	0.0%	1.3%	5.2%	5-7%
Impact scars	29.4%	45.0%	38.2% (1)	43-57%
No dorsal preparation	55.2%	71.2%	97.1 (1)	80-90%
Trimming	26.9%	15.0%	2.9% (1)	10-20%
Abrasion	17.9%	13.8%	0.0% (1)	0.0%
Corticated platform	10.6%	7.5%	17.7% (1)	31-37%
Plain platform	27.3%	33.8%	61.8% (1)	42-45%
Faceted platform	36.4%	36.3%	20.6% (1)	19-21%
Finely faceted platform	25.8%	16.3%	0% (1)	0.0%
Hinged terminations	17.8%	16.4%	16.7%	40-48%

Table 2.3. Technological key-figures for the operational schema of the assemblage from Area 1/Grid J; for comparison, the key-figures of two other late prehistoric assemblages from the Stoneyhill area are included (Ballin 2004b), as well as the key-figures of three LBA samples from the Raunds area, Northamptonshire (Ballin 2002). The populations have been sequenced according to their estimated dates. (1) percentage of platform blanks; (2) platform blanks/bipolar blanks.

Before and during the detachment of blanks, the platform-edge was prepared. This primarily took the form of fine faceting of the platform surface immediately behind the platform-edge (horizontal trimming), occasionally combined with, or replaced by, trimming (traditional, or vertical, trimming) and/or abrasion (rounding) of the platform-edge. The flakes and blades were then detached by the application of hard percussion, as demonstrated by the many pronounced bulbs, multiple bulbs and incipient cones or impact scars. As demonstrated by the average flaking-angle of the assemblage (ventrally *c.* 100°/dorsally *c.* 80°), the hammerstone met the platform at an almost right angle (Figure 2.19).

As noted by Manby (1974), Late Neolithic blanks are characterized by having finely faceted platform remnants, which is a direct consequence of the choice of core shape and the applied systematic core preparation. Most likely, platforms of Levallois-like cores were not rejuvenated by detaching traditional core tablets, and the 'core tablets' recovered in connection with this assemblage are most likely ordinary flakes which have been erroneously classified as a consequence of their finely faceted platform remnants (incorrectly perceived as traditional trimming) and their likeness to traditional platform rejuvenation flakes.

Occasionally, the Levallois-like cores were reorientated in an attempt to exhaust the cores completely. First, they were provided with a second, opposed platform and, later, possibly even a third platform, transforming them into irregular Levallois-like cores. Only in one case [CAT 885] was it attempted to exhaust a Levallois-like core by flaking its secondary face (the 'under-side'). As demonstrated by Table 2.1, the Late Neolithic Levallois-like cores were supplemented by a small number of traditional single-platform, opposed-platform, irregular and bipolar cores but, as suggested above (characterization of the site's cores), several of these may represent attempts at exhausting damaged Levallois-like cores. Though it cannot be ruled out that parallel blank production was carried out on traditional cores, it appears that, at Stoneyhill, seemingly traditional cores are *ad hoc* adaptations of the Late Neolithic Levallois-like approach.

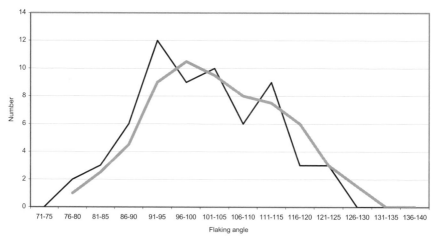

Figure 2.19. Flaking-angle of selected blanks from Area 1/Grid J. The fluctuating curve (black) is most likely the result of a 'smaller-than-ideal' sample size – to provide a more accurate impression of the trend a 'moving average' has been calculated and inserted (grey).

DISCUSSION

As indicated in the introduction, the main purpose of this chapter is to gain a deeper understanding of the British Late Neolithic 'Levalloisian'. To this end, four key questions were asked, and below it is attempted to address these questions on the basis of the evidence presented above, in conjunction with supplementary information from the archaeological literature.

The chronology of the post-Palaeolithic Levallois-like approach

In general, the Levallois-like approach is associated with two diagnostic elements, namely *petit tranchet* derivative arrowheads (Clark's (1934) *petit tranchet* derivative types B–D are referred to as chisel-shaped arrowheads, and types E–I as oblique arrowheads) and Impressed Ware / Grooved Ware pottery, indicating a mainly Late Neolithic date. Levallois-like cores do not seem to be a feature of the Bronze Age levels at Grimes Graves (Saville 1981, 47), and they are absent from Bronze Age contexts in East Anglia (Healy 1993). They are usually not reported from British Early Neolithic sites.

The precise dating of British Levallois-like cores is complicated by poorly defined, misleading or erroneous core classification. This problem predominantly relates to assemblages excavated and published prior to 1990, but some 'unhelpful' classification systems are still in circulation. The main problem, in this respect, is the use of the poorly defined core types D and E ('keeled cores') in Clark's core typology (Clark 1960). As discussed in Ballin (forthcoming c), the keeled core categories may include types such as Levallois-like, discoidal and bipolar cores, as well as rough-outs for platform cores with undetached crested guide ridges. In some cases, analysts have expanded Clark's type list to include an additional core type called tortoise, Levallois-like or Levalloisoid (e.g. Durden 1995, 425), but in most cases it is necessary to inspect the artefact illustrations of older sites to assess whether any Levallois-like cores were recovered from these locations. It is an additional complication that many older excavation reports do not include illustrations of the cores (or very few: e.g. Wainwright and Longworth 1971), or the cores were not dealt with at all (e.g. Fell 1952).

As mentioned above, the assemblage from Area 1/Grid J includes two chisel-shaped arrowheads (Types C1 and D), and a chisel-shaped arrowhead was recovered from surface contexts at Den of Boddam (Saville 1995, 364). Unfortunately, no diagnostic arrowheads were retrieved from Saville's excavations at Den of Boddam and Skelmuir Hill (1995; 2005). Scrutiny of artefact illustrations in reports on assemblages from the English later Neolithic period shows that, in most cases, the associated arrowheads belong to the various chisel-shaped categories, such as at Beacon Hill (Moore 1964), Hunstanton (Healy 1993) and Middle Harling (Healy 1995).

It is complicated to assess the small number of cases associating Levallois-like cores with oblique arrowheads, either as a result of incomplete reporting, absence of relevant artefact illustrations, or site/assemblage size. Some of the sites/assemblages combining Levallois-like cores and oblique arrowheads are fairly large and complex and may reflect multiple visits to the location (e.g. Durden 1995; Saville 1981). However, although it is difficult to know exactly what is included in the various core categories of assemblages like

Durrington Walls (Wainwright and Longworth 1971) and Storey's Bar Road (Pryor 1978), these assemblages with evolved oblique arrowheads *appear* not to include Levallois-like cores. This suggestion, in conjunction with the probability of the assemblage from Tye Field (Tye F: Healy 1985) embracing oblique arrowheads and Levallois-like cores, indicate that Levallois-like cores are largely associated with chisel-shaped arrowheads, and that they may have been phased out shortly after the introduction of oblique arrowheads.

At Hunstanton, a number of chisel-shaped arrowheads were associated with Grooved Ware (Healy *et al.* 1993, 34), suggesting that the common perception of chisel-shaped arrowheads being associated with Peterborough Ware (in Scotland: Impressed Ware) and oblique arrowheads with Grooved Ware may be an over-simplification (cf. discussion in Saville 1981, 49–50). This notion is further supported by the material from pits at Fengate, where chisel-shaped and oblique arrowheads were found together (e.g. Pit W17; Pryor 1978, 21), and Green (1980, 235–236) has documented the association of chisel-shaped arrowheads with the Clacton and Woodlands sub-styles. Probably, oblique arrowheads are associated exclusively with Grooved Ware pottery, whereas the simpler forms of the transverse arrowhead may appear in Peterborough Ware (Impressed Ware) as well as Grooved Ware contexts.

Levallois-like cores have traditionally been associated with Grooved Ware contexts (cf. Healy 1993, 33), but recent research – such as the excavation of East Lochside in Angus, and examination of the site's lithic and ceramic finds – associates the Levallois-like approach with Impressed Ware (Johnson and Ballin 2006). However, the entire East Lochside settlement was ploughed up, with no finds recovered in situ, and precise dating of this important diagnostic type requires the excavation and analysis of new undisturbed Late Neolithic sites. Presently, the only arrowhead type *certainly* associated with Levallois-like cores is the chisel-shaped point, suggesting a date of the Levallois-like approach in the earlier part of the Late Neolithic period.

Differences between the Levallois and Levallois-like approaches and their respective cores

The central difference between the two approaches is probably their general purpose. It is a truism that the primary purpose behind the traditional Levallois technique was to predefine the shape of either oval or pointed flakes removed from the central part of the Levallois cores' flaking-fronts (Figure 2.1; also Roe 1981, 78–89; however, also see Inizan *et al.* 1992, 48–56). This relatively limited scope is directly related to the limited tool spectrum, and thereby formal needs, of the later Acheulean and Mousterian periods.

The British Late Neolithic, on the other hand, is characterized by a much more varied tool spectrum, with *petit tranchet* derivatives, serrated pieces and scrapers being the three most important types (e.g. Honington (Fell 1952); Beacon Hill (Moore 1964); Hunstanton (Healy 1993); Middle Harling (Healy 1995)). As, for example, chisel-shaped arrowheads are based on broad, relatively thin flakes, and serrated pieces on long slender blades, it is most likely that the Late Neolithic Levallois-like approach had a dual purpose (*contra* Durden 1995, 411), namely the production of two distinctly different types of blanks on the same core type: blades from the crested areas of the cores; and broad flakes from the centre of the flaking-fronts (Fig 2.18). This suggestion is supported by the fact that, at Stoneyhill Area 1/Grid J, many crested blades were produced (11 pieces, or almost two per cent of the debitage), and one of the two serrated pieces has a surviving dorsal crest. The fact that the serrated pieces of British Late Neolithic flake industry are mainly on elegant blades was also noted by Healy (1993, 33; 1995, 37). The scrapers of this material culture are generally on oval, thick flakes – most probably waste flakes from the decortication of cores (*c.* 80% of the scrapers from Area 1/Grid J retain cortex).

The different purposes of the two core types, Levallois cores and Levallois-like cores, have a direct effect on the associated operational schemas, as the first step of the Levallois approach is to detach one or more flakes from the central part of the core's main flaking-front, whereas the first step of the Levallois-like approach is to detach the two lateral crests and, usually, a series of blades immediately next to and under the crests. As mentioned above, one of the 'design flaws' of the Levallois and Levallois-like approaches is that the flaking-front's flatness tends to produce many more plunging flakes than in connection with other reduction techniques. This flaw is counteracted (but not removed) by detaching the crests first, as this makes the flaking-front more domed and slightly less prone to plunging.

In terms of the general shape of the two core types, there are no fundamental differences, but the tortoise rough-outs of the later approach tend to have been more extensively prepared, with more carefully, more finely, faceted platforms, and more regular crests. The main differences appear in the later stages of the two operational schemas, largely as a consequence of the Levallois-like approach's focus on the production of crested blades and blades. The detachment of crests and their immediate surroundings removes major parts of the cores' lateral sides, and where a Levallois core frequently has surviving scars from the initial preparation of the core laterals (Figure 2.1.I), in most cases, these scars have been removed from the laterals of the Levallois-like cores. To the inexperienced specialist it may be difficult to acknowledge the later stages of Levallois-like cores for what they truly are, but these 'flat cores' are quite characteristic pieces (see presentation above). The most secure way of recognizing the application of Levallois-like reduction is by a full assemblage analysis, and by the combination of core rough-outs, 'flat cores', crested blades, finely faceted flakes and blades (see following section), and petit tranchet derivatives/serrated pieces. Usually, the lustre of the pieces will define them as either Palaeolithic or post-Palaeolithic specimens, as most of the former have a characteristic sheen, whereas most of the latter have reasonably fresh surfaces.

A more precise definition of the platform remnants of Late Neolithic flakes

As clearly stated by Manby (1974, 83), '*... narrow flake facets across the butt of flakes and tools ...*' are a characteristic feature of Late Neolithic assemblages. This trait is not always a dominating feature, as proven by Saville's (1981, 41) demonstration of low 'faceted butt ratios' in several sub-assemblages at Grimes Graves (*c.* 4-10%), but the main point is that these finely faceted pieces are *present* in Late Neolithic assemblages, whereas they are usually *absent* in assemblages from other prehistoric periods. The noticeable difference between the low ratios (*c.* 4–10%) of the Grimes Graves Late Neolithic levels and the high ratios (*c.* 50–60%) of the Late Neolithic Stoneyhill assemblages (Area 1/Grid J and Cairn 7/17 [Pit 7183]; Table 2.3) may reflect the different characters of the sites, with Grimes Graves being mainly a quarry-cum-factory site, whereas the Stoneyhill assemblages represent domestic or ritual depositions.

The main problem relating to the diagnosticity of the characteristic Late Neolithic flake butts is the fact that in some reports lithic analysts have excluded the word 'finely' from the description of these faceted platform remnants, and it may be claimed that a given assemblage includes Late Neolithic elements due to the presence of faceted butts. This is an unfortunate simplification, as faceted platform remnants are produced in practically all traditional lithic industries, where rejuvenation of platforms by detaching core tablets is practiced. Not all core tablets are complete, either by accident or by choice, and whenever partial core tablets are removed from platform surfaces, subsequent blanks tend to have faceted platform remnants. Obviously, the larger the platform remnant, the larger the possibility of that area becoming faceted. In other industries, small hinged flakes may have been detached immediately behind the platform-edge, either to adjust the platform-edge or to provide a more suitable 'seat' for a pressure-flaking punch, and the subsequent blanks from these cores may also acquire faceted platform remnants.

As suggested above, the fine faceting of Late Neolithic core platforms and flake butts should probably be seen as a form of horizontal trimming, and it is practically indistinguishable from traditional vertical trimming. Only *finely* faceted platform remnants are diagnostic of the British Late Neolithic.

The basic elements ('modules') of Late Neolithic flint-knapping

Even accepting that many of the keeled cores of the published Late Neolithic assemblages may be Levallois-like, it is obvious that flakes were also produced on other core forms. At Beacon Hill (Moore 1964, 194), for example, the flint collection includes 65 Levallois-like cores, as well as 100 more traditional fluted cores. Some of the traditional core types recovered from Late Neolithic sites may be exhausted Levallois-like cores, where the detachment of the lateral crests and the lateral sides have made positive identification difficult, and some may be adaptations of damaged Levallois-like cores (both examples represented in the assemblage from Area 1/Grid J; see above). However, there is little doubt that some production of ordinary flakes took place on traditional platform cores.

At present, it is not possible to assess the operational schemas of most published assemblages, as the majority of these were classified according to Clark's type schema from 1960, but the assemblage from Area 1/Grid J suggests that parallel production on traditional core types was less common than blank production on Levallois-like cores. In several cases, seemingly traditional cores are based on alteration or exhaustion of Levallois-like cores, and maybe as little as a handful of platform cores are traditional specimens formed specifically for the production of simple flakes. The frequent fine faceting of platforms on both core types indicates contemporaneity between traditional cores and their Levallois-like counterparts. The varying ratios between Levallois-like and traditional cores on Late Neolithic sites may be a reflection of different site activities, or Levallois-like cores may be particularly common in certain Late Neolithic phases.

FUTURE PERSPECTIVES

As indicated in the discussion above, it is quite possible to distinguish between Middle Palaeolithic Levallois cores and Late Neolithic Levallois-like cores. The two core types represent distinctly different industries, with the former aiming at the production of oval or pointed flakes and the latter at the production of long slender blades *as well as* broad flakes. The different aims lay the foundations of two different operational schemas, where the focus of the Levallois approach is the core's broad flaking-front, whereas the Levallois-like approach requires well-shaped lateral crests to allow the production of the industry's serrated blades as a supplement to the production of chisel-shaped arrowheads on broad blanks from the flaking-front.

However, the above characterization of the Levallois-like approach is based largely on one lithic assemblage, supported by finds from all parts of Britain. Most of these supplementary assemblages are chronologically mixed, poorly dated, or published without focus on the details relevant to the present investigation, and further scrutiny of the Levallois-like approach is clearly necessary.

Hopefully, the examination of additional assemblages with Levallois-like components may add detail to the operational schema outlined above, and the Beacon Hill assemblage from Flamborough Head in Yorkshire is a fine candidate for analysis. In the initial publication (Moore 1964), the site is presented as the focus of visits in the Late Neolithic as well as in the Beaker period. However, all the lithic finds, from both horizons, appear to represent a Late Neolithic Levallois-like assemblage, including chisel-shaped arrowheads as well as 'tortoise' cores. No flints from the buried horizons were datable to the Early Bronze Age. The pottery, on the other hand, was defined as a mixture of Western Neolithic, Peterborough, Rinyo-Clacton and Beaker Wares, and it is presently difficult to explain this contradictory situation. Most likely, judging from the composition of the worked flint presented in Moore's paper, the buried soils contain mainly Late Neolithic material, with some later finds recovered from higher levels, topsoil and surface contexts. The apparently unmixed lithic assemblage ought to be re-examined in the hope of adding detail to the Levallois-like operational schema sketched in this chapter. As the presentation of the site (Moore 1964, fig. 1) suggests that the Neolithic and Bronze Age finds may be separated horizontally, it may even be possible to make use of the lithics from the surface, by the application of 'horizontal stratigraphy', thus increasing the number of artefacts useful to this discussion.

Although the Levallois-like approach is clearly Late Neolithic, and associated with diagnostic elements like chisel-shaped arrowheads and Impressed Ware/Grooved Ware pottery, the industry needs to be dated more precisely. The suggested date of the earlier part of the Late Neolithic period is somewhat vague, and the later Late Neolithic assemblages included above are generally problematic in terms of their chronology, classification and/or manner of publication. Currently, it cannot be ruled out that blanks continued to be produced on Levallois-like cores after the introduction of oblique arrowheads. However, accurate definition of the beginning and end of the Late Neolithic Levallois-like approach requires radiocarbon dating of secure contexts associated with Levallois-like cores. This ought to be given some priority.

ACKNOWLEDGEMENTS

The author is grateful to Professor Derek Roe, University of Oxford, for kindly permitting the use of Fig. 2.1. Thanks are also owed to Ian Suddaby, CFA Archaeology Ltd, for cooperation in connection with the production of the original Stoneyhill lithics report, and to Beverley Ballin Smith, Glasgow University Archaeological Research Division, for photographing the artefacts.

BIBLIOGRAPHY

Ballin, T. B., 2002, Later Bronze Age flint technology: a presentation and discussion of post-barrow debitage from monuments in the Raunds area, Northamptonshire. *Lithics* 23, 3–28.

Ballin, T. B., 2004a, The Mesolithic period in southern Norway: material culture and chronology. In A. Saville (ed.), *Mesolithic Scotland and its Neighbours: the Early Holocene Prehistory of Scotland, its British and Irish Context, and some Northern European Perspectives*, 413–438. Edinburgh: Society of Antiquaries of Scotland.

Ballin, T. B., 2004b, *Stoneyhill Landfill Site, Peterhead, Aberdeenshire (COSL). The lithic assemblage.* Unpublished report: CFA Ltd, Edinburgh.

Ballin, T. B., forthcoming a, The lithic assemblage. In A. Cameron, Excavations at the Green, Aberdeen: a medieval Carmelite House revealed. *Internet Archaeology*.

Ballin, T. B., forthcoming b, The Quartz assemblage. In H. Moore and G. Wilson, *The Bayanne Project, Shetland.* Lerwick: Shetland Amenity Trust.

Ballin, T. B., forthcoming c, Struck flint from West Cotton, Irthlingborough and Stanwick: overview of the lithic evidence. In J. Harding and F. Healy (eds), *Raunds Area Project. The Neolithic and Bronze Age Landscapes of West Cotton, Stanwick and Irthlingborough, Northamptonshire.* London: English Heritage.

Ballin, T. B. and Johnson, M., 2005, Glentaggart, South Lanarkshire – discussion of a Scottish chert assemblage and its associated technology. *Lithics* 26, 57–86.

Bridgland, D. R., Saville, A. and Sinclair, J. M., 1997, New evidence for the origin of the Buchan Ridge Gravel, Aberdeenshire. *Scottish Journal of Geology* 33(1), 43–50.

Clark, J. G. D., 1934, Derivative forms of the petit tranchet in Britain. *Archaeological Journal* 91, 32–58.

Clark, J. G. D., 1960, Excavations at the Neolithic site at Hurst Fen, Mildenhall, Suffolk. *Proceedings of the Prehistoric Society* 26, 202–245.

Green H. S., 1980, *The Flint Arrowheads of the British Isles. A Detailed Study of Material from England and Wales with Comparanda from Scotland and Ireland.* Oxford: British Archaeological Reports (British Series 75i–ii).

Durden, T., 1995, The production of specialised flintwork in the later Neolithic: a case study from the Yorkshire Wolds. *Proceedings of the Prehistoric Society* 61, 409–432.

Fell, C. I., 1952, A Late Bronze Age urnfield and Grooved-Ware occupation at Honington, Suffolk. *Proceedings of the Cambridge Antiquarian Society* 45, 30–43.

Healy, F., 1985, The struck flint. In S. J Shennan, F. Healy, F. and I. Smith, The excavation of a ring-ditch at Tye Field, Lawford, Essex. *Archaeological Journal* 142, 177–207.

Healy, F., 1993, Lithic material [from Redgate Hill]. In R. Bradley, P. Chowne, R. M. J. Cleal, F. Healy and I. Kinnes, *Excavations on Redgate Hill, Hunstanton, Norfolk, and at Tattershall Thorpe, Lincolnshire*, 28–39. Gressenhall and Boston: East Anglian Archaeology Report 57.

Healy, F., 1995, Prehistoric material. In A. Rogerson, *A Late Neolithic, Saxon and Medieval Site at Middle Harling, Norfolk*, 32–40. Gressenhall: East Anglian Archaeology Report 74.

Inizan, M.-L., Roche, H. and Tixier, J., 1992, *Technology of Knapped Stone*. Meudon: Cercle de Recherches et d'Etudes Préhistoriques (Préhistoire de la Pierre Taillée 3).

Johnson, M., and Ballin, T. B. 2006, Gaining knowledge from the ploughsoil: a finds scatter from East Lochside, Kirriemuir. *Scottish Archaeology News* 51, 9.

Kesel, R. H. and Gemmell, A. M. D., 1981, The 'Pliocene' gravels of Buchan: a reappraisal. *Scottish Journal of Geology* 17(3), 185–203.

Manby, T. G., 1974, *Grooved Ware Sites in the North of England*. Oxford: British Archaeological Reports (British Series 9).

Moore, J. W., 1964, Excavations at Beacon Hill, Flamborough Head, East Yorkshire. *Yorkshire Archaeological Journal* 41, 191–202.

Pitts, M. W. and Jacobi, R. M., 1979, Some aspects of change in flaked stone industries of the Mesolithic and Neolithic in southern Britain. *Journal of Archaeological Science* 6, 163–177.

Pryor, F., 1978, *Excavations at Fengate, Peterborough, England: The Second Report*. Toronto: Royal Ontario Museum (Royal Ontario Museum Archaeology Report 5).

Roe, D. E., 1981, *The Lower and Middle Palaeolithic Periods in Britain*. London: Routledge & Kegan Paul.

Saville, A., 1981, *Grimes Graves, Norfolk. Excavations 1971/72: Volume II. The Flint Assemblage*. London: HMSO (Department of the Environment Archaeological Reports 11).

Saville, A., 1995, GB20 Den of Boddam near Peterhead, Grampian Region, Scotland, GB 21 Skelmuir Hill, Grampian Region, Scotland: prehistoric exploitation of flint from the Buchan Ridge Gravels, Grampian Region, north-east Scotland. *Archaeologia Polona* 33, 353–368.

Saville, A., 2003, Lithic resource exploitation for artefacts in prehistoric and early historic Scotland. In T. Stöllner, G. Körlin, G. Steffens and J. Cierny (eds), *Man and Mining – Mensch und Bergbau. Studies in Honour of Gerd Weisgerber on Occasion of his 65th Birthday,* 405–413. Bochum: Deutsches Bergbau-Museum (=*Der Anschnitt* 16).

Saville, A., 2005, Prehistoric quarrying of a secondary flint source: evidence from north-east Scotland. In P. Topping and M. Lynott (eds), *The Cultural Landscape of Prehistoric Mines,* 1–13. Oxford: Oxbow Books.

Saville, A., 2006, Flint technology associated with extraction sites in north-east Scotland. *In* G. Körlin and G. Weisgerber (eds), *Stone Age – Mining Age*, 449–454. Bochum: Deutsches Bergbau-Museum (=*Der Anschnitt* 19).

Suddaby, I., 2002, Stoneyhill Landfill, Longhaven, Peterhead (Cruden parish). Survey; evaluation. *Discovery and Excavation in Scotland 2002*, 9.

Suddaby, I., 2003a, Stoneyhill Landfill, Peterhead (Cruden parish). Prehistoric features. *Discovery and Excavation in Scotland 2003*, 17.

Suddaby, I., 2003b, *Stoneyhill Landfill, Peterhead, Aberdeenshire (COSL 3). Site Extension. Archaeological Evaluation. Updated Data Structure Report*. Report 753 (Revison 1). Unpublished report: CFA Ltd, Edinburgh.

Suddaby, I., 2003c, *Stoneyhill Landfill, Peterhead, Aberdeenshire (COSL 3). Site Extension. Stage 2: Excavation and Test-Pitting, Cells 2a–2c. Stage 3: Watching Brief, Laeca Burn re-route, Cells 2a–2c, Cells 3c–d. North Aldie Farm*. Data Structure Report. Report 788. Unpublished report: CFA Ltd, Edinburgh.

Suddaby, I. and Ballin, T. B., 2011, *Late Neolithic and Late Bronze Age Lithic Assemblages Associated with a Cairn and other Prehistoric Features at Stoneyhill Farm, Longhaven, Peterhead, Aberdeenshire, 2002–03*. Scottish Archaeological Internet Reports 45 [http://www.sair.org.uk/sair45]

Wainwright, G. J. and Longworth, I. H., 1971, *Durrington Walls: Excavations 1966–1968*. London: Society of Antiquaries of London (Reports of the Research Committee No. 29).

Chapter 3

The felsite quarry complex of Northmaven: observations from a fact-finding mission to Shetland

Torben Bjarke Ballin

In this chapter the felsite quarry complex of Northmaven, Shetland, is presented and discussed. Although the location represents one of the most extensive Neolithic procurement sites in Britain, its remote location has prevented detailed examination and discussion. Little is known about the site's specific proportions, its components or sub-sites, exact chronology, likely out-put volume, organization of the mining operations, as well as the exchange in and use of the quarried raw material. The purpose of this chapter is to summarize the presently available information on the Shetland felsites, in the hope that this may form the foundation of a future project delving into this matter.

INTRODUCTION

In 1968 Ritchie published his paper on 'The Stone Implement Trade in Third-Millennium Scotland', in which he discussed the sources and distribution of Rhum bloodstone, Arran pitchstone, Irish porcellanite, Perthshire hornfels, and Northmaven felsite. In the introduction, he states that this paper is not a full account, '... but rather ... a survey of what has been done and of future possibilities'. Aside from Ritchie's paper, Irish porcellanite has been dealt with fairly comprehensively (Cooney and Mandal 1998; Jope 1952; Meighan *et al.* 1993; Morey and Sabine 1952; Sheridan 1986), and the hornfels quarries at Creag na Caillich have now been described in detail (Edmonds *et al.* 1992). The procurement and distribution of Rhum bloodstone was discussed as part of the presentation of the lithic artefacts from Kinloch (Clarke and Griffiths 1990), and pitchstone has been touched upon in connection with the excavation of settlements and monuments on Arran (e.g. Barber 1997), as well as in connection with a separate pitchstone project (e.g. Ballin 2009). However, the archaeological aspects of the Northmaven felsites have not been dealt with at all.

The apparent lack of interest in the felsite outcrops probably mainly reflects the location of these geological sources in a remote – and very exposed – part of Shetland, combined with the fact that only a handful of *possible* felsite objects have been found outside the island group (Ritchie 1968; Ritchie and Scott 1988). The available archaeological and geological literature nevertheless gives the impression of a field of study with substantial research potential, and the author decided to investigate Northmaven's felsite sources, quarries, and workshops further. To allow the detailed definition of a future felsite project, a fact-finding mission to Shetland was required, partly to assess the holdings of felsite artefacts in the Shetland Museum in Lerwick, and partly to assess the source area of Northmaven in northernmost mainland Shetland.

The examination of the museum's felsite artefacts had as its main aims to gauge: 1) how much worked felsite actually exists; 2) which tool types were produced in this raw material; and 3) the date of these implements (via diagnostic elements). Expeditions to Northmaven had as their main aims to assess: 1) how many of the so-called 'dykes' have been exploited in prehistory; and 2) which activities, more specifically, were carried out at the individual locations in Northmaven (types of sites/types of features). The present chapter puts forward the preliminary results from this fact-finding mission, and outlines the framework of a future felsite project.

HISTORY OF RESEARCH

The archaeological discussion of the Northmaven complex has largely been limited to Ritchie's paper (1968) on the most significant lithic and stone raw materials exploited in the Scottish Neolithic period, supplemented by occasional notes in excavation reports (e.g. Calder 1950; 1956; 1963), monument records (see the online CANMORE database), and Shetland guide books (e.g. Fojut 1986).

The focus has generally been on the roofed knapping floor, or working gallery, at the Beorgs of Uyea, which was originally described by Scott and Calder (1952). The so-called 'axe factory' has never been subjected to closer archaeological scrutiny. To the lay visitor this roofed structure may easily be mistaken for an expedient form of chambered cairn, as, on the local Ordnance Survey map, the remains of a chambered cairn has been plotted in its vicinity, but not the working gallery itself. The walls of this (now un-roofed) cairn only survive to approximately half a metre and are easily missed in the rubble of the Beorgs of Uyea (cf. Henshall 1963, 156; RCAHMS 1946, 99; Scott and Calder 1952).

Although the various references to the Beorgs of Uyea 'axe factory' mention several knapping floors scattered across the hillside (e.g. Fojut 1986, 59; Turner 1998, 49), only the working gallery is described in any detail. In the online CANMORE database, for example, the heading 'Stone Implement Factory; Quarry' covers a description of the roofed structure, but does not mention the remaining quarry complex. Ritchie (1968) gives an account of the exploited raw material and the outcrops, but based wholly on reports from geological work carried out in the region (primarily Phemister *et al.* 1952).

The entire Northmaven area has been surveyed extensively by geologists, many of whom have shown great interest in the region's felsite occurrences (Mykura 1976; Mykura and Phemister 1976; Phemister *et al.* 1952; Phillips 1926). The felsites were defined in terms of petrology, chemical composition and visual attributes, and a number of north-south trending dykes were mapped, from Ronas Voe in the south to Calder's Head in the north (e.g. Phemister *et al.* 1952, fig. 1). However, although the maps may be accurate, in the sense that felsite dykes may be present in the vicinity of the mapped 'dykes', the author's inspection of several 'dykes' in the area between Collafirth Hill and Ronas Hill, as well as on the Beorgs of Uyea itself, suggests that these features are, in most cases, scree-like tailing piles and knapping floors, and not *in situ* geological features. This problem is discussed in more detail below.

In his paper on 'Aspects of intentional fracture', Lacaille (1938) discussed the flaking properties of 'Shetland porphyry'. It is thought that this material is either felsite (in the older archaeological literature referred to as 'Uyea porphyry') or the closely related quartz-feldspar porphyry (cf. Ritchie and Scott 1988).

THE NORTHMAVEN FELSITES

This section is mainly based on Phemister *et al.* (1952), Mykura and Phemister (1976), and Mykura (1976). The felsites exploited for Shetland's Neolithic axeheads and knives are generally discussed by geologists as part of the island group's minor intrusions. These intrusions include basic as well as acid members, with the former including principally basalts and dolerites and the latter felsites and quartz-feldspar porphyries, as well as spessartine, microdiorite and feldspar porphyrites. Dolerite is usually perceived as an excellent material for axeheads, but, on Shetland, felsite and quartz-feldspar porphyry were preferred for the manufacture of axeheads and polished knives, probably due to their striking visual qualities.

In northern Shetland, basic dykes are common in the southern half of Northmaven (south of Ronas Voe), whereas acid dykes are common on Vementry and Muckle Roe, immediately south of Northmaven, and north of Ronas Voe (North Roe). It appears that North Roe was favoured as a focus for the island group's stone implement production, as this area is particularly rich in colourful, strikingly patterned felsites. The reason for this, is the fact that many of the felsites of North Roe contain the sodic minerals riebeckite and aegirine, providing a blue, bluish-green, or purple colour. These so-called 'riebeckite felsites' are also frequently spherulitic and/or flow-banded. The exploitation of the area's non-riebeckite felsites and quartz-feldspar porpyries may simply be a consequence (a 'by-product') of the intense prospecting and quarrying activities forming part of the exploitation of the riebeckite felsites. In the following text, the term 'Northmaven' refers to the area north of Ronas Voe.

The acid dykes generally form parallel swarms, trending approximately north-south. The dykes are intrusive into the body commonly referred to as the Ronas Hill Granite. This area includes pockets of diorite, and it is surrounded by older metamorphic rock. The riebeckite-bearing dykes are limited to a four kilometre-wide lenticular zone, from Ronas Voe to Calder's Head. In the main, the acid dykes of Northmaven form four local groups or swarms: 1) the Collafirth Hill/Ronas Hill area; 2) the low-lying area between this area and the Beorgs of Uyea; 3) the Beorgs of Uyea; and 4) the area in the immediate vicinity of Calder's Head.

Mykura (1976, 95) suggests that the acid dykes are generally of late Caledonian, possibly Upper Devonian age (*c.* 350 Ma), whereas Finlay (1930, 693) suggests that the riebeckite felsites are of Tertiary age (<60 Ma). However, as Phemister *et al.* (1952) comment: 'since there are in Scotland riebeckite lavas and intrusions of Ordovician, Caledonian and Carboniferous, as well as Tertiary age, no conclusion on the question of age can be reached on the basis of mineralogical similarity'. In relative terms, the area's basic dykes, spessartites, microdiorites and porphyrites are older than the quartz-feldspar porphyries, and they are older than the felsites. The blue riebeckite-bearing felsites are younger than the white, pink, and dull felsites without riebeckite and aegirine. The acid dykes vary considerably in size, from a width of a few centimetres to about 18m, but some lenticular outcrops are locally up to 55m wide.

Though quartz-feldspar porphyry is closely related to felsite, this rock type is not felsite *sensu stricto*. However, due to petrographic and other similarities, Phemister *et al.* (1952, 365) chose to group Northmaven's quartz-feldspar prophyries with the area's non-riebeckite felsites, and, in the following text, the term 'felsite' is used as a generic term, embracing riebeckite-bearing and non-riebeckite felsites, as well as quartz-feldspar porphyries. In archaeological terms, this is a logical choice, as all three rock types were quarried in Northmaven and used, albeit selectively (see below), for axeheads and Shetland knives. In addition, some varieties from all three groups are so macroscopically similar, that it would require thin-section analysis to unequivocally define the individual artefacts as having been produced in one or the other type of rock, although the bluish specimens with the most stunning spherulites and patterning are almost certainly in riebeckite felsite.

Phemister *et al.* (1952) suggest the following general classification of felsites and related rock types (they did not include the group 'non-porphyritic, spherulitic felsites', but some knives are evidently in this type of rock):

1. Riebeckite-bearing felsites
   1.1. Non-porphyritic, non-spherulitic felsites
   1.2. Non-porphyritic, spherulitic felsites
   1.3. Porphyritic, spherulitic felsites
2. Felsites without riebeckite or aegirine
3. Quartz-feldspar porphyries

As mentioned above, the riebeckite-bearing varieties are usually in bluish colours, but dove-grey and stone-grey forms are common; the bluest varieties are usually from the chilled margins of the dykes. Type 1.1 specimens are generally of blue, purplish, or pale mauve colours; Type 1.2 specimens are commonly pinkish or stone-grey with spherulites in the size range of 1–10 mm; and Type 1.3 specimens frequently have a silver-grey matrix with tiny blue prisms of riebeckite, white, pink or red feldspar phenocrysts, clear blebs of quartz, and deep blue spherules of varying size. The non-riebeckite felsites are mostly white, pink, brown or red, occasionally with minor pockets of blue, or bluish margins. The majority of these felsite outcrops are spherulitic or sub-spherulitic. The quartz-feldspar porphyries, on the other hand, are non-spherulitic, but contain numerous, large phenocrysts of quartz and feldspar, and, occasionally, small amounts of biotite. For more detailed information on the petrography and chemistry of the felsites, see Phemister *et al.* (1952).

THE FACT-FINDING MISSION AND ITS RESULTS

During a visit to Shetland in September 2004, the author visited Shetland Museum in Lerwick. Office space was kindly provided by the museum, and access was granted to exhibitions as well as stores. During this visit, all artefacts in felsite were examined, and extensive notes were taken. In total, approximately 50 axeheads and 40 so-called Shetland knives were studied, in conjunction with a small number of other objects, such as arrowheads, scrapers, and hammerstones.

Following the examination of the museum's holdings of felsite artefacts, two general surveys were carried out in the Northmaven region: one of the area between Collafirth Hill and Ronas Hill, focusing on the Midfield summit and slopes, and one of the Beorgs of Uyea, in the northern part of Northmaven. On both occasions, the author was accompanied by Andy Duffus, Bressay, whose local knowledge ensured that the little time available was well spent, and Beverley Ballin Smith, Glasgow University, kindly assisted with the photographing of dykes/tailing piles/workshops and features on the Beorgs of Uyea. The inspection of the Neolithic 'axe factory' covered the area from the above-mentioned working gallery to the western boundary of the scheduled area. Due to time constraints, the low-lying area between the Collafirth Hill/Ronas Hill summits and the Beorgs of Uyea was not examined, although Phemister *et al.*'s map of Northmaven felsite occurrences indicate that, in this area, several 'dykes' (or quarries?) exist.

The examination of felsite implements in the Shetland Museum provided information as to: 1) the range of artefact types produced in this type of raw material; 2) which tool types were produced in which sub-types of felsite; and 3) the date of these objects and, indirectly, the date of felsite procurement in the Northmaven area. The Northmaven expeditions mainly provided information on: 1) the different types of felsite present in the different parts of the Northmaven area; and 2) the number, character and distribution of different types of sites and features.

Artefact types produced in felsite

The examination of the museum exhibitions and stores clearly demonstrated that felsite was largely reserved for the manufacture of axeheads and Shetland knives. Approximately 50 axeheads and 40 Shetland knives were examined, whereas other artefact categories only include small numbers of felsite specimens. This impression is supported by observations during the fieldwork in Northmaven, where rough-outs for axeheads and knives were noticed, but no other pre-forms or finished tools.

Though asymmetrical, or curved, adzeheads in felsite do exist, this general artefact category mainly consists of symmetrical axeheads. The felsite axeheads are mostly round- or pointed-butted specimens, with pointed-oval cross-sections and – in several cases – splayed edges (Figures 3.1–2). A small number of axehead-shaped pieces are exceptionally thin (e.g. ARC 65458, 65659, 65283), and it was thought that they could be axehead-shaped knives. However, as the sharp edge is at an end rather than along one of the lateral sides, they are more likely to be thin-bladed, pointed-butted axeheads.

The felsite knives are generally relatively large, but thin, polished pieces (thickness mostly *c.* 5mm), although more robust specimens (e.g. ARC 668) do exist (thickness up to *c.* 25mm). Usually the felsite knives are of a small number of related forms. Most likely, freshly shaped and polished pieces were of sub-rectangular form, more or less shaped like the so-called Piet Hein 'super-ellipse' (Figures 3.3, 4–6; cf. Vestergaard 2005). It is possible that the more asymmetrical and kidney-shaped forms developed during use, probably as a result of repeated sharpening of the edge. Usually, the slightly convex, straight or concave edges are blunt, and the distinctly convex edges sharp (contrary to, for example, traditional knives and sickles), supporting the interpretation of these pieces as flensing-knives related to the Greenland 'Ulu', but the find circumstances of

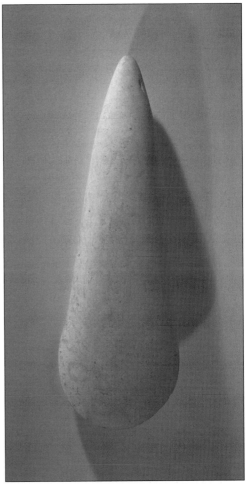

Figure 3.1. Typical round-butted stone axehead from Shetland (courtesy of Shetland Museum).

Figure 3.2. Typical pointed-butted stone axehead from Shetland (courtesy of Shetland Museum).

the knives, as deliberate depositions rather than loss, indicate use in the ritual sphere (cf. Fojut forthcoming).

A limited number of felsite arrowheads were noticed, distributed almost equally across small squat specimens with a rounded base, and small double-pointed, kite-shaped pieces. Although most of these specimens may be primary pieces, produced on small felsite waste flakes, at least one arrowhead rough-out (ARC 6618) has a polished face, indicating that it was made on a fragment from an abandoned axehead or knife. The museum collections held several felsite end-scrapers, which were mostly robust pieces with regularly convex, steep working-edges. Although pieces with a polished 'dorsal' face were noticed (ARC 65832 is polished on either face), most of the felsite scrapers have polished 'ventral' faces (e.g., ARC 1990–519, ARC 691), suggesting that this tool type may generally be based

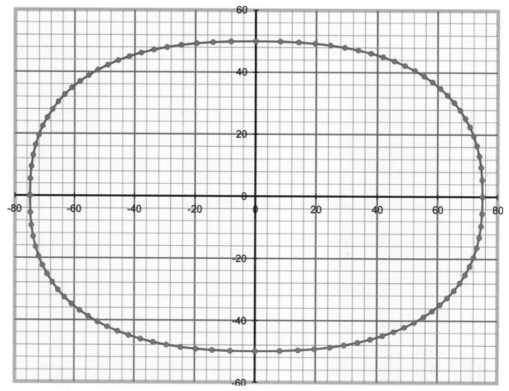

Figure 3.3. Piet Hein's 'super-ellipse' (courtesy of Erik Vestergaard, Haderslev Grammar School).

on scrap from abandoned polished axeheads. ARC 65828 is classified as a felsite 'core', but it has crush-marks at either end and is therefore more likely to be a hammerstone. A surviving knapping-seam at one end indicates that this piece may be the recycled fragment of a failed felsite axehead rough-out. An expedient felsite scraper with a polished 'ventral' face was recovered in connection with the excavation of the Scord of Brouster settlement (Ballin 2005).

Felsite sub-types and raw material preference

Examination of the museum's artefacts clearly demonstrated that different types of felsite were preferred for different implement types. Battle-axes and axe-hammers are generally not in felsite, though some exist. The Shetland battle-axes and axe-hammers are mainly in coarser-grained materials, supporting Fenton's general observations concerning Scottish pieces. He found that, in most cases, greywacke, basic and intermediate igneous rocks, and metabasites were used, supplemented by a small group of 'other' rock types (Fenton 1988, 108, table 35).

Scottish unperforated axeheads (Ritchie and Scott 1988), on the other hand, are mainly in fine-grained rocks, including some basic types of rock (quartz-dolerite), but with substantial numbers of axeheads being in acid igneous rocks (e.g. tuff and felsite) or metamorphic rocks (e.g. porcellanite and schist). Few Shetland axeheads have been analysed via thin-sectioning or chemical analysis, but macroscopic attributes indicate that, probably, most of the specimens in the museum exhibitions and stores are in felsite. The Shetland knives are generally so visually distinct (e.g. colour and spherulites) that there can be little doubt that they are almost exclusively in felsite.

However, different forms of felsite were apparently selected for the two implement types, axeheads and Shetland knives. The axeheads are generally in relatively plain, homogeneous forms of felsite, without spherulites, but frequently with small phenocrysts of quartz and feldspar, and their colours mainly vary between purple and dove-grey. The knives, on the other hand, are much more spectacular, with blue, blue-green, or purple colours dominating, and with above-average size spherulites, but mostly containing few phenocrysts. During the author's expeditions to Northmaven, some sources with medium-sized spherulites were located on the Beorgs of Uyea, but none with the large spherulites favoured by Neolithic people. This variety may either be generally rare, have been exhausted, or it may derive from sources in the unexplored area in the central parts of Northmaven. As most of the remaining tool types seem to be recycled axehead fragments, they are mostly in the same purple variety of felsite as those, with some phenocrysts but few spherulites.

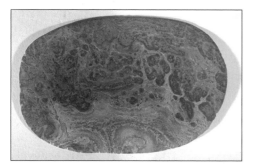

Figure 3.4. Typical Shetland knife (courtesy of Shetland Museum).

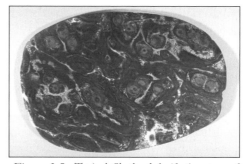

Figure 3.5. Typical Shetland knife (courtesy of Shetland Museum).

Figure 3.6. Typical Shetland knife (courtesy of Shetland Museum).

Possible dates of the felsite artefacts

The felsite objects, and thereby the felsite quarrying in Northmaven, have generally been dated to the later part of the Neolithic period, or even the Early Bronze Age, mostly through association with diagnostic pottery (e.g. Fojut 1986, 17–18; Turner 1998, 50). This date is being challenged by typological evidence, as several of the island group's leaf-shaped arrowheads are in felsite (e.g. Scott and Calder 1952, 176). These arrowheads are usually associated with the Early Neolithic period, but unfortunately few of the common leaf-shaped sub-types are diagnostic (within the Neolithic period). However, several of the Shetland pieces are kite-shaped, such as the pieces from 'Lerwick' (ARC 662) and Semblester in Sandsting (ARC 666). These points are usually associated with the later part of the Early Neolithic period (in northern England, the Towthorpe Burial Tradition (Green 1980, 85), or Early Individual Burials (Clarke *et al.* 1985, 63–67)), and with artefacts such as Seamer/Duggleby axeheads and polished flint knives.

The different types of felsite in the Northmaven area

During the author's expeditions to the Northmaven area, samples were collected from sources in the area's southern (Collafirth Hill/Ronas Hill) and northern parts (Beorgs of Uyea). Later examination of these samples indicates that distinct differences may exist between the felsites of southern and northern Northmaven. The macroscopic differences concern: 1) general colour; 2) grain-size of the matrix; 3) the presence, absence, number and size of phenocrysts; and 4) the presence, absence, number and size of spherulites. The following is not an exhaustive account, but a subjective first impression of a limited number of sources from the two main parts of the surveyed area.

1) COLOUR: The northern felsites are generally much more colourful than the southern ones. Although the former includes some dove-grey and dark-grey varieties, most are blue or blue-green; the latter are mostly either dove-grey or light- to dark-purple.

2) GRAIN-SIZE: Although some coarse-grained forms of felsite were recovered from the northern area, the felsites of that area are mostly fine-grained. In comparison, the southern felsites appear to have slightly coarser grain-sizes.

3) PHENOCRYSTS: Both areas comprise varieties with quartz and feldspar phenocrysts, with (in most cases) feldspar dominating. In the northern parts of Northmaven, some outcrops had no phenocrysts, whereas many contained small, mainly feldspar, crystals, and these were mostly either white or very light pink. The outcrops in the southern part of Northmaven generally had many more, larger, and more vividly pink or red feldspar phenocrysts, although pieces with white feldspar and quartz crystals were also found.

4) SPHERULITES: This element may be the most divisive attribute, as no felsites with spherulites were recovered from the southern area, whereas the northern area yielded samples with small, medium, and large spherulites, as well as spherulite-free samples. However, no outcrops appeared to have the very large spherulites favoured in the production of Shetland knives. Several pieces from the northern part of Northmaven were banded, a quality frequently associated with the presence of spherulites.

Figure 3.7. Rare remaining 'stubs' of two parallel felsite dykes.

The collected samples thus include the following felsite forms: 1) non-porphyritic, non-spherulitic felsites; 2) non-porphyritic, spherulitic felsites; and 3) porphyritic, spherulitic felsites. The presence of riebeckite is indicated by the colours, with riebeckite felsites usually being blue, green or purple, but certain identification would require thin-sectioning. However, the presence or absence of riebeckite may be more an academic than practical matter, as axeheads were clearly made in all forms of felsite, including riebeckite-free felsites and quartz-feldspar porphyries. It is the author's impression that it should be possible to define the various felsite sub-types by reference to the above macroscopic attributes, allowing reasonably precise sourcing of the museum's felsite artefacts.

The different types of sites and features of the Northmaven area

As briefly touched upon in the history of research section (above), most of the 'dykes' indicated on maps from geological surveys of Northmaven are either tailing piles or knapping floors. In some cases, *in situ* 'stubs' of felsite survive next to the tailing piles (Figure 3.7), or large loose boulders of felsite indicate that a dyke may exist, or have existed, in the vicinity. In a number of cases, linear depressions were noticed next to the tailing piles, occasionally covered by peat of a different (usually, greener) colour. It is the author's working hypothesis that these depressions may indicate the presence of the remains of a worked dyke, or the location of a now exhausted dyke, which were later covered by blanket peat.

The bluish felsite, whether loose or *in situ*, is clearly visible on the background of the area's pink granite, and it was possible to define a number of site or feature types:

1) THE BEORGS OF UYEA WORKING GALLERY: This feature is basically a lintelled-over trench, with one lateral side defined by a felsite dyke, and the other by dry-stone masonry (Figures

3.8–9). The floor was covered by felsite flakes and chips, as well as hammerstones and felsite rough-outs. It is thought that this feature represents a shelter in which a person '... could adopt a sitting posture inside in comparative comfort while, for instance, engaged in the manufacture of some kind of implement on the spot where a supply of the raw material of rock was readily to hand' (Scott and Calder 1952, 176). The structure has been illustrated in many archaeological publications, and it is described in detail in Scott and Calder (1952). The stone structure on top of the felsite dyke is most likely modern.

Figure 3.8. The Beorgs of Uyea working gallery (courtesy of Carol Christiansen).

Figure 3.9. The Beorgs of Uyea working gallery (courtesy of Carol Christiansen).

2) CIRCULAR/OVAL, OR SEMI-CIRCULAR, SHELTERS: At the western end of the scheduled area, two structures were noticed. One is circular to oval (Figure 3.10), and the other semi-circular, with a felsite boulder defining one side (Figure 3.11). The floor of the latter is strewn with knapping debris. It is thought that both are shelters intended to protect the Beorgs of Uyea quarriers/knappers from the wind at this exceedingly exposed location, much along the lines of the above roofed structure. As neither has an opening, however, they are unlikely to have been roofed.

Figure 3.10. Oval Shelter at Beorgs of Uyea.

Figure 3.11. Semi-circular shelter at Beorgs of Uyea.

The oval shelter in particular is well preserved, and it is possible that these structures could be modern shelters, used by hunters of, for example, ducks or geese. However, possible collapsed versions of these shelters were discovered during the survey of the Beorgs of Uyea (Figures 3.12–13), and this fact, in conjunction with the presence of knapping debris on the floor of the semi-circular shelter, suggests that the structures could be ancient. Nevertheless, the interior of these features, as well as their surroundings, should be tested for the presence of modern rubbish, such as shotgun and rifle cartridges, glass, plastic, etc.

Figure 3.12. Probably collapsed oval shelter at Beorgs of Uyea.

Figure 3.13. Probably collapsed oval shelter at Beorgs of Uyea (courtesy of Carol Christiansen).

3) TAILING PILES: The definition of these features follow Schneiderman-Fox and Pappalardo's (1996) detailed model for the investigation of prehistoric quarry sites, emphasizing the following activity areas:

  i. the quarry itself where material is extracted;
 ii. the tailing pile, just below the quarry face, containing blocks of quarried material;
iii. the ore dressing, milling, or transition area, located below and within 50m of the quarry face, where large blocks are broken down for transport; and
 iv. the lithic reduction site above the quarry face or on a level terrace adjacent to the quarry face, where reduced blocks are further reduced into preforms or final tools.

Figure 3.14. Tailing pile, with a linear depression immediately to one side.

Figure 3.15. Tailing pile, with a linear depression immediately to one side.

A cursory examination of the elongated concentrations of crude felsite blocks and fragments, zigzagging down the slopes of both surveyed areas (Figures 3.14–15), showed that they mainly contain unmodified blocks, although some rough axehead preforms were also noticed. It was therefore chosen to, preliminarily, refer to them as tailing piles, although the precise definition of the individual concentrations of felsite will require spot-check sampling of these, and detailed characterization of the fill of these concentrations. As mentioned above, several of the elongated concentrations are associated with linear depressions (Figure 3.16), which may represent the actual quarry areas, that is, the exploited or exhausted dykes, as well as surviving shelters, or the collapsed remains of such.

4) KNAPPING FLOORS: One concentration differs significantly from the elongated concentrations. It was discovered on the slopes of Midfield, in the general Collafirth Hill/Ronas Hill area, and it is roughly circular (Figure 3.17). It seems to be surrounded by large boulders, which may signify that the location has been cleared of 'clutter' before commencement of the actual production. Some degree of sorting appears to have taken place, with larger flakes and blocks mainly to one side, and smaller debris to the other side.

A small number of retouched pieces were found, one of which may be a broken rough-out for a Shetland knife. This type of site probably corresponds to Schneiderman-Fox and Pappalardo's Type iv activity area, the reduction site or knapping floor, '... where reduced blocks are further reduced into preforms or final tools'. It is characteristic of the Northmaven area that mainly preforms were produced, whereas the finished tools (axeheads and knives) seem to have been produced at the actual settlement site, probably off the central parts of Northmaven.

5) A POSSIBLE MODEL: Though Schneiderman-Fox and Pappalardo's (1996) terminology and nomenclature is helpful, their model may not necessarily fit all realities equally well, as it

Figure 3.16. Linear depression (enlarged section of Figure 3.15).

Figure 3.17. Knapping floor.

is possible that some of their activity areas may, in specific cases, have been combined by prehistoric quarriers. Their Type i sites (the actual quarry areas) are unproblematic, and, as mentioned above, it is thought that several of the exploited dykes may now be covered by blanket peat. Most likely, the linear depressions immediately adjacent to the tailing piles represent these dykes.

The elongated concentrations of relatively large-sized, angular debris, which in this chapter are referred to as tailing piles (Type ii), may, as indicated by the recovery of a small number of axehead rough-outs, be hybrid locations, including elements of Schneiderman-Fox and Pappalardo's Types ii and iii, and, to a lesser degree, Type iv. The circular concentration observed on the slopes of Midfield was referred to as a knapping floor, but it is probably most correct to define this type of location as a hybrid of Schneiderman-Fox and Pappalardo's Types iii and iv. The concentration contains larger as well as smaller pieces, in conjunction with numerous partially modified blanks, but no final tools, and the largest pieces suggest that some 'ore dressing, milling or transition' may have taken place as part of the breaking down ('quartering') of large blocks for transport. The main differences between the two forms of concentrations are: 1) size and shape (large/elongated – small/circular); 2) composition (size and type of debris); and 3) location (either immediately adjacent to a quarried outcrop or close to, but somewhat away from, the outcrop). Whether this interpretation is correct or not is testable by excavation, and other site types may be present in the unexplored parts of Northmaven.

By comparing the felsite quarry complex of Northmaven with the existing felsite artefacts in the Shetland Museum, and in National Museums Scotland, it becomes clear that there is a vast discrepancy between the number of recovered felsite implements and the prehistoric output from the Northmaven quarries and workshops. It is impossible to estimate the exact output from the quarry complex without undertaking a complete survey, mapping and quantification of the area's prehistoric sites, but it is apparent that the quarried felsite must be measured in thousands of tons. In comparison, known felsite axeheads probably number approximately 100 pieces, and felsite knives slightly less. Ian Tait of Shetland Museum, writes:

> *Our database yields 101 records on a search for felsite/porphyry/porphyrite/riebeckite. The vast majority of these entries are single items, so there's not likely to be more than say 120 individual items. Although we have uncatalogued excavation assemblages, there is virtually no felsite there. I would guess that 50% of the finds are axeheads, 40% knives, 10% others (maceheads, adzeheads, arrowheads). The percentages are likely to be somewhat skewed away from simpler items (scrapers and axehead roughouts mainly) because it is only in recent years that these have been recognized as stray finds and donated to us. Obviously, these totals only concern what we hold. National Museums Scotland have a great many Shetland felsite items, too (I guess from memory upper tens but less than 100). Again, axeheads and knives are the majority of the finds they have).*

A small number of possible felsite artefacts are known from mainland Scotland (Ritchie and Scott 1988), and some felsite implements may exist in private collections, but these individual specimens would not affect the existing discrepancy. Two possible interpretations of this situation are: 1) that the extraction of raw felsite was extremely exclusive, and therefore wasteful, as specific sub-types of raw material were required for the two main artefact groups (homogeneous spherulite-free felsite for the axeheads, and visually spectacular felsite with large spherulites and banding for the Shetland knives); or 2) large numbers of axeheads and knives were produced, but have not yet been rediscovered.

OUTLINES OF A FUTURE FELSITE PROJECT

As indicated above, this chapter is based on examination of the felsite artefacts in the Shetland Museum, in conjunction with a limited survey of the quarry complex. The artefact studies and the fieldwork resulted in the production of a number of impressions and working hypotheses, which are in need of testing (confirmation, rejection, adjustment). This requires the definition, organization, and implementation of a future felsite project, which could be selective and of limited scope, or all-embracing. The following tasks are considered potentially fruitful:

1) Full survey and mapping of the Northmaven area, including naming/numbering, and precisely locating (including NGRs) the individual quarries, tailing piles and workshops.
2) Definition and detailed characterization of the individual sites, following either the site typology of Schneiderman-Fox and Pappalardo (1996), or an adjusted version thereof (quarries, tailing piles, and workshop sub-forms).
3) Sampling of raw material from all sites and petrographic characterization. This descriptive process should possibly be combined with thin-section analysis.
4) Petrographic characterization and, possibly, thin-section analysis of artefacts from the Shetland Museum.
5) Excavation of at least two sites: i) a trench across one tailing-pile and its parallel linear depression (Beorgs of Uyea); and ii) a workshop (Midfield). Physical description of the two sites (quarry/tailing-pile and workshop), and characterization/quantification

of their composition and artefactual contents (types of waste, rough-outs, final tools, etc.), following an adapted version of the blank and debris types listed in Edmonds *et al.* (1992).

By undertaking the above tasks, it should be possible to:

1) pinpoint the position of the (now obscured) felsite dykes in relation to the still visible tailing piles and workshops;
2) construct a spatial model of the mining operations, and related activities, in Northmaven (where was the material quarried for axeheads, and where for knives, where were the preforms manufactured, shelters, etc.);
3) produce a time-line: not all the quarry sites and workshops would have been in use at the same time; it may be possible to produce a timeline, or at least group some sites chronologically, by associating specific morphological artefact types from the museum with specific sites in Northmaven;
4) discuss the actual quarrying techniques, and compare these with the techniques observed from other Neolithic quarries in Britain (the Great Langdale axe-factories in Cumbria, the porcellanite and porphyrite quarries of Northern Ireland, the Welsh axe-factory of Mynydd Rhiw, the Perthshire hornfels production site, etc.; see Bradley and Edmonds 1993; Cooney 2005; Edmonds *et al.* 1992; Houlder 1961; Jope 1952).

Presently the interest in prehistoric mining is gaining internationally (e.g. Topping and Lynott 2005), with quarry studies now being seen as central to the understanding of prehistoric settlement structure and activity patterns. Abbott *et al.* (forthcoming) write: 'data obtained from quarry sites serve as a baseline in which later production activities on other sites in the settlement system are measured. Without this basic level of information, lithic production models for specific populations will be suspect'. With its varied range of site types, an archaeological investigation of the Northmaven quarry complex is thought to be potentially fruitful, and of relevance to quarry analysts throughout the world.

ACKNOWLEDGEMENTS

The author is most grateful to: Andy Duffus on Bressay, Shetland, for guidance and good company during the author's expeditions to Northmaven; Jane Puckey and Stephen J. Pigott for help with accommodation during these expeditions; Tommy Watt and Ian Tait from the Shetland Museum in Lerwick, Shetland, for permission to use their photos of felsite artefacts;

Beverley Ballin Smith, Glasgow University Archaeological Research Division, for proof-reading the manuscript; Val Turner and Carol Christiansen, the Shetland Amenity Trust, for comments on the manuscript, Carol also for permission to use a number of her photos from a Northmaven inspection; Noel Fojut, Historic Scotland, for letting me see his manuscript and notes on Shetland knives; and Erik Vestergaard, Haderslev Grammar School, for permission to use his illustration of Piet Hein's super-ellipse.

BIBLIOGRAPHY

Abbott Jr., L. E., Cantley, C. E., and Jones, S., forthcoming, A reevaluation of quartz and silicate raw material acquisition along the South Atlantic Slope: going beyond the economics of expediency. Paper given at the Society for American Archaeology Conference 2001.

Ballin, T. B., 2005, Re-Examination of the Quartz Artefacts from Scord of Brouster. A Lithic Assemblage from Shetland and its Neolithic Context. *Scottish Archaeological Internet Reports (SAIR)* 17 (http://www.sair.org.uk/sair17/index.html).

Ballin, T. B., 2009, *Archaeological Pitchstone in Northern Britain*. Oxford: Archaeopress (British Archaeological Reports, British Series 476).

Barber, J. (ed.), 1997, *The Archaeological Investigation of a Prehistoric Landscape: Excavations on Arran 1978–1981*. Edinburgh: Scottish Trust for Archaeological Research (STAR Monograph 2).

Bradley, R. and Edmonds, M., 1993, *Interpreting the Axe Trade: Production and Exchange in Neolithic Britain*. Cambridge: Cambridge University Press.

Calder, C. S. T., 1950, Report on the excavation of a Neolithic Temple at Stanydale in the parish of Sandsting, Shetland. *Proceedings of the Society of Antiquaries of Scotland* 84 (1949–50), 185–205.

Calder, C. S. T., 1956, Report on the discovery of numerous Stone Age house-sites in Shetland. *Proceedings of the Society of Antiquaries of Scotland* 89 (1955–56), 340–397.

Calder, C. S. T., 1963, Cairns, Neolithic houses, and burnt mounds in Shetland. *Proceedings of the Society of Antiquaries of Scotland* 96 (1962–63), 37–86.

Clarke, A. and Griffiths, D., 1990, The use of bloodstone as a raw material for flaked stone tools in the west of Scotland. In C. R. Wickham-Jones, *Rhum. Mesolithic and Later Sites at Kinloch. Excavations 1984–86*, 149–156. Edinburgh: Society of Antiquaries of Scotland.

Clarke, D. V., Cowie, T. G. and Foxon, A., 1985, *Symbols of Power at the Time of Stonehenge*. Edinburgh: HMSO.

Cooney, G., 2005, Stereo porphyry: quarrying and deposition on Lambay Island, Ireland. In P. Topping and M. Lynott (eds), *The Cultural Landscape of Prehistoric Mines*, 14–29. Oxford: Oxbow Books.

Cooney, G. and Mandal, S., 1998, *The Irish Stone Axe Project, Monograph I*. Bray: Wordwell.

Edmonds, M., Sheridan, A. and Tipping, R., 1992, Survey and excavation at Creag na Caillich, Killin, Perthshire. *Proceedings of the Society of Antiquaries of Scotland* 122, 77–112.

Fenton, M. B., 1988, The petrological identification of stone battle-axes and axe-hammers from Scotland. In T. H. McK. Clough, and W. A. Cummins (eds), *Stone Axe Studies, Volume 2. The Petrology of Prehistoric Stone Implements from the British Isles*, 92–132. London: Council for British Archaeology (Research Report 67).

Finlay, T. M., 1930, The Old Red Sandstone of Shetland. Part II: north-western area. *Transactions of the Royal Society, Edinburgh* 56, 671–694.

Fojut, N., 1986, *A Guide to Prehistoric and Viking Shetland*. Lerwick: The Shetland Times Ltd.

Fojut, N., in prep., The Stourbrough Hill Hoard and other Polished Stone 'Knives' from Shetland.

Green H. S., 1980, *The Flint Arrowheads of the British Isles. A Detailed Study of Material from England and Wales with Comparanda from Scotland and Ireland*. Oxford: British Archaeological Reports (British Series 75i–ii).

Henshall, A., 1963, *The Chambered Tombs of Scotland 1*. Edinburgh: Edinburgh University Press.

Houlder, C. H., 1961, The excavation of a Neolithic stone implement factory on Mynydd Rhiw in Caernarvonshire. *Proceedings of the Prehistoric Society* 27, 108–143.

Jope, E. M., 1952, Porcellanite axes from factories in north-east Ireland: Tievebulliagh and Rathlin. *Ulster Journal of Archaeology* 15, 31–55.

Lacaille, A. D., 1938, Aspects of intentional fracture. *Transactions of the Glasgow Archaeological Society* 9(2), 313–341.

Meighan, I., Jamison, D. D., Logue, P. J. C., Mallory, J. P. and Simpson, D. D. A., 1993, Trace element and isotopic provenancing of North Antrim porcellanites: Portrush – Tievebulliagh – Brockley (Rathlin Island). *Ulster Journal of Archaeology* 56, 25–30.

Morey, J. E. and Sabine, P. A., 1952, A petrographical review of the porcellanite axes of north-east Ireland. *Ulster Journal of Archaeology* 15, 56–60.

Mykura, W., 1976, *Orkney and Shetland*. Edinburgh: HMSO (British Regional Geology 1).

Mykura, W. and Phemister, J., 1976, *The Geology of Western Shetland*. Scotland. Edinburgh: HMSO (Memoirs of the Geological Survey of Great Britain).

Phemister, J., Harvey, C. O. and Sabine, P. A., 1952, The riebeckite-bearing dikes of Shetland. *Mineralogical Magazine* 29 (1950–52), 359–373.

Phillips, F. C., 1926, Note on a riebeckite-bearing rock from the Shetlands. *Geological Magazine* 63, 72–77.

RCAHMS (Royal Commission on the Ancient and Historical Monuments of Scotland), 1946, *Twelfth Report, with an Inventory of the Ancient Monuments of Orkney and Shetland*. Edinburgh: HMSO.

Ritchie, P. R., 1968, The stone implement trade in third-millennium Scotland. In J. M. Coles and D. D. A. Simpson (eds), *Studies in Ancient Europe. Essays presented to Stuart Piggott*, 119–136. Leicester: Leicester University Press.

Ritchie, P. R. and Scott, J. G., 1988, The petrological identification of stone axes from Scotland. In T. H. McK. Clough and W. A. Cummins (eds), 1988, *Stone Axe Studies, Volume 2. The Petrology of Prehistoric Stone Implements from the British Isles*, 85–91. London: Council for British Archaeology (Research Report 67).

Schneiderman-Fox, F. and Pappalardo, A. M., 1996, A paperless approach toward field data collection: an example from the Bronx. *Society for American Archaeology Bulletin* 14.1 (http://www.saa.org/publications/saabulletin/14–1/index.html).

Scott, L. G. and Calder, C. S. T., 1952, Notes on a chambered cairn, and a working gallery, on the Beorgs of Uyea, Northmaven, Shetland. *Proceedings of the Society of Antiquaries of Scotland* 86 (1951–52), 171–177.

Sheridan, A., 1986, Porcellanite artifacts: a new survey. *Ulster Journal of Archaeology* 49, 19–32.

Topping, P. and Lynott, M. (eds), 2005, *The Cultural Landscape of Prehistoric Mines*. Oxford: Oxbow Books.

Turner, V., 1998, *Ancient Shetland*. Edinburgh: Historic Scotland.

Vestergaard, E., 2005, Vestergaards Matematiksider. Matematik for Gymnasiet og for Matematik-Interesserede (http://www.matematiksider.dk/index.html).

Chapter 4

The Sweet Track, Somerset, and lithic scatters: walking the land, collecting artefacts, and discovering the earliest Neolithic community

Clive Jonathon Bond

The Sweet Track, the earlier Neolithic trackway in the Somerset Levels excavated in the 1970s, has played a central role in discussions on the introduction of the Neolithic in southern Britain. However, despite this unique wetland site any attendant settlement pattern was rarely mentioned and not well understood. The results of the long-term field survey of the Shapwick Project (1989–1999) from the adjacent hills to this track have yielded over 2,500 lithic artefacts. This evidence can now be interpreted to indicate the extent of a broadly contemporary and attendant settlement pattern to the many earlier Neolithic trackways. These data reflect the seasonal mobility and attachment to places of the woodworking- and pottery-using earlier Neolithic peoples who inhabited this land from 3807 BC. Lithic scatters in this case have provided a means of reuniting the wet and dry zones of this much studied landscape. What are the implications for this earliest phase of the Neolithic in southern England?

INTRODUCTION

This chapter will discuss the influence of lithic artefacts, specifically lithic scatter data, on understanding the landscape context of the well-known trackways excavated in the Somerset Levels, south-west England (Figure 4.1). Over the last century numbers of trackways, platforms and single wooden artefacts were recorded during peat digging (Dewar and Godwin 1963; Godwin 1960), then recorded by the threat-led Somerset Levels Project between 1975 to 1989 (Coles 1989; Coles and Coles 1986). This evidence has entered the literature, for example recently in Malone (2001, 64) or Parker Pearson (1993, chapter 1), but is centred on excavation of the wetland sites, providing little wider landscape context. No broader understanding has been achieved on where the people who built these structures lived during their probable seasonal pattern of movements or their perception of the land. The contention here is that lithic scatters can provide this context. It is because of lithic scatters, their distribution, artefact numbers and time-depth (multi-period composition), and ease of recovery, that a landscape context can be accessed. Until recently, this was an undervalued and poorly investigated resource (Lisk *et al.* 1998; Schofield 1995; 2000). Research on the Sweet Track landscape provides a lesson in the value of lithic scatters.

Lithic scatters research alone, it is argued, can provide the evidence uniting the wet and dry landscapes of the Brue Valley (cf. Bond 2003; 2004a; 2004b; 2006; 2007a; 2007b). The systematic field survey completed by the Shapwick Project (Aston and Gerrard 1999; Gerrard and Aston 2007) facilitated walking the dry-land and the adjacent peat fields. This long-term project covering a decade of fieldwork; field walking/re-walking and excavation recovered artefact scatters across the Polden Hills and Somerset Levels landscape. This chapter will provide a summary of the findings. Themes moving from an introduction to the Shapwick Project, to methodology and the interpretation of a total earlier Neolithic landscape will be addressed.

LITHIC SCATTERS AND THE SHAPWICK PROJECT

Quantities of lithic artefacts have been recovered by three projects: The Shapwick Project (Bond 2007a); The Somerset Levels Project (Brown 1986); and a recent doctoral thesis (Bond 2006). The Shapwick Project was English Heritage-funded and surveyed the parish

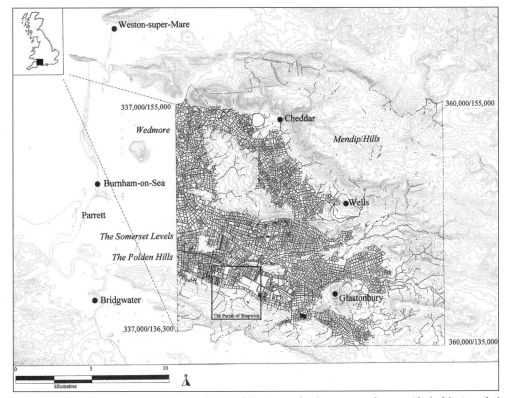

Figure 4.1. Location, south-west England, central Somerset, the Somerset study area (dashed-line) and the Parish of Shapwick (light black line); river, stream and rhyme system (black line); contour at 10m intervals (grey line). Ordnance Survey data Licence Number LA07683X.

in which the Sweet Track is located, Shapwick (Figure 4.2). This yielded struck flint and chert artefacts through systematic field survey, shovel test-pit survey, test pits, garden-bed investigations, and excavation (Bond 2007a). The Somerset Levels Project recovered small assemblages of lithic arterfacts by systematically walking peat cuttings, mineral islands protruding above the peat, and fields adjacent the peat. However, the excavated assemblages associated with structures, such as the Sweet Track (Coles *et al.* 1973), were central to this project; less attention was paid to the analysis of the surface finds (Brown 1986). Moreover, the threat-led brief of the project prohibited work on the adjacent dryland (Coles and Coles 1986). The doctoral research undertaken by this author provided an opportunity for analysis/re-analysis for the first time using a single methodology for all lithic artefacts across this wet/dry landscape. This also provided a broader study, a total landscape context, a survey transect from the Polden Hills, across the Somerset Levels to the Mendip Hills (Bond 2006). Combining the analysis of these lithic assemblages a total landscape context for the

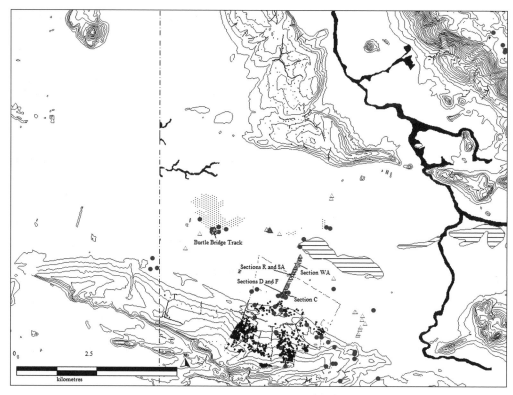

Figure 4.2. The Parish of Shapwick (dotted-line), with the Shapwick field survey results mapped (black dots); lithic scatters mostly from the Somerset Levels Project and amateur collections (grey dots); earlier Neolithic Trackways, including the line of the Sweet Track (grey triangle-open); Burtle Beds (dense dot islands); rock islands (horizontal lines); streams and silted river system (black lines and denticulate pattern); contour at 10m intervals (grey line); Ordnance Survey data Licence Number LA07683X.

Sweet Track and other later trackways can be achieved. As space is limited, this chapter will focus on the methodology for studying lithic scatters and the better understanding of the earlier Neolithic landscape in the Shapwick area.

Shapwick is a parish that straddles the wet and dry landscape (Figures 4.1–2) – to the south the light sandy slopes on lias bedrock, the Polden Hills; to the north the lower slopes, or Nidons and the peat moors (or Somerset Levels), inter-cut with mineral ridges, sand islands and further lias islands, such as Westhay, Meare and Godney. In the Shapwick Project systematic fieldwalking occurred across all available arable fields. Walking took place in autumn and spring. The main field methodology employed was line-walking and the traverse and stint approach. The sample interval of 25m 'stints' was used (the distance between fieldwalkers in Gerrard *et al.* 2007, 128). These 'stints' were also timed, being walked for 10 minutes. Most of the available fields in the parish were walked, totalling an area of 429.8 hectares (1060 acres). This represents one third of the total area of the parish. In total 96,452 artefacts were recovered by fieldwalking, of this 2377 (2.5%) were struck flint and chert artefacts. The largest proportion of the fieldwalked assemblage consisted of pottery (Gerrard *et al.* 2007, 148–151).

A detailed analytical approach towards lithic scatters has been critical to move the Shapwick data on from a damaged archaeology to an informative prehistoric dataset. As a simple definition, lithic scatters are multi-period assemblages of stone tools and waste, recovered from the ploughsoil disturbed by natural erosion or agricultural processes. When analysed as artefact assemblages by composition (date, technological attributes and typologies present) they can demonstrate the presence of a succession of episodes of flaking stone at different times and places from the Mesolithic into the Bronze Age (Schofield 1987; 1991). Over the past decade, or so, approaches have changed to lithic scatter analysis. Commonly emphasis has been on fieldwalking methods, systematic recovery and sampling the 'ploughzone' archaeology (Clark and Schofield 1991; Haselgrove *et al.* 1985), the interpretation (Ford 1987a; 1987b; Holgate 1985; Richards 1990; Schofield 1987; 1991), the archaeological potential (Schofield 1994; 2000) and the heritage/landscape importance (English Heritage 2000). Despite this, however, lithic scatters remain viewed as of secondary importance to excavation and are sidelined in mainstream debates on the coming of the Neolithic in the British regions (Thomas 1991; 1999). Only a few authors acknowledge their potential (Cooney 1997; Edmonds 1997; Whittle 1997). The quality of lithic scatter data has remained contentious, with few workers wanting to go beyond the preconception of it constituting 'bad data', poorly suited for recording the perfect Neolithic 'house' or 'dwelling'. At fault here, however, may be the questions asked of the record and assumptions about what was 'settlement' in the Neolithic and the seasonal and regional diversity in the record. There are also the pragmatics of fieldwork and funding – excavation can only ever cost-effectively sample small areas; the largest trenches will only ever be samples of complex palimpsests and due to current landuse landscape-wide studies will always need to revert to the analysis of artefact scatters. Thus, it is not the data that are poor, but the way the data are approached and deployed to answer research questions before and after fieldwork. Indeed, the lack of theory on the cultural formation process of lithic scatters is most telling (exceptions are: Bond 2004a; Bond 2004b; Edmonds 1995; Edmonds 1997; Edmonds *et al.* 1999; Pollard 1999; Whittle 1997). Study of the Neolithic period remains excavation-centred!

METHODS OF LITHIC ANALYSIS

The methodology adopted here to analyse artefacts from lithic scatters combines the use of raw material, technology, typology, and condition of flint and chert artefacts. This approach draws on a long tradition of scholarship. This tradition has attempted to relate and date lithic technologies and typologies (retouched forms), from surface collections by direct comparison with excavated and/or radiocarbon-dated assemblages. For example, within Somerset small assemblages have been excavated, associated with chronologically diagnostic pottery and/or radiocarbon dates: Brean Down (Saville 1990); Norton Fitzwarren hillfort (Saville 1989); the Sweet and Post Track, and other smaller assemblages, as at Skinner's Wood (Brown 1986); the Chew Lakes excavations (ApSimon 1977); Charterhouse Warren Farm Swallet (Levitan *et al.* 1988); the re-analysis of the assemblage excavated in the ditch of Gorsey Bigbury henge and *Bos* Swallet (ApSimon 1976; 1997); Aveline's Hole Cave (Jacobi 2005); other excavated Mesolithic open sites, as at Birdcombe Court and Hawkcombe Head (Gardiner in Hosfield 2005). These assemblages regionally demonstrate an understood change in flaking technology, blade to flake production within the Holocene (Ford *et al.* 1984; Pitts 1978; Pitts and Jacobi 1979). There is also a presence of certain retouched forms, the product of those lithic industries, broadly in keeping with other excavated and radiocarbon-dated assemblages in southern England.

The analysis of lithic scatters has varied but essentially can be seen to be divided into two camps; those who continue the diachronic approach of analysing excavated lithics on the basis of typology and technology (Clark and Higgs 1960), but using only typology to provide a date range for that material (Light *et al.* 1994; Schofield 1987; 1991; Tingle 1991; 1998), and those who attempt a 'whole assemblage' approach (cf. Gardiner and Shennan 1985, 66). The typology-centred approach is limited, as the emphasis of an assemblage is often described in terms of functional variability and the dating of that assemblage is of secondary importance. This problem arises as the assignment of period dates to lithic artefacts has traditionally only been inferred from what is generally the smallest proportion of a flaked-stone assemblage – the chronologically diagnostic retouched artefacts (i.e. the tools; Gardiner and Shennan 1985, 62). Moreover, these formal tools often represent less than 5 per cent of any flaked assemblage.

The 'whole assemblage' approach assesses the typology and technology, but also combines quantitative analysis (metric analysis, following Ford *et al.* 1984; Pitts 1978; Pitts and Jacobi 1979) and more subtly observed traits in the assemblage, such as the shape of flakes, the quality of flaking, evidence for core preparation and expediency of working. This is a typological, morphological-technological approach (Brown 1991), but combined with the whole assemblage approach (cf. Bradley in Richards 1978; Gardiner and Shennan 1985). The result is to infer a date to elements of the assemblage and function. Depending on the assemblage composition, chronological change may be ascribed to proportions of lithics including the traditionally viewed undated waste. This combined approach enables a statement on what is represented by a mixed-period lithic assemblage derived from the ploughsoil, making it possible to suggest a certain proportion of material, retouched forms (typology) and waste (technology), is most probably of a certain broad time-frame; for example, Mesolithic, later Mesolithic, early Neolithic, or even Beaker or indeterminate later Neolithic or early Bronze Age. This method has been applied in a number of regions, from the Wessex chalklands to more northern regions and the East Anglian Fen-edge (Table 4.1).

Study area	Publication date	Groups	Data quality and period filter descriptions	Technology	Typology	Metric analysis	Comparison to excavated assemblages	Lithic totals	Reference
Berkshire Downs, Berkshire	1978	4	1. Mesolithic, 2. early Neolithic, 3. later Neolithic/early Bronze Age, 4. Middle to early Bronze Age	X	X	X	X	2266	Bradley in Richards (1978, 17, table 3)
East Berkshire Survey, Berkshire	1987	7	1. Mesolithic, 2. Mesolithic/earlier Neolithic, 3. earlier Neolithic, 4. later Neolithic/earlier Bronze Age, 5. later Neolithic/Bronze Age, 6. later Bronze Age/Iron Age, 7. Undated	X	X	X	X	6533	Ford 1987, 13
North Stoke, Oxfordshire	1987	7	A. Mesolithic, B. Mesolithic or early Neolithic, C. later Neolithic, probably with some Mesolithic, earlier Neolithic or middle Neolithic present, D. late Neolithic, E. late Neolithic or earlier Bronze Age, F. later Bronze Age, G. undated	X	X	X	X	10158	Ford 1987, 106–107, 112, 115, Table 5
East Hampshire Survey, Hampshire	1985	4	1. Mesolithic, 2. Earlier Neolithic, 3. Later Neolithic/earlier Bronze Age, 4. Middle to late Bronze Age	X	X	X	X	2682	Gardiner and Shennan 1985, 66, 68, fig. 5.11
Stonehenge Environs, Wiltshire	1990	4	1. Mesolithic, 2. early Neolithic, 3. later Neolithic, Beaker, 4. later Bronze Age	X	X	–	X	102175	Richards 1990, 16, 18–19, 24–25, table 6, fig. 11
Maiden Castle field survey, Dorset	1991	2	1. earlier Neolithic, 2. middle to late Bronze Age	X	X	X	X	8384+ (sample areas 1–16)	Bellamy and Edmonds 1991, 32–34, tables 5 and 6; Woodward and Bellamy 1991, 24, 25, tables 3 and 4
Wissey embayment, Norfolk	1991	9	Predominately: Mesolithic, 2. earlier Neolithic, 3. Mesolithic and/or earlier Neolithic, 4. later Neolithic, 5. Beaker, 6. Bronze Age, 7. indeterminate later Neolithic or early Bronze Age, 8. Mixed or undated, 9. Non-site	X	X	–	X	15512	Healy 1991, 116–118, figs. 65–68, microfiche 2: 5–12
Milfield Basin, Northumberland	1999	4	1. Mesolithic, 2. late Mesolithic–early Neolithic transition, 3. late Neolithic–early Bronze Age, 4. unclassified	X	X	–	X	695	Waddington 1999, 57–58, table 4.8
Total								148405	

Table 4.1. A comparison of different approaches towards the analysis and interpretation of lithic scatters.

A review of the literature shows some variation in the application of the whole assemblage approach, mainly as a result of the type of lithic data, the condition of those data, and the regional landscape encountered. Clearly regional cultural variation in flaking technology over time and access to raw materials are further considerations. Two core aspects are shared (Table 4.1)

- *LITHIC GROUPS:* lithic data are assigned a group or data filter (ranging from 4 to 9 here), this relates to the chronological resolution accessible and data quality (different tools and waste give different signatures). The separate groups of material are then assigned to broad period and/or data filter descriptions. The quantification of these lithic groups enables an understanding of the main trends in the assemblage, the *predominant dating* and emphasis of the assemblage and industries present.
- *TECHNOLOGY, TYPOLOGY AND METRIC ANALYSIS:* most approaches attempt to integrate observations and quantitative data with technology and typology integrated with a sample of metric analysis (enabling a statement to be made on the proportion of blade and flake technology present that may also indicate a date range, cf. Ford *et al.* 1984; Pitts and Jacobi 1979). The dating within a region of lithic types, certain tools, or technology (the change from blade to flake-core technology) is also cross-checked with lithic industries derived from excavated, integral and dated contexts (for example, by radiocarbon dates or by analogy with pottery traditions).

To return to the lithic data in question, two aggregate units of analysis as part of this study have been analysed (Table 4.2); the Shapwick Project field survey data and the lithic scatter data drawn from the analysis of 150-plus lithic scatters from central Somerset. This second unit included lithic scatter data from the analysis of amateur collections recovered from the wider landscape – the Polden Hills, the Somerset Levels and mineral islands therein, including the Somerset Levels Project data re-analysed (cf. Brown 1986), and the Mendip Hills. This dataset is termed the Somerset study area referring to the broader survey transect (Figure 4.1).

In both datasets lithic scatters have been grouped and analysed into a total of 15 data quality and period filters (Table 4.2). The terms data quality and period filters are used primarily to emphasize that the lithic groups are organized as a hierarchical system. This straddles different groups of lithics with more or less quality of data inferred in terms of chronological resolution. This chronological resolution is supported by the presence of typologies, technologically diagnostic artefacts, metric analysis (and a demonstrated change in blade and flake shape) and condition of materials. In central Somerset it has been commented that surface lithic assemblages do exhibit a range of patina types, or presence/absence that can relate to the date of the industry (Brown 1986; Norman 2003). Table 4.3 summarizes the groups of lithic artefacts and attributes that have enabled the assignment of artefacts to each group. Note data quality and period filters may or may not overlap in time. However, the result is the ability to phase groupings of lithic artefacts relatively within a lithic scatter. This makes it possible to provide relative phasing of activity across the parish of Shapwick (Figures 4.2–4) and the broader Somerset study area (Figures 4.1–3). Both spatial and chronological variation can be isolated by mapping the discard of lithic artefacts at different periods across the regional landscape. A combined total of 20,531 lithic artefacts have been analysed across this landscape (Figure 4.3 and Table 4.2).

Study area	Groups	Data quality and period filter descriptions	Technology	Typology	Metric analysis	Surveyed and excavated assemblages compared	Lithic no.
Shapwick Project, Somerset	15	Excluding late Upper Palaeolithic material, data is divided into the following date quality and period filters: 1. ?Prehistoric, 2. Prehistoric, 3. Mesolithic, 4. early Mesolithic, 5. later Mesolithic, 6. later Mesolithic and/or earlier Neolithic, 7. earlier Neolithic, 8. earlier Neolithic and/or middle Neolithic, 9. middle Neolithic and/or later Neolithic, 10. later Neolithic, 11. Beaker, 12. indeterminate later Neolithic or early Bronze Age, 13. indeterminate early Bronze Age or middle Bronze Age, 14. indeterminate middle Bronze Age or later Bronze Age, 15. modern (gun-flints)	X	X	X	X	2377
Somerset study area	15	"	X	X	X	X	18154
Total							20531

Table 4.2. The data quality and period filter and methodology applied to the Shapwick Project and Somerset study area lithic scatter data.

No.	CAL. BC	DATA QUALITY AND PERIOD FILTERS	ABBREVIATIONS IN TEXT	TECHNOLOGY AND TYPOLOGY*	RETOUCHED FORMS	PATINA
1	–	?Prehistoric	?PREH	Irregular and angular flakes or chunks. This group includes material that is struck, but may not be humanly worked: flakes without diagnostic features; natural pebbles and 'timing flints' (irregular chunks, lumps and flakes, imported into the area from Wiltshire)	None	Heavy, medium and light
2	10,000–700	Prehistoric	PREH	Chronologically unclassified material, but definitely flaked. Waste dominated, with chunks, cores and core-nodules. More rarely retouched forms, such as scrapers	Scrapers, miscellaneous retouched flakes/blades	Heavy, medium, few light
3	10,000–4000	Mesolithic	ME	Dominated by waste; flakes, some cores and core fragments with some retouched forms, such as particular scrapers. Note, no diagnostic types, but given the degree of patination this group may be a residual element of the early Mesolithic. Other data filters: 4. EM; 5. LM	Scrapers, miscellaneous retouched flakes/blades	Heavy, medium, few light
4	10,000–6500	Early Mesolithic	EM	Diagnostic waste, with broad flake/blade scars on cores, microliths, typically 'Broad blade'. Common, end and end and side scrapers on flakes. Burins, microburins and miscellaneous retouched flakes. Other data filters: 3. ME	Obliquely blunted points (large), non-geometric forms, burins, microburins, end and end and side scrapers	Heavy to medium
5	6500–4000	Later Mesolithic	LM	Diagnostic waste, with narrow flakes/blades or bladelet scars on cores, microliths typically 'Narrow blade', small and thin non-geometric and geometric types. Small microburins (few). Other data filters: 6. LM/EN	Obliquely blunted points (small), crescents, scalenes, most geometric, small microburins, small round scrapers	Medium to light, to none
6	6500–2900	Later Mesolithic &/ or earlier Neolithic	LM/EN	Mostly not diagnostic; cores, flakes, narrow flakes, blades. Also some scrapers on flakes, other miscellaneous retouched flakes. Other data filters: 5. LM; 7. EN	Scrapers, miscellaneous retouched flakes/blades	Light to none
7	4000–2900 (3838 BC Post Track; 3806–07 BC Sweet Track)	Earlier Neolithic	EN	Group typically earlier Neolithic with typologically diagnostic retouched forms: leaf-shaped arrowheads, chipped and polished axes, as small and simples scrapers, such as the short scraper. Classic waste, includes narrow flake, blade-like flakes and some blades; evidence for core preparation and rejuvenation (for example, core tablets and core rejuvenation flakes). Other data filters: 6. LM/EN; 7. EN	Leaf-shaped arrowheads, chipped and polished axes, short scrapers	Light to none
8	2900–2500	Earlier Neolithic &/ or middle Neolithic	EN/MN	This grouping is less distinctive, with few retouched forms and waste dominating; cores, irregular waste, technologically narrow flake based. Other data filters: 7. EN; 9. MN/LN	Scrapers, miscellaneous retouched flakes/blades	Light to none
9	2900, 2500–2000	Middle Neolithic and/or later Neolithic	MN/LM	Lithics within this group are less diagnostic, but flakes do tend to be broad. Flakes are more squat and broad in shape, with little sign of core preparation. Blades are few. Waste dominates, with few retouched forms. Other data filters: 8. EN/MN; 10. LN	Scrapers, miscellaneous retouched flakes/blades	None

10	2500–2000	Later Neolithic	LN	Group typically includes particular later Neolithic retouched forms, such as the Petit tranchet arrowhead, chisel arrowhead and large scrapers (for example, the horse shoe scraper). Flakes are few, but tend to be large, hard hammer in type. This demonstrates technologically the shift from narrow to broad flake production, with a corresponding reduced emphasis on core preparation and maintenance. Other data filters: 9. MN/LN; 11. BK; 12. LN/EB; 13. EB/MB	Petit tranchet arrowheads, chisel arrowheads and large scrapers (for example, the horse shoe scraper)	None
11	2500–1800	Beaker	BK	This group is dominated by diagnostic retouched forms, including thumbnail scrapers and barbed and tanged arrowheads. Scale flaking is more evident on other forms of scraper, for example semi-circular scrapers and plano-convex knifes. Flakes, overlap in type with adjacent groups: broad and squat in shape, with limited platform preparation. Other data filters: 9. MN/LN; 10. LN; 12. LN/EB; 13. EB/MB	Thumbnail scrapers, other scale-flaked scrapers, plano-convex knifes, sickle knifes, daggers and all types of barbed and tanged arrowheads	None
12	2400–1500	Indeterminate later Neolithic or early Bronze Age	LN/EB	Waste would overlap with adjacent groups: broad and squat in shape, with limited platform preparation; some large flakes. Retouched forms on large flake blanks are present, for example, circular and sub-circular scraper forms. Other data filters: 9. MN/LN; 10. LN; 11. BK; 13. EB/MB	Large miscellaneous scrapers, miscellaneous large retouched flakes	None
13	2000–900	Indeterminate early Bronze Age or middle Bronze Age	EB/MB	Waste tends to be large or on irregular flakes, with hard hammer and low bulbar angle. Few pieces provide retouched edges, informal, coarse and short in execution. Miscellaneous retouched forms, scrapers, flakes are common. Within the study area examples are few from both excavated and ploughsoil assemblages. Other data filters: 12. LN/EB; 14. MB/LB	Few retouched forms; miscellaneous retouched flakes, coarse scrapers	None
14	1000, 900–700	Indeterminate middle Bronze Age or later Bronze Age	MB/LB	Waste tends to be large or on irregular flakes, with hard hammer and low bulbar angle. Raw material can be re-used, including thermal fractured flint. Expedient working demonstrated - poor technical skills, on ad-hoc flake blanks. Few pieces provide retouched edges, informal, coarse and short in execution. Miscellaneous retouched forms, scrapers, flakes are common. Within the study area examples are few from both excavated and ploughsoil assemblages. Other data filters: 13. EB/MB	Few retouched forms; miscellaneous retouched flakes	None
15	1600–1800 (AD)		MOD	This group consists of one class of artefact, without waste: the gun flints.	Gun flints	None

*Note on hierarchical system of data quality and period filters: In column 5 at the end of each statement the data filters that may or may not be contemporary with, or at least partly overlap in time with that data filter are listed. The late Upper Palaeolithic material is not included above.

Table 4.3. A description of the type of lithic artefacts, typologies and technological attributes grouped in the data quality and period filters: Mesolithic to indeterminate early Bronze Age or middle Bronze Age.

Importantly, it can also be argued to have successfully isolated the 'settlement' locales that served the Sweet Track and other broadly contemporary and later wooden structures (Figure 4.4). The stream-lines, springs/wells and the wetland/dryland interface of the low hillocks of the Nidons provide a frame in which prehistoric peoples moved, camped and gained access to the wetlands.

The result of the analysis of this lithic technology can be briefly summarized. A detailed statement is provided elsewhere (Bond 2006; 2007a). Several threads on technological and spatial change can be taken forward (Figures 4.3–4):

- *Raw materials:* The main raw material used was flint, specifically a green-black-grey variety. In a recent raw material survey (Bond 2004a; Bond 2005) this type of flint is located in the Dorset Downs, within Cranborne Chase and further east, specifically sourced to Hampshire and West Sussex downland nodular flint. Most flint is therefore introduced into central Somerset and Shapwick.
- *Technology and typology:* The dominant type of lithic technology is blade-core or narrow-flake core, from both datasets. There is little evidence for core-flake and squat-flake production occurring and high-quality core preparation is common (for example, the presence of core rejuvenation flakes; core tablets; prepared cores; fine cores with parallel-sided blade and narrow flake scars). With limited metric analysis this trend is confirmed, suggesting the majority of any lithic industry is pre-middle Neolithic or later Neolithic and this again is confirmed by the presence of typologically/chronologically diagnostic pieces: leaf-shaped arrowheads, end scrapers, miscellaneous retouched blades and flakes (see assemblage structure as typified by Shapwick survey derived data in Table 4.4). The smallest component in each individual assemblage tends to be later prehistoric: material that is middle Neolithic to later Bronze Age as summarized in Table 4.3 and also demonstrated in Table 4.4.

An overview is possible, contrasting the lithic data from the Shapwick Project with those from the Somerset study (Figure 4.3). The main trend in lithic scatter data, as plotted per data quality and period filter, is shared. The highest quantity of material occurs pre-middle Neolithic, with the largest peak in the earlier Neolithic to earlier Neolithic and/or middle Neolithic groupings (Figure 4.3).

The point of divergence is with higher amounts of early Mesolithic material in Shapwick (Figure 4.3), compared to the Somerset study area dataset. Moreover, there is also a higher number by *c.* 10 per cent of earlier Neolithic lithic artefacts in the Shapwick Project data, contrasting with the Somerset study area dataset. The reduction in lithics post-middle Neolithic is similar in trend, but marginally less in the Somerset study area dataset.

Importantly, as most of the Shapwick data is Polden Hill-based lowland and most (*c.* 70%) of the lithic scatters in the Somerset study area dataset is Mendip Hill-based this aggregate analysis does unite the wet and dry landscapes of central Somerset. What is apparent is that the broad trend in chronology – settlement pattern change is shared. Variation can be argued to reflect different settlement strategies operating between the upland (Mendip Hills) and lowland (Somerset Levels and Polden Hills) portions of this regional landscape. Different strategies, perhaps reflecting a drop of people in certain parts of the landscape, or less frequented visits may be argued for the early and later Mesolithic data in the Somerset

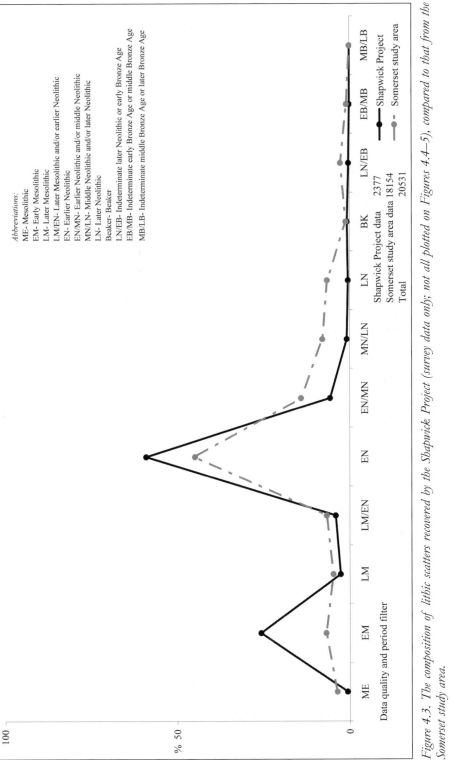

Figure 4.3. The composition of lithic scatters recovered by the Shapwick Project (survey data only; not all plotted on Figures 4.4–5), compared to that from the Somerset study area.

Levels and Polden Hills, contrasting with the Mendip Hills. This has been argued to be the result of a localized impact of marine flooding, changing seasonal forays into the lowlands in the later Mesolithic (Bond 2007a; Bond 2007b).

A further point is also that the peak in the line graph for both datasets in Figure 4.3 centres on the earlier to middle Neolithic. This is highly unusual, as where extensive field survey has occurred in adjacent regions, such as Wessex, the number of artefacts discarded after the earlier Neolithic is seen to increase. As a general rule, lithic scatters are larger in scale, less spatially diffuse (Edmonds 1995; Edmonds1997) with the highest proportion of material attributed to the later Neolithic to earlier-middle Bronze Age. This has been demonstrated on the Wessex chalklands, for example, in the Stonehenge Environs survey (Richards 1990), the Maiden Castle-Dorset Ridgeway survey (Woodward 1991; Woodward and Bellamy 1991), the Cranborne Chase survey (Barrett *et al.* 1991), the Marlborough Downs (Gingell 1992) and the Vale of the White Horse, Oxfordshire and Berkshire Downs (Gaffney and Tingle 1989; Tingle 1991). Other regional surveys have confirmed this accepted patterning in lithic composition, for example in north-east Devon (the Beer Head survey; Tingle 1998), in Hampshire (Gardiner and Shennan 1985; Schofield 1991), and in the East Anglian Fens and Fen-edge (Edmonds *et al.* 1999; Healy 1991 and 1996). Therefore, this method of lithic and landscape analysis does appear to provide new evidence for change in regional settlement patterns, contrasting with the accepted norm. This distinctive pattern of artefact discard over the long-term may be suggestive of a different relationship between social groups, their territories and seasonal movements, the central Somerset area versus the chalklands of Wessex.

DISCUSSION: WALKING THE LANDSCAPE AND SEEING THE PEOPLE, THEIR DWELLING PLACES AND PATHS

With the analysis of the two datasets it is apparent that earlier Neolithic lithic artefacts tend to be the largest component of any lithic scatter (Figures 4.3–5). The peak in the Shapwick lithic scatter dataset may therefore be argued to represent material that is broadly contemporary with the establishment of the first trackways in the Somerset Levels. These structures date, as with the Sweet Track and Post Track, to 3807 BC (Hillam *et al.* 1990) and with other structures such as the Bisgrove and Chilton Tracks (1–4) dated a few hundred years thereafter (Coles 1989). Most trackway use (establishment, maintenance and abandonment) has recently been argued by Coles and Coles to equate to a lifespan of *c.* 15 years maximum (1998, 6, fig. 4). At the Sweet Track 10–15 years was argued and is confirmed by dendrochronology (Coles and Coles in Hillam *et al.* 1990).

What of the process of settling this landscape? The lithic scatter data have been mapped using Geographical Information Systems software (Figures 4.4–5). These data, mapped across the Polden Hills, can be argued to represent the long sought after 'settlement' areas that Coles had aspired to find (1989, 19–27, fig. 13). By highlighting the location of four leaf-shaped arrowheads recovered during this project, the spatial ordering of the landscape can be considered (see in-filled squares representing the location of the leaf-shaped arrowheads in Figure 4.5). The movement and timing of routines, perhaps even choreography at the individual lithic scatter and between lithic scatters can be discussed. This new dataset, mapped across both dry and wet landscape, as interpreted here offers a

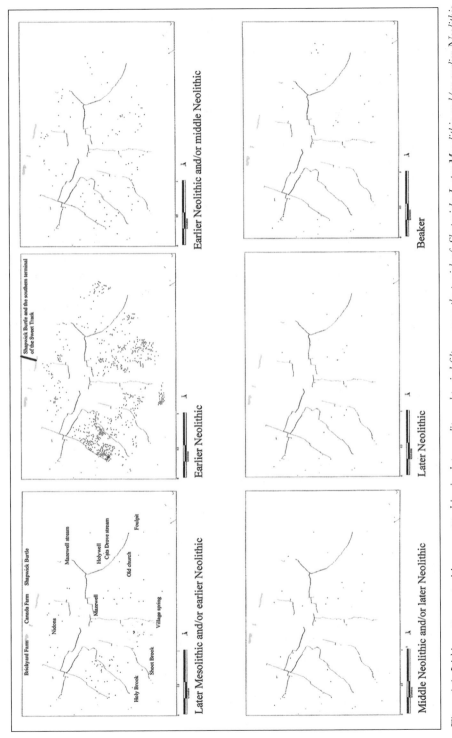

Figure 4.4. Lithic scatter composition as mapped in six data quality and period filters across the parish of Shapwick: Later Mesolithic and/or earlier Neolithic (6500–2900 BC) to Beaker (2500–1800 BC). Note insert top left has stream, spring, the named sand Burtles and the Nidons labelled; insert top middle indicates the extent of earlier Neolithic group lithics and their spatial relationship to Shapwick Burtle and the southern terminal of the Sweet Track.

new insight into the experienced past landscape, a socially constructed world (Tilley 1994, chapter 2) populated by highly mobile and small-scale communities. Lithic scatters regarded as 'locales' would have represented one form of nodual point in that world. These were humanized places, settled, visited, abandoned and perhaps returned to seasonally over generations (Bond 2004a, 2006, 2007a, 2007b).

Dense scatters are located along the north-south line of the Holy Brook and bounded to the east by the Shoot Brook (Figures 4.4–5). Other scatters are recorded, but less dense near the two springs above Church Field and Foulpit to the south-east. This distribution is focused on the Sherborne Series of calcareous soils. This light soil would be ideal for early, small-scale farming practice and/or hunting (lightly forested areas). Equally, this area would suit grazing, watering and the movement of herds from, or to, the wetland margin if a herding economy was present.

The remaining lithic scatters are located in a broad line of clusters of material at the lowest slopes of the Polden Hills on the Midelney Gley soils or bordering the Sedgemoor and Turbary Moor soils of the peat moor area near Shapwick Burtle (Figure 4.5). This area would also be suitable for hunting and grazing (see the leaf-shaped arrowhead to the north, just south of the Sweet Track and the Shapwick Burtle leaf-shaped arrowhead, Figures 4.4–5).

In the south-east around the springs in the field above Church Field and at the Foulpit there is dense activity with clusters of scatters, as a second focus of settlement. As an alternative to this dense activity in the middle-lower Polden Hill slopes there is little activity in the centre of the parish (this is perhaps masked by buildings or hill wash) Activity is recorded in a line on the Nidons forming the most northern distribution before Shapwick Burtle and the Sweet Track terminal located to the north in the Somerset Levels.

A main achievement with this earlier Neolithic lithic dataset is that it has located areas of potential settlement for the social group that cleared the woodland on the Polden Hills and a few generations later built the Post and Sweet Tracks (Coles 1989) and some generations later still perhaps the Bisgrove and Chilton Tracks. These lithic scatter data are crucial in order to understand the settlement pattern that is the landscape context of the Sweet Track. This settlement pattern starts to come alive demonstrating the different scales, duration of tasks, routines and movement of people along the stream lines using the sandy soils, the dry land slopes, perhaps woodland, and finally giving a context to the use of the wetlands. Coles's (1989) 'settlement' associated with the Sweet Track is found! The north-south streams-line, particularly mid- to upper-slope appear highly important. There is also, however, an area of low density activity that centres in the immediate vicinity of the village. This is suspected to be indicative of soil movement and building activity disrupting distributions of lithic scatters along streams-lines, associated with wells/springs (cf. Gerrard *et al.* 2007). These new data and a consideration of the symbiotic relationship between wet and dry landuse during the earlier Neolithic would accord well with Whittle's tethered mobility model (1997). Lithic scatters are interpreted here as evidence for repeated visits; episodes of seasonal settlement, perhaps part of a settlement cycle of visit, abandonment, discovery, and re-visit – activity over generations. These lithic scatters form locales on the northern Polden Hill slopes, focusing mainly on stream lines, springs or at the junction between the wet and dry ecologies on or near the Nidons.

The timing of events, flaking routines, the movement up and down the hillside are mapped (Figure 4.5). This will be discussed below. Also of some importance, away from the village there is little evidence for hillwash at any great depth (Bond 2007a; Gerrard *et al.* 2007), although experiments have shown this did exist and that artefacts, at least pottery, tested as part of that experiment had moved during annual tillage events (Marter 2007). This is not so much an issue, and is to be expected (Bosimier 1997; Clark and Schofield 1991), but the intensity of soil disturbance is an issue. Critical is the degree of artefact movement in the ploughsoil, the intensity of masking artefact distributions through soil movement from hill wash (colluviation), alluvial, building or manure activity. Although 'liming flints' (modern flint nodules) were present in the lithic assemblages, these were easily identified and slight in proportion to the total assemblage. Marling appeared to mostly affect the medieval pottery distributions. Thus, the lithic scatter spatial patterning exhibited in Figures 4.4–5 can be argued to be more ploughed in and disturbed, but certainly not ploughed out or covered by later deposition to any great degree. Given the complexity of deposits within the village only further work, such as test pits, shovel test-pits and re-walking, would clarify these lithic scatter density and distributions.

INTERPRETATION AT THE LOCALE: THE SWEET TRACK LANDSCAPE, CHOREOGRAPHY AND LITHIC TECHNOLOGY

The prehistoric landscape of this part of the Brue Valley, both wetland and dryland has been unified through lithic analysis. In the past the main focus has been wetland exploitation associated with trackways, the adjacent dryland of only marginal interest in narratives (Coles and Coles 1986). However, lithic scatters distributed across this total landscape, from hill slopes to mineral ridges/islands in the wetlands, demonstrate the total landscape was utilized. People, perhaps herd movements, with grazing on the Nidons and slopes can now be explored through lithic technology.

Four areas in total covering twenty fields, located in different topographical settings across the parish of Shapwick, all systematically fieldwalked can provide information on change in the composition of lithic assemblages (Table 4.5). The comparison between these sub-assemblages, part of the Shapwick dataset, can now provide a glimpse of change in use/function, perhaps visits to lithic scatter sites, and perception of different parts of this landscape in the earlier Neolithic. These data can be contrasted with that across the total parish landscape (Table 4.4).

Each area, or locale, consists of a number of interlinked lithic scatters, diverse in density and composition. These can be analysed, comparing activity from north to south, from the Nidons to upper hill slopes (Figure 4.5):

- *NIDONS*: The Nidons wetland interface is less than 350m south of Shapwick Burtle and the southern Sweet Track terminal (Coles *et al.* 1973). Retouch forms are low in proportion, as on the Mid-Slope (West) (Table 4.5). Here it may be that fewer tasks, or different tasks, may have occurred. Leaf-shaped arrowheads are present, as are other discarded single artefacts, for example scrapers. This may suggest single events, residues from forays at the wetland edge and mid-slope. At the Nidons the main balance of the assemblage is waste, with the highest percentage in the four areas on cores or core-related materials. As elsewhere, here non-cortical flakes are

Data quality and period filters	Cores	Irregular waste	Core trimming flakes	Flakes	Blades	Retouched forms	Other	Totals
?Prehistoric	–	104	2	166	–	–	92	364
	0.00%	28.50%	0.54%	45.60%	0.00%	0.00%	25.20%	
Prehistoric	1	56	2	116	–	7	15	197
	0.50%	28.40%	1.00%	58.80%	0.00%	3.50%	7.60%	
Mesolithic	–	2	–	3	–	7	–	12
	0.00%	16.60%	0.00%	25%	0.00%	58.30%	0.00%	
Early Mesolithic	5	27	106	299	4	20	–	461
	1.00%	5.80%	22.90%	64.8	0.80%	4.30%	0.00%	
Later Mesolithic	4	–	10	8	3	22	–	47
	8.50%	0.00%	21.20%	17.00%	6.30%	46.80%	0.00%	
Later Mesolithic &/or Earlier Neolithic	4	4	18	34	–	13	–	73
	5.40%	5.40%	24.60%	46.50%	0.00%	14.80%	0.00%	
Earlier Neolithic	47	80	321	465	10	135	2	1060
	4.40%	7.50%	30.30%	43.80%	0.90%	12.70%	0.10%	
Earlier Neolithic &/or Middle Neolithic	2	4	28	53	–	13	1	101
	1.90%	3.90%	27.70%	52.40%	0.00%	12.80%	0.90%	
Middle Neolithic &/or Later Neolithic	–	2	4	6	–	3	–	15
	0.00%	13.30%	26.60%	40.00%	0.00%	20.00%	0.00%	
Later Neolithic	–	–	–	–	–	8	–	8
	0.00%	0.00%	0.00%	0.00%	0.00%	100.00%	0.00%	
Beaker	–	–	–	–	–	13	–	13
	0.00%	0.00%	0.00%	0.00%	0.00%	100.00%	0.00%	
Indeterminate Later Neolithic or Early Bronze Age	–	–	–	1	–	4	–	5
	0.00%	0.00%	0.00%	20.00%	0.00%	100.00%	0.00%	
Modern	–	–	–	–	–	3	–	3
	0.00%	0.00%	0.00%	0.00%	0.00%	100/0%	0.00%	
Totals	63	279	491	1151	17	248	110	2359
	2.60%	11.80%	20.80%	48.70%	0.70%	10.50%	4.60%	

Table 4.4. Overall composition of lithic scatters, broken down to thirteen data quality and period filters: ?Prehistoric to Modern. The technological data are listed in eight columns: cores; irregular waste (for example, chunks, worked nodules, core fragments); core trimming flakes (for example, core rejuvenation flakes, core tablets, chips); flakes; blades (visually defined, but assuming a length / width ratio 1:3); retouched forms ('tools') and other (for example, pebbles, non-worked lumps, such as marting debris). Note 2359 lithic artefacts is only the total number of artefacts matched in Figures 4.2, 4.4, and 4.5. In total 2377 lithic artefacts were recovered by field-survey, but not all were able to be matched

high in number, but there are also a high percentage of completely cortical flakes (the highest amongst these locales). This may indicate that at the Nidons, within a flake technology of predominantly prepared cores, a proportion of the cores were worked down from whole cortex-covered nodules, leaving primary flakes. These may have been worked down prior to moving into the wetland, or moving south up-hill into dense woodland for hunting. Lithic scatters are distributed across the *c.* 1000m of the Nidons area as diffuse patches, with clusters covering *c.* 250 metres, but with a preponderance of single and isolated artefacts discarded (Figure 4.5).

- *MID-SLOPE (WEST)*: Moving up-slope, south-west towards the second locale, Mid-Slope (West), this area is between the *c.* 30m to *c.* 50m contour lines and some 2500m south of the Nidons. Perhaps a walk within a wooded landscape of an hour can be envisaged,

	TOOLS	WASTE	CORES	TOTALS	CORTEX:	0	1<50	50-100	TOTALS
NIDONS (NORTH)	4	29	8	41		16	10	3	29
	9.70%	70.70%	19.50%			55.10%	34.40%	10.30%	
MID-SLOPE (WEST)	28	351	40	419		237	80	27	344
	6.60%	83.70%	9.54%			68.80%	23.20%	7.80%	
UPPER-SLOPE (EAST)	20	81	12	113		55	22	2	79
	17.60%	71.60%	10.60%			69.60%	27.80%	2.50%	
UPPER-SLOPE (SOUTH)	7	36	9	52		27	8	0	35
	13.40%	69.20%	17.30%			77.10%	22.80%	0.00%	
TOTALS	59	497	69	625		335	120	32	487
	9.44%	79.52%	11.04%			68.78%	24.64%	6.57%	

Table 4.5. Composition of earlier Neolithic lithic scatters at four locales in Shapwick on the Polden Hills. Note the lithic data is selected from the earlier Neolithic data quality and period filter, n=1060 lithics (see Fig. 4.4); Column 1, lists the topographic setting and 'locales' cited in the text. The topographic settings listed in column 1 relate to the systematically line-walked lithic assemblages taken from adjacent fields in each locale: Nidons (North) – field nos. 8889, 2766, 2483, 6464, 0076, 0002; Mid-Slope (West) – field nos. 1264, 3553, 4974, 6000, 7123, 5488, EPC; Upper-Slope (East) – field nos. 51600, 4200, 0068, 5700; Upper-Slope (South) – field nos. 2534, 4334, 6435. Details of fields surveyed, other artefacts recovered are to be found in Gerrard and Aston (2007); Column 2, lists the number of lithic artefacts attributed to retouched forms ('tools'); Column 3, lists the number of lithic artefacts attributed to waste (incorporating: irregular waste, core trimming flakes, flakes, blades); Column 4, lists the number of lithic artefacts attributed to cores; Column 5, lists the total number of lithic artefacts per 'locale'; Column 7 to 10 covers the flaking stage per 'locale'. Column 7, lists all complete flakes, core rejuvenation flakes and blades that had no cortex on their dorsal surface; Column 8, lists all complete flakes, core rejuvenation flakes and blades that had less than 50% cortex on their dorsal surface; Column 9, lists all complete flakes, core rejuvenation flakes and blades that had between 50% and 100% cortex on their dorsal surface; Column 10, lists the total number of lithic artefacts selected from the earlier Neolithic sub-assemblage for this analysis. A full analysis of the total technological attributes and flaking stage data is published in Bond (2007a).

from the Nidons to mid-slope (Figure 4.5). The Holy Brook stream is to the east of the lithic scatters; these are denser up-hill. Here retouch forms are low as a proportion of the assemblage, but near equal with core and core-related materials (Table 4.5). Waste dominates the assemblage, even more so than at the Nidons. There is also less of an emphasis on partly-cortical and cortical flakes. This may suggest more of an emphasis on flaking prepared cores; flakes are commonly associated with core-related material, including core rejuvenation flakes. Of interest is the wider range of retouched forms compared to the Nidons: a leaf-shaped arrowhead; an axehead/adzehead; more scrapers; and a borer. The denser clusters of lithics, often with multiple artefacts recovered at one findspot are set away from the river-stream. The lithic scatters are spatially more discrete than on the Nidons and commonly set within an area of *c.* 250m. The combined lithic scatters are in the shape of patches, perhaps with ribbons of activity therein, distributed across a similar area as the Nidons,

- *Upper-Slope (East)*: From this area, some *c.* 3.5 kilometres to the south-east, crossing the Holy Brook, Shoot Brook, and village stream-spring, the Upper-Slope (East) locale provided a different picture (Figure 4.5). This may be envisaged as some three to four hours walk away, perhaps a morning from the Nidons in a densely wooded landscape. Here a spring is located in Church Field, a draw for repeated episodes of activity over generations with potential panoramic views North, at the c. 40–50 metres contour line. Here, as elsewhere waste remains high, but the highest proportion of retouched forms must be significant (Table 4.5). Similar proportions of cores and core-related materials are present at the Nidons locale. However, the stage of flaking within this locale lacks primary cortical flakes. Here quantities of axehead / adzehead-related artefacts are present for the first time; scrapers continue to be recorded, but no arrowheads in contrast to the Nidons and Mid-Slope (West). Spatially lithic scatters are less discrete than lower down the slope, but there are also a high number of single artefact findspots. Multiple findspots are recorded, especially for flakes, mirroring the pattern at the Mid-Slope (West) locale. This area, although providing flakes and cores, also has axehead/adzehead material. The low percentage of primary flakes, suggests prepared core reduction, but also in a setting higher up slope where either adzeheads or axeheads are deployed, re-worked (axehead flakes), or maintained,

- *Upper-Slope (South)*: To move further south, up-hill, from the Upper-Slope (East) locale, two lithic scatters (one dense, one diffuse) constitute the fourth and final locale, Upper-Slope (South). This is on and above the 60m contour line, to the east of the village spring (Figure 4.5). Here the lowest proportions of waste within the four locales are recorded, but also a high percentage of cores as on the Nidons (Table 4.5). The elevated site, with potential panoramic views north to the Levels, Burtle islands, Wedmore, and Mendip, may have been highly significant to mobile, hunters or even herding peoples, following paths from the Polden Hill ridge down to the wetland. The similar proportions of cores here and the Nidons may link the same areas to similar core-reduction activity, although here there is more working of prepared cores evident (although partly-cortical flakes occur at each locale). Findspots are multiple, both in the dense cluster in the western field (6435) and at the diffuse cluster. There is an isolated scatter of flakes. Flake reduction, cores and core-related material are recovered with few retouched artefacts – a scraper and miscellaneous retouched flakes.

Figure 4.5. The Sweet Track and its landscape context, the Nidons, the Polden Hills and the earlier Neolithic lithic scatters. Note labelled are selected streams, springs and the Nidons; Shapwick Burtle, the result of shovel test pitting on Shapwick Burtle (the leaf-shaped arrowhead) and the location of the southern terminal of the Sweet Track (cf. Coles et al. 1973). The four locales referred to in Table 4.5 are labelled in italics: Nidons (North), Mid-Slope (West), Upper-Slope (East) and Upper-Slope (South).

Systematic knapping of prepared cores at a highly elevated locale seems plausible – a setting from which to gear-up assemblages, preparing to graze herds on the lower slopes and Nidons and prepare for hunting or fowling forays into the wetland. From this locale a good view northwards would be gained. The spring would be significant as a landscape feature – a stopping place on a well-known path down from the hill ridge to the river-streams and wetland beyond.

The four locales discussed here provide an insight into an earlier Neolithic landscape, most probably occupied seasonally by cattle-herding peoples, the same people who created and maintained the Sweet Track, if only during annual visits. A classic earlier Neolithic lithic technology was employed at the Sweet Track (Bond 2003, 2–8, 12, figs. 1.4 and 1.6; Brown 1986; Coles *et al.* 1973). In the broader landscape the same lithic technology was discarded including axeheads, leaf-shaped arrowheads, small end scrapers and narrow flakes, struck with precision from well-maintained prepared cores (cf. Bond 2004b, 45–46, fig. 4).

CONCLUSION

Above, the physicality of the Shapwick landscape has been expressed, as movements and time between four locales, from the Nidons to the upper slopes of the Polden Hills. Lithic technology as mapped and analysed across the landscape and at each locale demonstrates a complex interwoven pattern of activity; most probably representing episodes of visits, re-visits and abandonment, from one season to another, one generation to another. Through carefully walking this landscape, systematically collecting lithic artefacts over a decade and considering the composition of lithic scatters, an assessment sympathetic to the landscape has been achieved. Prior to this study all that existed were islands of knowledge, centred on excavation and wetland case studies. Their landscape context and broader social meaning were unexplored. Lithic scatters mapped and re-thought as humanized and socially constructed places offer a means of better understanding the earlier Neolithic way of settling the Brue Valley.

The broader context of the Sweet Track has begun to be revealed with this more comprehensive dataset (Figure 4.5). The implication of this is that the regional characteristic of the earlier Neolithic settlement pattern will become clearer; the Sweet Track and its structures, together with lithic scatter data, relate to a specific regional Neolithic, a way of being (Bond 2003, 2004b, 2006, 2007a, 2007b). This case study contrasts with that of other much studied regions such as Wessex (Thomas 1991; Thomas 1999). The composition of lithic scatters, as analysed here, suggests a disjuncture with the patterning/phasing of settlement activity in the Wessex chalklands (cf. Darvill 2003; Whittle 1990) and this will require further explanation.

To date the Sweet Track remains part of an island of timber structures within a wetland ecology, with little reference in textbook syntheses to the broader landscape frequented by its builders (e.g. Malone 2001, 64, 70, fig. 40). This landscape narrative can now be re-written and a debate initiated on the links between dry-land and wet-land, and between the scale of local and regional communities (Bond 2003; 2004a; 2004b; 2005; 2006; 2007a; 2007b). A total social landscape can be accessed (Figure 4.5). The people and community who walked this land, with their stone tools, pottery and wood-crafting skills are now beginning to be revealed some 34 years after the discovery of the Sweet Track. Lithic artefacts and lithic scatters have enabled that community prehistory to be mapped and re-interpreted afresh.

BIBLIOGRAPHY

ApSimon, A. M., 1976, Archaeological reassessment. In A. M. ApSimon, J. H. Musgrave, J. Sheldon, E. K. Tratman and L. H. van Wijngaarden-Bakker, Gorsey Bigbury, Cheddar Somerset: radiocarbon dating, human and animal bones, charcoals, archaeological reassessment. *Proceedings of the University of Bristol Spelaeological Society* 14(2), 169–181.

ApSimon, A. M., 1977, The finds: Palaeolithic, Mesolithic, Neolithic and Bronze Age. In P. A. Rahtz and E. Greenfield, *Excavations at Chew Valley Lake, Somerset*, 171–193. London: HMSO (Department of the Environment Archaeological Report No. 8).

ApSimon, A. M., 1997, Bos Swallet, Burrington, Somerset: boiling site and Beaker occupation site. *Proceedings of the University of Bristol Spelaeological Society* 21(1), 43–82.

Aston, M. A. and Gerrard, C. M., 1999, 'Unique, traditional and charming'. The Shapwick Project, Somerset. *Antiquaries Journal* 79, 1–58.

Barrett, J., Bradley, R. and Hall, M. (eds), 1991, *Papers on the Prehistoric Archaeology of Cranborne Chase*. Oxford: Oxbow Books (Monograph 11).

Bond, C. J., 2003, The coming of the earlier Neolithic, pottery and people in the Somerset Levels. In A. M. Gibson (ed.), *Prehistoric Pottery. People, Pattern and Purpose*, 1–27. Oxford: Archaeopress (British Archaeological Reports International Series 1156/Prehistoric Ceramic Research Group Occasional Publication No. 4).

Bond, C. J., 2004a, The supply of raw materials for later prehistoric stone tool assemblages and the maintenance of memorable places in central Somerset. In E. A. Walker, F. Wenban-Smith and F. Healy (eds), *Lithics in Action: Papers from the Conference Lithic Studies in the Year 2000*, 124–139. Oxford: Oxbow Books/Lithic Studies Society Occasional Paper No. 8.

Bond, C. J., 2004b, The Sweet Track, Somerset: a place mediating culture and spirituality? In T. Insoll (ed.), *Belief in the Past. The Proceedings of the 2002 Manchester Conference on Archaeology and Religion*, 37–50. Oxford: Archaeopress (British Archaeological Reports International Series 1212).

Bond, C. J., 2005, 'The Gift was stone'. Socio-economic complexity and exchange between Neolithic and Bronze Age polities in the South-West and Wessex. Paper given at the weekend conference 'Defining Social Complexity: approaches to power and interaction in the archaeological record', McDonald Institute, Department of Archaeology, University of Cambridge, 11–13 March 2005. Accessed at: http://www2.eng.cam.ac.uk/~djo31/saw33/secure.htm

Bond, C. J., 2006, Prehistoric Settlement in Somerset. Landscapes, Material Culture and Communities 4300 to 700 cal. BC (Vols. I–II and DVD). Unpublished Ph.D. thesis. Winchester: Department of Archaeology, Faculty of Social Sciences, The University of Winchester.

Bond, C. J., 2007a, Lithics. In C. M. Gerrard and M. A. Aston (eds), *The Shapwick Project, Somerset. A Rural Landscape Explored*, 687–728. Leeds: Maney Publishing (Society for Medieval Archaeology Monograph 25).

Bond, C. J., 2007b, Walking the track and believing: the Sweet Track as a means of accessing earlier Neolithic spirituality. In D. A. Barrowclough and C. Malone (eds), *Cult in Context. Reconsidering Ritual in Archaeology*, 158–166. Oxford: Oxbow Books.

Boismier, W. A., 1997, *Modelling the Effects of Tillage Processes on Artefact Distributions in the Ploughzone*. Oxford: British Archaeological Reports (British Series 259).

Brown, A. G., 1986, Flint and chert small finds from the Somerset Levels, Part 1: The Brue Valley. *The Somerset Levels Papers* 12, 12–27.

Brown, A. G., 1991, Structured deposition and technological change among the flaked stone artefacts from Cranborne Chase. In J. Barrett, R. Bradley and M. Hall (eds), *Papers on the Prehistoric Archaeology of Cranborne Chase*, 101–133. Oxford: Oxbow Books (Monograph 11).

Clark, J. G. D. and Higgs, E. S., 1960, Flint industry. In J. G. D. Clark, Excavations at the Neolithic Site at Hurst Fen, Mildenhall, Suffolk (1954, 1957 and 1958). *Proceedings of the Prehistoric Society* 26, 214–226.

Clark, R. H. and Schofield, A. J., 1991, By experiment and calibration: an integrated approach to archaeology of the ploughsoil. In A. J. Schofield (ed.), *Interpreting Artefact Scatters: Contributions to Ploughzone Archaeology*, 93–105. Oxford: Oxbow Books (Monograph 4).

Coles, J. M., 1989, The Somerset Levels Project 1973–1989. *Somerset Levels Papers* 15, 5–61.

Coles, J. M. and Coles, B. J., 1986, *Sweet Track to Glastonbury. The Somerset Levels in Prehistory*. London: Thames & Hudson.

Coles, B. J. and Coles, J. M., 1998, Passage of time. *Archaeology in the Severn Estuary 1998. Annual Report of the Severn Estuary Levels Research Committee* 9, 3–16. (Lampeter, Department of Archaeology, University of Wales.)

Coles, J. M., Hibbert, F. A. and Orme, B. J., 1973, Prehistoric roads and tracks in Somerset, England: 3. The Sweet Track. *Proceedings of the Prehistoric Society* 39, 256–293.

Cooney, G., 1997, Images of settlement and the landscape in the Neolithic. In P. Topping (ed.), *Neolithic Landscapes*, 23–31. Oxford: Oxbow Books (Monograph 86/Neolithic Studies Group Seminar Papers 2).

Darvill, T., 2003, Analytical scale, populations and the Mesolithic-Neolithic transition in the far northwest of Europe. In L. Bevan and J. Moore (eds), *Peopling the Mesolithic in a Northern Environment*, 95–102. Oxford: Archaeopress (British Archaeological Reports International Series 1157).

Dewar, H. S. L. and Godwin, H., 1963, Archaeological discoveries in the raised bogs of the Somerset Levels, England. *Proceedings of the Prehistoric Society* 29, 17–49.

Edmonds, M., 1995. *Stone Tools and Society. Working Stone in Neolithic and Bronze Age Britain*. London: Batsford.

Edmonds, M., 1997, Taskscape, technology and tradition. *Analecta Praehistorica Leidensia* 29, 99–110.

Edmonds, M., Evans, C. and Gibson, D., 1999, Assembly and collection – lithic complexes in the Cambridgeshire Fenlands. *Proceedings of the Prehistoric Society* 65, 47–82.

English Heritage, 2000, *Managing Lithic Scatters. Archaeological Guidance for Planning Authorities and Developers*. London: English Heritage.

Ford, S., 1987a, *East Berkshire Archaeological Survey*. Newbury: Department of Highways and Planning, Berkshire County Council (Occasional Paper 1).

Ford, S., 1987b, Flint scatters and prehistoric settlement patterns in south Oxfordshire and east Berkshire. In A. G. Brown and M. R. Edmonds (eds), *Lithic Analysis and Later Prehistory: Some Problems and Approaches*, 101–135. Oxford: British Archaeological Reports (British Series 162).

Ford, S., Bradley, R., Hawkes, J. and Fisher, P., 1984, Flint-working in the metal age. *Oxford Journal of Archaeology* 3(2), 157–173.

Gaffney, V. and Tingle, M., 1989, *The Maddle Farm Project. An Integrated Survey of Prehistoric and Roman Landscapes on the Berkshire Downs*. Oxford: British Archaeological Reports (British Series 200).

Gardiner, J. and Shennan, S., 1985, The Mesolithic, Neolithic and Earlier Bronze Age. In S. Shennan, *Experiments in the Collection and Analysis of Archaeological Survey Data: the East Hampshire Survey*, 47–72. Sheffield: Department of Archaeology and Prehistory, University of Sheffield.

Gerrard, C. M. and Aston, M. A. (eds), 2007, *The Shapwick Project, Somerset. A Rural Landscape Explored*. Leeds: Maney Publishing (Society for Medieval Archaeology Monograph 25).

Gerrard, C. M., Aston, M. A., Gidney, L., Gutiérrez, A. and King, A., 2007, Fieldwalking. In C. M. Gerrard and M. A. Aston (eds), *The Shapwick Project, Somerset. A Rural Landscape Explored*, 124–177. Leeds: Maney Publishing (Society for Medieval Archaeology Monograph 25).

Gingell, C., 1992, *The Marlborough Downs: A Later Bronze Age Landscape and its Origins*. Devizes: Wiltshire Archaeological and Natural History Society (Monograph 1).

Godwin, H., 1960, Prehistoric wooden trackways of the Somerset Levels: their construction, age and relation to climatic change. *Proceedings of the Prehistoric Society* 26, 1–36

Haselgrove, C., Millett, M. and Smith, I. (eds), 1985, *Archaeology from the Ploughsoil: Studies in the Collection and Interpretation of Field Survey Data*. Sheffield: Department of Archaeology and Prehistory, University of Sheffield.

Healy, F., 1991, Appendix 1: lithics and pre-Iron Age Pottery. In R. J. Silvester, *The Fenland Project, Number 4: The Wissey Embayment and the Fen Causeway, Norfolk*, 116–139. Gressenhall: East Anglian Archaeology Report 52.

Healy, F., 1996, *The Fenland Project, Number 11: The Wissey Embayment: Evidence for Pre-Iron Age Occupation*. Gressenhall: East Anglian Archaeology Report 78.

Hillam, J., Groves, C. M., Brown, D. M., Baille, M. G. L., Coles, J. M. and Coles, B. J., 1990, Dendrochronology of the English Neolithic. *Antiquity* 64, 210–220.

Holgate, R., 1985, Identifying Neolithic settlements in Britain: the role of field survey in the interpretation of lithic scatters. In C. Haselgrove, M. Millett and I. Smith (eds), *Archaeology from the Ploughsoil: Studies in the Collection and Interpretation of Field Survey Data*, 51–57. Sheffield: Department of Archaeology and Prehistory, University of Sheffield.

Hosfield, R., 2005, Palaeolithic and Mesolithic. In C. J. Webster (ed.), *South West Archaeological Research Framework: Draft Resource Assessment*, 22–61. Taunton: Environment Department, Somerset County Council.

Jacobi, R. M., 2005, Some observations on the lithic artefacts from Aveline's Hole, Burrington Combe, North Somerset. *Proceedings of the University of Bristol Spelaeological Society* 23(3), 267–295.

Levitan, B. M., Audsley, A, Hawkes, C. J., Moody, A., Moody, P., Smart, P. L. and Thomas, J. S., 1988, Charterhouse Warren Farm Swallet, Mendip, Somerset: exploration, geomorphology, taphonomy and archaeology. *Proceedings of the University of Bristol Spelaeological Society* 18(2), 172–239.

Light, A., Schofield, A. J. and Shennan, S. J., 1994, The Middle Avon survey: a study in settlement history. *Proceedings of the Hampshire Field Club and Archaeological Society* 50, 43–101.

Lisk, S., Schofield, J. and Humble, J., 1998, Lithic scatters after PPG16 – local and national perspectives. *Lithics* 19, 24–32.

Malone, C., 2001, *Neolithic Britain and Ireland*. Stroud: Tempus.

Marter, P., 2007, CD-ROM – Appendices, 23. Artefact scatters at Shapwick: an experiment in ploughzone archaeology. In C. M. Gerrard and M. A. Aston (eds), *The Shapwick Project, Somerset. A Rural Landscape Explored*, 1114–1118. Leeds: Maney Publishing (Society for Medieval Archaeology Monograph 25).

Norman, C., 2003, Mesolithic to Bronze Age activity at Parchey Sand Batch, Chedzoy. *Proceedings of the Somerset Archaeological and Natural History Society* 145, 9–38

Parker Pearson, M., 1993, *English Heritage Book of Bronze Age Britain*. London: Batsford/English Heritage.

Pitts, M. W., 1978, Towards an understanding of flint industries in post-glacial England. *University of London Institute of Archaeology Bulletin* 15, 179–197.

Pitts, M. W. and Jacobi, R. M., 1979, Some aspects of changes in flaked stone industries of the Mesolithic and Neolithic of southern England. *Journal of Archaeological Science* 6, 163–173.

Pollard, J., 1999, These places have their moments: thoughts on settlement practices in the British Neolithic. In J. Brück and M. Goodman (eds), *Making Places in the Prehistoric World. Themes in Settlement Archaeology*, 76–93. London: University College London.

Richards, J., 1978, *The Archaeology of the Berkshire Downs: An Introductory Survey.* Reading: Berkshire County Council (Berkshire Archaeological Committee Publication No. 13).

Richards, J., 1990, Surface collections. In J. Richards, *The Stonehenge Environs Project*, 15–30. London: English Heritage (Archaeological Report No. 16).

Saville, A., 1989, The flint and chert artefacts. In P. Ellis, Norton Fitzwarren Hillfort: a report on the excavations by Nancy and Philip Langmaid between 1968 and 1971. *Proceedings of the Somerset Archaeological and Natural History Society* 133, 18–23.

Saville, A., 1990, The flint and chert artefacts. In M. Bell (ed.), *Brean Down Excavations 1983–1987*, 152–157. London: English Heritage (Archaeological Report No. 15).

Schofield, A. J., 1987, Putting lithics to the test: non-site analysis and the Neolithic settlement of southern England. *Oxford Journal of Archaeology* 6(3), 269–286.

Schofield, A. J., 1991, Lithic distributions in the Upper Meon Valley: behavioural response and human adaptation on the Hampshire chalklands. *Proceedings of the Prehistoric Society,* 57(2), 159–178.

Schofield, A. J., 1994, Looking back with regret; looking forward with optimism: making more of surface lithic scatter sites. In N. Ashton and A. David (eds), *Stories in Stone*, 90–98. London: Lithic Studies Society (Occasional Paper No. 4).

Schofield, A. J., 1995, Settlement mobility and la longue durée: towards a context for surface lithic material. In A. J. Schofield (ed.), *Lithics in Context: Suggestions for the Future Direction of Lithic Studies*, 105–113. London: Lithic Studies Society (Occasional Paper No. 5).

Schofield, A. J., 2000, Reflections on the future for surface lithic artefact study in England. In J. L. Bintliff, M. Kuna and N. Venclová (eds), *The Future of Surface Artefact Survey in Europe,* 45–55. Sheffield: Sheffield Academic Press.

Thomas, J. S., 1991, *Rethinking the Neolithic.* Cambridge: Cambridge University Press.

Thomas, J. S., 1999, *Understanding the Neolithic.* London: Routledge.

Tilley, C., 1994, *A Phenomenology of Landscape: Places, Paths and Monuments.* London: Routledge.

Tingle, M., 1991, *The Vale of the White Horse Survey.* Oxford: British Archaeological Reports (British Series 218).

Tingle, M., 1998, *The Prehistory of Beer Head. Field Survey and Excavations at an Isolated Flint Source on the South Devon Coast.* Oxford: British Archaeological Reports (British Series 270).

Waddington, C., 1999, *A Landscape Archaeological Study of the Mesolithic-Neolithic in the Milfield Basin, Northumberland.* Oxford: British Archaeological Reports (British Series 291).

Whittle, A. W. R., 1990, A model for the Mesolithic-Neolithic transition in the upper Kennet Valley, North Wiltshire. *Proceedings of the Prehistoric Society* 56, 101–110.

Whittle, A. W. R., 1997, Moving on and moving around: Neolithic settlement mobility. In P. Topping (ed.), *Neolithic Landscapes,* 15–22. Oxford: Oxbow Books (Monograph 86/Neolithic Studies Group Seminar Papers 2).

Woodward, P. J., 1991, *The South Dorset Ridgeway. Survey and Excavations 1977–84.* Bridport: Dorset Natural History and Archaeological Society (Monograph Series 8).

Woodward, P. J. and Bellamy, P., 1991, Artefact distribution. In N. H. Sharples, *Maiden Castle: Excavations and Field Survey 1985–86*, 21–32. London: English Heritage (Archaeological Report No. 19).

Chapter 5

New discoveries at the Mynydd Rhiw axehead production site

Steve Burrow, Heather Jackson, and Nigel Blackamore

Mynydd Rhiw is one of Britain's smaller axehead production sites and the assumed source of Group XXI axeheads. It was discovered in the late 1950s and promptly published in 1961, but has not featured strongly in subsequent interpretations of axehead production and exchange in Britain (e.g. Bradley and Edmonds 1993; Pitts 1996; but see Darvill 1989, 28, 35). This oversight might be a consequence of the limited number of axeheads thought to be derived from the site, in contrast to the much more extensive distributions from larger sources in Gwynedd and Cumbria. It might also be because the original excavations had apparently identified and adequately investigated all evidence for axehead production on the hill, deterring subsequent fieldwork. This chapter reports on the discovery of further quarrying activity on the hill which may date to the Neolithic and which it is hoped will open up new avenues of research at the site. It also summarizes difficulties which exist in the current status of Group XXI, a group which Chris Houlder, the excavator of the site, thought of as potentially 'not a natural group' (1961, 114), for reasons discussed below.

BACKGROUND

Mynydd Rhiw is a high hill at the western end of the Lleyn peninsula in northwest Wales (highest point, 304m AOD at SH 2285 2938) (see Figure 5.1). On clear days it commands extensive views west to Ireland's Wicklow Hills, north up the coast of Anglesey, and south down the sweep of Cardigan Bay. The inherent disadvantage of such a dramatic situation is that the hill is extremely exposed and inhospitable in poor weather.

The hill is composed of dolerite from the Gallt y Mor and Maen Gwenonwy sills, which have been traced, by magnetometer survey, from the coast to the ground north-eastwards from Porth Ysgo to Mynydd Rhiw (Brown and Evans 1989). This dolerite was intruded into wet sediments which on Mynydd Rhiw are represented by the Trygarn Formation. The sediments comprise an altered tuffitic siltstone (referred to by Houlder and throughout this chapter as baked shale) and, to the west, a band of Mynydd Rhiw Rhyolitic Tuff. Due to the nature of the intrusion, the dolerite and sediments outcrop in alternating bands following the strike of the hillside.

There are four stone piles on Mynydd Rhiw's eastern flanks. These are scheduled as Bronze Age round cairns, although two differ little in character from the natural screes which partially cover this side of the hill. A further cairn was recorded in 1939 on the

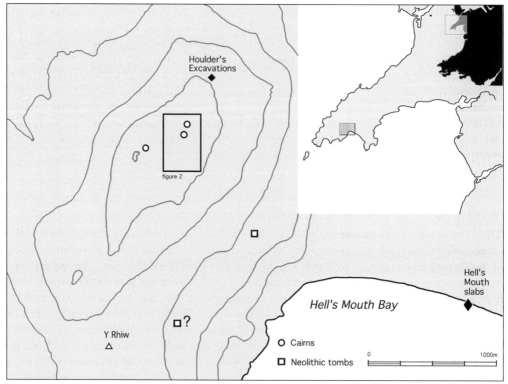

Figure 5.1. Location map of Mynydd Rhiw in relation to Wales, with local archaeological features indicated. This map contains Ordnance Survey data and is reproduced with the permission of Ordnance Survey on behalf of the Controller of Her Majesty's Stationery Office © Crown copyright. All rights reserved National Museum of Wales 100017916.

highest point of the hill, but this has since been destroyed by the construction of a radio relay station. Low on the south side of the hill is the Neolithic tomb of Tan y Muriau, a portal dolmen with lateral chamber and surviving cairn behind it (RCAHMW 1964, 105), and *c.* 1km southwest of this at Plas-yn-Rhiw is a collapsed chamber recorded by Lynch (1969, 305) as being 'so ruined as to be unintelligible'.

The possibility of Neolithic exploitation of the hill itself was first raised by A. H. A. Hogg of the Royal Commission on Ancient Monuments in Wales and Monmouthshire, who discovered debris from stone axehead manufacturing in the banks of what were then interpreted as round houses. This discovery led to two seasons of fieldwork by Chris Houlder (1958 and 1959), which revealed the round houses to be spoil dumps from a line of quarry pits (Houlder 1961).

These quarry pits were positioned on the edge of a seam of sediment, which had been baked by the intrusion of dolerite adjacent to it, forming a white-weathering porcellanous zone. This baked shale was easily flaked, being fine-grained, homogenous and highly silicic in character. In total, five quarry pits were identified, with one being examined in detail (Site

B). Site B was a quarry 3.3m deep; the upper 1.4m had been dug through drift deposit, and the remainder followed the junction of the dolerite and the shale which fell away at an angle of 25°. The band of material exploited was only *c.* 0.7m thick and examination of samples collected during the excavations indicate that it varied in quality across this thickness. The quarry had been partially backfilled with drift from the digging of the next pit in the line, and contained debris from stone tool manufacturing, including flakes, 'domestic' tools, and axehead-making debris.

In contrast to the extensive workings at Tievebulliagh, Langdale and Graig Lwyd, the five quarry pits at Mynydd Rhiw seem to reflect a small scale and short lived enterprise.

GROUP XXI

The baked shale seam exploited in Houlder's pits was designated Group XXI by the CBA implement petrology group, and a general description of the rock was produced on the basis of two samples of bedrock. Eighteen flakes were selected as type specimens for the Group.

Comparison of this material with CBA implement petrology records available at the start of the 1960s showed that twenty five axeheads, or parts of axeheads, could belong to Group XXI (Houlder 1961: 142–3). In 1988, this figure had risen to thirty three (Clough and Cummins 1988), with further identifications being added subsequently (e.g. Allen 1990, 171).

This sparse material is found across Wales, with a concentration in the Borders, particularly in Herefordshire (Shotton 1988, 51). This unexpected concentration led Shotton to question whether Mynydd Rhiw was indeed the source of all implements matching this petrological description, a point which had already been noted by Houlder who observed that the thermal metamorphism which would result in suitable material 'could result elsewhere in the formation of axe material exactly similar to that quarried at Mynydd Rhiw' (Houlder 1961, 114).

A further difficulty observed during reanalysis of the CBA thin sections by one of the authors (HJ) is that the axeheads which have, in the past, been ascribed to Group XXI are not homogenous, but actually contain a range of rock types. Further study of Houlder's type specimen thin sections has also shown that the baked shale band at Mynydd Rhiw is itself not strictly homogenous, and could be reclassified into at least three sub-groups. These difficulties cast doubt on the validity of Group XXI as it, and its products, are currently defined. The problems resulting from this realisation have acted as a stimulus to the current programme of work, which includes the aim of mapping in more detail the petrology of the Mynydd Rhiw area.

DATING HOULDER'S QUARRY PITS AND GROUP XXI

Houlder's quarry pits contained large quantities of axehead working debris, making it clear that they were dug in the Neolithic, but they remain undated within this broad span of time. The only radiocarbon dates which Houlder obtained from his excavations were taken from charcoal in a hearth in the tertiary fills of Site B. Two determinations were obtained:

1700–1050 cal. BC and 1500–900 cal. BC (3155±110bp and 3012±110bp, calibrated to two standard deviations using the curve of Stuiver *et al.* 1998; both dates were given the laboratory code Q-387). These dates clearly relate to secondary activity which Houlder viewed as being the product of a 'nomadic people making use of a convenient hollow for rest and shelter' (1961, 121). But it should also be noted that this activity might be related to the use of the Bronze Age cairns on the hill.

Houlder's excavations took place at the very beginning of the development of radiometric dating in Britain, when comparatively large samples were required. But he also retained smaller quantities of charcoal from a range other contexts; these are still in the excavation archive. These would now allow nine samples from Site B to be dated, including the uppermost hearth in the secondary fills (Hearth I), a hearth cutting the primary fills (Hearth IV), as well as charcoal present in the upper part of the primary fills themselves (Layer Ie). This charcoal would not decisively date the digging of the quarry pits themselves, but should provide a tighter *terminus ante quem* for this Neolithic phase.

All of the axeheads and flakes so far identified as belonging to Group XXI have been stray finds, with the exception of three flakes recovered from an earlier Neolithic occupation level at Gwaenysgor in Flintshire (Glenn 1914: 253; Piggott 1935; Powell 1954) and one artefact from an earlier Neolithic level at Dyserth Castle (Glenn 1915). The precise nature of this last object is uncertain as it seems to have been destroyed during thin sectioning and no drawings were made prior to this.

One artefact which might have a bearing on the use of Houlder's pits and the currency of Group XXI is a broken wristguard discovered during the excavation of the tomb at Dyffryn Ardudwy, 36km to the east across Tremadog Bay. This presumably accompanied a secondary burial at the site (see Burrow 1999; Powell 1973). Macroscopic examination suggests that the wristguard is made of a baked shale, similar in character to that derived from Houlder's quarry pits. The difficulty of accurately identifying fine-grained material on the basis of macroscopic identification should be noted, but if the identification is correct then two possibilities present themselves. Either the maker of the wristguard reused an old Neolithic axehead as a convenient blank, or Mynydd Rhiw itself was still active as a source of raw material in the Early Bronze Age.

On present evidence, it therefore seems likely that baked shale was used to produce axeheads in the earlier Neolithic, and it seems it was still being used in the second half of the 3rd millennium BC, although this later use need not imply continued quarrying of the rock.

NEW DISCOVERIES

Although detailed survey work has been undertaken over Houlder's quarry pits since his excavations (Muckle and Jocelyne 2001), and the end of the Lleyn peninsula has been resurveyed by the British Geological Survey (Gibbons and McCarroll 1993), the authors have been unable to find references to subsequent archaeological survey of the wider landscape at Mynydd Rhiw. In consequence, one of the authors (SB) paid a speculative visit to the hill in June 2005. During the visit, an outcropping rock with a substantial conchoidal fracture was noted, 400m south of Houlder's pits. This was initially thought to be a southward extension of Houlder's baked shale, but was subsequently recognized as a parallel seam of Mynydd Rhiw Rhyolitic Tuff.

Confirmation of the find's potential came from geologists at the National Museum of Wales and members of the Implement Petrology Group and, in October 2005, the area was surveyed with a Total Station and sampled geologically over four days. The aim was to define the nature of this new material and map its extent more precisely (Figure 5.2).

The survey identified several features of interest. Numerous outcropping rocks were located along a 400m line, running on a curve from north-northeast to south along the side of the hill. These rocks were crossed by lines of weakness caused by structural geological processes and a superimposed cleavage resulting from the intrusion of the dolerite, causing them to break easily into slabs of sufficient size for the production of stone axeheads. Geological samples were taken at outcrops along the seam and these are currently undergoing XRD analysis.

A series of twelve quarry scoops was identified along this line of outcrops, each one around 10m in diameter at its widest point, and cutting into the steep slope of the hill (unlike Houlder's pits which were cut vertically at a point where the ground was almost level).

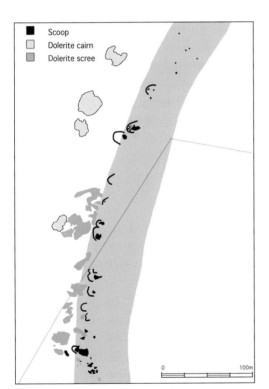

Most of these scoops contained loose debris and some of those on the steepest part of the hill have screes beneath them. Unfortunately, deep vegetation prevented the mapping of these screes at all points, although they could be felt underfoot. Vegetation also limited the survey area at its northern and southern ends, where the depth of heather made it impossible to identify further surface features.

The survey's remit was limited to the collection of geological samples, and no attempt was made to remove vegetation or disturb screes, but even so a single flake with a clear conchoidal fracture was found which had been produced from the Mynydd Rhiw Rhyolitic Tuff member. A search of the National Museum of Wales's archaeology collections revealed a further flake of this material which had been found on Mynydd Rhiw in 1933 (Figure 5.3). The Mynydd Rhiw Rhyolitic Tuff member is more silicic than the baked shale and consequently has superior conchoidal fracture and produces sharper flakes. However, microtextures in the tuff result in a slightly less homogenous fabric in the tuff than the baked shale, the structure of which has been homogenized during thermal metamorphism.

Figure 5.2. Results of 2005 survey on Mynydd Rhiw. The dark band is the Mynydd Rhiw Rhyolitic Tuff member, and the quarry scoops and their associated screes cut this band. For location of survey see detail on Figure 5.1.

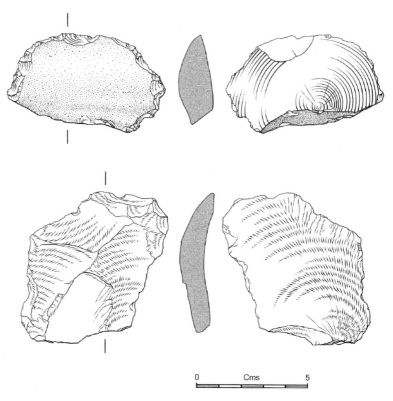

Figure 5.3. Prehistoric flakes struck from the Mynydd Rhiw Tuff member. The top example was discovered in 1933, the lower example was found during the course of the 2005 survey.

DATING THE DISCOVERIES

Given the evidence for Neolithic quarrying on Mynydd Rhiw it is tempting to assume that the new quarries also date from this period. The rock would certainly have been suitable for the manufacture of small tools or axeheads, and the presence of a large conchoidal fracture on one of the outcrops and on two flakes suggest that the seam was worked for this purpose. But conclusive evidence is still lacking, and it is important to consider the possibility that the quarries relate to activities in other periods.

First, there are the Early Bronze Age cairns which show that Mynydd Rhiw's rocks were still being used, albeit as building material in this period. These cairns were built on the crest of the hill around 30m from the newly discovered quarries and are aligned broadly parallel to them. But examination of their make-up shows that they were constructed from the dolerite screes that cover the hillside, rather than from quarried material from the rhyolitic tuff member. Houlder's radiocarbon dates from his quarry pit also indicate later Bronze Age activity on Mynydd Rhiw, but again, this cannot be linked to the new quarries. The only other notable archaeology on the top of Mynydd Rhiw is a series of post-medieval walls, one of which crosses the line of quarry pits. Like the cairns these were built from the abundant dolerite screes on this part of the hill.

Circumstantial evidence would therefore suggest that the newly discovered quarries date to the Neolithic, although a question mark remains as to what purpose the quarried material served. The natural assumption is that the quarrying relates to axehead production, but examination of all likely candidates within the CBA's implement petrology collection for Wales has failed to find a single match for this rock among sectioned axeheads. This raises several possibilities:

- First, the quarried material might indeed have been used to make Neolithic axeheads, but none of these have yet been thin sectioned. If this is the case it raises significant questions about the extent to which the implement petrology programme in Wales has created a true reflection of the materials used in the manufacture of Neolithic axeheads.
- Second, since the authors have not checked thin section records in England, Scotland or Ireland, it is possible that matches exist with axeheads in these areas. This seems unlikely, since all other grouped axes show a clustering around their source locality, and it is hard to see why these axeheads would have been treated differently.
- Third, the quarried material may have been used to make artefacts other than axeheads. This possibility is worth exploring since the tuff does naturally cleave into slabs. These slabs may have been valued in their own right, for example as polishing surfaces. To date, polishing slabs have only been recorded in Wales from excavations at Llandegai (Lynch and Musson 2001, 45), Bryn yr Hen Bobl (Hemp 1935, 292) and Gwernvale (Britnell and Savory 1984, 134). Like stone axeheads, it seems probable that the majority of polishing slabs would survive as stray finds, not in sealed contexts. But the likelihood of non-descript polishing slabs being recognised by casual collectors and passed to museums is far less than for stone axeheads, which have a distinctive shape. If the tuff was indeed being used to make polishing slabs, these products could easily have evaded the attention of archaeologists to date.
- Lastly, of course, there remains a strong possibility that the quarries are not Neolithic, like all the other options, this can only be settled by excavation.

CONCLUSION

In conclusion, it has been over 40 years since Houlder published his excavations at Mynydd Rhiw. Since this time there have been significant advances in our understanding of the archaeology of Neolithic axehead production sites (e.g. Preseli Hill: David and Williams 1995; Graig Lwyd: Williams and Davidson 1998; Killin: Edmonds *et al.* 1992; and Lambay Island: Cooney 2005), as well as in the interpretation of the distribution of axehead products (e.g. Bradley and Edmonds 1993; Darvill 1989). A re-evaluation of the archaeology on Mynydd Rhiw, and of the products currently ascribed to it would seem timely given these developments. This chapter has discussed several of the approaches that might be taken, and these can be summarized as follows:

- A small radiocarbon dating programme on material from Houlder's excavations would help to date more closely the quarrying activity he discovered.
- Review of the material currently included under the heading of Group XXI would resolve outstanding questions regarding the distribution of products from Mynydd Rhiw.
- Excavation of the new quarries (whether they are Neolithic or not), would help to expand our awareness of the complexity of the hill's archaeology.

A final approach which should be addressed is the examination of other tuff seams known from geological mapping to exist on and around Mynydd Rhiw. An illustration of the necessity of this work was provided during a short walk on the beach at Hell's Mouth, 3.5km from Mynydd Rhiw, at the end of the survey programme reported here.

During this walk several large, and relatively unweathered slabs of rock were found which are petrologically indistinguishable from that found in Houlder's quarry pits (Figure 5.1). It is possible that these were carried down to the coastal plain from the Mynydd Rhiw quarries during the Neolithic and have since eroded from the soft cliffs onto the beach. But it seems more likely that they are derived from one of the several other seams in the area and that they eroded into the sea naturally. Further survey work is needed to locate this petrologically important seam (or seams) and to check whether there is any sign of quarrying along its length.

The authors hope to undertake this work in the near future. (Addendum: further excavation at Myndd Rhiw has confirmed the Neolithic date of the features described here. See Burrow 2011).

ACKNOWLEDGEMENTS

The finds and samples recovered from Houlder's excavations, as well as the CBA implement petrology archive for Wales are housed at the National Museum of Wales. Permission to undertake survey at Mynydd Rhiw was granted by the John Latham of the National Trust and Mr and Mrs Pugh of Neigwl Plas. The authors are especially grateful to the members of the Implement Petrology Group and other professionals who visited Mynydd Rhiw before and during the survey and who offered much constructive comment: Vin Davis, David Field, Jana Horak, David Jenkins, Frances Lynch, Pete Topping, John Ll Williams. Figures 5.1–2 were produced by Tony Daly, and Figure 5.3 by Jackie Chadwick.

BIBLIOGRAPHY

Allen, J. R. L., 1990, Three Neolithic axes from the Severn Estuary. *Transactions of the Bristol and Gloucestershire Archaeological Society* 108: 171–174.

Bradley, R. J. and Edmonds, M., 1993, *Interpreting the Axe Trade: Production and Exchange in Neolithic Britain*. Cambridge: Cambridge University Press.

Britnell, W. J. and Savory, H. N., 1984, *Gwernvale and Penywyrlod: Two Neolithic Long Cairns in the Black Mountains of Brecknock*. Cardiff: Cambrian Archaeological Association (Monograph 2).

Brown, M. J. and Evans, A. D., 1989, *Geophysical and Geochemical Investigations of the Manganese Deposits of Rhiw, Western Llyn, North Wales*. British Geological Survey Technical Report, WF/89/14.

Burrow, S., 1999, Reuniting the Dyffryn Ardudwy pendants. *Archaeologia Cambrensis* 148, 203–6.

Burrow, S., 2011, The Mynydd Rhiw quarry site: recent work and it's implications. In V. Davis and M. Edmonds (eds), *Stone Axe Studies III*, 247–260. Oxford: Oxbow Books

Clough, T. H. McK. and Cummins, W. A., 1988, *Stone Axe Studies, Volume 2. The Petrology of Prehistoric Stone Implements from the British Isles*. London: Council for British Archaeology (Research Report 67).

Cooney, G., 2005, Stereo porphyry: quarrying and deposition on Lambay Island, Ireland. In P. Topping and M. Lynott (eds), *The Cultural Landscape of Prehistoric Mines*, 14–29. Oxford: Oxbow Books.

Darvill, T. C., 1989, The circulation of Neolithic stone and flint axes: a case study from Wales and the mid-west of England. *Proceedings of the Prehistoric Society* 55, 27–43.

David, A. E. U. and Williams, G., 1995, Stone axe-head manufacture: new evidence from the Preseli Hills, West Wales. *Proceedings of the Prehistoric Society* 61, 433–60.

Edmonds, M., Sheridan, A. and Tipping, R., 1992, Survey and excavation at Creag na Caillich, Killin, Perthshire. *Proceedings of the Society of Antiquaries of Scotland* 122, 77–112.

Gibbons, W. and Mc Carroll, D., 1993, *Geology of the Country Around Aberdaron, Including Bardsey Island*. Memoir of the British Geological Survey, Sheet 133 (England and Wales).

Glenn, T. A., 1914, Exploration of Neolithic station near Gwaenysgor, Flintshire. *Archaeologia Cambrensis* new series 6:14, 247–270.

Glenn, T. A., 1915, Prehistoric and historic remains at Dyserth Castle. *Archaeologia Cambrensis* new series 6:15, 47–86.

Hemp, W. J., 1935, The chambered cairn known as Bryn yr Hen Bobl, near Plas Newydd, Anglesey. *Archaeologia* 85, 252–292.

Houlder, C. H., 1961, The excavation of a Neolithic stone implement factory on Mynydd Rhiw in Caernarvonshire. *Proceedings of the Prehistoric Society* 27, 108–143.

Lynch, F. M., 1969, The megalithic tombs of North Wales. In T. G. E. Powell, J. X. W. P. Corcoran, F. M. Lynch and J. G. Scott (eds), *Megalithic Enquiries in the West of Britain*, 107–148. Liverpool: Liverpool University Press.

Lynch, F. and Musson, C., 2001, A prehistoric and early medieval complex at Llandegai, near Bangor, North Wales. *Archaeologia Cambrensis* 150, 17–142.

Muckle, P. and Jocelyne, N., 2001, *Measured Survey of the Prehistoric Axe Factory at Mynydd Rhiw*. Unpublished report for the National Trust.

Piggott, S., 1935, Report on the pottery from Dyserth and Gwaenysgor. *Archaeologia Cambrensis* 90, 212–213.

Pitts, M., 1996, The stone axe in Neolithic Britain. *Proceedings of the Prehistoric Society* 61, 311–371.

Powell, T. G. E., 1954, Excavations at Gwaenysgor (Flints), 1951. *Archaeologia Cambrensis* 103, 109–11.

Powell, T. G. E., 1973, Excavation of the megalithic chambered cairn at Dyffryn Ardudwy, Merioneth, Wales. *Archaeologia* 104, 1–50.

RCAHM(W), 1964, *Caernarvonshire, Volume 3: West*. London: HMSO.

Shotton, F. W., 1988, The petrological identification of stone implements from the West Midlands: third report. In T. H. McK. Clough and W. A. Cummins, *Stone Axe Studies, Volume 2. The Petrology of Prehistoric Stone Implements from the British Isles*, 49–51. London: Council for British Archaeology (Research Report 67).

Stuiver, M., Reimer, P. J., Bard, E., Beck, J. W., Burr, G. S., Hughen, K. A., Kromer, B., McCormac, G., van der Plicht, J. and Spurk, M., 1998, INTCAL98 radiocarbon age calibration, 24,000–0 cal BP. *Radiocarbon* 40, 1041–1077.

Williams, J. L. and Davidson, A., 1998, Survey and excavation at the Graiglwyd Neolithic axe factory, Penmaenmawr. *Archaeology in Wales* 38, 3–21.

Chapter 6

Stonehenge, looking from the inside out: a comparative analysis of landscape surveys in southern Britain

Benjamin Tun-Yee Chan

INTRODUCTION

Recent work on Stonehenge and its landscape has emphasized the need to study the monuments, not in isolation, but as part of a complex in which each locale is but a point in a network of significant places (Cleal *et al.* 1995; Exon *et al.* 2000; Darvill 1997; Parker Pearson and Ramilisonina 1998; Thomas 1999). Within Neolithic and Bronze Age studies in general, a further emphasis has also been placed upon understanding the positions of monuments within wider landscapes of human activities or 'taskscapes' (Edmonds 1997; 1999; Ingold 1993). Despite this, the majority of accounts of Stonehenge and its environs have failed to grasp the extent and nature of utilitarian activities and have also been limited in terms of their comparisons with other contemporary landscapes (Chan 2003, Chap. 2). However, there is a material that is often inadequately dealt with, which carries the potential to help us resolve both of these issues. This material is comprised of the lithic scatters that occur in abundance in the ploughsoil assemblages of the Stonehenge environs and other landscapes across Britain.

The main focus of this chapter is the analysis of the character of inhabitation of the Stonehenge landscape through a comparison with other landscapes in southern Britain. This will provide an alternative means for not only understanding the conditions under which people came to places like Stonehenge but also the wider variations in inhabitation patterns in Neolithic and Bronze Age landscapes.

COMPARING LANDSCAPES

At the most general level archaeological assemblages are often interpreted through analysis of the presence or absence of variation over time and/or space. For landscape survey projects and ploughsoil assemblages spatial variation can be understood at two main levels. That is variation *within* a single landscape and variation *between* different landscapes/regions.

Analysis of both levels of variation is important as it facilitates the investigation of different types of questions. The study of variability within a single landscape is necessary for the understanding of the organization of lithic working practice at a micro-scale. This is particularly important as it allows the composition and scale of ploughsoil assemblages to be understood in relation to landscape, topography and most archaeological contexts or sites.

Analysis of variability in ploughsoil assemblages between different landscapes frames questions at a regional and inter-regional scale. Unlike questions posed at a micro-scale this analysis allows the understanding of a specific landscape context *in relation* to other landscapes. This provides the potential for an assessment of how typical or unusual the overall nature of activity within a landscape may be.

The ability to tack back and forth between intra- and inter-regional analytical scales is particularly important in the study of the Neolithic and Early Bronze Age as societies may have retained a significant degree of mobility. For example, visits to flint mines, stone axehead sources, the gathering of seasonal foodstuffs and the movements of herds would have required certain members of communities to visit a variety of different landscapes on a periodic basis. Hence, it is wrong to talk of groups as inhabiting any single landscape or location. If the Stonehenge landscape is understood to be just one amongst a number of places that Neolithic and Bronze Age people would have visited then the full character of its inhabitation can only be understood through reference to other landscapes.

In practice what the interpretation of differences in ploughsoil assemblages between landscapes or regions requires is the analysis of material collected by different projects. Whilst in an ideal case this analysis might involve the direct comparison of the actual material from different projects, this is impossible in practical terms. Therefore, what is required is the comparison of assemblages based upon published data.

It seems obvious that such comparisons should be made given that in southern Britain, and in Wessex in particular, the 1980s witnessed a mass of large, ploughsoil-based survey projects aimed at providing details of a poorly understood settlement context (e.g. Barrett *et al.* 1991; Gaffney and Tingle 1989; Gardiner 1984; Holgate 1988; Richards 1990; Sharples 1991; Woodward 1991). Several of these (the South Dorset Ridgeway Survey, the Maiden Castle Survey and the Stonehenge Environs Project) were specifically designed as sister projects whose methodologies and therefore results were intended to be comparable. In addition, as the number of such projects grew so did the basic awareness of ploughsoil assemblages and there was some attempt to standardize collection methodologies. This is witnessed in the acceptance by several projects of a standardized collection grid (spaced at 25m intervals aligned on the National Grid) based upon the then Trust for Wessex Archaeology field collection system (e.g. Ford 1987a, 11; Gaffney and Tingle 1989, 15; cf. Woodward 1978). However the assemblages from these projects remain relatively poorly understood and more importantly, stand in isolation from each other.

Given the above it is indeed surprising that a comparative analysis of these landscape surveys has not previously been attempted in any detail. Even the South Dorset Ridgeway Survey and the Stonehenge Environs Project ultimately failed to directly compare their results. Indeed in general Woodward felt that analysis of such a:

> ...*mass of data...would require considerable processing and assessment to allow detailed cross correlation and comparison.* (Woodward 1991, 122)

The veracity of Woodward's statement should be questioned. As will be seen there are of course problematic issues involved in the comparison of material from different projects. However, the extent to which they are considered insurmountable depends largely on how directly comparable in 'statistical' terms one wants the results to be. It will be shown that a relatively rapid comparison can be made between projects and although there may be some issues involved with the final results they are not serious enough to negate the overall significance of the findings.

THE ANALYSIS METHODOLOGY

Project selection

Due to the nature of the analysis the first limiting issue in choosing projects for the analysis was that they needed to be published in sufficient detail. I have also attempted to select projects from the same broad region, some of which have similarity in terms of their chalkland settings and Neolithic and Early Bronze Age archaeology and others which incorporated a wider range geologies and densities of archaeological monuments.
The projects selected for analysis were:

- The East Berkshire Survey (Ford 1987a)
- The Holgate and Thomas Survey (Holgate 1987)
- The Maddle Farm Project (Gaffney and Tingle 1989)
- The Maiden Castle Survey (Sharples 1991)
- The Middle Avon Valley Survey (Schofield 1987; 1988)
- The North Stoke Survey (Ford 1987b)
- The Stonehenge Environs Project (Richards 1990)
- The South Dorset Ridgeway Survey (Woodward 1991)
- The Upper Meon Valley Survey (Schofield 1988)
- The Windmill Hill Survey (Whittle *et al.* 2000)

All of these projects investigated landscapes within the central part of southern Britain (Figure 6.1). The projects also all involved the survey of chalkland landscapes except the East Berkshire and North Stoke surveys which contained extensive areas of varied drift deposits representing a range of different geologies.

In terms of prehistoric archaeology the projects can be split into two rough groups. The Holgate and Thomas Survey, the Maiden Castle Survey, the South Dorset Ridgeway Survey the Stonehenge Environs Project and the Windmill Hill Survey were conducted in areas with dense distributions of monuments and monumental complexes that incorporate the full range of Neolithic and Bronze Age ritual and funerary monuments. In contrast, the remaining projects all contain Neolithic and Early Bronze Age monuments but with relatively sparse distributions and lower frequencies

The basis of the analysis

The analysis was originally conducted as part of a PhD research project (Chan 2003, Chap. 7). The analysis was aimed at assessing two simple factors; namely the *scale* of activity, assessed through differences in the density of surface material and the *character* of activity, assessed through the composition of assemblages. The aspect of the analysis that will be presented here refers to the scale of activity. The assessment of the variation in the

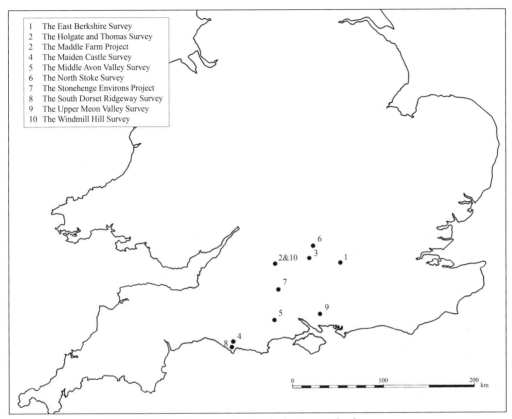

1   The East Berkshire Survey
2   The Holgate and Thomas Survey
2   The Maddle Farm Project
4   The Maiden Castle Survey
5   The Middle Avon Valley Survey
6   The North Stoke Survey
7   The Stonehenge Environs Project
8   The South Dorset Ridgeway Survey
9   The Upper Meon Valley Survey
10 The Windmill Hill Survey

Figure 6.1. Location map showing the location of landscape surveys.

composition of assemblages yielded mixed results mainly as it was hampered by the lack of the necessary published data for many of the projects involved in the analysis. It is felt that this aspect of the analysis could still provide useful results, however it requires access to individual project archives. Such work was outside the remit of the current analysis.

METHODOLOGICAL ISSUES OF COMPARABILITY

Although it was suggested above that there was an attempt by some projects to standardize collection grids, it will be shown that there is a potential for variation in just about every aspect of the collection, analysis, and presentation of ploughsoil assemblages. Therefore, in order to understand the archaeological significance of the comparison between different survey projects it is first necessary to understand how the data were derived.

The variation occurring between projects that affect the data used in the analysis can be considered to be resulting from differences in:

- Project objectives
- Collection methodologies
- Analysis methodologies
- Data presentation
- Post-depositional processes

Analysis methodologies refer to variation in the techniques of lithic analysis and the definitions of analytical categories, whilst data presentation refers to ambiguities and inconsistencies in the manner in which data are presented within project reports. Both of these issues affect data involved in the analysis of assemblage composition. As this part of the analysis will not be presented here further details of these issues will not be discussed.

Project objectives

Project objectives are perhaps the most influential of all factors affecting variation between different projects. It is an essential part of question-led methodologies that early choices concerning project objectives underlie all subsequent decisions made during a project. Therefore, many of the methodological issues listed above are directly influenced by project objectives, as they are the tools with which they are supposed to be met.

Particular examples of the effect of differing project objectives are the choices over the area of the landscape to be investigated and the proportion of this landscape that will be sampled. These obviously vary from project to project according to their original objectives. For example the Stonehenge Environs Project set out:

> ...*to show that the area [was] also unique in terms of its prehistoric settlement record, demonstrating a range and density of human activities hitherto unstudied and essentially unknown.* (Richards 1990, 9)

Therefore, the choice of the study area centred around a coherent landscape determined partially by the extent of the concentration of monuments and partially by previous work through the acceptance for the most part of the RCHME's definition of the 'Stonehenge Environs' (an area of roughly 8 × 6km: RCHME 1979; Richards 1990, 1). Hence, the coverage of the project is comparatively intense with survey area boundaries predicated to a certain extent by the character of the archaeology in the area as opposed to any topographical or geological variation.

In contrast, other projects set out with quite different objectives. Both the East Hampshire Survey (Shennan 1985) and the East Berkshire Survey (Ford 1987a) were carried out in areas where, compared to the Stonehenge environs, little was known of the archaeology. Both also lacked the range and density of monuments of the latter landscape. In addition, both explicitly set out to examine the relationship between human exploitation and ecological variables understood through surface geology (Ford 1987a, 5; Shennan 1985, 5). It was this decision that determined the extent and location of the survey areas in that both were designed to take in as large a variation in surface geology as possible. Due to this, and also probably because the general density of material in the areas was relatively low, the survey areas for these projects are much larger than that chosen for the Stonehenge Environs Project. The East Hampshire Survey covered an area of 15 × 10km, whilst the

East Berkshire Survey covered a single transect of roughly 25 × 6km. As a corollary of the size of the sample areas, the intensity of surface sampling within the study areas was lower than that of the Stonehenge Environs Project. Ultimately the East Berkshire Survey involved walking three times as many hectares as the Stonehenge Environs Project but resulted in the collection of only a fraction of the material (Tables 6.1–2).

AREA NAME	AREA No.	GEOLOGY	TOTAL FLINT	HECTARES WALKED (HA.)	LINE SPACING (M)	FLINT/HA
Winterbourne Stoke Crossroads	50	Middle Chalk	4493	17.6	25	254.92
Coneybury Hill	51	Middle Chalk	7588	42.6	25	178.02
N. of Cursus	52	Middle Chalk	11655	27.3	25	427.71
S.H. Triangle	54	Middle Chalk	8748	33.5	25	261.13
South of S.H.	55	Middle Chalk	1639	31.1	25	52.66
Normanton Down	56	Middle Chalk	466	26.8	25	17.42
King Barrow Ridge	57	Middle Chalk	4373	34.1	25	128.15
The Diamond	59	Middle Chalk	4068	20.8	25	196.05
Woodhenge	60	Middle Chalk	2934	16.6	25	176.48
Normanton Gorse	61	Middle Chalk	300	10.5	25	28.57
Cursus West End	62	Middle Chalk	2366	64.3	25	36.82
Fargo Road	63	Middle Chalk	3591	34.1	25	105.23
Horse Hospital	64	Middle Chalk	2977	21.0	25	141.76
Durrington Down	65	Middle Chalk	3031	26.4	25	114.92
Sewage Works	66	Middle Chalk	482	8.6	25	55.88
Normanton Bottom	67	Middle Chalk	2529	12.1	25	208.58
West Field	68	Middle Chalk	3856	24.6	25	156.59
King Barrow Ridge East	69	Middle Chalk	2330	19.9	25	117.23
Nile Clump	70	Middle Chalk	1265	15.0	25	84.33
Railway	71	Middle Chalk	3335	19.5	25	171.03
Home Fields	72	Middle Chalk	3409	20.8	25	164.29
Whittles	73	Middle Chalk	806	6.8	25	119.41
Pig Field	74	Middle Chalk	475	6.5	25	73.08
Bunnies Playground	75	Middle Chalk	1466	8.0	25	183.25
Destructor	76	Middle Chalk	473	9.0	25	52.56
The Ditches	77	Middle Chalk	2752	6.1	25	449.31
Spring Bottom	78	Middle Chalk	5594	23.6	25	236.78
Aerodrome	79	Middle Chalk	753	16.4	25	45.98
Ammo Dump	80	Middle Chalk	540	13.9	25	38.92
King Barrow Ridge Addit.	81	Middle Chalk	484	4.0	25	121.00
Rox Hill	82	Middle Chalk	4279	27.3	25	157.03
Well House	83	Middle Chalk	1313	4.9	25	269.33
Luxenborough	84	Middle Chalk	1661	13.9	25	119.71
South of Cursus	85	Middle Chalk	380	12.8	25	29.80
Rox Hill (unsown)	86	Middle Chalk	2254	11.4	25	198.15
New King	87	Middle Chalk	1655	20.8	25	79.76
Normanton East	88	Middle Chalk	1274	29.5	25	43.19
Lake Bottom	89	Middle Chalk	199	2.0	25	99.50
Wood End	90	Middle Chalk	382	10.8	25	35.53
Total	-	-	102175	754.5	-	135.42
Mean	-	-	2620	19.3	-	139.23

Table 6.1. Surface flint densities from the Stonehenge Environs Project.

Project	Area Sub-division	Geology	Total Flint	Ha. Walked	Line Spacing (m)	Flint/ ha	Adjusted flint/ ha.	Data taken or calculated from
SDR Survey	All	Varied: Mostly Upper Chalk some River Gravels	38659	231.2	10	167.25	66.90	Woodward 1991
SDR Survey	1	Varied: River Gravels and Alluvium	3634	51.8	10	70.22	28.09	Woodward 1991
SDR Survey	1b	Mainly Chalk	1390	10.7	10	130.52	52.21	Woodward 1991
SDR Survey	2	Upper Chalk	3498	44.5	10	78.61	31.44	Woodward 1991
SDR Survey	3	Upper Chalk	2147	13.5	10	159.04	63.61	Woodward 1991
SDR Survey	4a	Upper Chalk	4106	27.8	10	147.96	59.19	Woodward 1991
SDR Survey	4b	Upper Chalk	15570	42.8	10	364.21	145.68	Woodward 1991
SDR Survey	4c	Upper Chalk	8314	40.3	10	206.56	82.62	Woodward 1991
Maiden Castle Survey	All	Mostly Upper Chalk	46789	322.6	25	145.04	145.04	Sharples 1991
Maiden Castle Survey	W107	Unclear	30350	184.7	25	164.32	164.32	Sharples 1991
Maiden Castle Survey	W156A	Unclear	9756	69.4	25	140.58	140.58	Sharples 1991
Maiden Castle Survey	W156B	Unclear	6683	68.5	25	97.65	97.65	Sharples 1991
Middle Avon Valley Survey	All	Mainly Chalk	6450	402.4	15	16.74	10.04	Schofield 1987; 1988
Middle Avon Valley Survey	1	Gravel & Alluvium	566	28.0	15	20.21	12.13	Schofield 1987; 1988
Middle Avon Valley Survey	2	Valley Gravels	1833	70.6	15	25.96	15.60	Schofield 1987; 1988
Middle Avon Valley Survey	3	Lower Chalk	652	39.9	15	16.34	9.78	Schofield 1987; 1988
Middle Avon Valley Survey	5	Gravels & Sands	1992	141.8	15	14.05	8.43	Schofield 1987; 1988
Upper Meon Valley Survey	All	Upper & Lower Chalk	5217	260.7	15	20.01	12.01	Schofield 1988; 1991
Upper Meon Valley Survey	1	Upper Chalk	3026	80.9	15	49.60	29.76	Schofield 1988; 1991
Upper Meon Valley Survey	2&3	Lower Chalk	2191	179.8	15	14.50	8.70	Schofield 1988; 1991
East Berkshire Survey	All	Very Varied	6533	2119.0	25	3.08	3.08	Ford 1987a

Project	Area Sub-division	Geology	Total Flint	Ha. Walked	Line Spacing (m)	Flint/ ha	Adjusted flint/ ha.	Data taken or calculated from
E. Berkshire Survey	-	Thames Gravel	783	202.0	25	3.88	3.88	Ford 1987a
E. Berkshire Survey	-	Upper Chalk	3378	452.0	25	7.47	7.47	Ford 1987a
E. Berkshire Survey	-	London Clay	387	964.0	25	0.40	0.40	Ford 1987a
E. Berkshire Survey	-	Reading Beds	1912	358.0	25	5.34	5.34	Ford 1987a
North Stoke Survey	All	Very Varied	9097	968.0	25	9.39	9.39	Ford 1987b
North Stoke Survey	-	Gravel	1355	145.0	25	9.35	9.35	Ford 1987b
North Stoke Survey	-	Lower Chalk	4604	436.0	25	10.56	10.56	Ford 1987b
North Stoke Survey	-	Middle Chalk	2079	228.0	25	9.12	9.12	Ford 1987b
North Stoke Survey	-	Upper Chalk	103	11.0	25	9.39	9.39	Ford 1987b
North Stoke Survey	-	Older Coombe	796	88.0	25	9.05	9.05	Ford 1987b
Windmill Hill Survey	-	Middle and Lower Chalk	1091	71.0	50	15.37	30.73	Whittle *et al.* 2000
Maddle Farm Project	All	Chalk	39955	1792.0	25	22.30	22.30	Gaffney and Tingle 1989
Maddle Farm Project	Area 1	Lower Chalk	199	43.0	25	4.63	4.63	Gaffney and Tingle 1989
Maddle Farm Project	Area 2	Middle Chalk	219	24.0	25	9.13	9.13	Gaffney and Tingle 1989
Maddle Farm Project	Area 3	Middle and Some Upper Chalk	2053	62.0	25	33.11	33.11	Gaffney and Tingle 1989
Maddle Farm Project	Area 4	Upper Chalk & prob. Clay-with-Flints	563	11.6	25	48.26	48.26	Gaffney and Tingle 1989
Maddle Farm Project	Area 5	Upper Chalk & some Clay-with-Flints	1674	40.5	25	41.33	41.33	Gaffney and Tingle 1989
Maddle Farm Project	Area 6	Middle & Upper Chalk and Clay-with-Flints	503	27.0	25	18.63	18.63	Gaffney and Tingle 1989
Maddle Farm Project	Area 7	Upper Chalk & Clay-with-Flint	1392	17.3	25	80.70	80.70	Gaffney and Tingle 1989
Maddle Farm Project	Area 8	Middle Chalk	1369	14.5	25	94.41	94.41	Gaffney and Tingle 1989

Table 6.2. Surface flint densities from landscape surveys in southern Britain.

At the opposite range of the spectrum, some fieldwalking projects have not been conducted as part of such large-scale surveys. They have instead been targeted towards answering more specific questions or have taken place within ongoing projects whose approaches are not so heavily orientated towards surface collection. The work that has taken place around Avebury by, amongst others, Alasdair Whittle and Joshua Pollard is an example of just such a project (e.g. Whittle 1993; 1994; 1997a; Whittle *et al.* 1993; 1999; Whittle and Pollard 1998). Although the work has concentrated largely on excavated contexts and field monuments, some detailed systematic field collection has occurred on a relatively small scale. The main example of this was the collection from a single field on the south slope of Windmill Hill called North Field, which covers an area of roughly 1km^2 (Whittle *et al.* 2000).

As can be seen, the geographical scale of different episodes of surface collection varies immensely according to individual project objectives. For larger projects there is an inevitable variation in the intensity of prehistoric activity over the large areas of the landscape covered by projects like the East Berkshire Survey (Ford 1987a). This can make comparisons with episodes of much more focused collection such as that carried out adjacent to Windmill Hill (Whittle *et al.* 2000) problematic in statistical terms. This is mainly because it is not known whether collections from smaller areas are representative of the ploughsoil assemblages in their wider landscapes. However, most of the projects included in the current analysis are large scale, which should make the results broadly comparable in these terms. Despite the small scale of the collection the results of the Windmill Hill Survey (Whittle *et al.* 2000) are included because of the importance of the area, particularly when making comparisons with the Stonehenge landscape. In addition, for the first time data are available for Holgate and Thomas's survey (Holgate 1987), which provides data for the wider Avebury landscape and allows the Windmill Hill data to be placed in context (see below).

COLLECTION METHODOLOGIES

Collection methodologies determine the proportion of the surface from which material will be picked up. For any sort of comparative analysis the most basic requirement is for a consistent and systematic collection of material on a regularly spaced grid. Without the use of a regularly spaced grid it is not possible to calculate the proportion of the surface that has been walked and hence statistical comparison between different survey projects is not possible. For these reasons all of the data included here are from projects that utilized a regular collection grid.

Whilst different decisions have often been made about the appropriate dimensions of collection grids (i.e. the *spacing* and *length* of collection lines), it is not the grid that affects the amount of material collected and concurrently the comparative compatibility of projects. The size of the collection grid determines the spatial *resolution* with which collected material can later be *analysed*, whereas the spacing of the collection lines determines what *proportion* of the surface material is *collected*. As the basis of this analysis is the density of surface material it is essential to know what proportion of the surface material was collected by different projects.

Despite the fact that all of the projects included in this analysis used systematically spaced collection lines, their spacing varies from 10–50m apart. Before the data from the projects can be considered to be comparable it is necessary to compensate for the differences in the spacing of collection lines. As the spacing of collection lines is constant within individual projects a simple calculation is all that is required to reconfigure the densities of material as if they had all been collected on the same basis. For the sake of convenience all of the figures have been recalculated as if they were collected from lines spaced 25m apart, the spacing used by the Stonehenge Environs Project (Richards 1990, 11).

The other main issue concerning collection methodologies that affects the comparative potential of different landscape surveys is the imposition by certain projects of collection corridors. As discussed, the proportion of surface material collected depends upon the spacing of collection lines. However, it also relies upon the distance either side of those lines from which material is collected. In this respect, there are some inconsistencies in suggestions of the size of a fieldwalkers 'natural' collection corridor. Whilst some estimate it to be a corridor roughly 2–2.5m wide (Richards 1985; Tingle 1987, 89), others suggest only a 1m corridor (Ford 1987a, 11).

In general, differences in estimations of the size of collection corridors do not affect the comparability of data from different survey projects as we may assume that disregarding unpredictable variation (e.g. lighting, surface visibility, individual ability etc.) people will collect material from a roughly equal area. However, some projects such as the Windmill Hill Survey (Whittle *et al.* 2000) and the Avebury Survey (Holgate 1987) have purposefully imposed a collection corridor. In both cases collection took place along 1m wide strips spaced 50m apart (Holgate 1987, 260; Whittle *et al.* 2000, 137). Accordingly, in this case estimates of a walkers 'natural' collection corridor are important. If, as some suggest, a walker would normally collect from a 2m wide area then the aforementioned surveys would have collected from half the area of the surface as the other projects.

There is no immediate resolution to this issue. It is enough for now to be aware of the problem and to take it into account when viewing the data presented in this analysis. This factor will be brought back into the discussion during the presentation of results.

Post-depositional processes

The post-depositional processes that affect ploughsoil assemblages have been a major concern for the last 20 years (e.g. Allen 1991; Clark and Schofield 1991; Schofield 1988). Literature on the topic is concerned with the range of factors that affect materials in the period between their original deposition and their eventual collection from the surface of the ploughsoil. The major factors in this respect are landuse history, topography, geology and soil type (cf. Boismier 1991, 15). These factors may vary locally and quantification of their relative effects between different survey projects is almost impossible to assess given the scope of the current analysis. However, as far as possible there is some coherency within regional areas defined by broad similarities in 'environment, climate and the nature and intensity of agricultural use' (Clark and Schofield 1991, 94). This is part of the reason that, within the current analysis, areas have been selected which are reasonably close geographically and there has been a preference for projects conducted in chalkland landscapes.

One other factor warranting consideration is a post-depositional process of quite another kind. The actions in the past of avid collectors working on an unsystematic basis, who sometimes left little or no record of their activities, obviously affect the material remaining to be collected today. Such collections can be localized and may have taken place over a considerable number of years. An example of one such collector was the Reverend H.G.O. Kendall, Rector of Winterbourne Bassett, who collected in the Avebury region during the early twentieth century (Gillings and Pollard 2004, 175; Holgate 1987; Whittle *et al.* 2000). It must be said that he was a conscientious man and we are lucky as he apparently collected all struck flint and recorded the locations from which they were found. However, it is still not possible to quantify the impact of such persistent action on the quantities and composition of material collected from the surface today. Equally, as the precise locations and collection methodologies he used are not known we cannot use the information from his collections to compare with current surveys (Holgate 1987; cf. Gardiner 1984)

In the Avebury region in general and around Windmill Hill in particular the problem is compounded because Alexander Keiller was openly willing to pay Kendall and others for surface collected material (Whittle *et al.* 2000, 134). Over the years thousands of artefacts entered his collection in this way. As payment was on the basis of the perceived quality of pieces it seems inevitable that collection in this area was biased towards certain artefact types.

These types of activities were quite localized, often poorly recorded and probably concentrated around areas already of interest due to the presence of upstanding monuments. Unfortunately the effects of such collections are essentially an unquantifiable factor affecting the comparability of ploughsoil assemblages from different areas. However, many of these types of large-scale amateur collections took place before the Second

Field No.	Geology	Total Flint	Ha. Walked	Line Spacing (m)	Flint/ ha	Adjusted flint/ ha.
1	Middle and Lower Chalk	29	13	50	2.23	4.46
2	Middle and Lower Chalk	205	6	50	34.17	68.33
3	Middle and Lower Chalk	15	29	50	0.52	1.03
4	Middle and Lower Chalk	4	27.1	50	0.15	0.30
5	Middle and Lower Chalk	9	7.9	50	1.14	2.28
6	Middle and Lower Chalk	75	9.2	50	8.15	16.30
7	Middle and Lower Chalk	26	16.5	50	1.58	3.15
8	Middle and Lower Chalk	20	6.2	50	3.23	6.45
9	Middle and Lower Chalk	39	13	50	3.00	6.00
10	Middle and Lower Chalk	59	20	50	2.95	5.90
11	Middle and Lower Chalk	140	15.6	50	8.97	17.95
12	Middle and Lower Chalk	156	10.1	50	15.45	30.89
13	Middle and Lower Chalk	184	25.8	50	7.13	14.26
14	Middle and Lower Chalk	6	20	50	0.30	0.60
15	Middle and Lower Chalk	29	35	50	0.83	1.66
15A	Middle and Lower Chalk	11	6.2	50	1.77	3.55
16	Middle and Lower Chalk	116	6.9	50	16.81	33.62
17	Middle and Lower Chalk	11	15.2	50	0.72	1.45
18	Middle and Lower Chalk	126	12	50	10.50	21.00
19	Middle and Lower Chalk	32	11.8	50	2.71	5.42
20	Middle and Lower Chalk	15	25.6	50	0.59	1.17
Total	-	1307	332.1	-	3.94	7.87
Mean	-	62.2	15.8	-	5.85	11.70

Table 6.3. Surface flint densities from the Holgate and Thomas Survey.

World War (Holgate 1988, 91–92) and it was not until after this time that mechanized ploughing seriously increased the extent and depth of ploughing. As this process would have dramatically altered the amount of material that was incorporated into the ploughsoil, it could be argued that the problems connected with the early collectors are limited.

Chronology

The object of this analysis is to utilize the data from ploughsoil assemblages to provide a means for the comparison of the character of inhabitation of different landscapes in southern Britain. For the full significance of the results of the analysis to be realized it is also necessary to have some understanding of the chronology of the assemblages in question. In the following analysis there is a broad assumption that the comparison is of *contemporary* landscapes. In other words, that the lithic scatters in the landscapes under question were all derived from activity within the same broad period. This period is the later Neolithic and Bronze Age.

Unfortunately the chronological aspects of ploughsoil assemblages will always remain difficult to assess (Ford 1987c) and being palimpsests it is likely that the lithic scatters under question also contain Early Neolithic material. In this respect, the main contention of this analysis is that the *majority* of the material relates to Late Neolithic and Bronze Age activity. This suggestion is backed up by the general understanding that the use of flint in the Late Neolithic became more profligate than it had been in the Early Neolithic (Edmonds 1998, 255). This is reflected, amongst other things, in our understanding that in many landscapes in southern Britain Early Neolithic lithic scatters are smaller than those of the later period (Barrett *et al.* 1991, 60; Edmonds 1995, 80; 1998, 256). Hence if a landscape was occupied during both the Early and Later Neolithic it might be assumed that the majority of the material in the ploughsoil would be derived from the later period.

In addition to these general arguments, the quantity of chronologically distinctive tools in ploughsoil assemblages such as those in the Stonehenge environs are heavily weighted towards the Late Neolithic. Nearly 70% of all diagnostic tools collected by the Stonehenge Environs Project are attributable to the period (Chan 2003, 274). Furthermore the frequency of activity in landscapes such as Stonehenge and Avebury, as measured by the number and size of monuments, also seems to increase in the Late Neolithic and Early Bronze Age in comparison to the Early Neolithic. Therefore there is some basis for suggesting that the majority of the activity in the landscapes in question occurred during the later Neolithic and Bronze Age.

Summary

As discussed, there are many issues that militate against the direct comparison of the data from different survey projects. They are wide ranging and many are difficult to quantify. This is probably why Woodward (1991, 122), amongst others, felt that to conduct such a project would be immensely time-consuming, and hence why this has not been done before. However, the current contention is that these issues will be resolved by keeping the comparative analysis relatively more simple rather than by making it more complicated. That is why the elements of survey data that have been used in this analysis are directed towards the understanding of the simple factor of the scale of lithic artefact producing activities. In a similar fashion, as fine chronological definitions are unlikely to ever be yielded by the analysis of ploughsoil assemblages, the understanding of chronology is kept intentionally broad.

It should be realized that the aim of the analysis is not to generate an exact index of the intensity of occupation of the landscapes in question. The object is not to suggest that one landscape witnessed exactly ten times more occupation than another; rather it is enough to talk of gross differences in scale. The clearest assessment of the validity of this approach is the character of the results themselves and the degree of differences between different landscapes that they suggest.

THE COMPARATIVE ANALYSIS

The main objective of the analysis is an assessment of the relative scale of activities within different landscapes. Scale is a simple measurement in that it is an assessment of the density of worked surface flint per hectare. The results of the analysis indicate large-scale variability with the numbers of worked flint artefacts collected per hectare ranging from 0.3 flints per hectare to nearly 450 flints per hectare for individual collection areas (Tables 6.1–3). When the densities of individual collection areas are averaged for each survey project the data indicate a minimum of 3.1 flints per hectare for the East Berkshire Survey and a maximum of 145.0 flints per hectare for the Maiden Castle Survey (Figure 6.2). Comparison of the geology and archaeology of the landscapes in question indicates several different sources for this variation in flint density.

Variability Relating To Surface Geology

The first area of variability correlates closely with surface geology. In this respect the density of surface flint increases in areas with a chalk surface geology and within chalkland landscapes it increases in areas of flint-bearing chalk. The observation may be unsurprising but essentially the amount of worked surface flint increases in areas where the raw material itself is abundant. The effects of this factor can also be seen within localized landscape contexts such as within the Upper Meon Valley. In this valley, flint occurred naturally only in the areas of Upper Chalk, whereas the surveyed areas of Lower Chalk contained no flint sources but stood only 4–5km away. Despite their reasonable proximity the differences in the density of material is marked (Table 6.2; cf. Schofield 1991).

Assessing the covariation between surface geology and surface density highlights a key aspect of the analysis. The analysis is orientated towards the assessment of variation in the scale of inhabitation of various landscapes through the densities of surface flint. However, it should be realized that in the strictest terms surface density does not relate to the scale of inhabitation, rather it is an indication of the scale of lithic artefact producing activities. Hence the results are indicative of not only the scale of occupation of an area, but also of the overall character of lithic reduction strategies.

In respect to the above, the patterning for surface geology and flint density suggests two distinct possibilities: either inhabitation was preferentially located in flint-bearing chalkland

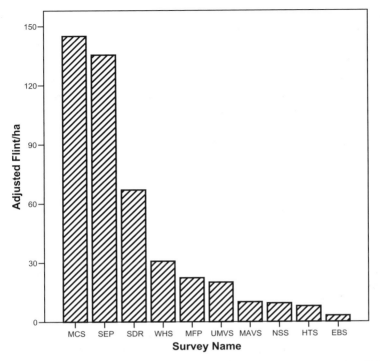

Figure 6.2. The adjusted amount of flint per hectare collected by field survey projects in southern Britain (MCS= Maiden Castle Survey; SEP: Stonehenge Environs Project; SDR= South Dorset Ridgeway Survey; WHS= Windmill Hill Survey; UMVS= Upper Meon Valley Survey; MAVS = Middle Avon Valley Survey; NSS= North Stoke Survey; HTS= Holgate and Thomas Survey; EBS= East Berkshire Survey).

areas, or flint use in those areas was more profligate. The most likely scenario is that both factors were in play. There is also the potential for a chronological element to be involved as there is a general understanding that flint use in the Late Neolithic was more profligate than in the Early Neolithic, and this is a pattern that may well have been exaggerated in areas with abundant raw materials. Hence there is a possibility that those landscapes with lower-density flint scatters may also be ones in which occupation in the Early Neolithic did not continue into the later Neolithic.

Variability relating to archaeology

Beyond the level of variation related to surface geology there is an additional level of difference. This is indicated by the fact that there is still gross variation in the amounts of worked surface flint within areas of flint-bearing chalk. For example, Upper Chalk areas of the Upper Meon Valley Survey and the Stonehenge Environs Project, both of which are flint-bearing landscapes, had average surface densities 29.8 flints per hectare and 135.4 flints per hectare respectively.

The differences within landscapes in which flint occurs naturally appear to correlate with the character of the archaeology in the different areas and their associated variations in density are of an order of magnitude above those discussed for surface geology. In this respect, two main groups can be distinguished. One group consists of the Stonehenge environs, the South Dorset Ridgeway and Maiden Castle, and the other contains all of the other landscapes. The average density of surface flint for the first group is nearly 116 flints per hectare, whilst the average density for the second group is just 15 flints per hectare (Figure 6.2).

The difference between these groups in terms of their upstanding archaeology is clear. The areas which have the high concentrations of surface lithic artefacts are those that have dense concentrations of monuments which make up ritual complexes. Within this group the area that has the highest average density of surface flint is that covered by the Maiden Castle survey (Sharples 1991). One of the reasons behind this is potentially that this survey concentrated on a single, large, and more or less continuous area centred on Maiden Castle. It may be the tight spatial focus of the project that explains its high average density.

Bearing this last factor in mind it should be noted that in contrast to the Maiden Castle Survey the Stonehenge Environs Project covered a large spatial area and its collection areas were spread across the landscape. This makes the densities of flint in the Stonehenge area, which nearly equal those around Maiden Castle, all the more significant. In this respect it is of interest that the South Dorset Ridgeway Survey, which surveyed the wider area around Maiden Castle, recorded densities of worked flint roughly half those recorded around Stonehenge.

Comparing the Stonehenge and Avebury landscapes

So far I have identified variations in the data that correlate with both the surface geology and archaeology. Given this correlation it is significant that there is an area that, whilst it shares both similar geology and archaeology to the Stonehenge environs and the South Dorset Ridgeway, it does not appear to share the density of lithics producing activities. This area is Avebury. Until recently, comparisons between the ploughsoil assemblages of Stonehenge and Avebury have been limited as the only sizable published data were from the area of land on the south slope of Windmill Hill (Whittle *et al.* 2000). The small size of the collection area of this project made comparisons with the more extensive Stonehenge Environs Project material difficult. A more widespread collection within the Avebury area was conducted during the 1980s by Holgate and Thomas (Holgate 1987), but the data from this collection remained unpublished. This meant that comparison could only be conducted based upon the published distribution map (Figure 6.3). However, the required data have been supplied from the project archive held in the Alexander Keiller Museum and is published here. For the first time this allows a significant comparison to be made between the ploughsoil assemblages of the Stonehenge and Avebury landscapes.

The first interesting comparison that can be made is between the Windmill Hill survey data and the Holgate and Thomas Survey (Tables 6.2–3). There is an excellent correlation between the two datasets in terms of surface density. The density of surface flint for the Windmill Hill survey is 30.73 flints per hectare, whilst in the Holgate and Thomas Survey the field (Field 12) that is nearest to the Windmill Hill Survey area has a density of 30.89 flints per hectare. The similarity in the data indicates the validity of the comparisons that

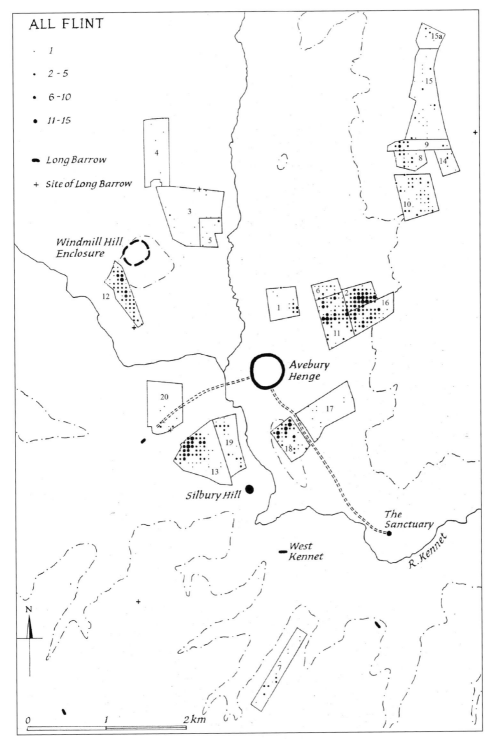

Figure 6.3. Distribution of surface flint from the Holgate and Thomas Survey indicating collection areas (after Holgate 1987, 261, fig.1; copyright Antiquity Publications Ltd, used with permission).

can be made between the two surveys. Furthermore, the wider coverage of the Holgate and Thomas Survey allows the Windmill Hill data to be placed in its wider landscape setting. This indicates that the density of surface flint in the area is actually higher than all but two of the collection areas in the rest of the Avebury landscape.

Overall the average density of surface flint for the Holgate and Thomas Survey is 7.9 flints per hectare with the lowest density of just 0.3 flints per hectare occurring to the north of Windmill Hill and the highest of 68.3 flints per hectare occurring to the northeast of Avebury. These data can be compared with the material collected from the Stonehenge Environs Project where the average density is 135.4 flints per hectare with the lowest being 17.4 flints per hectare and the highest being a massive 449.3 flints per hectare. To put the differences into perspective, the collection area with the highest density in the Thomas and Holgate Survey has a density of surface flint lower than all but eleven of the 39 sample areas of the Stonehenge Environs Project.

The differences between the data for Avebury and Stonehenge are stark. The reasons behind such significant variation would not appear to be due to any of the methodological issues outlined above. The survey areas are broadly comparable, being roughly 8 × 6km for the Stonehenge Environs Project and 9 × 5km for the Holgate and Thomas Survey. The collection areas differ slightly, with a total collection area of 754.5 hectares for the Stonehenge Environs Project and 332.1 hectares for the Holgate and Thomas Survey, but both are extensive enough to produce statistically representative data. As previously mentioned, the most significant factor that may affect the comparability of the data is the imposition by the Avebury surveys of a 1m-wide collection corridor. As discussed this leaves the possibility that the Avebury surveys may have only collected from half of the surface area compared to the Stonehenge Environs Project. As this is only a possibility the data have not been recalculated to reflect this. Furthermore it is clear from the contrasts in the data that even if the totals for surface flint for the Avebury surveys were doubled there would still be a massive difference with those in the Stonehenge landscape.

The analysis shows an interesting and hitherto hardly discussed difference between the Avebury and Stonehenge landscapes, two areas which have most often been seen as similar in many other respects. These data indicate that there was a significant difference in the manner in which these two landscapes were inhabited in the Neolithic and Bronze Age. The hope is that the understanding of variation in inhabitation that this leads to may ultimately provide new avenues of interpretation for southern Britain's two most studied later prehistoric landscapes.

DISCUSSION: THE INHABITATION OF THE STONEHENGE ENVIRONS

Hopefully the importance of the current analysis is now beginning to become clear. For the first time the material from the Stonehenge environs can be set in its wider context. The character of inhabitation can now be understood in relation to the scale of occupation of other areas. The importance of this perspective is realized when it is considered that the density of material in areas such as Normanton Down, which in the context of the Stonehenge ploughsoil assemblages is characterized as an almost total lack of activity, in other landscapes such as that of the Middle Avon Valley would be considered to be densely occupied.

From this analysis it is now clear that there were major differences in the scale of stoneworking activities in the landscapes around Stonehenge and the South Dorset Ridgeway compared to other contemporary landscapes. This immediately places the Stonehenge landscape within a more informed context of regional inhabitation patterns. In this respect, the landscape appears to be unusual not only in relation to the range and density of monuments in the area, but also because of the intensity of other activities. The Stonehenge environs must have been a relatively 'busy' place.

Now that the scale of inhabitation of the Stonehenge landscape has been established it is necessary to consider its nature. It is perhaps helpful to imagine two idealized forms of inhabitation that might have occurred, these are: permanent long-term occupation; or intermittent long- or short-term occupation. In other words it is necessary to decide whether we wish to talk about the construction and use of the monuments in the Stonehenge landscape by a permanent 'Stonehenge Population' or by a supra-community group who gathered in the area on an intermittent basis.

Permanent occupation in the Stonehenge landscape

When considering the possibility for permanent occupation in the Stonehenge environs during the Later Neolithic and Bronze Age it is necessary to examine the settlement evidence that exists beyond the lithic scatters themselves. Until recently, besides the timber circles at Durrington Walls (Wainwright and Longworth 1971) and scattered pits concentrated mainly around King Barrow Ridge and Durrington (Harding 1988; Stone and Young 1948; Vatcher 1969), there was no evidence in the Stonehenge landscape for anything that could be argued to be settlement evidence. Even the interpretation of these features as the remains of settlement structures was highly contentious. However, the picture has changed dramatically in recent times due to the work being carried out by the Stonehenge Riverside Project (Parker Pearson 2004; Parker Pearson *et al.* 2006a; 2006b). Now it appears that the first house floors have been discovered immediately outside of the eastern entrance to Durrington Walls (Parker Pearson *et al.* 2006a, 252). The floors of the houses lie in close association with a midden, roughly 20 × 10m across, that yielded massive quantities of animal bone, pottery, and worked flint. At present, six structures interpreted as houses have been found at Durrington Walls (Parker Pearson *et al.* 2006a) and, given the massive size of the site and the high proportion of it that remains unexcavated, there is a potential that there were a great many more. The ramifications of these findings are yet to be fully realized and it is too early to suggest definitively whether or not they relate to permanent occupation of the area. However, for reasons that will be discussed below, early findings suggest that Durrington Walls was not permanently occupied.

Returning to the matter at hand, it should be realized that in terms of the ploughsoil assemblages the greatest concentrations occur away from Durrington Walls and are spread over considerable areas. These dense scatters occur in locations such as north of the Stonehenge Cursus, around the Winterbourne Stoke Crossroads, and even within the Stonehenge Triangle close to the monument itself. Hence, whilst the nature and scale of the activities at Durrington Walls appear to be remarkable it should be remembered that the lithic scatters probably dwarf the current findings at Durrington Walls in terms of size and potentially also in terms of the density of activity. Hence to explain the nature of the lithic scatters in the area it might be necessary to imagine some of the types of things found around Durrington Walls occurring across many different locales within the Stonehenge landscape.

Intermittent occupation in the Stonehenge landscape

The possibility for intermittent occupation of the Stonehenge landscape is perhaps more attractive than the idea of permanent occupation for a number of reasons. For example, it is in keeping with the idea that the monuments themselves are the product of communal labour gathered from a wider region. The strong connection between the monuments in the area with both lunar and solar alignments (Ruggles 1997) implicates people in the wider landscape on a seasonal basis. Although traditionally research on the solar alignments at Stonehenge has had an emphasis upon the midsummer solstice, recent research has also indicated the potential importance of the midwinter solstice (Parker Pearson *et al.* 2006b, 234–240). This is backed up by findings from Durrington Walls of the alignment of the newly discovered Durrington Walls Avenue (Parker Pearson *et al.* 2006b, 239). In addition, analysis of the growth stages of teeth from a sample of pig jaws from Durrington Walls also suggests that the majority were slaughtered during midwinter (Albarella and Payne 2005). This potential needs to be understood in conjunction with the existing suggestion that the animal bones from the site represent the remains of feasting (Wainwright and Longworth 1971, 232). Therefore it would appear that Durrington Walls may well have been inhabited on a seasonal basis and that it was the site of massive feasting episodes. The sheer scale of these activities and their unusual nature lends itself towards the interpretation that the gatherings that took place were of supra-community groups from a widespread region.

Although Durrington Walls represents only one site within the Stonehenge environs it has suggested that it is an integral part of a much wider sacred landscape (Parker Pearson and Ramilisonina 1998). Hence it seems applicable to utilize the high resolution of the excavated material from Durrington Walls to provide insight into the inhabitation of the wider area. Therefore, if inhabitation of Durrington Walls was on a seasonal basis then so too may have been that of the rest of the Stonehenge landscape.

From a more general standpoint, the idea of seasonal visits is also in keeping with ideas of a tethered mobility practiced amongst Neolithic populations (Edmonds 1999; Thomas 1999, 222; Whittle 1997b). Gatherings at Stonehenge may well have been fitted into a seasonal cycle of activities, which set the tempo for the wider movements of populations across many different landscapes.

Another aspect of the idea of intermittent occupation is that it fits in many ways with what we know about the constructional history of Stonehenge. Thanks to recent work our knowledge of its construction is more detailed than ever before (Cleal *et al.* 1995). From this work it is clear that it was a messy project, never fully planned and never finished. At certain points the site was abandoned for long periods and stone settings were put up, taken down, and rearranged a number of times. The work at the Stonehenge took place over hundreds of years and appears to have been conducted on an intermittent basis. Perhaps this feature of Stonehenge provides a clue that the wider occupation of the landscape took place in a similar manner.

CONCLUSION

During the first half of this chapter a series of methodological issues involved in this analysis were presented. Many of these issues are essentially unquantifiable. It is hoped that despite the issues encountered the clear variability in the data validates the analysis. Even if some of the patterning of the data is due to methodological issues, the variation is so extensive that it must still be considered meaningful in archaeological terms. This variation has been described as correlating to both the surface geology and upstanding archaeology of the landscapes in question. Ultimately though it is hoped that that the data are seen as describing loose details of the patterns of inhabitation of prehistoric populations. This is an analysis that can be built on in future and to which the data from past and future landscape surveys can be added allowing us an alternative method for contrasting different prehistoric landscapes.

The analysis has ultimately been directed towards an understanding of the inhabitation of the Stonehenge environs. Two potential forms of occupation have been hypothesized. These are to be seen as idealized forms of inhabitation and given the duration of use of the Stonehenge landscape there is of course the potential that populations may have drifted over time between the two extremes of permanent and intermittent occupation. Further work in the Stonehenge area will hopefully provide continued insights into the nature of the inhabitation of the landscape. However, at the current time I tend to favour the idea of the intermittent occupation of the area as it best fits our wider understandings of the period and the excavated evidence we have from sites within the Stonehenge landscape.

Perhaps the most important statement that arises from the suggestion of intermittent occupation is that this means that groups must have visited Stonehenge from elsewhere. They may have even come to Stonehenge from some of the other landscapes included in this comparative analysis. Reconstructing these patterns of movement and the temporality of prehistoric life is one of the central concerns of this research.

By placing Stonehenge within a regional settlement context it is also clear that the landscapes, which visitors to Stonehenge came from, were much less densely occupied than the one they came to. In this sense it may be appropriate to imagine that gatherings in the Stonehenge landscape were aggregations of supra-community groups from a widespread region. In this respect, at certain times the landscape around Stonehenge must have seemed a busy place. More people may have aggregated around Stonehenge than in any other contemporary landscape, and hopefully now for the first time the shear scale of these gatherings can begin to be understood rather than assumed. Disparate groups may have come together; old faces would have been recognized and relationships would have needed to be renewed. Where normally one might not have seen any but immediate kin for long periods of time, around Stonehenge the smoke from many different camps must have risen into the sky.

Unlike many accounts of the Stonehenge landscape this discussion has not centred on ritual observance and monument building. The majority of the remains of lithic scatters are probably concerned with a very different and potentially more quotidian set of activities. Whilst moments of construction and ritual observance undoubtedly took place, it was also necessary to attend to many more mundane practices whilst dwelling amongst the monuments. If the construction of monuments was not the most important part of activity in the Stonehenge environs then, given the character of the data, it can perhaps be suggested that it was the act of gathering itself that was meaningful. Amongst relatively small and dispersed communities drawing upon ideas of being part of a much larger group may have served to provide a strong sense of belonging and provided a context in which relationships could be renegotiated. In metaphorical terms the strength and ability of the wider community was set in stone through the communal labour involved in constructing monuments such as Stonehenge. However, these associations were also embodied in the act of aggregation and rather than seeing such gatherings as serving other causes perhaps they should be understood as end points in themselves.

ACKNOWLEDGEMENTS

The data for the Holgate and Thomas Survey were kindly retrieved from the archive held in the Alexander Keiller Museum at Avebury by Michele Drisse, Jim Gunter, and Ros Cleal. This analysis was originally conducted as part of my PhD research at the University of Sheffield and I would like to thank my supervisors Mark Edmonds and John Barrett for their comments on earlier versions of this work.

BIBLIOGRAPHY

Albarella, U. and Payne, S., 2005, Neolithic Pigs from Durrington Walls, Wiltshire, England: a biometrical database. *Journal of Archaeological Science* 32(4), 589–599.
Allen, M. J., 1991, Analysing the landscape: a geographical approach to archaeological problems. In A. J. Schofield (ed.), *Interpreting Artefact Scatters: Contributions to Ploughzone Archaeology*, 39–57. Oxford: Oxbow Books (Monograph 4).
Barrett, J. C., Bradley, R. J. and Green, M., 1991, *Landscape, Monuments and Society. The Prehistory of Cranborne Chase*. Cambridge: Cambridge University Press.
Boismier, W. A., 1991, The role of research design in surface collection: an example from Broom Hill, Braishfield, Hampshire. In A. J. Schofield (ed.), *Interpreting Artefact Scatters: Contributions to Ploughzone Archaeology*, 11–25. Oxford: Oxbow Books (Monograph 4).
Chan, B. T.-Y., 2003, Understanding the Inhabitation of the Stonehenge Environs: the Interpretative Potential of Ploughsoil Assemblages. Unpublished PhD thesis, University of Sheffield.
Clark, R. H. and Schofield, A. J., 1991, By experiment and calibration: an integrated approach to archaeology of the ploughsoil. In A. J. Schofield (ed.), *Interpreting Artefact Scatters: Contributions to Ploughzone Archaeology*, 93–105. Oxford: Oxbow Books (Monograph 4).
Cleal, R. M. J., Walker, K. E. and Montague, R., 1995, *Stonehenge in its Landscape: Twentieth-Century Excavations*. London: English Heritage (Archaeological Report 10).
Darvill, T. C., 1997, Ever increasing circles: the sacred geographies of Stonehenge and its landscape. In B. Cunliffe and C. Renfrew (eds), *Science and Stonehenge*, 167–202. London: British Academy (=*Proceedings of the British Academy* 92).
Edmonds, M. R., 1995, *Stone Tools and Society: Working Stone in Neolithic and Bronze Age Britain*. London: Batsford.
Edmonds, M. R., 1997, Taskscape, technology and tradition. *Analectia Praehistoria Leidensia* 29, 99–110.

Edmonds, M. R., 1998, Sermons in stone: identity, value and stone tools in Later Neolithic Britain. In M. R. Edmonds and C. Richards (eds), *Understanding the Neolithic of North-Western Europe*: 248–276. Glasgow: Cruithne Press.

Edmonds, M. R., 1999, *Ancestral Geographies of the Neolithic: Landscapes, Monuments and Memory*. London: Routledge.

Exon, S., Gaffney, V., Woodward, A. and Yorston, R., 2000, *Stonehenge Landscapes: Journeys Through Real-and Imagined Worlds*. Oxford: Archaeopress.

Ford, S., 1987a, *East Berkshire Archaeological Survey*. Berkshire: Department of Highways and Planning (Berkshire County Council Occasional Paper No. 1).

Ford, S., 1987b, Flint scatters and prehistoric settlement patterns in south Oxfordshire and east Berkshire. In A. G. Brown and M. R. Edmonds (eds), *Lithic Analysis and Later British Prehistory*, 101–135. Oxford: British Archaeological Reports (British Series 162).

Ford, S., 1987c, Chronological and functional aspects of flint assemblages. In A. G. Brown and M. R. Edmonds (eds), *Lithic Analysis and Later British Prehistory*, 67–86. Oxford: British Archaeological Reports (British Series 162).

Gaffney, V. and Tingle, M., 1989, *The Maddle Farm Project: An Integrated Survey of Prehistoric and Roman Landscapes on the Berkshire Downs*. Oxford: British Archaeological Reports (British Series 200).

Gardiner, J. P., 1984, Lithic distributions and Neolithic settlement patterns in central and southern England. In R. J. Bradley and J. P. Gardiner (eds), *Neolithic Studies: A Review of Some Current Research*, 15–40. Oxford: British Archaeological Reports (British Series 133).

Gillings, M. and Pollard, J., 2004, *Avebury*. London: Duckworth.

Harding, P., 1988, The chalk plaque pit, Amesbury. *Proceedings of the Prehistoric Society* 54, 320–326.

Holgate, R., 1987, Neolithic settlement patterns at Avebury, Wiltshire. *Antiquity* 61, 259–263

Holgate, R., 1988, *Neolithic Settlement of the Thames Basin*. Oxford: British Archaeological Reports (British Series 194).

Ingold, T., 1993, The temporality of the landscape. *World Archaeology* 25(2), 152–174.

Parker Pearson, M., Pollard, J., Richards, C., Thomas, J., Tilley, C. and Welham, K., 2006a, Stonehenge, its river and its landscape: unravelling the mysteries of a prehistoric sacred place. *Archäologischer Anzeiger* 1, 237–258.

Parker Pearson, M., Pollard, J., Richards, C., Thomas, J., Tilley, C., Welham, K. and Albarella, U., 2006b, Materializing Stonehenge: The Stonehenge Riverside Project and new discoveries. *Journal of Material Culture* 11(1–2), 227–261.

Parker Pearson, M. and Ramilisonina, 1998, Stonehenge for the Ancestors: the stones pass on the message. *Antiquity* 72, 308–326.

RCHME (Royal Commission on Historical Monuments, England), 1979, *Stonehenge and its Environs: Monuments and Land Use*. Edinburgh: Edinburgh University Press.

Richards, J., 1985, Scouring the surface: approaches to the ploughzone in the Stonehenge environs. *Archaeological Review from Cambridge* 4, 27–42.

Richards, J., 1990, *The Stonehenge Environs Project*. London: English Heritage (Archaeological Report No. 16).

Ruggles, C., 1997, Astronomy and Stonehenge. In B. Cunliffe and C. Renfrew (eds), *Science and Stonehenge*, 203–229. London: British Academy (=*Proceedings of the British Academy* 92).

Schofield, A. J., 1987, Putting lithics to the test: non-site analysis and the Neolithic settlement of southern England. *Oxford Journal of Archaeology* 6(3), 269–286.

Schofield, A. J., 1988, The Interpretation of Surface Lithic Collections: Case Studies from Southern England. Unpublished PhD thesis, University of Southampton.

Schofield, A. J., 1991, Lithic distributions in the Upper Meon Valley: behavioural response and human adaptation on the Hampshire chalklands. *Proceedings of the Prehistoric Society* 57(2), 159–178.

Sharples, N. M., 1991, *Maiden Castle. Excavations and Field Survey 1985–6*. London: English Heritage (Archaeological Report No. 19).

Shennan, S., 1985, *Experiments in the Collection and Analysis of Archaeological Survey Data; The East Hampshire Survey*. Sheffield: Department of Archaeology and Prehistory, University of Sheffield.

Stone, J. F. S. and Young, W. E. V., 1948, Two pits of Grooved Ware date near Woodhenge. *Wiltshire Archaeological and Natural History Magazine* 52, 287–306.

Thomas, J. S., 1999, *Understanding the Neolithic*. London: Routledge.

Tingle, M., 1987, Inferential limits and surface scatters: the case of the Maddle Farm and Vale of the White Horse fieldwalking survey. In A. G. Brown and M. R. Edmonds (eds), *Lithic Analysis and Later British Prehistory*, 87–99. Oxford: British Archaeological Reports (British Series 162).

Vatcher, F. de M., 1969, Two incised chalk plaques from Stonehenge Bottom. *Antiquity* 43, 310–311.

Wainwright. G. J. and Longworth, I. H., 1971, *Durrington Walls: Excavations 1966–1968*. London: Society of Antiquaries of London (Reports of the Research Committee 29).

Whittle, A., 1993, The Neolithic of the Avebury area: sequence, environment, settlement and monuments. *Oxford Journal of Archaeology* 12, 29–53.

Whittle, A., 1994, Excavations at Millbarrow chambered tomb, Winterbourne Monkton, north Wiltshire. *Wiltshire Archaeological and Natural History Magazine* 87, 1–53.

Whittle, A., 1997a, *Sacred Mound, Holy Rings. Silbury Hill and the West Kennet Palisade Enclosures: A Later Neolithic Complex in North Wiltshire*. Oxford: Oxbow Books (Monograph 74).

Whittle, A., 1997b, Moving on and moving around: Neolithic settlement mobility. In P. Topping (ed.), *Neolithic Landscapes*, 15–22. Oxford: Oxbow Books (Monograph 86/Neolithic Studies Group Seminar Papers 2).

Whittle, A. and Pollard, J., 1998, Windmill Hill causewayed enclosure: the harmony of symbols. In M. R. Edmonds and C. Richards (eds), *Understanding the Neolithic of North-Western Europe*, 231–247. Glasgow: Cruithne Press.

Whittle, A., Rouse, A. J., Evans, J. G., 1993, A Neolithic downland monument in its environment: excavations at the Easton Down long barrow, Bishops Cannings, north Wiltshire. *Proceedings of the Prehistoric Society* 59, 197–239.

Whittle, A., Pollard, J. and Grigson, C., 1999, *The Harmony of Symbols: the Windmill Hill Causewayed Enclosure*. Oxford: Oxbow Books.

Whittle, A., Davies, J. J., Dennis, I., Fairbairn, A. S. and Hamilton, M. A., 2000, Neolithic activity and occupation outside Windmill Hill causewayed enclosure, Wiltshire: survey and excavation 1992–93. *Wiltshire Archaeological and Natural History Magazine* 93, 131–180.

Woodward, P. J., 1978, Flint distribution, ring ditches and Bronze Age settlement patterns in the Great Ouse Valley: the problem, a field survey technique and some preliminary results. *Archaeological Journal* 85, 32–56.

Woodward, P. J., 1991, *The South Dorset Ridgeway: Survey and Excavation 1977–84*. Dorchester: Dorset Natural History and Archaeological Society (Monograph 8).

Chapter 7

Shining water, shifting sand: exotic lithic material from Luce Sands, southwest Scotland

Diana Coles

This chapter will examine the exotic lithic materials of Neolithic date from the dune system of Luce Sands, to ascertain what light these may shed on activities within the area. Luce Sands is located towards the western end of the southwest Scottish mainland peninsula in the former county of Wigtownshire and comprises the dune and beach area at the north side of Luce Bay (Figure 7.1).

The Luce Sands dunes lie at the heart of a rich and complex Neolithic landscape (Figure 7.2). To the north is the ceremonial site of Dunragit. First noted through aerial photography in the nineties and partially excavated from 1999 to 2002, the construction and use of this massive timber complex spanned a large part of the Neolithic through into the Bronze Age (Thomas 2002). To the northwest is Fox Plantation. This has a similar range of features and appears to span an even longer period (Cullen and James 1995; MacGregor

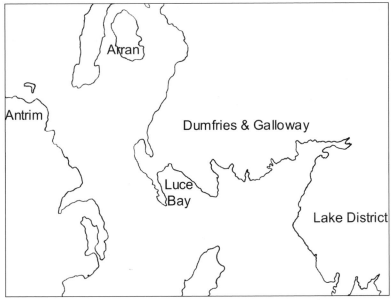

Figure 7.1. Location of Luce Bay, southwest Scotland.

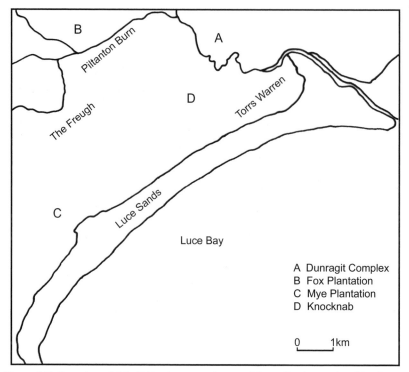

Figure 7.2. Location of Neolithic sites on and around Luce Sands mentioned in the text.

1996). Both lie to the north of the Piltanton Burn while the dunes lie to the south. To the west is the puzzling site of Mye Plantation. This consisted of an alignment of pits containing sharpened stakes with tool-marks from stone axeheads. It has been variously and unsatisfactorily interpreted as a series of pit dwellings or deadfall pits for trapping game (Mann 1903, 401–402), and has recently been dated to 2500–2230 cal BC (3913±39 BP; UB-3882) from a sample of wood from a pit excavated by Ritchie and Atkinson in 1951 (Sheridan 2005). This is in agreement with the Late Neolithic date indicated by the flint artefacts and Grooved Ware pottery recovered. The Piltanton Burn both divided the landscape and provided a means for moving through it. Flowing through the low ground it could have taken boats with a shallow draft most of the way across the neck of the isthmus to Loch Ryan and the sea routes to the north, never rising over 15m above mean sea level (Figure 7.3).

The area of study itself is on and around Torrs Warren, an area which forms the western part of the Luce Sands dune system. It is bounded by water, with the sea to the south, the Piltanton Burn to the north, and the Mye Burn to the west. Between the Piltanton Burn and the dunes lay the mires of the Freugh. The highest and oldest dunes lie to the north; those dunes closest to the sea have formed more recently. Separating the two is a flat area which is the postglacial raised beach. The dunes are covered by coarse grasses and other plants characteristic of dune heathland (Cowie 1996, 12–14; Idle and Martin 1975). Until

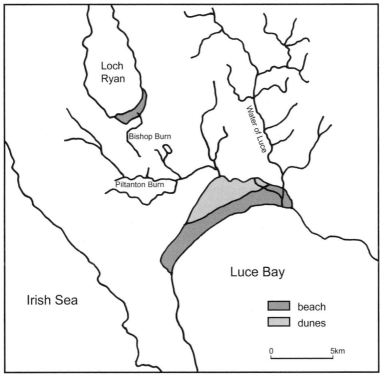

Figure 7.3. Location of the main river systems on the isthmus showing the potential for utilizing the low-lying waterways as an overland crossing.

recently they were an area of rough grazing. However, in recent years they have been under the control of the Ministry of Defence and access to them has been limited.

Within the dunes are horizons of buried soils. These buried soils are sandwiched between layers of sand and they undulate, indicating that the soil layers formed above existing dunes and were later themselves covered by fresh sand-blow. These soils contain dense concentrations of prehistoric material which differ markedly both in quantity and kind from any of the assemblages found elsewhere in the southwest peninsula.

Any damage to the surface vegetation makes the area prone to blowouts when sand and underlying soil are eroded rapidly by wind action. This exposes the prehistoric material and, in consequence, the dunes became a favourite area for collectors to search for artefacts of pottery, metal, and worked stone (Atkinson 1952; Black 1894; Maxwell 1885; Wilson 1876; 1878; cf. Murray 2005, 154). Large collections, particularly of the latter, have been donated to both the national and local museums. Much of this material is of locally obtained pebble flint. However, there are also a number of exotics, that is to say artefacts manufactured from imported material. The exotics are predominantly of Langdale tuff from Cumbria to the south and pitchstone from the island of Arran to the north, together with some of flint of non-local origin, and it is these exotics that this chapter will examine.

AXEHEADS

A search in the collections or the catalogues of Glasgow Museums, National Museums Scotland in Edinburgh, and the museums at Stranraer and Dumfries, reveals that over 240 stone axeheads have been discovered in the Wigtownshire area, the majority of them known or presumed to be of Group VI rock (cf. Ritchie and Scott 1988, 87). As most are antiquarian finds, many cannot be provenanced with any degree of accuracy; of those which can, a high proportion was found in the vicinity of Luce Sands.

Darvill has noted with reference to the distribution of axeheads within Wales and the mid-west of England that the greatest variation of axehead sizes occurs in regions with easy access to the source of the material, with the largest axeheads being found closest to the production sites (Darvill 1989). The Group VI sample from Wigtownshire demonstrates a marked variation in size (cf. Stevenson 1950). At the larger end of the scale is a fine axehead in National Museums Scotland from Kirkcolm on the north Rhinns, which is 315mm in length (Anon. 1885, 336). At the other end of the scale is a tiny axehead, measuring a mere 55mm, found by Wilson together with a polishing stone 'near the sandhills in Stoneykirk' (Wilson 1881, 263; cf. Anderson 1886, 350; Black 1894, 21). In order to test whether this phenomenon was observable in the Wigtownshire sample, the collection of locally provenanced Group VI axeheads at Stranraer Museum was compared with a collection of eleven Group VI axeheads from the lower Thames valley held in the Museum of London collection (Figure 7.4). These latter were discovered in the Thames and are considered to have been deliberately deposited there. Four were collected by Layton in the nineteenth century. The remaining seven were provenanced to the Thames and are considered to be probable ritual deposits (Jon Cotton pers. comm.). The Wigtownshire sample included only axeheads with a known findspot within the area and excluded those from the collection

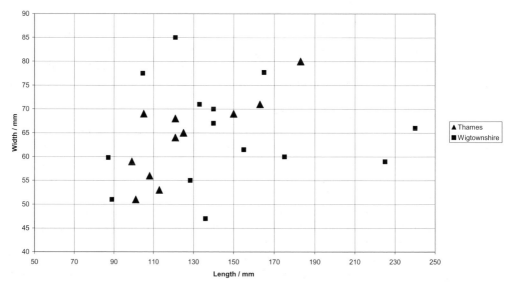

Figure 7.4. A comparison of Group VI axeheads from Wigtownshire and the lower Thames Valley.

of Lord Stair, since there is a possibility that some of his collection may not be of local derivation (John Pickin pers. comm.).

Whilst the samples in both cases were very small, the results of this comparison were marked. The axeheads from Wigtownshire are, on average, 16 per cent greater in length than the axeheads from the Thames region. The mean length of the Wigtownshire axeheads is *c.* 146mm and for the Thames axeheads it is *c.* 126mm. The shortest Wigtownshire axehead is 10mm shorter than the shortest Thames axehead and the longest Wigtownshire axehead is over 50mm longer than the longest Thames axehead. Because the two samples were so small, and consequently statistically unreliable, it would be unwise to draw firm conclusions from these results but it would appear that the Wigtownshire axeheads have a greater average length and are more varied both in size and length/width proportions.

If the findings in southwest Scotland are considered to be analogous with those of Darvill (1989) for Wales and the mid-West, it might suggest that Group VI axeheads were being brought the 60 miles from the Lake District directly to Wigtownshire by water, rather than coming overland through Dumfriesshire and the Stewartry. The relative paucity of Group VI axeheads from elsewhere in Galloway could be seen to confirm this.

Within the Luce Sands dunes themselves the occurrence of flakes and cores from damaged axeheads is far more frequent than that of entire axeheads. At the turn of the nineteenth century Ludovic McLellan Mann collected large numbers of these, 20 from Knockdoon, 57 from Torrs, and 49 from his unlocated 'Star' site, all of which are now in the Glasgow Museums collection. National Museums Scotland has a further 90 or so surface finds, and pieces turn up frequently in other collections, for example 27 from William Cormack's collection (Dumfries Museum) and 16 from the Knocknab excavation. A small number have been found elsewhere in Wigtownshire, including five in a hoard at Ersock Loch and 12 from Blairbuie, but they have for the most part been found in the area of the dunes.

It has been suggested that the number of axehead fragments may indicate 'workshops' for the reworking of damaged axeheads (Williams 1970). At Dunragit a large number of timbers of up to half a metre in diameter were used to construct monuments which were destroyed by burning and replaced several times during the period when the monument was in use (Thomas 2002). This level of woodworking would have taken a heavy toll of the tools employed and might therefore support this type of scenario. However, it is apparent that much of the axehead material from the dunes does not result from reworking use-damaged axeheads. Some pieces are clearly cores from which a number of flakes, such as elegant blades, have been removed in a way that could not have been the result of accidental damage. The Neolithic practice of deliberately flaking axeheads to destruction is well-attested from a number of sites, particularly causewayed enclosures (Edmonds 1998; Mercer 1980; Pryor 1998), but also from such contexts as the old land surface below the Wayland's Smithy tomb (Whittle 1991, 92). Edmonds (1998, 267) has suggested that the practice may have been associated with rituals for the dead. The quantity of deliberately damaged axehead material from Luce Sands suggests that this may also have been a significant place for ceremonies involving the destruction of precious and socially charged objects.

It is also interesting to consider the previously mentioned *polissoir* and Group VI axehead of an unusually small size discovered by Wilson (1881, 263). It has been noted that a very small number of axehead roughouts has been found in the southwest peninsula (Adkins and Carlyle 1982), and there is a paucity of evidence to suggest that Group VI axeheads were being imported in an unfinished state. Edmonds has commented that the occurrence of *polissoirs* at a number of Neolithic sites indicates 'that the finishing of certain axeheads may occasionally have been undertaken in the context of other important events' (Edmonds 1998, 267). What cannot be ascertained is whether these items had been deliberately placed within a depositional context although it would seem reasonable to suppose that this may well have been the case.

Although the majority of the axehead flakes are unretouched, a small number have been fashioned into artefacts, including a leaf-shaped Neolithic arrowhead (National Museums Scotland collection) and, from Knocknab, a very fine scraper made on a large Group VI flake which retains polishing on the entire dorsal face. It is only possible to speculate about the circumstances in which these particular flakes had been selected for this treatment.

There are only a possible nine porcellanite axeheads from the whole of Wigtownshire, and several of these are of doubtful provenance (John Pickin pers. comm.). It may be questioned why these numbers are so small with the Antrim source only some 32km from the west coast of the Rhinns – considerably closer that the Langdale region. The answer is almost certainly in part due to the topography of the area. The direct route from Luce Bay to Antrim involves crossing the Rhinns, a journey over relatively difficult terrain rising to over 100m above mean sea level, whilst the sea route involves sailing around the Rhinns which would add over 50km to the journey across what is a particularly treacherous sea crossing.

Also, it has been observed that, during the Neolithic period, certain materials were valued for qualities other than functionality (Bradley and Edmonds 1993). The Antrim porcellanite axeheads may only have come into wider circulation after the population of southwest Scotland had become habituated to using Langdale axeheads, which by then may have acquired a cultural resonance that was not easily superseded.

PITCHSTONE

The other exotic material that this chapter will consider is Arran pitchstone. This is a shiny volcanic material, similar to obsidian in appearance and physical properties, which occurs as dykes in several locations on the Isle of Arran. The Corriegills dyke which produces the most suitable pitchstone for knapping is over 180m long and up to 6m thick (Mann 1918; Williams Thorpe and Thorpe 1984). Worked pitchstone is found widely over Scotland and northern England. It was also present in quantity at Ballygally in County Antrim (Simpson and Meighan 1999). Within Arran itself, pitchstone has been found in association with the Clyde cairns while poor-quality pitchstone was found in abundance during excavations on Machrie Moor (Haggarty 1991).

Luce Sands is the major location for finds of worked pitchstone on the Scottish mainland (Table 7.1; cf. Williams Thorpe and Thorpe 1984). Most pieces were unstratified surface finds and it has proved impossible to ascertain any precise location for them. However, there is evidence that both Group VI axehead material and pitchstone were located in specific, discrete areas within the dunes and, at least in one instance, were to be found in association with each other. In 1992–1994 a small rescue excavation was undertaken at Knocknab,

Glasgow Museums	97 pieces
National Museums Scotland	183+ pieces
Hunterian Museum, Glasgow	13 pieces
Stranraer Museum	10 pieces
Dumfries Museum	659 pieces Cormack collection
Dumfries Museum	17 pieces McCracken collection
Knocknab excavation	255 pieces
Total	1234+ pieces

Table 7.1. Collection summary of pitchstone finds from Luce Sands.

where an exposed soil horizon containing prehistoric features was rapidly being destroyed by animal and wind action. This excavation produced 250 pieces of pitchstone together with 16 axehead fragments. Unlike the rest of the pitchstone artefacts from the area these pieces were found in context and indicate that the material was being worked *in situ*. Two discrete scatters of mixed blades, flakes and cores were found and it was possible to refit several of the pieces. This working area, which also produced scatters of pot and quantities of flint artefacts, was associated with a pit containing flint and charcoal (Crane Begg pers. comm.). The survival of this intact working-floor may result from a contemporary and possibly very localized inundation of storm-driven sand.

A detailed examination of the pitchstone from Luce Sands yields several points of interest. First it must be noted that the assemblage is markedly different from that excavated at Machrie Moor on Arran, both in the nature of the material and the way in which it has been utilized. The Machrie Moor assemblage contained a considerable quantity of porphyritic pitchstone with large phenocrysts, including both unmodified lumps and worked pieces. Most of this was either brown or grey-green in colour. Despite its coarse quality, the worked material included a number of finished and retouched pieces including scrapers and arrowheads as well as waste flakes. The pieces measured up to 98 × 73mm and no weathered outer surfaces were observable, suggesting that the raw material may have been quarried directly from a pitchstone dyke.

Aphyric pitchstone on the other hand only occurred in the Machrie Moor assemblage as small pieces including narrow blades and flakes. Some showed evidence of retouch, including a scraper made on a narrow flake which can most probably be attributed to the Mesolithic period. It seems likely that the porphyritic pitchstone comes from the source at Tormore, on the west side of the island, close to Machrie Moor, whilst some of the aphyric material may have occurred as 'pockets' within the Tormore dykes or have come from Corriegills (Torben Ballin pers. comm.). It does seem probable, however, that much of the latter was derived from a pebble source, as at the Mesolithic site of Auchareoch on Arran (Affleck *et al.* 1988, 46), since small highly-weathered pebbles which had been split open were present in the assemblage.

In contrast with the Machrie Moor assemblage, nearly all the pitchstone examined from Luce Sands is aphyric and of very high quality, generally densely black with only a few, very small, phenocrysts. A small number of the flakes were pale or dark green. The only piece of porphyritic material was a transverse arrowhead, exactly analogous to those

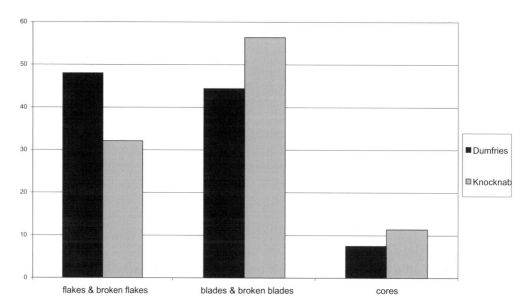

Figure 7.5. Proportions of blades, flakes and cores from: a) Cormack's surface collection; and b) the excavated assemblage from Knocknab.

from Machrie Moor. This fine quality aphyric pitchstone is visually very different from the porphyritic material and it was utilized very differently. It had been knapped to produce a high proportion of narrow blades and bladelets and many cores had been worked to tiny flattened cones showing blade scars. This bias towards the production of blades and bladelets is extremely marked (Figure 7.5) and the pattern is repeated in all the collections examined, namely those from National Museums Scotland, Dumfries Museum, Stranraer Museum, and the as yet unpublished Knocknab assemblage. This latter was retrieved using a full collection policy so the assemblage is free from the possible biases affecting the composition of the surface collections. The quantities of chips and small debris recovered together with the numbers of cores, rejuvenation flakes and refittable pieces indicate that onsite knapping was occurring.

The size of the original cores from which the blades and flakes were being struck can only be estimated from the longest surviving flakes, particularly the plunging blades which utilize the entire length of the core from which they were struck. These rarely exceed 30mm. One unworked pebble in the Cormack collection, among the largest of the pieces recovered, measures 39 × 31 × 17mm and weighs 23.7g. From this it would seem likely that the pitchstone was being brought to the sands as unworked but comparatively small pieces.

Despite the lack of direct dating evidence for any of the pitchstone from the Sands, it is possible to infer that it is of Neolithic, rather than Mesolithic, date, despite the predominance of narrow blades. Firstly, no pitchstone microliths have been found in the lithic material from the dunes. Nor is there any of the debitage characteristic of a Mesolithic blade-industry present. A comparison of this assemblage with that at Auchareoch on Arran, where aphyric pitchstone was also utilized, reveals a markedly different assemblage with a far higher proportion of flakes to blades as well as a number of carefully retouched pieces (Affleck *et al.* 1988, 46–50). Secondly, two Late Mesolithic sites, Low Clone and Barsalloch, have been excavated on the east side of Luce Bay. Had pitchstone been in widespread use in the Luce Bay area during the Mesolithic period, it might be expected to have been present on these sites, but at neither was any pitchstone discovered (Cormack 1970; Cormack and Coles 1967, 56–66). Indeed, it is arguable whether any of the pitchstone found in southwest Scotland is Mesolithic, as none of it has been found in contexts that can be demonstrated to be exclusively of this period (Saville 2003a, 345). Finally, pitchstone blades and bladelets *were* demonstrably being produced in the southwest peninsula during the Neolithic as indicated by their recovery from datable contexts. The 100 or so pieces from Marshall's excavation at Auchategan fall into a similar pattern to that from Luce sands (Marshall 1978; also see Ballin 2006). These artefacts were of fine quality aphyric pitchstone with a marked focus on the production of unretouched narrow blades. Interestingly, here the excavator also found two badly damaged Group VI axeheads. A flake, apparently from the blade end of one of the axeheads was recovered from the base of an ashy 'hearth' deposit together with pitchstone and half a lignite bead (Marshall 1978:41). The single date given for this phase of the site is 2300±110 uncal BC (I-4705), which, although providing an unfortunately wide calibrated date range, falls securely within the Neolithic period. Similarly at Carzield, near Dumfries, a deposition pit contained two pitchstone bladelets in association with Group VI axehead fragments. Charcoal from the pit gave an early fourth millennium BC date (Maynard 1993).

An examination of undamaged blades from the Luce Sands collections reveals a relatively low proportion of well-knapped blades with over three-quarters showing various forms of miss-strikes (Figure 7.6). It is likely that pitchstone would have been relatively unfamiliar to those who were trying to work it. Experiment has ascertained that the local pebble flint, which would have been the usual medium of the knappers, requires a heavy hand to achieve results (John Lord pers.comm.). The number of plunging blades and abrupt terminations may reflect the difficulties in working with an unfamiliar material that responded very differently to the flint that they were used to. This together with an overriding concern to maximize the length of the blades may well have resulted in the unusually high incidence of over-forceful knapping.

The nature of the material recovered demonstrates the importance attached to pitchstone by the prehistoric knappers. The emphasis on blade production and core curation alone indicate it was regarded as a valuable and limited resource. Some blades were as much as 32mm in length by 7mm in width demonstrating the desirability of slender blades. Nevertheless, many of the cores continued to be worked to little more than nubbins, which would have produced only tiny bladelets and many cores were not abandoned until completely exhausted.

To summarize, it seems evident that pitchstone was being worked in order to produce blades and flakes which were rarely retouched. Although comparatively large blades were produced, the raw material continued to be worked until the cores were completely exhausted. Very little of the pitchstone demonstrates secondary working. Of over 900 pieces examined from Luce Sands, less than half a dozen showed evidence for rather crude retouch along one edge. The pitchstone arrowhead in National Museums Scotland is the

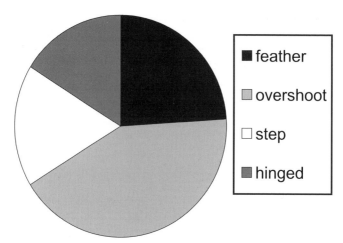

Figure 7.6. Proportion of termination types from undamaged blades and bladelets in the Cormack collection, Dumfries Museum.

only piece made from porphyritic pitchstone. The lack of any waste flakes of this coarser pitchstone strongly suggests that the arrowhead may have been imported as a finished piece, whilst the aphyric Corriegills material was being worked locally. It appears that unretouched flakes and, more particularly, blades of fine aphyric pitchstone were the desired end product. From this it may be assumed that the main attribute sought was maximum sharpness and that the flakes and blades were perhaps to be used once and then discarded.

Simpson suggested that 'it is possible that the pitchstone was used for bodily mutilation for social and/or religious ceremonies' (Simpson and Meighan 1999). Scarification, like tattooing, is widely used in a number of cultures as a means of asserting tribal and individual identity, and has often played a part in rites of passage, when individuals acquire changed or enhanced status within their society. Empirical evidence would inform potential Neolithic practitioners that a single use of each flake would minimize the risk of infection. Such a use would account for both the form of the worked pitchstone and the status it seems apparent that it was accorded, but in the absence of clear evidence this must remain speculative. The association on a number of sites of pitchstone with Group VI material strongly suggests that the pitchstone shared in the metaphorical importance that attached to axeheads from the Langdales.

It would be correct to say that the entire assemblage of pitchstone found outside Arran would fit easily into a shoe box. And yet within Arran the pitchstone source is both extensive and easily accessible. This suggests a number of possibilities. One is that all the pitchstone was brought into mainland Scotland at one time by a single intrepid traveller. This may seem intrinsically unlikely, but if the material were being used for a specialized purpose such as scarification it is possible that a very few individuals were responsible for transporting it to Luce Sands. The excavator of Knocknab has suggested the idea of specialists carrying their stock-in-trade (Crane Begg pers. comm.). Alternatively, access to the source may have been highly controlled by the inhabitants of Arran themselves. By limiting the availability of pitchstone, its status as a rare and desirable material would have been enhanced. This in turn would have enhanced the status of those who controlled access to it.

It seems very likely that the ceremonies that led to the manufacture of narrow pitchstone blades and possibly also the destruction of Group VI axeheads occurred over a specific and limited period. The dates from the Carzield pit would suggest that this fell within the Early Neolithic (Maynard 1993).

FLINT

Flint artefacts from Luce Sands, which are numerous, appear in the main to be made from pebble flint, which is readily available on the local beaches. There is some evidence, however, for contact with Yorkshire, in the form of a Seamer-type flint axehead from Stoneykirk and a discoidal knife of possible Yorkshire flint from the dunes. The evidence for material imported from Ireland is somewhat ambivalent. It is observable that specifically Irish forms are generally absent from the assemblage. A Bronze Age exception is a very fine barbed arrowhead of Irish type from Machermore Loch, to the east of Luce Sands, in National Museums Scotland (Wilson 1878, 30; cf. Murray 2005, 162). Two hoards of Antrim flint were discovered at Portpatrick, on the west coast of the Rhinns (Saville 1999, 117–123), but little has been positively identified from Luce Sands. It should be recognized that it can be hard to distinguish between flint actually from Antrim flint and the light grey variety of pebble flint from the Scottish coast at and adjacent to Luce Bay (Saville 2003b). Large pieces may be assumed to have a non-local origin as may those with cortex that does not show chatter marks consistent with water rolling. However, smaller pieces and those with chatter-marked cortex cannot be precluded from originating in Antrim (Saville 1999, 86, 99). Thus it is possible that many Antrim pieces have remained unidentified within the various assemblages.

Furthermore, examination of the Knocknab material revealed a number of particularly large and well-made pieces including backed knives and scrapers that were positively identified as being of Antrim flint (Alan Saville pers. comm.). These all occurred within close proximity of each other and the presence of a primary flake would seem to indicate that the raw material may have been imported for knapping on site, although it may be that flakes were imported as blanks for tool manufacture. The evidence would thus seem to suggest an exchange which was predominantly material rather than cultural in its nature. This might imply that contact was indirect, with flint and axehead material both passing through an intermediary before reaching Luce Sands.

CONCLUSION

Within Luce Bay the lithic evidence suggests a structured Neolithic landscape, zoned into areas where different activities occurred, divided from each other by water, the medium that both defines and divides the landscape of western Galloway. Luce Sands itself contains a wealth of material that provides a glimpse of the complex activities taking place there, and this abundance is contrastingly absent from the Dunragit complex, which provided a theatre for other ceremonies. This difference may be consequent upon spatial or temporal difference.

There are also indications that deposition patterns observable within the dunes may be repeated elsewhere in the southwest of Scotland. Both axehead fragments and pitchstone indicate that exotic materials were being brought into the area and used in specific ways that served the spiritual rather than the practical needs of the users. The apparent similarities with practices at causewayed enclosures raises the question whether, within southwest Scotland, other spaces within the landscape were being used for particular gatherings of people for activities that could include what Edmonds has termed 'rites of passage' (Edmonds 1998, 268). The nature and the quantity of the exotic lithic material from Luce Sands clearly indicate that for at least part of the Neolithic period, this was far from being simply a domestic occupation site. Further work may be able to elucidate further the part that Luce Sands played within the local and regional Neolithic landscape.

ACKNOWLEDGEMENTS

I have received much generous help in writing this chapter. My thanks are due to Jon Cotton at the Museum of London, John Pickin at Stranraer Museum, Alan Saville and Alison Sheridan at National Museums Scotland, and Joanne Taylor at Dumfries Museum, who have all made their collections available to me and answered innumerable queries. Jane Murray has offered invaluable advice and acted as a guide on a tour of the dunes themselves. Crane Begg has kindly allowed me full access to all of his material from Knocknab. John Lord undertook experimental work on flint pebbles from Luce Bay, providing insights into the nature of the local raw materials. Torben Ballin provided the answers to my many queries about pitchstone. Richard Bradley has read through preliminary drafts and given invaluable help and guidance.

Finally, thanks to Mr Alex McCracken and to Mrs Sheila Cormack, wife of the late William Cormack, who provided further information on their collections.

BIBLIOGRAPHY

Adkins R. A. and Carlyle D., 1982, A roughout Neolithic axe from Glenluce, Dumfries and Galloway. *Transactions of the Dumfriesshire and Galloway Natural History and Antiquarian Society* 62, 84.

Affleck T., Edwards K. J. and Clarke A., 1988, Archaeological and palynological studies at the Mesolithic pitchstone and flint site of Auchareoch, Isle of Arran. *Proceedings of the Society of Antiquaries of Scotland* 118, 37–59.

Anderson, J., 1886, *Scotland in Pagan Times: the Bronze and Stone Ages*. Edinburgh: David Douglas.

Anon., 1885, Purchases for the Museum. *Proceedings of the Society of Antiquaries of Scotland* 19 (1884–1885), 329–336.

Atkinson, R. J. C., 1952, Notes on archaeological material from Dumfriesshire, Kirkudbrightshire, and Wigtownshire, in the Bishop Collection: part II – surface-finds from the Luce Sands, Wigtownshire. *Transactions of the Dumfriesshire and Galloway Natural History and Antiquarian Society* 30, 176–178.

Ballin, T. B., 2006, Re-examination of the Early Neolithic pitchstone-bearing assemblage from Auchategan, Argyll, Scotland. *Lithics* 27, 12–32.

Black G. F., 1894, Descriptive catalogue of antiquities found in Ayrshire and Wigtownshire and now in the National Museum, Edinburgh. *Archaeological and Historical Collections relating to Ayrshire and Galloway* 7, 1–47.

Bradley, R. and Edmonds, M., 1993, *Interpreting the Axe Trade. Production and Exchange in Neolithic Britain*. Cambridge: Cambridge University Press.

Cormack, W. F., 1970, A Mesolithic site at Barsalloch, Wigtownshire. *Transactions of the Dumfriesshire and Galloway Natural History and Antiquarian Society* 47, 63–80.

Cormack, W. F and Coles, J., 1967, A Mesolithic site at Low Clone, Wigtownshire. *Transactions of the Dumfriesshire and Galloway Natural History and Antiquarian Society* 45, 44–71.

Cowie T. G., 1996, Torrs Warren, Luce Sands, Galloway. *Transactions of the Dumfriesshire and Galloway Natural History and Antiquarian Society* 81, 11–105

Cullen, I. and James, R., 1995, Scotland to Northern Ireland Pipeline – Twynholm to Portnaughan Bay Section: geophysical survey, trial trenching, fieldwalking and excavation. *Discovery and Excavation in Scotland 1995*, 22.

Darvill, T. C., 1989, The circulation of Neolithic stone and flint axes: a case study from Wales and the mid-west of England. *Proceedings of the Prehistoric Society* 55, 27–43.

Edmonds, M., 1998, Sermons in stone: identity, value, and stone tools in Later Neolithic Britain. In M. Edmonds and C. Richards (eds), *Understanding the Neolithic of North-Western Europe*, 248–276. Glasgow: Cruithne Press.

Haggarty, A., 1991, Machrie Moor, Arran: recent excavations at two stone circles. *Proceedings of the Society of Antiquaries of Scotland* 121, 51–94.

Idle, E. T. and Martin, J., 1975, Vegetation and land use history of Torrs Warren. *Transactions of the Dumfriesshire and Galloway Natural History and Antiquarian Society* 51, 1–9.

MacGregor, G., 1996, Fox Plantation (Inch parish), prehistoric settlements excavation. *Discovery and Excavation in Scotland 1996*, 29–30.

Mann L. MacL., 1903, Report on the excavation of prehistoric pile structures in pits in Wigtownshire. *Proceedings of the Society of Antiquaries of Scotland* 37 (1902–1903), 370–415.

Mann L. MacL., 1918, The prehistoric and early use of pitchstone and obsidian. *Proceedings of the Society of Antiquaries of Scotland* 52 (1917–1918), 140–149.

Marshall, D. N., 1978, Excavations at Auchategan, Glendaruel, Argyll. *Proceedings of the Society of Antiquaries of Scotland* 109 (1977–1978), 36–74.

Maxwell H. E., 1885, Ancient weapons, instruments, utensils and ornaments of Wigtownshire. *Archaeological and Historical Collections relating to Ayrshire and Galloway* 5, 21–55.

Maynard, D., 1993, A Neolithic pit at Carzield, Kirkton, Dumfriesshire. *Transactions of the Dumfriesshire and Galloway Natural History and Antiquarian Society* 68, 25–32.

Mercer, R. J., 1980, *Hambledon Hill – A Neolithic Landscape*. Edinburgh: Edinburgh University Press.

Murray J., 2005, The William McDowall Selby Collection. *Transactions of the Dumfriesshire and Galloway Natural History and Antiquarian Society* 79, 147–171.

Pryor, F., 1998, *Etton: Excavations at a Neolithic Causewayed Enclosure near Maxey, Cambridgeshire 1982–7*. London: English Heritage (Archaeological Report 18).

Ritchie, P. R. and Scott, J. G., 1988, The petrological identification of stone axes from Scotland. In T. H. McK. Clough and W. A. Cummins, *Stone Axe Studies, Volume 2. The Petrology of Prehistoric Stone Implements from the British Isles*, 85–91. London: Council for British Archaeology (Research Report 67).

Saville, A., 1999, A cache of flint axeheads and other flint artefacts from Auchenhoan, near Campbeltown, Kintyre, Scotland. *Proceedings of the Prehistoric Society* 65, 83–123.

Saville, A., 2003a, Indications of regionalisation in Mesolithic Scotland. In L. Larsson, H. Kindgren, K. Knutsson, D. Loeffler and A. Åkerlund (eds), *Mesolithic on the Move: Papers presented at the*

Sixth International Conference on the Mesolithic in Europe, Stockholm 2000, 340–350. Oxford: Oxbow Books.

Saville, A., 2003b, A flint core-tool from Wig Sands, Kirkcolm, near Stranraer, and a consideration of the absence of core-tools in the Scottish Mesolithic. *Transactions of the Dumfriesshire and Galloway Natural History and Antiquarian Society* 77, 13–22.

Sheridan, A., 2005, Pitfalls and other traps … why it's worth looking at museum artefacts again. *The Archaeologist* 58, 20–21.

Simpson, D. and Meighan, I., 1999, Pitchstone – a new trading material in Neolithic Ireland. *Archaeology Ireland* 48, 26–30.

Stevenson, R. B. K., 1950, Stone axe from Dhuloch. *Transactions of the Dumfriesshire and Galloway Natural History and Antiquarian Society* 28 (1949–1950), 186–187.

Thomas, J., 2002, Dumfries and Galloway excavations website. Dunragit 1999/2000/2001/2002 (http://orgs.man.ac.uk/research/dunragit).

Whittle, A., 1991, Wayland's Smithy, Oxfordshire: excavations at the Neolithic tomb in 1962–63 by R. J. C. Atkinson and S. Piggott. *Proceedings of the Prehistoric Society* 57(2), 61–102.

Williams J., 1970, Neolithic axes in Dumfries and Galloway. *Transactions of the Dumfriesshire and Galloway Natural History and Antiquarian Society* third series 47, 111–122.

Williams Thorpe, O. and Thorpe, R. S., 1984, The distribution and sources of archaeological pitchstone in Britain. *Journal of Archaeological Science* 11, 1–34.

Wilson, G., 1876, Notes on a collection of stone implements and other antiquities, from Glenluce, Wigtownshire, now presented to the museum. *Proceedings of the Society of Antiquaries of Scotland* 11.2 (1875–1876), 580–587.

Wilson, G., 1878, Notes on the ancient stone implements of Wigtownshire. *Archaeological and Historical Collections relating to Ayrshire and Galloway* 1, 1–30.

Wilson, G., 1881, Notes on a collection of implements and ornaments of stone, bronze, etc. from Glenluce, Wigtownshire. *Proceedings of the Society of Antiquaries of Scotland* 15 (1880–1881), 262–276.

Chapter 8

Seamer axeheads in southern England

David Field

INTRODUCTION

In his *History of Warwickshire* published in 1656, Sir William Dugdale reported the discovery of a flint axehead from Hartshill, Nuneaton, near Coventry (Dugdale 1656, 778; 1730, 1081). This appears to have been the first occasion on which a ground flint axehead had been described and illustrated in print in Britain and it is unfortunate that the axehead itself it is now missing. The legend alongside Dugdale's illustration (Figure 8.1) suggests that it was passed to his son-in-law Elias Ashmole, later founder of the Ashmolean Museum, but whose original collection of coins, seals, medals, books, and other antiquities was lost in a fire at his chambers at Middle Temple in London in 1679 (Ovenell 1986, 13). The axehead is depicted as neat and symmetrical with a broad crescentic butt and blade, both having angular junctions with the sides. Dugdale described it as 'about four inches and a half in length, curiously wrought by grinding, or some such way, into the form here expressed; at one end shaped much like the edge of a Pole Axe'. The grinding occurs at the cutting-edge

Figure 8.1. The first ground flint axehead to be illustrated in Britain – a Seamer type from Hartshill, Nuneaton – from Dugdale's Antiquities of Warwickshire, first published in 1656.

and as the blade is wider than the butt, the sides taper and are slightly concave. The piece falls into that category now generally referred to as 'Seamers', a type of Neolithic axehead brought to attention by Terry Manby in his work on Grooved Ware sites and their associations in Yorkshire (Manby 1974). Named after similar axeheads in the Seamer Moor hoard, the major characteristics are concave sides, wide (in plan view) butts, slender form, grinding and sometimes polishing of the blade-edge, along with unusually striking raw material.

The Hartshill axehead was found immediately north of Oldbury hillfort at Hartshill, where '…have been found by plowing divers Flint Stones' implying that other material was also recovered from the site and this, together with a further axehead recovered during the 1930s, appears to represent more than casual losses. The find is perhaps unusual in that, as Dugdale observed, it is made of flint, the nearest exposure of which is some 100km distant and which appears in stark contrast to the locally available knappable stone deposits. The local diorite is certainly suitable for axehead manufacture and flakes of it were noted during field investigation at several points in the vicinity (Brown and Field nd). There is some evidence that the local stone was exploited and perhaps moved great distances earlier than in the Neolithic period. An anvil-stone of quartzite from the Mesolithic sites at Oakhanger in Hampshire was thought to derive from Hartshill (Rankine 1961, 64). The Geology Survey report considered it 'similar to a specimen in our collections from Hartshill Quarry, north-east of Nuneaton', and two further pebble rubbers were said to be similar to Hartshill quartzite. These aside, the geological deposits around Oldbury comprise Upper Cambrian rocks with dykes of diorite and were considered to be one of the potential sources of Group XIV camptonite (Shotton 1959, 136–137; 1988, 49). Thus the presence of such a piece at a location with its own potential attractions might be considered to signal something beyond mundane activity.

The axehead was complete and presumably not simply discarded as a result of damage. For it to survive at great distance from its material source the flint must have been carefully used and conserved during its active life, then perhaps placed in a protected location such as a pit, cist, or burial deposit. Unfortunately, the nature of the site is now impossible to determine as it has been quarried away.

Other Seamer-type axeheads have been recovered from the Midlands (Appendix 1), emphasizing that such artefacts were not restricted to Yorkshire, although there has been a tendency to consider them rare outside that county. This is somewhat surprising as Manby indicated that the distribution extended into Scotland as well as to East Anglia and Wessex (1974, 95). The axeheads from Scotland have recently been considered and summarized by Kenworthy (1979; 1981) and Sheridan (1992), but Seamer axeheads are also present elsewhere in northern England (Appendix 1 and 2).

The ground axeheads of East Anglia are sadly under-studied, particularly that enormous and important group, the distribution of which is focused on the fen edge, but Seamer axeheads are certainly present. Several come the fens; Burwell, Burnt Fen, Chatteris, Iselham, Bottisham and Sedge Fen are catalogued below (Appendix 1), while from Weeting, Norfolk, not far from the flint extraction site of Grimes Graves, a neat example with flared blade was recovered. Pitts (1976, fig. 11a) illustrated a 'classic' Seamer-type axehead from Tunstead, whilst from Mildenhall, Suffolk, two pieces, a blade as well as the butt of probable Seamer axeheads were found. Among this greater distribution of finds the Yorkshire axeheads continue to stand out as an important focus. In terms of numbers Manby lists 14 from East Yorkshire alone, as well as 11 adzeheads, but it is evident that it is just part of a much wider picture.

SEAMER SERIES AXEHEADS FROM SOUTH OF THE THAMES

Ground axeheads are certainly numerous across southern England. Some 461 are listed as being found in the Cotswold Hills, 49 of them complete (Tyler 1976). Over 1175 come from the south Wessex area alone and it might be considered surprising that despite the well-known Neolithic monuments in the region, there has been a lack of investigation into these implements. Over 368 have been recovered from the River Thames (Adkins and Jackson 1979) and in addition to these there are 150 on-land finds from the London area (MacDonald 1976, 26) as well as 503 complete and fragmentary examples from Surrey (Field and Woolley 1984). The most comprehensive coverage of Neolithic ground axeheads is that by Pitts (1996), whose extremely useful inspection and detailed analysis of some 3500 examples nationwide did not consider Seamer axeheads as a type. Instead well-known waisted axeheads such as that in the Canewden hoard were simply assigned to his cluster 6 (Pitts 1996, 365). Here axeheads of this form and their distribution have been assessed from the inspection of collections in museums, primarily although not exclusively from south of the Thames, and from Kent as far west as Devon.

At least a dozen Seamer axeheads, and possibly as many as 17 depending upon the definitions that one accepts, have been recovered from the River Thames itself. Almost all derive from the great west London meanders of the river between Hampton and Southwark, where the largest concentration of prehistoric artefacts occurs. Most come from areas where there are distinct sub-groups of other ground axeheads and of Neolithic flint-work generally. Three form part of a major cluster of material at Teddington; one is part of the major group at Kingston; and two form part of a smaller cluster at Richmond. The reasons for the presence of prehistoric finds in this reach of the Thames have been discussed by others (Adkins and Jackson 1979; Bradley 1990; Field and Woolley 1984; Needham and Burgess 1980) and while no definitive conclusion has been reached, there is currently an emphasis on most being ritual deposits. It is evident that this stretch of Thames riverside was considered a particularly attractive location for several millennia. There is little direct evidence of ceremonial activity, at least in terms of the presence of large monuments, although the deep alluvium masks archaeology and signs of settlement and other forms of occupation are increasing as a result of commercial interventions (see essays in Cotton and Field 2004). There is now some evidence of riverside activity at Kingston (Penn *et al.* 1984; Serjeantson *et al.* 1992), Twickenham (Sanford 1970), Putney (Warren 1977) and Ham (Field 1983). The latter site, known from surface and gravel-pit collections, includes three possible broken Seamer axehead pieces while excavations at Putney revealed the butt of one amongst a mixed assemblage of material. Axeheads from the Thames, both Seamer-type and others, are for the most part complete – chance or protected context perhaps – but something that is quite unusual, for as the examples from Ham and Putney indicate, finds made on land are invariably broken or fragmented.

Few Seamer axeheads are currently recorded from the Essex or Kent banks. One was found as part of the hoard of axeheads from a gravel-pit adjacent to the River Crouch at Canewdon, near Southend, in Essex in 1923 (Anon 1931, 57–58). A further example, a thin edge-ground and almost rectangular axehead found at Cavenham, Margate, although striking in appearance, does not quite fall into a Seamer category. Other than this there is a single waisted example from Orpington. Seamer axehead distribution, therefore, is not particularly strong adjacent to the estuary and there is no real indication of influence from the continent.

To the west of London, greater numbers come from Surrey, where the river finds continue to provide the major focus, but others occur along the tributary terraces at, for example, Woking, where an axehead was recovered from a depth of 1.5m in the gravel. Further into the hinterland a greater number occur on the Greensand that fringes the Weald. Seven fragmented examples come from the Limpsfield area, for example, but the location also possesses a larger grouping of Neolithic material including 34 complete and fragmentary ground axeheads (Field and Cotton 1987, fig. 4.3). Similarly, the central Greensand location around Peaslake, where three broken examples have been recovered, is also the focus for much other Neolithic material including a cache of (non-Seamer) unground axeheads from Burrows Cross (Bruce-Mitford 1938) and numbers of other broken and rechipped ground axeheads (Field and Cotton 1987, fig. 4.7). Smaller though no less significant numbers occur on the west Surrey Greensand, from Hindhead, Hindhead Common, and Godalming Common, as well as two (one broken) from Seale (Figure 8.2). The role of the Greensand in the Neolithic settlement of southern England has been partly overlooked, as the major communal monument complexes have focused archaeological attention on the chalk. However, these warm, easily tilled soils, especially those along the spring-line at the foot of the chalk escarpment, are thought to have been ideal for early cultivation (Wooldridge and Linton 1933). It is not only in the Weald where the Greensand harbours greater clusters of Neolithic material, but Wessex also has significant concentrations of material on this deposit, for example around Tisbury and Hindon, Wiltshire (collections in Salisbury museum). There are, however, fewer Seamer axeheads known from Sussex where there has been less archaeological investigation of the Greensand deposit. Nevertheless, two have been found in coastal locations; a 'classic' Seamer from Bevendean, Brighton is illustrated by Curwen (1937, 145) and another from Goring. A further example comes from an unknown location on the South Downs.

In north Wessex few Seamer axeheads appear to be present around the Severn or upper Thames drainage, but collections in Oxfordshire museums have not been investigated although Tyler (1976) illustrated one from Aston Bampton. There are single examples from Windmill Hill and Amesbury, otherwise the monument complexes appear to be devoid of Seamer axeheads. In terms of distribution there are a few from north

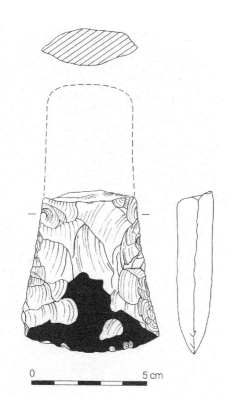

Figure 8.2. Seamer axehead from Seale in Surrey (private collection). Marbled pale-grey / white flint with ground-edge on an expanding blade which is exaggerated by concave waisting (Illustration by D. Cunliffe from a measured drawing by S. Needham).

Wiltshire, one with a very marked junction between the blade and sides found at Lye's Green, Corsley (Burchard 1973): others were found at Colerne Down and on the edge of the chalk escarpment at Heddington not far from Kings Play long barrow.

Of the ground axeheads from southern Wessex, that is the area of the Solent drainage pattern, just 120 are edge-ground, of which 42 are of the Seamer type. One half of the examples known from the region were recovered from the Higher Chalk of Dorset and Hampshire, particularly from the areas around Basingstoke and Cranborne Chase. Like the Surrey examples many of these are not isolated finds, but they form part of a wider array of artefacts found on the surface in clusters around the headwater springs and streams of the Rivers Test and Stour respectively. The material comprises rough crudely struck flakes and scrapers, waisted and Y-shaped pieces, occasional blunt edge or tranchet forms, fabricators, chisels, and axeheads. Some of these scatters, such as at Dummer, Hampshire, are very large indeed and the Seamers from the site form only part of an assemblage that includes 12 other broken ground axeheads, six chipped axeheads, two tranchet axeheads, 80 fabricators, eight Y-shaped tools, and eight waisted tools (Field 2004), most of which would traditionally be taken as indicating extensive domestic activity.

The rest are located on the lower ground (Figure 8.3), including nine from coastal locations that enhance and extend the thin coastal distribution noted in Sussex. Amongst them are examples from Thornhill, Southampton, its butt snapped in antiquity (Feachem 1975, 29), from Bakers Island, Hayling Island, Shirley, Southampton, and a number from the mouth of the Avon around Christchurch and Bournemouth spreading as far west as Bere Regis, Dorset (Smith 1969, 174). Apart from the west London group, the concentrations of the south do not quite meet the density of finds from East Yorkshire, but they are nevertheless significant in terms of numbers, particularly from the Greensand of the northern Weald and Wessex.

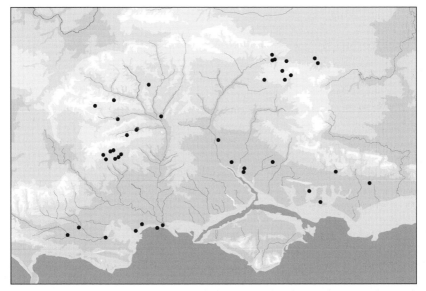

Figure 8.3. Map of central southern England showing the distribution of Seamer flint axeheads.

DISCUSSION

The context of the Seamer hoard

The Seamer Moor hoard was discovered by Lord Conyngham in 1848 during a campaign of excavations into the mounds on the moorland near Scarborough, Yorkshire. After digging at a number of sites to the southwest of the beacon on Seamer Moor, he turned his attention to two mounds situated in the adjacent parish, just on the southern edge of the moor (Conyngham 1849). They were 'lying in a field called Ayton East Field', previously known locally as 'the Sparrow Flat'. The two barrows were said to be 'at a very slight distance from each other', the easternmost being the smaller of the two, measuring just 15.8m in length by 12m in width. Even then its height had been greatly reduced by the plough. The larger, westernmost mound reached 29.9m in length and 16.7 in width, which is towards the smaller end of the long barrow range. On digging into this larger mound, Conyngham found a 'circle of large irregular stones, these were placed at the base of a cairn of large stones, topped by limestone rubble'. He excavated the entire cairn and found that the rubble on the eastern half of the cairn had been converted into lime by fire, but amongst it was pottery, animal and human bones, and ashes 'mixed into one mass'. In the centre towards the north, two groups of decomposed human bones were noted among the rubble and with each a flint projectile point. A little west of centre, at just 0.2m below the surface, a thin flat stone, 0.5m by 0.4m, partly covered a further mass of bones. With these were the flint axeheads and other artefacts that are now known as the Seamer Moor hoard.

Reginald Smith was evidently the first to interpret the mound as a long barrow (Smith 1922, 121; 1926, 104) presumably basing this on Conyngham's description, and Elgee (1930) subsequently listed the site as among the long barrows in the Scarborough area and remarked that the only barrow standing in Ayton East Field at the time of his visit must have been the mound in question.

Excavation at a long barrow on Seamer Moor (located at NGR TA 000864) carried out by Mrs F. de M. Vatcher in 1961 revealed a mortuary house of stone and wood, with drystone walls flanking the mound and forming a forecourt. The latter was later enclosed and used for cremations (Vatcher 1961, 345; Inspectorate of Ancient Monuments 1961, 69). Ian Kinnes subsequently listed the site as a round barrow and referred to it as Ayton East Field in his study of Neolithic round barrows (Kinnes 1979), but as an oval barrow in his report on the finds (Longworth and Kinnes 1985), while Terry Manby felt that the 'richly furnished inhumation' described by Conyngham had been inserted into the top of a long barrow, which had subsequently been enlarged into a round barrow (Manby 1988, 59).

Conyngham certainly appeared to describe a circular cairn, perhaps set around with stone, and described this as within the mound. However, this contrasts in some degree with the descriptions supplied by Vatcher. Whilst it may be that the circular feature once lay on top of the features excavated in the 1960s and had been levelled in the interim, it could alternatively be that Vatcher's excavation was of the smaller barrow. Further comment must await full publication and analysis of the material.

The Seamer Moor axeheads were therefore part of a burial deposit inserted at a late, probably final, stage of activity at what appears to have been a relatively short long barrow. Whether the deposit in a mound with 'stacked-up' ancestral significance signals some appropriate importance for the axeheads is unclear. An almost identical situation occurred at Whitegrounds, Burythorpe, Yorkshire, where a Seamer axehead and jet slider accompanied a burial in a round barrow that overlay an entrance grave (Brewster 1992); and probably at Duggleby Howe, Yorkshire, where the waisted adzehead was associated with a burial, lozenge arrowhead, and antler macehead at the top of a shaft containing earlier material (Kinnes 1979; Manby 1988). No similar burial-associated deposit is known in the south of England, although a burial in a round barrow, Handley Down 26, Dorset, was accompanied by a jet slider and Mortlake-ware sherds were recovered from both mound and ditch (Pitt Rivers 1898). The major related monuments, however, might be those at the Pistle Down, Dorset, long barrow, which was opened in 1828 and in which four lozenge arrowheads similar to those in the Seamer hoard were recovered (Warne 1866, 5, 16); and Winterbourne Stoke 35, where a burial at the west end was accompanied by a lozenge- and three leaf-shaped arrowheads (Thurnam 1867).

The Seamer axehead series

The finds from Seamer Moor have been considered by a number of authorities (Ashbee 1970, 76, fig. 4; Elgee 1930, 440–441; Kinnes 1979; Piggott 1954, 356–357; Smith 1922, 121–123; 1926) and most comprehensibly by Ian Longworth and Ian Kinnes in their catalogue of artefacts in the William Greenwell collection held by the British Museum (Longworth and Kinnes 1985, 147). The four edge-ground axeheads have a thin lenticular section formed by neat invasive bifacial flaking. In each case the cutting edges are broad and rounded, and the butts are also broad (thin in profile), though less so than the blade.

Remnants of cortex on three of the four axeheads, along with the small size of the pieces (two at *c.* 100mm; the others reach just over 130mm), indicate that there was some restriction imposed by the raw material and that they may have been made on large flakes. The wider axeheads are symmetrical, the larger piece of raw material presumably allowing a little greater scope in the reduction process, whilst the narrow axeheads are less so – one is asymmetrical with one side slightly concave, the other marginally convex. Generally the sides on the other examples are straight or just imperceptibly concave. It is this concave feature, exaggerated in some examples from elsewhere, that has become one of the most distinctive features of 'Seamer' axeheads. Yet, in contrast to other examples, the axeheads from the type site hardly appear waisted at all. The cutting-edge of each axehead is carefully ground and sometimes this extends across a considerable portion of the median ridge. The ground area has a gloss or sheen that may take it beyond simple grinding. In axeheads from elsewhere, for example that found in the River Thames opposite Hampton Church (Figure 8.4), it can be almost mirror like. Whether this was part of a deliberate process of 'burnishing' the surface to provide an aesthetically pleasing and reflective product is unclear. One possibility is that the final stage of grinding was carried out without a whetting agent and that friction caused the surface to fuse and become glass-like.

Pieces of similar plan form but with curved profile were referred to by Manby (1974, 95) as a special though related type after the example from burial G at Duggleby Howe, Yorkshire. This, the 'Duggleby' adzehead, is over twice as large as the axeheads from Seamer Moor, but flaked and edge-ground in a similar manner (see illustration in Kinnes 1979, fig. 18.8). The extent to which this implies a certain kind of use is unclear. The term 'adzehead' is used here without prejudice to actual use which could, for example, be as a mattock, hoe, ploughshare, or wood adze, and is simply an indication that it might be hafted in a different way (see for example Crosby 1977; or in a Seamer context Kenworthy 1981). Some were deliberately knapped to a D-shaped or triangular cross-section, which in part appears to be the product of reducing a trapezoidal cross-sectioned flake and there are examples of this from Shirley, Hampshire, and Amesbury, Wiltshire. Manby (1974, fig. 42.1) illustrates a 'Duggleby'-type blade from Potter Brompton, Yorkshire, with a D-shaped cross-section that can only have been used as an adze.

Figure 8.4. Seamer axehead found in the River Thames opposite Hampton Church (drawing by D. Williams).

Inspection of Neolithic axeheads in museum collections reveals that great numbers were made on large sturdy flakes, even those from flint mines where the extremely large nodules need to be reduced quite considerably to make functional artefacts. The asymmetry and small size of the 'Cissbury' type axehead, for example, appear to relate to their being formed in this manner on large flakes (examples in Pitt-Rivers Collection, Quaternary Research Centre, Oxford). As noted above, the small size of the axeheads in the Seamer Moor hoard – remarked upon by Smith (1922) – is likely to be the result of being made on flakes. Kenworthy (1981) thought that the Knappers, Aberdeenshire, axehead may have been formed on a struck flake, and Evans (1872, 67, fig. 22) suggested the same for an expanded-blade axehead from Thetford Warren, Suffolk. In contrast, however, the great size of the Duggleby Howe example suggests that it was made from a nodule. Asymmetry here may have been intentionally fabricated and it appears, therefore, that both adzehead and axehead forms of Seamer were deliberately contrived. It is not evident whether the difference in form was necessarily functional or whether these pieces were entirely ceremonial and symbolic, as both adzeheads and axeheads are known from burial contexts.

Of central importance in defining the 'Seamer' type is the hoard of artefacts found at York in 1868. This included arrowheads, spearheads, scrapers, flakes, and at least 15 axeheads, but unfortunately they have been partially dispersed and only seven could be reported on (Radley 1968; RCHME 1972). One of these, illustrated by Manby (1974, 98, fig. 42.3), has the considerable waisting of the Canewdon and Duggleby examples, along with a wide crescentic blade and butt that mirror each other. This is the axehead that has become the 'classic' Seamer type.

A number of different though related types emerge. All are well-knapped, slender, have lenticular cross-sections and grinding at the blade edge. Discussing ground axeheads from the East Midlands, Moore (1979, 86) sub-divided them according to the shape of the cutting edge; some had a rounded blade and others a curved blade meeting the sides at an angle. In her report on the Whitegrounds, Yorkshire, axehead (in Brewster 1992), Elizabeth Healey also described two types: a), those with splayed blades; and b), those with concave sides, broad butts, and rounded blades. Seamer-type axeheads from the Thames were not referred to as such in the catalogue produced by Adkins and Jackson (1978), but were placed into three of their categories. Their type J had straight almost parallel sides not unlike those in the Seamer Moor hoard, the width of blade and butt being similar; type K was almost identical, but had concave sides and a broad butt; and type Q had an exaggerated waisted appearance with expanded blade and butt formed in a similar manner to that of the Whitegrounds axehead. Of course there might be some local or regional style preference; there appear to be no axeheads from the Thames with the dramatically splayed blades mentioned by Healey, for example, and the rounded blades described by both Healey and Moore seem to be less in evidence in the south. Alternatively, it may be that raw material had some influence on form, or perhaps use was different.

The principal stylistic features are concave sides, splayed blades and, most importantly, well and neatly formed broad (plan), thin (profile) butts, although whilst the butt form is standard there is no strict consistency regarding the other features and, as is often the case, attributes merge one into the other. Some, such as those in the Seamer Moor hoard, taper towards the butt, yet in others the width of the blade simply mirrors the butt. The rounded edge of the axeheads in the Seamer Moor hoard is present on some, for example an axehead from the Thames at Strand-on-the-Green (Adkins and Jackson 1978, no.189), but more frequently the edge is crescentic with a marked angle with the sides, as in the example from the York hoard (Manby 1974, 99, fig. 42.3) or that from Thornhill, Southampton (Feachem 1975, 29). The importance of waisting is emphasized by the exaggeration given to some. Such a form precluded any grinding of the side edges, although it is possible that grinding took place prior to final retouching of the sides.

The two-fold division is useful, although less emphasis is placed here on the shape of the cutting edge than others have done. The 'classic' waisted type has a wide crescentic butt that lies symmetrical to the cutting edge with the concave sides each reduced by some 5 or 6mm. Good examples are that in the York hoard, or the Thames at Hampton (Figure 8.4). In contrast, others have a flared blade (i.e. much wider at the blade than the butt) sometimes exaggerated by deliberate concave waisting, such as the example from the Thames at Kingston (Adkins and Jackson 1978, no.185) or that from Seale (Figure 8.2). The range, however, covers variations between these two extremes, including those with almost straight and sometimes parallel sides and little or no blade flaring such as those in the Seamer hoard itself and similar examples from the Thames. Excluded, for the moment, are those edge-ground axeheads with a narrow butt, even where other characteristics such as striking raw material is present, although further investigation may result in the need to modify this.

There are a few examples that have been ground all over, in some cases completely erasing the flake scars: an unprovenced artefact in the National Museum of Wales, two from East Anglia and two from Northumberland. In contrast, there are a several in museum collections that are flaked with concave sides, yet have no edge-grinding (Appendix 2). These may be pre-forms, but it is equally likely that they represent finished tools. Evans (1872, 67, fig. 22) figured examples from Thetford Warren, Suffolk, Burwell Fen, Cambridgeshire, and from near Bournemouth. A similar example, with splayed cutting edge, comes from Newhaven, Sussex, and others recovered from the Thames at Teddington, Brentford, and Waterloo Bridge (Adkins and Jackson 1978, nos 237–239) indicates that these are relatively widespread. Some have an exaggerated waist and on one from the Thames at Waterloo Bridge this feature is quite severe. Of similar form, at least in terms of initial preparation, is the axehead found in a pit adjacent to the Fir Tree Field shaft, Down Farm, Dorset (Green and Allen 1997, 128, fig. 5), where the exaggerated waist is reduced by as much as 9mm. This is a coarser piece than those noted above, atypical in terms of slender form and neat flaking, and is quite short and stumpy.

The reason for the neat concave waist is quite unclear, but waisting of axeheads and other tools is by no means uncommon in the Neolithic (e.g. illustrations in Field *et al.* 1990, figs 4–5; Gardiner 1987, fig. 5.1; Green 2000, fig. 40), and indeed much earlier in the Mesolithic (Field 1989). It may be that the feature is related to a method of hafting that used much binding to hold the piece in position. This would certainly ensure that the butt half was secure and might explain the clean breaks across some axes, but it would also obscure much of the elaborate knapping from view. The 'classic' examples, such as that in the York hoard, are well proportioned and balanced with similar weight at each end. Even where the blade is flared the butt is usually sufficiently wide to retain the balance of the piece. The tendency towards splayed blades implies the need for a wide cutting-edge relative to the size of the axehead, but the small size and light weight of most indicates that any function must be relatively refined. None have been subject to microwear study, but from inspection of micro-scars Kenworthy suggested that little use had been made of the adzehead from Knappers, Dunbartonshire (Kenworthy 1981, 190).

Raw material

One of the characteristics of Seamer axeheads originally identified by Manby (1974; 1988) was the good quality, unusual, often coloured and distinctive flint that was used as raw material. The raw material of most of the examples in Yorkshire is thought likely to derive from nodules in the boulder clay rather than the chalk (Manby 1979, 71), although the axeheads in the Seamer Moor hoard itself are all corticated (patinated) and the nature of the flint obscured, but otherwise apparently undistinguished. Kenworthy suggests that a number of Seamer type axeheads in Scotland, including that from Greenbrae, Cruden, Aberdeenshire, were of flint imported from south of the border (Kenworthy 1979, 85). In contrast to these areas, flint in the south is ubiquitous and rarely is there anything outstandingly special about it. Differences in colour derive from mineral saturation of secondary flint sources, for example, gravel terraces, but in many cases it is difficult to determine whether staining of a piece occurred prior to, or after, knapping. A number of finds have an ochreous surface, for example, that from Shedfield, Hampshire, or Corsley,

Wiltshire, where the orange-brown flint was thought to have been obtained from an area of local Gault Clay (Burchard 1973). Sometimes a mottled effect is produced, such as in the axeheads from Lake Clay Pits, Hamworthy, or Bridford, Devon. There are a few, however, one from south Hampshire with brown banding in the grey flint, one from Hayling Island in pink and brown flint, that do appear to have been made on unique raw material, but most are on variations of the standard grey southern flint, corticated to varying degrees according to the deposit in which they were located. Some axeheads found on the Surrey Greensand appear to be made of a more cherty material, but none appear to be made on Bullhead Beds flint, with its orange band beneath dark cortex being the most striking raw material available in the region. The material of a Seamer series axehead from Lound Run, Belton, Suffolk, was analysed as part of a trace-element sourcing programme and considered to derive from the floorstone at Grimes Graves (Craddock and Cowell 2004, 18–21), but given the enormous number of axeheads that must have been produced from this material it need not be considered out of the ordinary. Occasionally it can be certain that the staining is post-manufacture where, for example, it occurs on one face only, being the side in contact with the ground, such as on the example from Walderton, Sussex, and many from the Thames are stained by peat or gravel deposits. Like the Smerrick type of ground axehead, which employs banded and mottled flint (Saville 1999; 2004), Seamer axeheads in striking materials do occur, but in the south there appears to be no greater emphasis on unusual material than in any other type of ground flint axehead.

Date and associations

It was formerly thought that, based on the expanding blade form, Seamer axeheads were likely to be an imitation of flat metal axeheads and therefore of Early Bronze Age date (Bruce-Mitford 1938, 283). Needham (1996) places the introduction of metal at *c.* 2500 BC and, although it remains possible that influences from the continent were absorbed around the turn of the fourth to third millennium, there is no evidence for such early use of copper in Britain. The early copper axehead found with the 'iceman' in the Italian Alps was rectangular in cross-section (Spindler 1994, 205) and its otherwise straight sides only flared at the blade as a result of hammering the edge. In form it reflects the north European flint axeheads rather than anything from the UK. Any suggested mimicry carries with it an implication that the flint versions were less prestigious than the real thing, but given the number of flint Seamer type axeheads from across the country and the corresponding lack of flat metal axeheads with an appropriate early date, it seems rather unlikely that they were influenced by metal prototypes.

From his seriation of finds from Neolithic burial contexts, Kinnes (1979) placed edge-ground axeheads in Stage D of his progression. This had associations with Mortlake ware, lozenge- and leaf-shaped arrowheads, ground-edge knives, plano-convex knives, serrated blades, stone rubbers, boars tusk blades, jet belt sliders and antler maceheads. The Seamer Moor hoard figured prominently here, as did the Whitegrounds burial and adzehead from Duggleby Howe (burial G), but also included are the finds from Liff's Low, near Biggin, Yorkshire, a burial with two accompanying flint edge-ground axeheads; two flint arrowheads, two edge-ground flint knives (one of which was serrated), a small and unusual decorated cup with Mortlake affinities, and an antler macehead (Kinnes 1979, fig.

18.7). The Whitegrounds axehead was also found with a jet slider (Brewster 1992, 12), an artefact sometimes associated with Peterborough pottery and a male burial with a single radiocarbon determination of 3500–2900 cal BC (HAR-5587). Recent reassessment of the date of Mortlake pottery suggests currency around *c.* 3400–2500 cal BC (Gibson and Kinnes 1997). The evidence regarding the date of the axeheads is slender, but what there is pulls it forward into the middle Neolithic. Manby considered that the genesis of the 'Duggleby horizon' was in effect from the beginning of his Meldon Bridge Period, from around 3000 until 2750 BC (Manby 1988, 37). The Whitegrounds axehead might fall into the earlier part of that time frame, but could equally have been manufactured in the 4th millennium.

Of those objects directly associated in the Seamer hoard, tusk knives are rare in the south, though a few ground and polished flint knives do occur and accompany the Seamer distribution (Appendix 3). A lozenge arrowhead from Mudeford close to the mouth of the Avon is also relevant as it is partly ground on both faces (Red House Museum, Christchurch, Hampshire). There is no clear association with discoidal ground knives, either in Yorkshire or elsewhere. In Yorkshire, the incidence of such knives is frequent, but that from Carnaby Top site 12 is the only one from an excavated context, a line of swallow holes that contained Beaker pottery and a sherd of Grooved ware, although Peterborough ware was also present on site (Manby 1974). The knife, however, is retouched at the sides and may have been reworked. Varndell (2004) discussed the few secure contexts elsewhere in the country. One occurred in the Great Baddow hoard, Essex, along with ground and edge-ground axeheads, none of which are of the Seamer series.

The cache from Canewdon, Essex, comprised two edge-ground axeheads and a ground chisel (Anon 1931, 57–58). One of the axeheads has a flared blade and concave sides, the extent of the concavity being uncertain as the butt is missing. The other is slightly asymmetrical in plan with one concave and one convex side tapering to a narrow butt, not unlike the narrower pieces in the Seamer Moor hoard. With them was a cigar-shaped chisel, ground at the pointed butt end rather than the blade end, which was left rough. The implication is that it was the pointed end that was used, in which case the tool must have been some kind of punch. An axehead with expanding blade and concave sides from Newmarket Heath, Cambridgeshire, although not as neat as other examples, was found 'together' with a chisel, this time edge-ground (Fox 1925), although as surface finds little weight can be placed upon them.

Social implications

Varndell (2004: 121) considered that the association of different axehead types with a discoidal knife in the Banham and Great Baddow hoards simply 'related to more than one activity' and were not part of a toolkit, and the same may apply to the association of chisels (if we accept the narrow axeheads as chisels) and axeheads in the Canewden and Seamer Moor hoards. Given that the 'Seamer' template was widely adopted, for almost identical axeheads occur in the north and south of the country, it must have been a relatively easy matter to provide several of a single type should that have been desirable. That different forms were found together implies different uses and by implication Seamer axeheads both with and without flared blades were deliberately contrived types that served a certain function inappropriate to other axeheads.

It is interesting that when considering the Oldbury find, Dugdale drew comparison with poleaxes. Methods of animal slaughter is a subject not often touched upon in the archaeological literature, though it should be noted that elsewhere special tools were often used for bloodletting and sacrifice (e.g. Saunders 1994, 176). An edge-ground axehead found embedded in the forehead of a *Bos primigenius* at Roche, Burwell Fen, Cambridgeshire (Figure 8.5; Babbington 1864) demonstrates that there may be a wide and unexpected range of functions for axeheads beyond cutting down trees.

The highly distinctive nature of these artefacts has resulted in the view that they were socially prestigious with a role to play in ceremony (Manby 1988). The neat appearance, shallow flaking, form, and ground edges that sometimes bear a high gloss polish beyond anything required for practical use implies a concern with aesthetics, and the slender form makes each piece highly breakable. It is of course easy to dismiss mundane function in the face of aesthetic effort and perhaps incautious to uncritically assign a ceremonial function on looks alone. However, presence in prominent burial mounds in Yorkshire lends support to the view that these were prestigious artefacts and were not used in a casual manner. Both Whitegrounds and Duggleby Howe artefacts accompany single burials and whether deposisted at the time of death or subsequently (despite the burnt limestone cairn, the hoard at Seamer Moor was not burnt although one axehead has a slightly creamier-coloured cortication) they provide a link even if only in terms of memory. In the south, where there is no similar association with burials, several axeheads of this series have been recovered

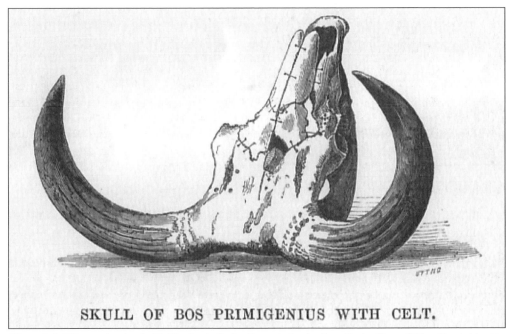

SKULL OF BOS PRIMIGENIUS WITH CELT.

Figure 8.5. Flint axehead embedded in the skull of a Bos primigenius from Roche, Burwell Fen, Cambridgeshire (from Babbington 1864).

from the River Thames. All are complete and may have been deliberately deposited in the river as part of some ceremony.

Manby (1988: 59) pointed to the exceptional mastery of the knapping process in the production of these and associated pieces. The distinctive types may point to a few individual craftsmen and, as Topping has pointed out, flint knapping of certain objects may be restricted by sex, class or social position and conditioned by 'secret knowledge' concerning procedures and ceremonies (Topping 2004; 2005 for ethnographic examples). It may be that with careful study of flaking technique, the signature of certain individuals might be identified. Certainly there are numbers of axeheads, on for example the Surrey Greensand, that appear to be, at least superficially, very similar.

SUMMARY THOUGHTS

Seamer forms are widespread across the country and are no less numerous in the south than in Yorkshire. The distribution is essentially riverine, particularly along the west London Thames, but there is also a significant scatter along the south coast that may focus on the mouth of the Avon at Christchurch. Others accumulate around the headwaters of the rivers Stour and Test in Wessex and the Darent and Wey in the Weald. They do not appear to mark the location of overtly special or religious centres and the known monument complexes do not figure as an important component. Instead, away from protected environments, fair wear and tear on axeheads has resulted in broken and fragmentary examples that are a minor component of the total ground axehead population for each site. Unlike northern examples, the ubiquity of flint as a raw material in the south negates any value as a prestigious material, although such value may have increased the further north from the chalk that one travelled. Use of unusual coloured or patterned flint certainly occurs, but no more than in other types of ground axehead. This by no means indicates that Seamer axeheads did not have an important or specific role to play. The forms were clearly intended and the distribution right across the UK suggests a widely understood template rather than something restricted to a local group, but it widens the range of social possibilities which might differ according to the proximity to source material. The flint axehead from Oldbury Camp Warwickshire, with which this essay was introduced, is likely to have had considerably greater impact on the contemporary local population of the west Midlands, just as it did on Dugdale, than it would have done further south.

ACKNOWLEDGEMENTS

My fascination with Seamer type axeheads was kindled over 25 years ago after encountering the outstanding axehead from the Thames opposite Hampton Church in Kingston Museum. Since then I have annoyed countless curators who have very kindly allowed me to inspect their collections. Sometimes I have benefited from certain other projects. The RCHME flint mine project for example allowed a trawl of museums in Northumberland, while more recently PhD research at the University of Reading under the supervision of Richard Bradley included visiting museums in south Wessex. In a few cases, particularly for East

Anglia, the catalogue has been supplemented by details of axeheads from Mike Pitts's extensive catalogue of ground axeheads now held in the National Monuments Record at Swindon, while Terry Manby kindly supplied details of others held by the Cambridge University Archaeological and Ethnographical Museum. I would like to thank Pete Topping of English Heritage and Gill Varndell of the British Museum as well as Terry Manby for casting their respective critical eyes over an earlier draft of the manuscript, Stuart Needham for allowing me to use his illustration of an axehead from Seale, Deborah Cunliffe and David Williams for providing finished drawings and, by no means least, Alan Saville for accepting this chapter at a very late point in proceedings.

APPENDIX 1. EDGE-GROUND SEAMER AXEHEADS

Where the precise findspot is unknown the grid reference has been taken to the appropriate place-name.

Provenance	NGR	Type/Notes	Location/Source
Berkshire			
Maidenhead	SU 8781		Liverpool Museum 44.23.2
Tilehurst	SU6673		Reading Museum 57.51
Cambridgeshire			
Burwell Fen	TL5767		Cambridge A&E Museum
Burnt Fen	TL6087		Cambridge A&E Museum
Chatteris, Longwood Hill	TL4185		Wisbech Museum
Swaffham Prior Fen	TL5467		Ashmolean Museum
Isleham Fen	TL6276		British Museum 478
Bottisham Fen	TL5265		British Museum
Sedge Fen	TL5674		Cambridge A&E Museum
Burwell	TL5966	Duggleby adze	Cambridge A&E Museum
Ditton	TL4960	Duggleby adze, pink flint	Cambridge A&E Museum
Fordham	TL6270	Duggleby adze	Cambridge A&E Museum
Reach Fen	TL5666	Duggleby adze	Cambridge A&E Museum
Cornwall			
Knil Steeple, St Ives	SU5138	Curved profile	Truro Museum
Bolventor	SX1876	Curved profile	Plymouth Museum 72,24,31
Chyanghued, Lelant	SW5437		Truro Museum
Cumbria			
Ainstable, The Harras	NY540461		Richardson 1990, 73-4
Devon			
Bridford, Roborough	SS 5635	Straight tapered sides	Exeter Museum 258/1960
North Tawton	SS 6601		(Evans 1872, 84)
Throwleigh, Cawsand Beacon	SX6391		Plymouth Museum 1074

Provenance	NGR	Type/Notes	Location/Source
DORSET			
Bere Regis	SY 862918		(Smith 1969, 74)
Bournemouth	SZ 052891	Butt	British Museum 65
Bournemouth nr			Red House Museum, Christchurch 34
Bournemouth, Redhill	SZ 1391	Curved profile	Hampshire Museum Service 1/1965
Bournemouth, Winton	SZ 0993		Red House Museum, Christchurch 91/1968
Bussey Stool	ST 931154	Blade, possible Seamer	Down Farm Museum, Dorset (M.Green coll.)
Farnham Newtown	ST 943163	Blade, possibly Seamer	Down Farm Museum, Dorset (M.Green coll.)
Hamworthy, Lake Clay Pits	SY 990907	Not waisted	Poole Museum
Woodcutts, Down Farm	ST 996148	Blade, possibly rechipped Seamer	Down Farm Museum, Dorset (M.Green coll.)
Woodcutts, Down Farm	SU 004146	Mid portion, possible Seamer	Down Farm Museum, Dorset (M.Green coll.)
Woodcutts, Handley	ST 9618	Blade edge missing	Salisbury Museum 2032d
DYFED			
Cilymaenllwyd, Ael-y-bryn	SN164278		National Museum Wales 77.14H
ESSEX			
Canewdon	TQ 8994		(Anon 1931)
Langham, Park Lane Fm	TM0231	One side straight	Colchester Museum 116.43
Great Horkesley	TL9730		Colchester Museum
GREATER LONDON			
Ham	TQ 1772	Fragment of flat thin example, with traces of grinding	Museum of London 60.176/403
Ham	TQ 1772	Middle portion of very well flaked axehead with concave sides, ends crushed	Museum of London 60.176/305
Ham nr church	TQ 179717	Butt missing, very thin, one side straight the other concave, possibly a Seamer	Museum of London 60.176/31
Orpington	TQ 4565		Orpington Museum (Eldridge coll.)
Putney, Sefton St	TQ 232760	Butt	Wandsworth History Society Museum
HAMPSHIRE			
Ashe, Overton	SU 5350	Mid section	Hampshire Museum Service
Baker's Island	SU 695035		Portsmouth Museum (Chris Draper coll.)
Christchurch, Latch Farm, Mill Plain	SZ154935	Butt ground, chert	Poole Museum Nii6
Deane, Deane Down	SU 5450	Blade	Hampshire Museum Service

Provenance	NGR	Type/Notes	Location/Source
Deane, Deane Down	SU552513	Mid portion	Hampshire Museum Service
Dummer	SU 5846	Blade	Hampshire Museum Service
Dummer	SU6042		Hampshire Museum Service
Cobley, Foresters Cottage	SU 5244	Blade	Down Farm Museum, Dorset (M.Green coll.)
Farleigh Wallop	SU 6246	Butt	Hampshire Museum Service
Farleigh Wallop	SU 6149	Blade	Hampshire Museum Service
Greywell, Bidden Water	SU 7151	Mid portion	Hampshire Museum Service
Hayling Island	SU 7200		Portsmouth Museum unnumbered
Lavant	SU 8508	Butt	Chichester Museum
Longwood Manor, Winchester		Butt missing, ?Seamer	Winchester City Museum
Odiham, Isnam's Farm	SU 7249	Butt	Hampshire Museum Service
Romsey, Cupernham	SU 3622		Liverpool Museum 44.23.227
Christchurch, probably		Blade	Red House Museum, Christchurch
Shedfield, Winchester Rd	SU 563144		Portsmouth Museum 1979/702
Shirley	SU 4013	Adze, D-cross section	Salisbury Museum 2005
Southampton, Sholing	SU 46821156	Rough example	
Southampton, Thornhill	SU 4612		(Feachem 1975)
South Hampshire		Butt missing	Portsmouth Museum 25/50/59

Lancashire			
Bacup, Tooter hill	SD 8622		(Jackson 1928)

Leicestershire			
Stanton-under-Barden, Cliffe Hill	SK4710		Leicester Museum 39.1861
Lubenham/Mkt Harborough			Leicester Museum 25. 1914
Ratby, Holywell Farm	SK5005		Leicester Museum 4.IL.1929

Lincolnshire			
Tattershall Thorpe	TF2258		British Museum
Barholme	TF0910		Cambridge A&E Museum
Belton	SK9239		Scunthorpe Museum 81.19
North Kelsey	TA0401		Scunthorpe Museum
Woodhall Spa	TF1963		

Norfolk			
Weeting	TL 7789	Trapezoidal type, corticated (patinated) white, neat	Gunnersbury Park Museum, London (Sadler coll.)
Tunstead	TG 2921		Norwich Castle Museum 308.958

Provenance	NGR	Type/Notes	Location/Source
North Walsham, Knapton	TG291318		Norwich Castle Museum
Thetford	TL8883		Cambridge A&E Museum
Sporle	TF8411		See M Pitts catalogue
Edingthorpe	TG3232	Exaggerated waist	Norwich Castle Museum
West Beckham	TG1438	Found 6 feet deep	Norwich Castle Museum
Cranwich	TL7894		Norwich Castle Museum
Watton	TF9100	Ground all over	British Museum 441
NORTHUMBERLAND			
Berwick	NT 9952	Straight blade edge, waisted, neatly knapped, dark grey mottled flint	Society of Antiquaries Museum, Newcastle University 1984.8a
East Thirston Moor	NZ 1999	Prob Seamer butt missing, ochreous	Alnwick Castle Museum
Ponteland, Chillingham	NZ 1673		Chillingham Castle Museum
Burradon	NT9806	Ground all over	British Museum 469
Eachwick	NZ1171	Ground all over	British Museum
OXFORDSHIRE			
Aston Bampton	SP 358017		(Tyler 1976, 10)
Goring	SU 6081		Reading Museum 150.47
POWYS			
Llanwrin	SH787062		National Museum Wales 59.526/1
RIVER THAMES			
Hampton Church	TQ 141694	Adkins & Jackson No.188 Type K	Kingston Museum 833
Kingston	TQ 2276	Adkins & Jackson No.185 Type K	
Long Wittenham reach	SU 5493	Adkins & Jackson No.184 Type K	Salisbury Museum (Pitt Rivers coll.)
Mortlake	TQ 2075	Adkins & Jackson No.191 Type K	British Museum SG 85
Penton Hook	TQ 0469	Adkins & Jackson No.180 Type J	Museum of London 36.217/13
Richmond	TQ 1874	Adkins & Jackson No.181 Type J ?Seamer	British Museum
Richmond	TQ 1874	Adkins & Jackson No.182 Type J	Museum of London 49.107/126
Strand on the Green	TQ 1977	Adkins & Jackson No.189 Type K	British Museum 1965, 2-9, 55
Surbiton	TQ 1767	Adkins & Jackson No.177 Type J ?Seamer	Museum of London 49.107/95
Teddington	TQ 1670	Adkins & Jackson No.186 Type K	British Museum WG 87
Teddington	TQ 1670	Adkins & Jackson No.237 Type Q exaggerated	Museum of London 49.107/5

PROVENANCE	NGR	Type/Notes	LOCATION/SOURCE
Teddington Lock	TQ 1671	Adkins & Jackson No.187 Type K ?Seamer	Cheltenham Museum 1915.109
Twickenham	TQ 1573	Adkins & Jackson No.178 Type J	British Museum WG 73
Waterloo Bridge	TQ 3179	Adkins & Jackson No.238 Type Q exaggerated waist	Museum of London 0.221
Woolwich	TQ 4379	Adkins & Jackson No.190 Type K	British Museum

SUFFOLK			
Hockwold, Leylands Farm	TL7587		Bury St Edmunds Museum
Bury St Edmunds	TL8564		British Museum 1965, 2-9,95

SURREY			
Godalming	SU 9643	Butt, wide, slight & gentle curve	Godalming Museum B980.580.2
Hindhead	SU 8836		Haslemere Museum
Hindhead Common	SU 895354	Thin, expanded blade	Haslemere Museum
Knap Hill	SU958582		Guildford Museum AS110
Limpsfield	TQ 4151	Highly polished edge	Pitt Rivers Museum, Oxford
Limpsfield	TQ 4153	Neat, very fine, straight sides, rounded blade. Similar to Seamer hoard type	Pitt Rivers Museum, Oxford
Limpsfield Common	TQ 410525	Blade fragment possibly from Seamer	Pitt Rivers Museum, Oxford
Limpsfield, Paine's Hill	TQ 4151	Mid section – neat-no polish	Pitt Rivers Museum, Oxford
Limpsfield, Paines Hill	TQ 414517	Mid section – extremely neat	Pitt Rivers Museum, Oxford
Limpsfield, Paines Hill	TQ 414517	Mid section straight, sides neat, very well flaked, small patch of grinding	Pitt Rivers Museum, Oxford
Limpsfield Common	TQ 4152	Blade possibly Seamer	Pitt Rivers Museum, Oxford
Oxted	TQ 3952	Blade of possible Seamer, neat but a little thick, ground and burnt edge	Pitt Rivers Museum, Oxford
Peaslake, Far Corner	TQ 0844	Fragment mid-portion, neat and fine	Guildford Museum G3868
Peaslake, Far Corner	TQ 0844	Butt from possible Seamer flint axehead, battered on butt	Guildford Museum G5263
Seale area, probably		Blade only	Guildford Museum G789
Seale	SU 8947	Blade	Stuart Needham pers. comm.
Woking, Oriental Road	TQ 005586	Large with wide butt, flared edge-ground blade, olive with black patches, cortex at butt and on each face	Weybridge Museum 52.1980

SUSSEX			
Brighton, Bevendean	TQ 3406		(Curwen 1937)
Goring-by-sea	TQ 1103	Blade	Worthing Museum 705
Horsed Keynes	TQ3825		Lewes Museum

Provenance	NGR	Type/Notes	Location/Source
South Downs			Alexander Keiller Museum, Avebury
Walderton Down, Walderton	SU7911		Portsmouth Museum 351/1976

Suffolk			
Belton, Lound Run	TG 4802		(Craddock & Cowell 2004)
Cavenham,	TL 7669	? Seamer	Alexander Keiller Museum, Avebury
Mildenhall	TL 7175	Blade, brown flint	Bournemouth NHS Museum
Mildenhall	TL 7175	Butt of ?Seamer, patterned brown / grey flint	Bournemouth NHS Museum
Newmarket Heath	TL 6162		(Fox 1925)
Lakenheath		Duggleby adze, ground all over	Cambridge A&E

Unprovenanced			
Unprov.			Farnham Museum
Unprov.		Well ground all over, not flint	National Museum Wales 29.276

Warwickshire			
Alcester, Oversley	SP 0857		(Shotton 1934, 44).
Hartshill, Oldbury	SP 3194		(Dugdale 1656)

Wiltshire			
Amesbury, west of Stonehenge	SU 1142	Adze. D-cross section	Salisbury Museum
Avebury, Windmill Hill	SU785613	Blade edge-ground, possibly Seamer	Keiller Museum, Avebury
Bishopstone	SU 0725	Butt missing, probably Seamer	Salisbury Museum 1025
Bishopstone	SU 0725	Adze, D-cross section	Salisbury Museum 1013a
Broad Chalke	SU0323	Butt missing	Salisbury Museum 41/60
Colerne Down	ST 8377	Blade expanding	Devizes Museum 50.1968
Corsley, Lye's Green	ST 81674625	Waisted axehead with butt missing, ochreous	Devizes Museum case 17
Cranborne Chase, Scrubbity Copse	SU 9717	Butt missing 4/10/83, from Ring barrow 10, found at depth of 1ft 7in	Salisbury Museum (Pitt Rivers coll.)
Fovant	SU 9929	Blade only, probably Seamer	Salisbury Museum 86/1971
Handley Down	SU 0117	Found at centre of Angle Ditch enclosure	Salisbury Museum (Pit Rivers coll.)
Heddington	SU 015667	Blade expanding	Devizes Museum 63.1970
Highworth, Rag Farm	SU202909		Swindon Museum B77/228
Hindon	ST 9133		Salisbury Museum (Newell coll.)
Salisbury	SU 1430		Red House Museum, Christchurch
Stockton Earthworks	SU 970362	Blade, from rabbit hole	Salisbury Museum 44/46

Yorkshire			
See Manby 1974, 128-9			

APPENDIX 2. UNGROUND SEAMER AXEHEADS

Provenance	NGR	Type/Notes	Location/Source
Cambridgeshire			
Burwell Fen	TL 5767		(Evans 1872)
Dorset			
Bournemouth, Rush Corner			University Museum of Archaeology & Anthropology, Cambridge 36.390
Hampshire			
Bussey Stool	ST 9315		Down Farm Museum, Dorset (M.Green coll.)
Dummer	SU 5846	Blade	Hampshire Museum Service
Dummer	SU 5846	Blade	Hampshire Museum Service
Dummer	SU 602467	Blade.	Hampshire Museum Service
Dummer	SU 6042	Blade.	Hampshire Museum Service
Ellisfield	SU 6345	Centre	Hampshire Museum Service
Ellisfield	SU 6345	Fragment	Hampshire Museum Service
Farleigh Wallop	SU 6246	Blade	Hampshire Museum Service
Overton, King Overton	SU 5149		Hampshire Museum Service
Preston Candover	SU 6342	Blade	Hampshire Museum Service
Upton Grey, Bidden Water	SU 7151	Centre	Hampshire Museum Service
Surrey			
Peaslake	TQ 0844	Mr Daniels garden. Fragment mid-portion	Guildford Museum G3384
Farnham, Caesars Camp	SU835505		British Museum 61,8-21,2
Sussex			
Eastbourne	TV6199		British Museum 29, 7-9, 25
Newhaven	TQ 4401		Alexander Keiller Museum, Avebury
Suffolk			
Thetford Warren	TL 8383		(Evans 1872, 67)

APPENDIX 3. EDGE-GROUND FLINT KNIVES

(for Yorkshire see Manby 1974, 111-6)

PROVENANCE	NGR	TYPE/NOTES	LOCATION/SOURCE
Christchurch, Hampshire	SZ 1592		Red House Museum, Christchurch 800

PROVENANCE	NGR	TYPE/NOTES	LOCATION/SOURCE
Christchurch, Hampshire	SZ 1592		Red House Museum, Christchurch
Donhead St Andrew, Wiltshire	ST 9222		Down Farm Museum, Dorset (M.Green coll.)
Donhead St Andrew, Wiltshire	ST 9222		Down Farm Museum, Dorset (M.Green coll.)
Highham, Kent	TQ 7171		Maidstone Museum BA8
Malling East, Kent	TQ 7057		Maidstone Museum
Ryton, Northumberland	NZ 1564	2 fragments	Society of Antiquaries Museum, Newcastle University 1970
Southampton, Hampshire	SU 3914		Ordnance Survey records
Winterbourne Basset, Wiltshire	SU 132741	fragment	Devizes Museum 1986.27.115
Woodcutts, Wiltshire	SU2014		Down Farm Museum, Dorset (M.Green coll.)

BIBLIOGRAPHY

Adkins, R. and Jackson, R., 1978, *Neolithic Stone and Flint Axes from the River Thames: An Illustrated Corpus*. London: British Museum (Occasional Paper 1).

Anon., 1931, Neolithic hoard from Essex. *Antiquaries Journal* 11(1), 57–58.

Anon., 1961, Seamer Moor, Yorkshire. *Proceedings of the Prehistoric Society* 27, 345.

Ashbee, P., 1970, *The Earthen Long Barrow in Britain*. London: Dent.

Babbington, C., 1864, On a skull of *Bos primigenius* associated with flint implements. *Proceedings of the Cambridge Antiquarian Society* 2, 285–288.

Bradley, R., 1990, *The Passage of Arms*. Cambridge: Cambridge University Press.

Brewster, T. C. M., 1992, *The Excavation of Whitegrounds Barrow, Burythorpe* (2nd edition). Leeds: East Riding Archaeological Research Trust.

Brown, G. and Field, D., n.d., *An Investigation and Earthwork Survey at Hartshill Hayes, Warwickshire (SP39SW6)*. Swindon: English Heritage.

Bruce Mitford, R. L. S., 1938, A hoard of Neolithic axes from Peaslake, Surrey. *Antiquaries Journal* 18(3), 279–284.

Burchard, A., 1973, A waisted flint axe from Corsley. *Wiltshire Archaeological and Natural History Society Magazine* 68, 118–119.

Conyingham, Lord A. D., 1849, Account of discoveries made in barrows near Scarborough. *Journal of the British Archaeological Association* 4, 101–107.

Cotton, J. and Field, D. (eds), 2004, *Towards a New Stone Age: Aspects of the Neolithic in South-east England*. York: Council for British Archaeology (Research Report 137).

Cottrill, F., 1941, Another Bronze Age Beaker from Leicestershire. *Antiquaries Journal* 21(3), 232–234.

Craddock, P. and Cowell, M., 2004, 'Cutting edge'. *British Archaeology* 79, 18–21.

Crosby, E., 1977, An archaeologically oriented classification of ethnographic material culture. In R. V. S. Wright (ed.), *Stone Tools as Cultural Markers: Change, Evolution and Complexity*, 83–96. Canberra: Australian Institute of Aboriginal Studies / New Jersey: Humanities Press.

Curwen, E. C., 1937, *The Archaeology of Sussex*. London: Methuen.

Dugdale, W., 1656, *The Antiquities of Warwickshire*. London.

Dugdale, W., 1730, *The Antiquities of Warwickshire* (2nd edition). London.

Elgee, F., 1930, *Early Man in North-East Yorkshire*. Gloucester: John Bellows.

Evans, J., 1872, *The Ancient Stone Implements, Weapons, and Ornaments of Great Britain*. London: Longmans, Green, Reader and Dyer.

Feachem, R. W., 1975, A late Neolithic axe from Thornhill, Southampton. *Proceedings of the Hampshire Field Club* 30, 29.

Field, D., 1983, Ham: the Edwards Collection. *Surrey Archaeological Collections* 74, 169–184.

Field, D., 1989, Tranchet axes and Thames picks: Mesolithic core tools from the west London Thames. *Transactions of the London and Middlesex Archaeological Society* 40, 1–26.

Field, D., 2004, Use of Land in Central Southern England during the Neolithic and Early Bronze Age. Unpublished PhD thesis, University of Reading, UK.

Field, D. and Cotton, J., 1987, Neolithic Surrey: a survey of the evidence. In J. Bird and D. Bird (eds), *The Archaeology of Surrey to 1540*. Guildford: Surrey Archaeological Society.

Field, D., Nicolaysen, P., Waters, K., Winser, K. and Ketteringham, L. L., 1990, Prehistoric material from near Slines Oak and Worms Heath, Chelsham. *Surrey Archaeological Collections* 80, 133–145.

Field, D. and Woolley, A. R., 1984, Neolithic and Bronze Age ground stone implements from Surrey: morphology, petrology and distribution. *Surrey Archaeological Collections* 75, 85–110.

Fox, C., 1925, Flint axe and 'chisel' found at Newmarket Heath. *Proceedings of the Prehistoric Society of East Anglia* 5, 79.

Gardiner, J., 1987, Tales of the unexpected: approaches to the assessment and interpretation of museum flint collections. In A. G. Brown and M. R. Edmonds (eds), *Lithic Analysis and Later British Prehistory: Some Problems and Approaches*, 49–65. Oxford: British Archaeological Reports (British Series 162).

Gibson, A. and Kinnes, I., 1997, On the urns of a dilemma: radiocarbon and the Peterborough problem. *Oxford Journal of Archaeology* 16(1), 65–71.

Green, M., 2000, *A Landscape Revealed: 10,000 Years on a Chalkland Farm*. Stroud: Tempus.

Green, M. and Allen, M., 1997, An early prehistoric shaft on Cranborne Chase. *Oxford Journal of Archaeology* 16(2), 121–132.

Inspectorate of Ancient Monuments, 1961, Brief summary of excavations. *Archaeological News Letter* 7, 69–71.

Jackson, W., 1928, Flint adze from Bacup. *Antiquaries Journal* 8(1), 90.

Kenworthy, J. B., 1979, A reconsideration of the 'Ardiffery' finds, Cruden, Aberdeenshire. *Proceedings of the Society of Antiquaries of Scotland* 108 (1976–1977), 80–93.

Kenworthy, J. B., 1981, The flint adze-blade and its cultural context. In J. N. G. Ritchie and H. C. Adamson, Knappers, Dunbartonshire: a reassessment. *Proceedings of the Society of Antiquaries of Scotland* 111, 189–192.

Kinnes, I. A., 1979, *Round Barrows and Ring-Ditches in the British Neolithic*. London: British Museum (Occasional Paper 7).

Lawrence, G. F., 1929, Antiquities from the middle Thames. *Archaeological Journal* 86, 69–98.

Longworth, I. H. and Kinnes, I. A., 1985, *Catalogue of the Excavated Prehistoric and Romano-British Material in the Greenwell Collection*. London: British Museum Publications.

MacDonald, J., 1976, Neolithic. In D. Collins, J. MacDonald, J. Barratt, J. Canham, R. Merrifield and J. Hurst, *The Archaeology of the London Area: Current Knowledge and Problems*, 19–32. London: London and Middlesex Archaeological Society (Special Paper 1).

Manby, T. G., 1974, *Grooved Ware Sites in the North of England*. Oxford: British Archaeology Reports (British Series 9).

Manby, T. G., 1979, Typology, materials and distribution of flint and stone axes in Yorkshire. In T. H. McK. Clough and W. A. Cummins (eds), *Stone Axe Studies: Archaeological, Petrological, Experimental and Ethnographic*, 65–81. London: Council for British Archaeology (Research Report 23).

Manby, T. G., 1988, The Neolithic period in eastern Yorkshire. In T. Manby (ed.), *Archaeology in Eastern Yorkshire: Essays in Honour of T. C. M. Brewster*, 35–88. Sheffield: Department of Archaeology and Prehistory, University of Sheffield.

Moore, C. N., 1979, Stone axes from the East Midlands. In T. H. McK. Clough and W. A. Cummins (eds), *Stone Axe Studies: Archaeological, Petrological, Experimental and Ethnographic*, 83–86. London: Council for British Archaeology (Research Report 23).

Ovenell, R. F., 1986, *The Ashmolean Museum 1683–1894*. Oxford: Clarendon Press.

Penn, J., Field, D. and Serjeantson, D., 1984, Evidence of Neolithic occupation in Kingston: excavations at Eden Walk, 1965. *Surrey Archaeological Collections* 75, 207–224.

Phillips, P., Cummins, W. A. and Keen, L., 1988, The petrological identification of stone implements from Yorkshire: second report. In T. H. McK. Clough and W. A. Cummins (eds), *Stone Axe Studies Volume 2: the Petrology of Prehistoric Stone Implements from the British Isles*, 52–59. London: Council for British Archaeology (Research Report 67).

Piggott, S., 1954, *Neolithic Cultures of the British Isles*. Cambridge: Cambridge University Press.

Pitt-Rivers, A. L. F., 1898, *Excavations in Cranborne Chase, Volume IV*. Privately printed.

Pitts, M., 1996, The stone axe in Neolithic Britain. *Proceedings of the Prehistoric Society* 62, 311–372.

Radley, J., 1968, The York hoard of flint tools, 1868. *Yorkshire Archaeological Journal* 42, 131–132.

Rankine, W. F. R., 1938, Tranchet axes of south western Surrey. *Surrey Archaeological Collections* 46, 98–113.

Rankine, W. F. R., 1961, Mesolithic folk movements in southern England: further evidence from Oakhanger, Hants. Phase II. *Archaeological News Letter* 7(3), 63–65.

RCHME (Royal Commission on Historical Monuments, England), 1972, *An Inventory of the Historical Monuments in the City of York. Vol. III. South-west of the Ouse.* London: HMSO.

Richardson, C, 1990, A catalogue of acquisitions to Carlisle and reported finds from the Cumbrian Area *Transactions Cumberland and Westmorland Antiquarian and Archaeological Society* 90, 1–98.

Sanford, R., 1970, Neolithic Twickenham. *London Archaeologist* 1(9), 199–201.

Saunders, N., 1994, At the mouth of the obsidian cave: deity and place in Aztec religion. In D. L. Carmichael, J. Hubert, B. Reeves and A. Schanche (eds), *Sacred Sites, Sacred Places*, 172–183. London and New York: Routledge.

Saville, A., 1999, An exceptional polished flint axehead from Bolshan Hill, near Montrose, Angus. *Tayside and Fife Archaeological Journal* 5, 1–6.

Saville, A., 2004, A polished flint axehead from near Hayscastle, Pembrokeshire, Wales, and its typological context. In R. Cleal and J. Pollard (eds), *Monuments and Material Culture: Papers in Honour of an Avebury Archaeologist – Isobel Smith*, 225–230. East Knoyle: The Hobnob Press.

Serjeantson, D., Field, D., Penn, D. and Shipley, M., 1992, Excavations at Eden Walk II Kingston: environmental reconstruction and prehistoric finds. *Surrey Archaeological Collections* 81(1991–1992), 71–90.

Sheridan, A., 1992, Scottish stone axeheads: some new work and recent discoveries. In N. Sharples and A. Sheridan (eds), *Vessels for the Ancestors: Essays on the Neolithic of Britain and Ireland in Honour of Audrey Henshall*, 195–212 Edinburgh: Edinburgh University Press.

Shotton, F. W., 1934, Stone implements of Warwickshire. *Transactions and Proceedings of the Birmingham Archaeological Society* 58, 37–52.

Shotton, F. W., 1959, New petrological groups based on axes from the west Midlands. *Proceedings of the Prehistoric Society* 25, 135–143.

Shotton, F. W., 1988, The petrological identification of stone implements from the west Midlands: third report. In T. H. McK. Clough and W. A. Cummins (eds), *Stone Axe Studies Volume 2: the Petrology of Prehistoric Stone Implements from the British Isles*, 49–51. London: Council for British Archaeology (Research Report 67).

Smith, I. F., 1969, A flint axe from Bere Regis. *Proceedings of the Dorset Natural History and Archaeological Society* 91, 174.

Smith, R. A., 1922, Hoards of celts. *Archaeologia* 71(1921–22), 113–124.

Smith, R. A., 1926, *A Guide to Antiquities of the Stone Age in the Department of British and Medieval Antiquities* (3rd edition). London: British Museum.

Spindler, K., 1994, *The Man in the Ice*. London: Weidenfeld & Nicolson.

Thomas, N., 1974, An archaeological gazetteer for Warwickshire: Neolithic to Iron Age. *Transactions of the Birmingham and Warwickshire Archaeological Society* 86, 16–48.

Thurnam, J., 1867, Leaf and lozenge-shaped flint javelin-heads from an oval barrow near Stonehenge. *Wiltshire Archaeological and Natural History Society Magazine* 11, 40–49.

Topping, P., 2004, The South Downs flint mines: towards an ethnography of prehistoric flint extraction. In J. Cotton and D. Field (eds), *Towards a New Stone Age: Aspects of the Neolithic in South-east England*, 177–190. York: Council for British Archaeology (Research Report 137).

Topping, P., 2005, Shaft 27 revisited: an ethnography of Neolithic flint extraction. In P. Topping and M. Lynott (eds), *The Cultural Landscape of Prehistoric Mines*, 63–93. Oxford: Oxbow Books.

Tyler, A., 1976, *Neolithic Flint Axes from the Cotswold Hills*. Oxford: British Archaeological Reports (British Series 25).

Varndell, G., 2004, The Great Baddow hoard and discoidal knives: more questions than answers. In A. Gibson and A. Sheridan (eds), *From Sickles to Circles: Britain and Ireland at the Time of Stonehenge*, 116–122. Stroud: Tempus.

Warne, C., 1866, *The Celtic Tumuli of Dorset*. London: Russell Smith.

Warren, S. E., 1977, Excavation of a Neolithic site at Sefton Street, Putney, London. *Transactions of the London and Middlesex Archaeological Society* 28, 1–13.

Wooldridge, S. W. and Linton, D. L., 1933, The loam-terrains of southeast England and their relation to its early history. *Antiquity* 7(3), 297–310.

Chapter 9

Neolithic territories and lithic production: some examples from the Paris basin and neighbouring regions

François Giligny

INTRODUCTION

This study is part of an ongoing research project on the archaeology of the Paris basin, carried out by the CNRS unit *Archéologies et sciences de l'antiquité*, based at the Maison de l'Archéologie et de l'Ethnologie, Nanterre. The broad aim of the project is to study territories, exchange, and communication networks within this unique geographical and historical entity, from the Palaeolithic up to modern times.

The particular aim here is to examine territories and the role of lithic raw material extraction and production sites in the Seine basin during the Neolithic. Whilst 'producer' sites are indeed central to the diffusion process, they are not necessarily located in the geographical centre of a territory, and their distribution should be analysed in relation to other sites such as settlements, burials, and places of communal assembly. A number of territorial models have been established in the Neolithic contexts of Linear Pottery (LBK) or flint mines. This article will review models of territory which take into account the organization of lithic production, and will apply these models to Neolithic use of Bartonian Tertiary flint in a sector of the Seine valley, in the north Yvelines.

The Paris basin chronological sequence includes the successive early Neolithic phases (LBK and Villeneuve-Saint-Germain), then the middle Neolithic I (Cerny, Rössen and post-Rössen), middle Neolithic II (Chasséen or Michelsberg), late Neolithic (Seine-Oise-Marne) and final Neolithic (Gord-Bell Beaker) (Figure 9.1). The emergence of flint mines, a significant moment in the development of lithic production systems, dates to the beginning of the middle Neolithic in the mid-5th millennium BC. Little is known about earlier extraction modes. However, specialized manufacturing sites controlling the distribution of lithic products were already present in the early Neolithic.

THE START OF THE NEOLITHIC: LBK AND VILLENEUVE-SAINT-GERMAIN

In the LBK of the Hesse region and the Rhineland, certain lithic production sites are considered to be central in a territory. This pattern is also apparent after the LBK, in the Villeneuve-Saint-Germain of the Paris basin.

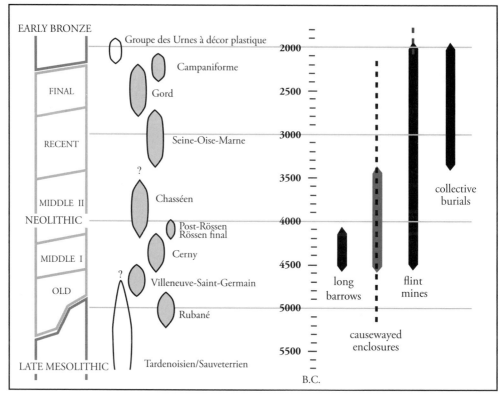

Figure 9.1. Chronology of the Seine valley Neolithic, showing the main cultural developments.

The Hesse and Rhineland LBK

Current models for the LBK portray settlement as a set of hierarchical spatial structures, increasing in size and function. The notion of settlement group has been put forward to describe the concentration of sites within a small region still termed 'micro-area' (Lüning 1998, fig.1).

Andreas Zimmerman was the first to use lithic data to identify internal organization and central places within a micro-area, on the basis of evidence from the Aldenhoven plateau (Kegler-Graiewski and Zimmerman 2003; Zimmerman 1995). Here, settlements are grouped along the middle Merzbach valley, with seven or eight sites for an area covering six square kilometres. Zimmerman observed that the quantity and quality of flint materials and debitage products varied between sites and that, in particular, greater quantities of tools were produced on the site of Langweiler 8. This settlement was seen as a flint 'producer' and distributor site, showing favoured relations with the Rijckohlt flint sources (Figure 9.2a). In fact this settlement is the largest in surface area (up to 7 ha at any one time) and has the longest occupation sequence. It is also the founder site, since it was the earliest occupation of the micro-area in the 'Flomborn' stage. According to the model, the other sites, termed 'secondary', also probably specialized in certain products which were exchanged with the central site. These may have included pottery or an unidentified product which required the digging of special narrow pits (*Schlitzgruben*). The central place would have maintained favoured relations with the outside in terms of procurement and redistribution. These relations are seen by Zimmerman as 'hereditary in character', and his interpretation is that this was a ranked society (Zimmerman 1995, 106–107). Other less common features such as enclosures and ovens may well have had functions indicating complementarity between sites. The relative diversity of pottery decoration in the Langweiler 8 enclosure, compared to other features on the settlement, could reflect the micro-regional role, suggesting that the enclosure was used by people other than the inhabitants of the site itself.

This notion of central place has been applied to Hesse by Kneipp (1995), using data from surface survey. The central places in this region are characterized by items such as figurines, grindstones and polishers, and seem more likely to be associated with cemeteries. There are favoured long-distance relations involving materials and certain settlements are located near raw materials sources, such as quartzite (Figure 9.2b).

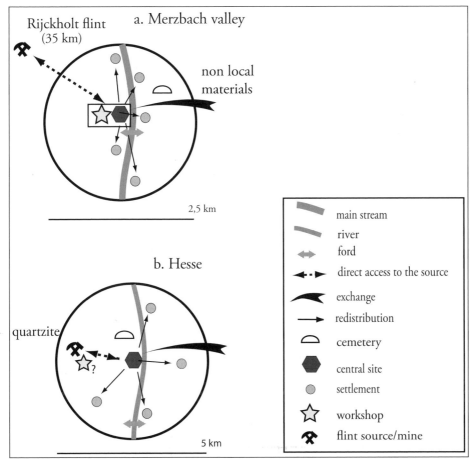

Figure 9.2. Models of micro-area territories for (a) the Merzbach valley and (b) Hesse, from the point of view of flint sources and production sites.

The Villeneuve-Saint-Germain in the Paris basin

The Villeneuve-Saint-Germain (VSG) follows after the LBK in the Paris basin. Françoise Bostyn, who has undertaken major studies of the lithic industries of this culture, applies the principle of central sites to the system of production-distribution of blades in Bartonian flint (Bostyn 1994; 1997; 2003a).

On the basis of a sample of 20 sites for which she studied the lithic industry and six other sites used for comparison, Bostyn has defined the characteristics of lithic production for this period. Raw materials were used for distinct products, depending on their source, which could either be local (0–5 km), regional (5–50 km) or exogenous (outside the Paris basin):

- local material, often flint of Secondary origin, is brought back on to the site for knapping;
- regional or extra-regional material is treated in a more variable manner – either unmodified blocks, shaped blocks or finished products (generally blades) are brought onto the settlement sites;
- exotic materials can be brought back from long-distance expeditions (>50 km); and
- exogeneous material from outside the Paris basin reaches the sites as finished products (unmodified or retouched flint blades, adze or axeheads in hard stone).

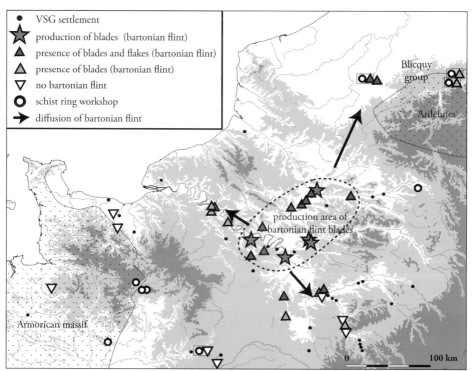

Figure 9.3. Geographical distribution of Villeneuve-Saint-Germain and Blicquy group sites, in relation to categories of Bartonian flint present (after Bostyn 1997, modified).

Two types of production occur together – production of flakes and blades and sometimes a few pieces made on blocks (bifacial tools). Materials also undergo different treatments, according to their origin. Flake production, which is predominant, is almost always on local flint. Blade production is on better quality flint, either Secondary or Tertiary Bartonian. Contrary to the *chaînes opératoires* for Secondary flint, the production of long, regular blades (>200 mm) in Bartonian flint is probably the work of specialist knappers in a village mode of production.

Only a few sites can be termed 'producer' sites for Bartonian flint blades. These are Jablines 'La Pente du Croupeton', Trosly-Breuil 'Les Obeaux' and Rungis 'ZAC des Antes', to which one can now add Epône 'La Mare-aux-Chevaux' and Ocquerre 'La Rocluche' (Bostyn 1997; Martial 1997a; Praud *et al.* 2002).

The production of these long blades in Bartonian flint is probably organized at regional scale from 'producer' sites which distribute blades or cores, or the knappers themselves travel (Figure 9.3). The blades are distributed as far as the Armorican massif and the Ardennes. Both the latter regions provide exogenous materials, such as the schist bracelets, which are mainly found on the 'producer' sites, notably in the form of roughouts and manufacturing waste. Circulation in two directions suggests that reciprocity was involved. The 'producer' sites for long blades would have played the role of redistributing to consumer sites not only Bartonian flint blades, but also schist bracelets and perhaps other items (Figure 9.4).

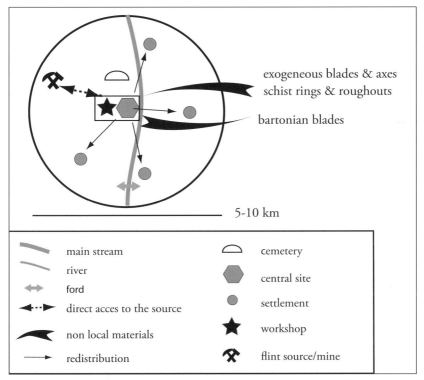

Figure 9.4. Territorial model for regions producing Bartonian flint blades in the Villeneuve-Saint-Germain.

The Mauldre basin in the Villeneuve-Saint-Germain

A research project underway since 1998 on the Neolithic in the Yvelines has led to the discovery of many new sites, and a territorial model has been elaborated (Bostyn *et al.* 2003; Giligny *et al.* 1998). Covering a surface area of about 600 km², the study region is located between Paris and Mantes, on the plateaux alongside two tributaries of the Seine, the Mauldre and the Vaucouleurs.

A blade 'producer' site has been identified at Epône 'La Mare-aux-Chevaux', providing almost 80 per cent of blades recorded in collections from the region. Field-walking on the site has recovered almost 30 blade cores and 400 blades or fragments. Other sites contain either a few cores and blade debitage waste, or blades with no debitage waste (Figure 9.5).

Two sites excavated at Neauphle-le-Vieux (Martial 1997b) and Bailly (unpublished) contain the same types of product in Bartonian flint: blade cores, partially cortical flakes and flakes without cortex, flake tools, crested blades, unmodified blades and blade tools. These products suggest that some of the blades were locally produced and show that the raw material source is relatively close to the site (distributed in the form of shaped blocks or cores?).

Furthermore, there is a dense concentration of schist ornaments in the north-west Yvelines. Surface collections and finds from recent excavations include over 200 fragments

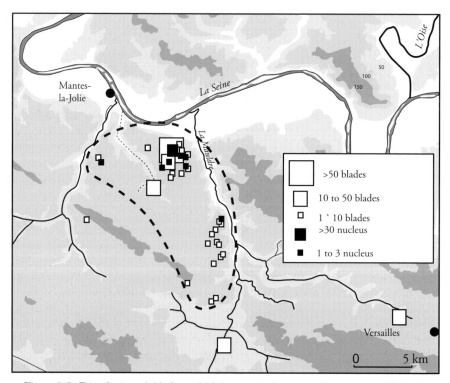

Figure 9.5. Distribution of blades and blade cores in Bartonian flint in the north Yvelines.

of schist bracelets, in a region over 150 km from the nearest outcrops of raw material, which occur close to Alençon. A first study of the source of these materials has identified the origin of some of the production (Fromont 2003 & 2008; Giligny *et al.* 1998; Praud 2000); this is a facies of mottled schist with cordierite, widespread in the thermo-metamorphic belts surrounding the granite massifs of the eastern Armorican massif (Vire, Athis, la Ferté-Macé region). Other materials, including ochre and blades in Bathonian flint, may also have come from lower Normandy. This evidence shows the contacts and exchange networks that were maintained between the two regions, Île-de-France and lower Normandy, in the early Neolithic.

The territory identified in the Yvelines region is organized around the blade 'producer' site of Epône, overlooking the river Seine, whilst other settlements occur on the fertile plateaux to the south and south-west, on the left bank of the Mauldre. It also appears that on the other bank of the Seine, as far as the Vexin and the Epte valleys, Bartonian flint blades are rare. The Seine seems to represent not only a territorial limit but also a factor constraining the circulation of products. These blades circulated downstream along the Seine as far as the Vaudreuil bend, just before the Eure-Seine confluence. They have been found in some Villeneuve-Saint-Germain sites here, such as Poses and Incarville (Bostyn 2003b).

FLINT MINES AND ENCLOSURES IN THE MIDDLE NEOLITHIC

The questions addressed by research on territories of the mid-5th millennium onwards – the middle Neolithic of the local Paris basin chronology – are territory size, and the identification of central sites and of the various entities making up a typical territory.

The development of enclosures and the question of their function are important aspects of territorial models in the Paris basin. Enclosures are unevenly distributed and are concentrated in certain zones such as the Yonne, Marne, Aisne and Oise valleys (Dubouloz *et al.* 1991). The models proposed distinguish types of site related to different levels of social integration (household, village, region), depending on their nature and size: large enclosures in valleys, plateau-edge enclosures, small enclosures in valleys, large villages in valleys, small occupations in valleys (Dubouloz 1989). Collective input increases with site rank. These sites also vary in terms of occupation remains.

The 'mining complex' concept emerged in France through analysis of data provided by large-scale rescue excavations. The term mining complex has been used to describe either a large group, 'within a single geomorphological entity', of similar or complementary sites involved in lithic production (extraction sites, knapping areas, *polissoirs*), as well as settlements and megaliths (Labriffe and Thébault 1995, 49), or a smaller group of 'sites exploiting the same flint, in more or less the same geological and topographical conditions' (Bostyn and Lanchon 1992, 221).

Both these definitions are illustrated by evidence from regions including the Pays d'Othe, the river Vanne in the Yonne, the Caen plain in Calvados, the Marne/Grand Morin confluence in the Seine-et-Marne, and the Mauldre valley in the Yvelines (Figure 9.6). In some regions mines are found together with enclosures, in others this is not the case. Several territoral models have been elaborated in the regions where there are both mines and

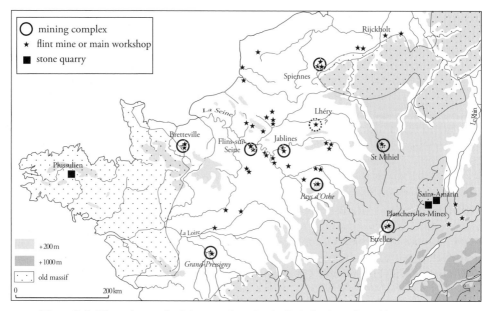

Figure 9.6. Flint mines and mining complexes in the Paris basin and neighbouring regions.

enclosures, such as the Yonne valley or the Caen plain. The example of products in quartz-pelite from the Vosges offers further illustration of the role of enclosures in the diffusion and control of mineral resources which also include salt. The discussion here will be limited to flint mines and the reader is referred to work published elsewhere for other aspects of this theme (e.g. Pétrequin and Jeunesse 1995; Pétrequin et al. 1998; Weller 2000).

The Yonne valley in the Cerny and Chasséen

A reconstruction of territorial organization in middle Neolithic I has been proposed for the Yonne valley, using evidence from excavations and aerial photographic survey. Enclosures and monumental cemeteries of Passy type attributed to the Cerny have been mapped (Delor *et al.* 1997). This region is close to one of the most important mining complexes in the Paris basin, the 'Pays d'Othe' complex in Burgundy. Several mines are adjacent to the Yonne valley (Labriffe and Thébault 1995).

In these models, 'sectors of favoured occupation' are described, consisting of spatial groups constrained by geomorphological features such as confluences, dry valleys and slopes. For the Cerny period of middle Neolithic I, the territory is composed of the following entities: long funerary monuments of Passy type, settlements, small and medium enclosures, and family cemeteries, as well as complementary natural features or resources, including confluences, fords, meanders, communication routes, forest, pasture, mines and groups of *polissoirs*. The territorial unit is modelled as a circle 30 km in diameter, thus covering about 700 km2 (Figure 9.7). This territorial model is transformed in middle Neolithic II, with the appearance of large enclosures such as Noyen-sur-Seine (Seine-et-Marne), which complete or replace certain elements of the earlier territorial unit. The large enclosures are located near the earlier monumental cemeteries of the Cerny, 'taking advantage of the clustering of population around the previously created poles' (Delor *et al.* 1997, 392). These authors interpret the segmentation of the territory in terms of social entities – 'the distribution of monumental enclosures could in fact confirm the division of the valleys into equidistant zones, in segments controlled by a "governing caste"' (Delor et al. 1997, 392), a social model similar to the ranked society evoked by Zimmerman.

The interest of this model is the integration of lithic production sites, mines and groups of *polissoirs* within territorial units. In this model, mines are located on the periphery rather than in the centre of territories. The schematic illustration (Figure 9.7) presents mines and *polissoirs* in separate but neighbouring entities, implying movement and complementarity, or even partial specialization of territories either in mining and roughout manufacture or in polishing. This dichotomy between producers and users has been suggested for other archaeological and ethno-archaeological models (Pétrequin and Jeunesse 1995).

In the absence of enclosures and Passy-type cemeteries, this model is not directly applicable to the Yvelines. It can be applied, however, to the Marne valley, which presents the same characteristics as the Yonne: a zone colonized by the LBK, densely occupied in the Villeneuve-Saint-Germain, with a mine, a Passy-type cemetery, and middle Neolithic II enclosures.

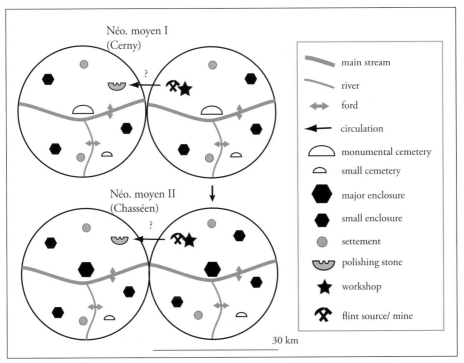

Figure 9.7. Territorial model for the Yonne valley in the Cerny and Chasséen phases (after Delor et al. 1997).

The mining complex on the Caen plain

In other regions, there is sufficient evidence to examine relations between mines and the other sites. This is the case with the Caen plain, to the south of the present-day city, between the rivers Laize and Laizon. This area was densely occupied in the Neolithic and the large numbers of sites can be used to establish a model for territories at the time when mining began, at the start of the middle Neolithic (Desloges 1986; 1999). On the plateaux on either side of the Laize there are several large flint-working and extraction sites, as well as fixed *polissoirs*, in proximity to an enclosed plateau-edge site (Figure 9.8).

The best known mine in this region is Bretteville-le-Rabet, an important site because the traces of mining activity cover almost 50 ha (Desloges 1999). The flint exploited is of Jurassic age, located in the middle Bathonian levels. Dating of the first use of the Bretteville mine is early and goes back to the Cerny phase, as does occupation on the 'Mont-Joly' plateau-edge enclosure at Soumont-Saint-Quentin. This site also has evidence for axehead production.

Other knapping sites and mines are known in this area, distributed around 'Mont-Joly' (Les Longrais, Olendon, Soignoles, Potigny). The diffusion zone where this raw material predominates has yet to be identified, however. Some axeheads have recently been found above the Seine valley. At a distance of 1–5 km there are drystone cairns dated to the Cerny or Chasséen at Ernes/Condé-sur-Ifs and Fontenay-le-Marmion, reflecting the attraction of this region and the state of development of local populations.

The mining complex at the Marne/Grand-Morin confluence

East of Paris, the mine of Jablines 'Le Haut Château' was excavated in 1979–1981 and 1989–1990, the second campaign covering an extensive surface in advance of high-speed

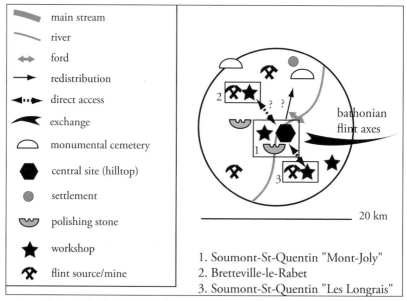

Figure 9.8. Territorial model for the mining complex on the Caen plain.

train-line construction (Bostyn and Lanchon 1992; Bulard *et al.* 1986). This is a large mine linked to the manufacture of axeheads, and these excavations have provided excellent data on extraction features and products. The material exploited is Bartonian flint, also used in the Villeneuve-Saint-Germain for blade production on another site nearby the mine at Jablines 'La Pente du Croupeton' (Bostyn 1994). Additional extraction sites have been found along a tributary of the Marne, the Grand-Morin, including Coupvray 'Les Chauds Soleils', and there are other possible sites known from field-walking around Couilly, Pont-aux-Dames and Bouleurs (Bostyn and Lanchon 1992, fig.215). With shafts covering an area of almost 15 ha, the Jablines mine is of considerable size. Around 800 extraction features were identified in the area investigated in 1989–1990, which represents 20 per cent of the mine. The features range from simple pits to bell-shaped pits and shafts with galleries up to 7m deep. Although most of the 17 radiocarbon dates fall between the late 5th and the first half of the 4th millennium BC, corresponding to the middle Neolithic, three dates from the area excavated in 1979–1981 lie close to 3000 BC (cf. Padzur in Bostyn and Lanchon 1992, 234).

The role of the various sites, mines and working areas and the diffusion of axeheads produced at Jablines and the surrounding region is not well known, because inventory work on surface collections and surveys of unexcavated sites have yet to be undertaken. On the other hand, there have been extensive excavations on settlements in the Marne valley in advance of gravel quarrying. The recent excavation of a middle Neolithic II enclosure at Vignely 'La Noue Fenard', not far from the Jablines mine and contemporary with it, raises the problem of the relationship between enclosure and mine in this region (Lanchon *et al.* 2001).

The status of products and producers is illustrated by graves found in the region. Radiocarbon dated to the middle Neolithic, several of these contain axeheads in Bartonian flint, quite probably originating from the Jablines mine. A single burial at Dampmart contained a flaked axehead (Brézillon 1973); a single burial of a child about five years old at Vignely 'La Porte aux Bergers' was accompanied by two partially polished axeheads, an axehead roughout and a flint flake (Bouchet *et al.* 1996, 38); and another undated burial on the same site contained a large polished axehead (Bouchet *et al.* 1996, 38). The grave of the young child suggests that community or family social status may have been connected with axehead production.

The mine at Flins-sur-Seine and the Mauldre mining complex

The mine at Flins-sur-Seine was first recognized as a flint-knapping site in 1926 by Silvestre de Sacy and M. Baudouin (1926; 1927), who noted similarities with finds from the Jablines mine. The raw material used is in fact Bartonian flint and the axehead roughouts closely resemble examples from Jablines. The actual presence of mine shafts was first revealed by aerial photography undertaken by the Yvelines *Service Archéologique Départemental* in 2000. Subsequently, a programme of fieldwalking and geophysical survey was initiated, revealing that the surface area with knapping waste covers 15 ha and the mine shafts cover between 3 and 5 ha. So far there has been no excavation on the site. Surface finds include a range of waste and abandoned items reflecting all the technical stages of axehead manufacture (bifacial preparations, roughouts, flaked axeheads), apart from polished objects. In addition, there are large tools on wide, thick blanks which may have been used for activities connected with mining, such as preparing the timbers required for shafts and galleries. Domestic tools are rare, and there are practically no sherds, polished tools, or grinding equipment. So this is a specialized extraction and knapping site, with the nearest settlements located 1.5 km away on the opposite bank of the river Mauldre, on the Epône plateau.

Further knapping sites producing axeheads in Bartonian flint are known in the region at Jumeauville 'La Croix de Jumeauville', Montainville 'La Fauconnerie' and 'Bloche', and Beynes 'Bois de Carcassonne' (Figure 9.9). Finds from these sites are identical to those from the Flins-sur-Seine mine, although there are smaller quantities of knapping waste. The sites are over 10 km from the mine and are located on the same geological formation, Saint-Ouen limestone. Whilst extraction sites in this geological context have yet to be discovered, they are likely to exist around the plateaus of the Mauldre, Vaucouleurs and Ru de Senneville, close to the axehead production sites. Sites working Campanian Secondary flint are also known, and a few mine shafts excavated at Maule 'Pousse-Motte' have been dated to between the end of the Neolithic and the early Bronze Age (Simon 1986). If

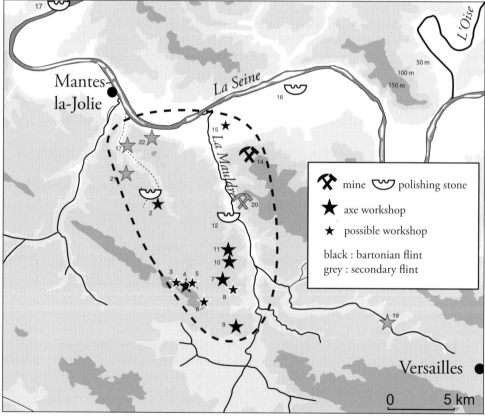

Figure 9.9. The Mauldre mining complex.

there had been another mine as important as the one at Flins in this region, it is hard to understand how it could have escaped discovery in an agricultural region explored by several generations of fieldwalkers. It thus seems probable that the Flins mine was the only major mining site and that it was worked for a long period of time.

The question must be raised of the possible existence of a central site controlling the system of production and diffusion of Bartonian flint axeheads in the Mauldre valley. Although no enclosures or hilltop sites are known in the Yvelines, one can look for potentially favourable locations for this kind of site. The most likely candidate is Jumeauville 'La Croix de Jumeauville', due not only to its geographical position and topography, but also to the fact that this was as an axehead 'producer' settlement occupied throughout most of the Neolithic (Figure 9.10). Close by the site, there are *in situ* sandstone *polissoirs* and on the site itself axehead roughouts as well as large numbers of pecking tools, presumably used for shaping the edges of roughouts. The site would have played a role not only in the production of roughouts, but also of polished axeheads, and was probably involved in their diffusion. From the geographical point of view, the site is centrally located on the plateau, at an equal distance from the Mauldre and the Vaucouleurs, with access to the Seine along the Senneville stream. Bounded to the east and west by fairly steep slopes, the site forms a triangular area of about 25 ha, overlooking the stream and a dry gully. It may have been enclosed on the south side by a bank and ditch system. This hypothesis will be tested by future geophysical survey. Even without a system of ditch, bank or palisade, the site certainly played a central role in the production and circulation of Bartonian flint axeheads in the Mauldre basin.

Study of surface collections (Lo Carmine 2002) has shown that Bartonian flint axeheads were widely distributed throughout the north Yvelines and beyond, in the Val d'Oise,

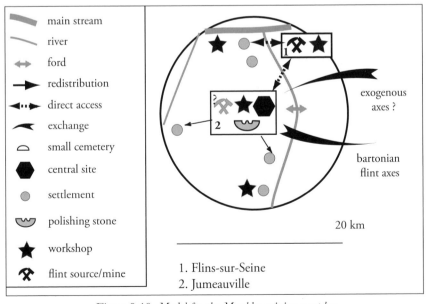

Figure 9.10. Model for the Mauldre mining complex.

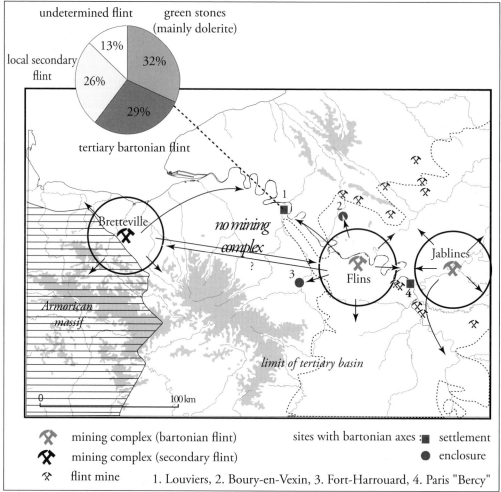

Figure 9.11. Geographical organization of Neolithic axehead productions in the north-west Paris basin.

Eure, and Eure-et-Loire. There are still connections with lower Normandy, indicated by the presence in the Yvelines and Val d'Oise of a few Bathonian flint axeheads similar to those from the Bretteville-le-Rabet mine. Bartonian flint axeheads must have circulated in the opposite direction, since a small number have been found in lower Normandy (Figure 9.11).

Diffusion eastwards is difficult to evaluate, however. The raw material worked at Flins is identical to the flint from Jablines and the axehead types are very similar.

CONCLUSION

The various examples described here illustrate the importance for territorial organization of sites specialized in lithic extraction and/or production, in the same manner as the 'producer' sites of the Rhineland LBK or the Paris basin Villeneuve-Saint-Germain. However, the extraction sites are frequently located in marginal situations and some lie outside the territory.

From the second half of the 5th millennium BC in France, corresponding to the Paris basin middle Neolithic, there is an obvious link between the development of hierarchically organized territories and intensification of lithic production, notably of axeheads. The relation between increasing social complexity and spatial patterning of product and territories is quite clear. Although it is not always the case, the network of central sites of enclosed type seems denser in regions with mining complexes. These regions are often close to the first areas of Neolithic colonization and to areas with the highest population.

It remains to be seen to what extent flint axehead production influenced social developments and the regional organization of territories from the beginning of the Paris basin middle Neolithic. More needs to be known too about the relationship between the flint axehead network and stone axeheads originating from both the Armorican massif and the Alps. The Seine valley can well be seen as a circulation and exchange route, serving as a geographical interchange for the diffusion of Armorican and Alpine axeheads.

BIBLIOGRAPHY

Bostyn, F., 1994, Caractérisation des productions et de la diffusion des industries lithiques du groupe néolithique du Villeneuve-Saint-Germain. Thèse de Doctorat, Université de Paris X, 2 vols.

Bostyn, F., 1997, Characterization of flint production and distribution of the tabular Bartonian Flint during the early Neolithic (Villeneuve-Saint-Germain period) in France. In R. Schild and Z. Sulgostowska (eds), *Man and Flint. Proceedings of the VIIth International Flint Symposium*, 171–183. Warszawa: Institute of Archaeology and Ethnology, Polish Academy of Sciences

Bostyn, F., 2003a, De la lame à la hache: contextes geologiques et socio-économiques des productions en silex tertiaire bartonien du bassin parisien au néolithique. In F. Surmely (ed.), *Les matières premières lithiques en préhistoire, Table-ronde internationale, Aurillac (20–22 juin 2002)*, 63–70. Préhistoire du Sud-Ouest, supplément n°5.

Bostyn, F. (ed.), 2003b, *Le village Villeneuve-Saint-Germain de Poses 'Sur la Mare' et les sites de la boucle du Vaudreuil*. Paris: Société Préhistorique Française (Travaux 4).

Bostyn, F. and Lanchon, Y. (eds), 1992, *Jablines, Le Haut Château (Seine-et-Marne): une minière de silex au Néolithique*. Paris: Maison des Sciences de l'Homme (Documents d'Archéologie Française 35).

Bostyn, F., Giligny, F., Lo Carmine, A., Martial, E. and Praud, I., 2003, Production et circulation des objets en silex tertiaire bartonien dans le nord des Yvelines. In F. Surmely (ed.), *Les matières premières lithiques en préhistoire, table-ronde internationale, Aurillac (20–22 juin 2002)*, 51–62. Préhistoire du Sud-Ouest, supplément n°5.

Bouchet, M., Brunet, P., Jacobieski, G., and Lanchon, Y., 1996, *Il y a 7000 ans en vallée de Marne... Premiers labours, premiers villages...* Catalogue de l'exposition, APRAIF/Musée municipal de Lagny-sur-Marne/SHALE.

Brézillon, M., 1973, Information archéologiques. Région parisienne. *Gallia Préhistoire* 16, 346.

Bulard, A., Degros, J. and Tarrête, J., 1986, Premières fouilles sur le site néolithique d'extraction du silex du Haut-Château à Jablines (Seine-et-Marne). *Revue Archéologique de l'Ouest*, supplément n°1, 55–70 (Actes du Xe Colloque Interrégional sur le Néolithique, Caen 1983).

Delor, J.-P., Genreau, F., Heurteaux, A., Jacob, J.-P., Lerrede, H., Nouvel, P. and Pellet, C., 1997, L'implantation des nécropoles monumentales au sud du Bassin parisien. In C. Constantin, D. Mordant, and D. Simonin (eds), *La culture de Cerny, nouvelle économie, nouvelle société au Néolithique*: 381–395. Nemours: APRAIF (Memoirs du Musée de Préhistoire d'Île-de-France 6).

Desloges, J., 1986, Fouilles de mines à silex sur le site néolithique de Bretteville-le-Rabet (Calvados), *Revue Archéologique de l'Ouest*, supplément n°1, 73–101 (Actes du Xe Colloque Interrégional sur le Néolithique, Caen 1983).

Desloges, J., 1999, Une mine de silex au Néolithique. L'exemple de Bretteville-le-Rabet. In G. San Juan and J. Maneuvrier, *L'exploitation ancienne des roches dans le Calvados : histoire et archéologie*, 53–77. Couleurs Calvados: SDAC-Société historique de Lisieux.

Dubouloz, J., 1989, Problématique de recherche sur les enceintes néolithiques de la vallée de l'Aisne: un exemple représentatif du Bassin parisien. In A. D'anna and X. Gutherz (eds), *Enceintes, habitats ceinturés, sites perchés du néolithique au bronze ancien dans le sud de la France et les régions voisines*, 55–67. Montpellier: Mémoire de la Société Languedocienne de Préhistoire, n°2.

Dubouloz, J., Mordant, D. and Prestreau, M., 1991, Les enceintes 'néolithiques' du Bassin Parisien. In A. Beeching, D. Binder and C. Blanchet (eds), *Identité du Chasséen (Actes du colloque international de Nemours 1989)*, 211–229. Nemours: Apraif (Mémoires du musée de Préhistoire de l'Île de France 4).

Fromont, N., 2003, Anneaux en pierre et culture de Villeneuve-Saint-Germain/Blicquy: premiers éléments sur la structuration des productions et la circulation des matières premières entre Massif armoricain et Massif ardennais. In F. Surmely (ed.), *Les matières premières lithiques en préhistoire, Table-ronde, Aurillac (20–22 juin 2002)*, 177–183. Préhistoire du Sud-Ouest, supplément n°5.

Fromont, N., 2008, Les anneaux du Néolithique bas-normand et du nord-Sarthe: production, circulation et territoire. *Bulletin de la Société Préhistorique Française* 105(1), 55–86.

Giligny, F., Martial, E. and Praud, I., 1998, Premiers éléments sur l'occupation des Yvelines au Néolithique. *Internéo 2*, 43–55 (Journée d'information du 14 novembre 1998, Paris).

Kegler-Graiewski, N. and Zimmermann, A., 2003, Exchange systems of stone artefacts in the European Neolithic. In L. Burnez-Lanotte (ed.), *Production and Management of Lithic Materials in the European Linearbandkeramik*, 31–35. Oxford: British Archaeological Reports (International Series 1200).

Kneipp, J., 1995, Frühbäuerliche Siedlungsverbände an Diemsel, Esse und unterer Fulda. Gedanken zur sozialen und wirtschaftlichen Struktur vor 7000 Jahren. *Zeitschrift des Vereins für hessische Geschichte und Landeskunde* 100, 1–19.

Labriffe, P.-A. de and Thébault, D., 1995, Mines de silex et grands travaux, l'autoroute A5 et les sites d'extraction du Pays d'Othe. In J. Pelegrin and A. Richard (eds), *Les mines de silex au Néolithique en Europe: avancées récentes*, 47–67. Paris: CTHS.

Lanchon, Y., Brunet, V., Brunet, P. and Chambon, P., 2001, Le site néolithique de Vignely 'La Noue Fenard' (Seine-et-Marne). In Service Régional de l'Archéologie d'Île-de-France, *Actes des Journées Archéologiques d'Île-de-France*, 64–77. Paris : Institut d'art et d'archéologie.

Lo Carmine, A., 2002, *Grandes lames de haches et ateliers de fabrication dans le nord des Yvelines*. Mémoire de DEA de l'Université de Paris 1 Panthéon-Sorbonne.

Lüning, J., 1998, L'organisation régionale des habitats rubanés: sites centraux et sites secondaires (groupements de sites). *Anthropologie et Préhistoire* 109, 163–185.

Martial, E., 1997a, Une production laminaire en silex tertiaire du Villeneuve-Saint-Germain à Epône 'La Mare aux Chevaux' (Yvelines). *Bulletin du Centre de Recherches Archéologiques de la Région Mantaise* 14, 25–45.

Martial, E., 1997b, L'industrie du silex. In F. Giligny (ed.), Les occupations pré- et prothistoriques du Vallon de la Guyonne, Neauphle-Le-Vieux 'Le Moulin de Lettrée' (Yvelines), 209–248. (Document Final de Synthèse, unpublished)

Pétrequin, P. and Jeunesse, C. (eds), 1995, *La hache de Pierre. Carrières vosgiennes et échanges de lames polies pendant le Néolithique (5400–2100 av. J.-C.)*. Paris: Errance.

Pétrequin, P., Pétrequin, A.-M., Jeudy, F., Jeunesse, C., Monnier, J.-L., Pelegrin, J. and Praud, I., 1998, From the raw material to the Neolithic stone axe: production processes and social context. In M. Edmonds and C. Richards (eds), *Understanding the Neolithic of North-Western Europe*, 277–311. Glasgow: Cruithne Press.

Praud, I., 2000, Les Bracelets en schiste du néolithique ancien Villeneuve Saint-Germain (V.S.G.) dans les Yvelines. *Bulletin du Centre de recherches archéologiques de la région mantaise* 15, 17–24.

Praud, I., Bostyn, F., Martial, E. and Michel, L., 2002, Un site Villeneuve-Saint-Germain dans la vallée de l'Ourcq. *Internéo* 4, 13–22.

Silvestre De Sacy, L. and Baudouin, M., 1926, La station campignienne du Clos, à Flins-sur-Seine (Seine-et-Oise). *Bulletin de la Société des Sciences de Seine-et-Oise*, fasc. 4, 2e série, t. VII, 49–62.

Silvestre De Sacy, L. and Baudouin, M., 1927, La station campignienne du Clos, à Flins-sur-Seine (Seine-et-Oise). *Bulletin de la Société des Sciences de Seine-et-Oise*, fasc. 4, 2e série, t. VIII, 50–58.

Simon, P., 1986, Le site protohistorique de Pousse Motte à Maule (Yvelines), *Bulletin de la Société Préhistorique Française* 83, 271–280.

Weller, O., 2000, Produire du sel par le feu: techniques et enjeux socio-économiques dans le Néolithique européen. In P. Pétrequin, P. Fluzin, J. Thiriot and P. Benoit (eds), *Arts du feu et productions artisanales*, 565–584. Antibes: Editions ADPCA.

Zimmerman, A., 1995, *Austauschsysteme von Silexartefakten in der Bandkeramik Mitteleuropas*. Bonn: Habelt (Universitätsforschungen zur prähistorischen Archäologie 26).

Chapter 10

Why do people use exotic raw materials? The case of obsidian in the Near East during the Halaf Period

Elizabeth Healey

INTRODUCTION

Recent studies of lithic raw materials in Europe have demonstrated the potential of comprehensive and integrated studies which combine raw material characterization, acquisition at source, manufacturing techniques, function and context (among others Andrefsky 1994; Bradley and Edmonds 1993; Pétrequin *et al.* 1998; Tykot and Ammerman 1997). Preliminary results of the analyses of two lithic assemblages of late Neolithic date in south-eastern Turkey, in which obsidian, an exotic raw material, has a numerically minor role, and a third assemblage where obsidian is more commonly used, suggest along with analogous studies at other sites (e.g. Carter *et al.* 2006a; Maeda 2003), that our understanding of how and why obsidian usage was so widespread could be greatly enhanced through such an approach.

The location of obsidian sources in Anatolia together with the distribution of artefacts made of these obsidians throughout the Near East have been studied since the 1960s and most recently summarized in Cauvin *et al.* (1998). On the basis of this information various models of distribution have been constructed which have shaped our interpretation of the relevance of obsidian as a raw material (see Cauvin 1998, 259–260 for an overview). However, there are inherent problems with these broad models in that in most instances not only is there little consideration of the geography, the environment or the nature of society (Chataigner *et al.* 1998, 535), but also only a few artefacts from any one site have been analysed and we often do not know if they are representative of the assemblage as a whole and we have no idea of the proportion from each source or whether some sources were preferred above others. Indeed in later periods the assemblages are not well known at all. Also, some of the sources are not too well characterized (Chataigner 1998; Chataigner *et al.* 1998; Poidevin 1998) because only a few geological samples may have been analysed, sometimes even without precise location, so that intra-source variation may be masked. There are a number of factors which may explain this situation including the expense of analysis, its often destructive nature, and export difficulties, particularly for any quantity of material or for museum-quality artefacts. The case-studies outlined below, together with a review of the wider picture, suggest ways of overcoming some of these constraints and of understanding obsidian within a wider framework and so allow us to begin to address the question of why exotic raw materials were so attractive to prehistoric peoples.

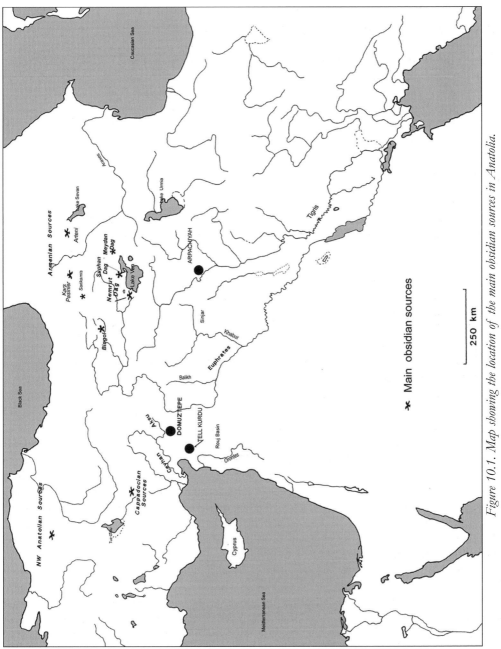

Figure 10.1. Map showing the location of the main obsidian sources in Anatolia.

OVERVIEW

The obsidian sources in Anatolia

Most of the sources were originally distinguished from each other using binary diagrams plotting certain elements such as zirconium and barium against each other using a logarithmic scale (Renfrew *et al.* 1966; 1968) or through other ratios (Blackman 1984) or multivariate analaysis, although now the preferred way of presenting data is though multi-elemental spidergrams normalized to the earth's crust (Chataigner *et al.* 1998, 518).

The principle sources of obsidian exploited for artefact manufacture in the Near East are shown in Figure 10.1. Most were first characterized by Renfrew (Renfrew *et al.* 1966; 1968) and comprise sources in central Anatolia (principally Göllüdağ-east and Nenezi Dağ, but other sources too), in south-east Anatolia (Bingöl calc-alkaline, Bingöl/Nemrut Dağ per-alkaline, and Meydan Dağ), and in north-east Anatolia and Armenia (Pasinler, Kars and Arteni). New sources have recently been identified north of Ankara, for example Yaklar and Sakaeli (Poidevin 1998, 107–109), and at Bayburt near Pasinler (Brennan 2000) as well as elsewhere in eastern Anatolia (Kobayashi and Sagona 2007). There are also unlocated sources established through artefact analysis such as Renfrew's 3d source probably located in eastern Turkey (Chataigner *et al.* 1998, 534). We are also now, thanks to an integrated programme of research on the Göllüdağ-east source area (Binder and Balkan-Atlı 2001), coming to appreciate the geological complexity of the obsidian there. For example, at least six flows are now known (Poidevin 1998, 115–121), even though at the moment it is not possible to distinguish them geochemically (Poupeau *et al.* 2005). Also there is still some difficulty in separating some of the flows on Nemrut Dağ (Poidevin 1998, 141). However, the separation of the Nemrut Dağ and the Bingöl per-alkaline obsidians, for a long time not easily distinguishable, is now possible both through dating the flows and through more precise geo-chemical analysis (Chataigner *et al.* 1998, table 1; Poidevin 1998, 140–141). This will allow differences in distribution of each source to be identified (Chataigner *et al.* 1998, 530).

Quarrying and workshops

Generally speaking little is known about workshops at sources especially in eastern Anatolia, but recently a major advance has been made in Cappadocia at the Göllüdağ-east source. So far no evidence of quarrying or extracting obsidian has been found (Binder and Balkan-Atlı 2001, 3; Binder pers. comm.). However, there are a number of things which suggest that quarrying was practised, for example substantial deposits of workshop debitage – it is estimated that for a single production unit involving the manufacture of 1500 points and 4500–6000 prismatic blades about 10 tonnes of debitage would be produced (Binder 2002, 80) – have been carefully disposed of in what are presumed to be previously quarried areas, indicating careful management of the quarrying space (Balkan-Atlı *et al.* 1999, 140). Also it is probable that the highly standardized techniques of blade production practised at one workshop (see below) would require large blocks of unaltered obsidian (rather than surface or weathered blocks) for successful detachment and consistent results and it is considered that they are likely to have been obtained by quarrying (Binder pers. comm.). Selective use of sources and quarry planning and management are of course documented in other circumstances, for example at Great Langdale and elsewhere in the European Neolithic (Bradley and Edmonds 1993, chap. 4), including flint mines such as Grimes Graves (Barber *et al.* 1999, 47), as well as ethnographically. A key to our understanding of the complexity of obsidian acquisition and distribution is provided by the workshops at, and sites near, the Göllüdağ-east and Nenezi Dağ sources where a number of different reduction technologies have been identified.

Particularly interesting are two workshops (Bitikeler and Kaletepe) at different outcrops on Göllüdağ (Kayırlı and Kömürcü) both of which have plentiful and excellent quality obsidian. Each workshop had distinctive products and different dispersal patterns. Products from the Bitikeler workshop are found in central Anatolia throughout the PPNB in the Levant and Cyprus (Balkan-Atlı and der Aprahamian 1998, 241–247; Binder and Balkan-Atlı 2001, 14–15) whereas the eponymous and highly specialised naviform blades produced at the Kaletepe workshop can be paralleled in the Levant (Balkan-Atlı *et al.* 1999, 139; Binder 2002, 81; Binder and Balkan-Atlı 2001, 12). At this stage it is not clear whether this is due to chronological differences or other factors.

Nevertheless, and despite these important discoveries, most of our understanding of the dispersal of obsidian is very general and subject to change as source areas and assemblages are studied. Still very little is known about workshops at or dispersal from the eastern sources although the study of caches of blades from the PPNB and PN sites of Tell Sabi Abyad II and Tell Damishliyya has led to the suggestion that, in some instances at least, small bundles of blades may have been exchanged rather than blade production taking place at each site or through localized redistribution systems (Astruc *et al.* 2007, 335ff).

Obsidian use – an overview

Obsidian was used in the Palaeolithic period at or near sources (see for example Balkan-Atlı *et al.* 1999, 137; Yalçinkaya 1998) but thus far there is no clear evidence of wide dispersal of obsidian before the Epi-palaeolithic. Around 10,000 cal BC, however, blades and fragments of blades of Göllüdağ-east obsidians are found in small quantities in the Levant some 900 km from source – probably the result of exchange between mobile groups rather than trade (Cauvin and Chataigner 1998, 331). At about this time at Pinarbaşı on the Konya Plain there is clear evidence of working of obsidian from Cappadocian sources (Baird 2006). Similarly in eastern Anatolia, at about the same time the village of Hallan Çemi (which generally showed connections with the earlier Zarzian industries rather than those of the Levant) used obsidian obtained from Nemrut Dağ and both the Bingöl calc-alkaline and per-alkaline sources at least 100 km distant, for about 50 per cent of its tool-kit (Rosenberg 1994, 225; 1999). Obsidian from the Bingöl/Nemrut Dağ region reaches the Levant a little later in the early Pre-Pottery Neolithic at Aswad and Mureybit, where obsidians from both source areas are found (Cauvin and Chataigner 1998, 333). More extensive use of obsidian begins in the Pre-Pottery Neolithic (PPN) and reaches its peak in the early to middle PPNB when 70 per cent of the known sites have obsidian (Chataigner *et al.* 1998, 535), corresponding to the spread of agriculture into sites in the Taurus (Binder and Balkan-Atlı 2001, 15). Çayönü, for example, shows an increase in the use of obsidian through time coupled with a change in technology (Caneva *et al.* 1994, 263) and sites in upper Mesopotamia such as Tell Magzaliyah (300 km from the sources) also have a large amount of obsidian

(Cauvin 2000, 174–75). By the Halaf period (late Neolithic) a change in emphasis in the distribution patterns can be seen – eastern sources are preferred and new sources start to be exploited such as the Meydan Dağ source, the obsidians from which often accompany the per-alkaline obsidians from Nemrut Dağ (Cauvin and Chataigner 1998, 345; Chataigner 1998, 313; Renfrew *et al.* 1966, 48).

In brief, the exploitation of the obsidians from Cappadocian sources and those from eastern Anatolian sources seem to have started independently and in general terms the distributions seem to continue to respect each other, although there is an overlap in the Levant where the middle Euphrates forms the dividing line between the eastern and western distribution areas (Figure 10.2), with very rare occurrences of Göllüdağ obsidian reported in the eastern area (Chataigner *et al.* 1998, fig. 3) or eastern obsidians in the west (although a few pieces have been identified at Catalhoyuk (Carter pers. comm.)).

With this background in mind the following discussion will focus on the approaches used in the study of three Halaf period (end of the Pottery Neolithic) sites to identify the different obsidians present and the milieu in which they were worked and used.

CASE-STUDIES

The assemblages to be considered are from the recently excavated Halaf levels of the sites of Domuztepe, near Kahramanmaraş, and Tell Kurdu in the Amuq, both in south-east Turkey. Data from a recent study of the lithic artefacts from the broadly contemporary site of Tell Arpachiyah in northern Iraq are also included (Figure 10.1). 'Halaf' is a term used to describe a late Neolithic culture (sixth millennium BC) in northern Mesopotamia (Figure 10.3) believed to have had wide-spread connections and characterized by highly painted pottery, figurines, and stamp seals. The sites are generally small (under 10 ha) although occasionally there are larger ones such as Domuztepe, Tell Kurdu and Kazane (Breniquet 1996; Campbell 1997; 1999).

Domuztepe is a long, low mound of about 20 hectares located in the valley of the Aksu river. Excavation began in 1995 by a joint team from the University of Manchester, UK, and the University of California, Los Angeles (Campbell 1999), and is ongoing. The excavated levels span about 500 years between *c.* 6000–5500 cal BC and are divided into three phases (A-1, A-2, A-3). So far about 1900 sq m have been excavated – approximately one per cent of the site, the largest single exposure (Operation I) is 1600 sq m (Figure 10.4) – and most of the lithic artefacts discussed below come from this area. Architecturally there are rectilinear one- or two-roomed buildings and less common circular buildings (often termed 'tholoi'), probably used for special functions including storage. There is a rich assemblage of artefacts including painted ceramics – some of the decoration showing a high degree of sophistication – stamp seals, bijouterie, stone bowls, axeheads and mace-heads, as well as bone tools, ground-stone, and chipped-stone assemblages of both flint and obsidian. Most of the raw materials used are of local or regional origin but obsidian originates from much further afield (obsidian from sources 250 km to 900 km away are documented), as do materials such as silver and marine shells. The pottery shows the clearest links with northern Mesopotamia but there are also links to the Levant and lesser ties to central Anatolia (Campbell pers. comm.).

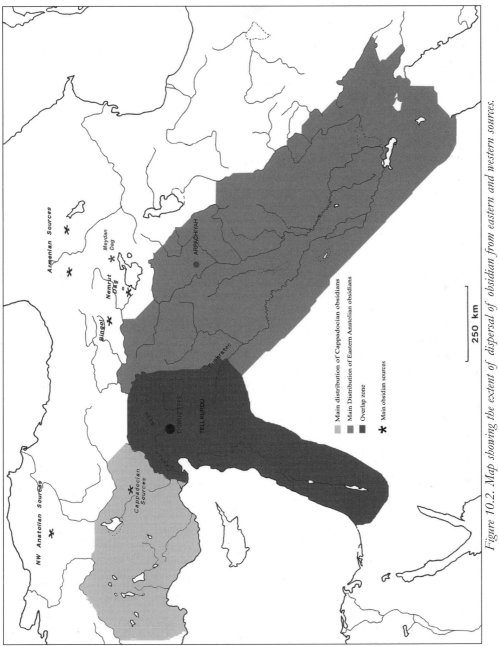

Figure 10.2. Map showing the extent of dispersal of obsidian from eastern and western sources.

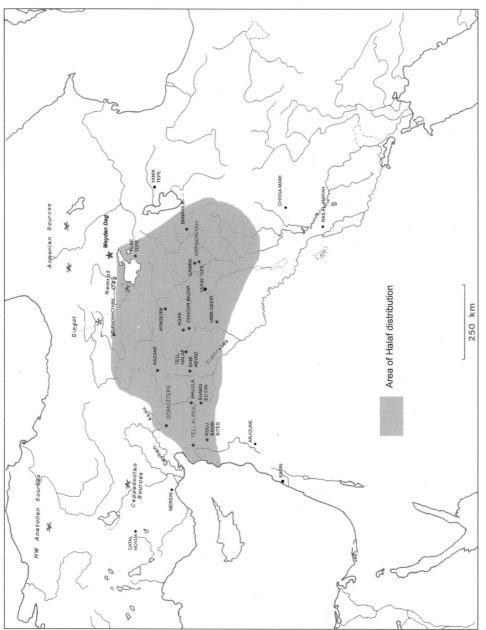

Figure 10.3. Map showing the extent of the Halaf culture and the sites and areas mentioned in the text.

The Halaf (Amuq C) levels of Tell Kurdu were excavated in 2001 under the direction of Rana Özbal, Northwestern University, Chicago (Özbal *et al.* 2004). Tell Kurdu is a 15-hectare mound in the centre of the Amuq valley in the province of Hatay. The Halaf settlement appears to cover the entire mound, and the 2001 excavations exposed a coherent settlement of houses, courtyards, streets and alleys on the northern part of the mound (Özbal *et al.* 2004, fig. 2). They belong to a single phase in the early part of the Halaf period, thus approximately contemporary with the earliest Halaf levels of Domuztepe. The ceramics show a strong local tradition with a Halaf component looking to eastern Syria rather than to the Mediterranean as did the pre-Halaf ceramics (Diebold 2004, 55). The material culture is broadly similar to, though less rich than, that of Domuztepe.

Tell Arpachiyah, located in northern Iraq near Mosul, is a small tell excavated in the 1930s by Sir Max Mallowan (Mallowan and Rose 1935). It is more or less contemporary with

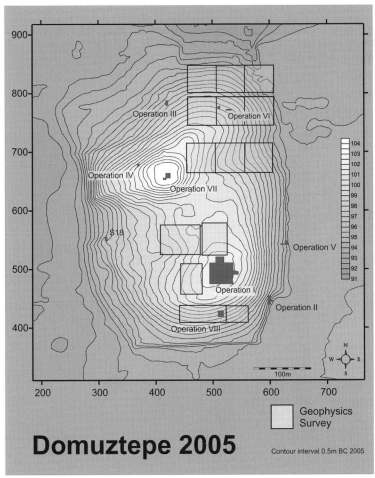

Figure 10.4. Site plan of Domuztepe showing the extent of the excavations up to 2005.

Domuztepe and is important both because it has long been a key site in the interpretation of Halaf culture, and because a rich collection of material was preserved *in situ* in burnt buildings in the area designated TT6, some of which can be compared to Domuztepe. The lithic artefacts were not fully published but it is considered that the collections now housed in the Institute of Archaeology, University College London, represent the bulk of the artefacts recovered apart from those listed as being elsewhere, for example in the Iraq Museum in Baghdad and in the British Museum (Campbell 1992,153; 2000, 21–22).

THE CHIPPED-STONE ASSEMBLAGES

The compositions of the assemblages from the first five seasons at Domuztepe, from the 2001 excavations at Tell Kurdu and from the material I have examined in London from Tell Arpachiyah are given in Figures 10.5–10.9. At Domuztepe and Tell Kurdu flint is the predominant raw material, obsidian forming less than a quarter of the raw materials, whereas at Arpachiyah obsidian is 'at least as common as flint' (Mallowan and Rose 1935, 102). Furthermore, judging from the number of early-stage pieces, flint at both Domuztepe and Tell Kurdu was acquired in a relatively unprepared state whereas the obsidian was probably

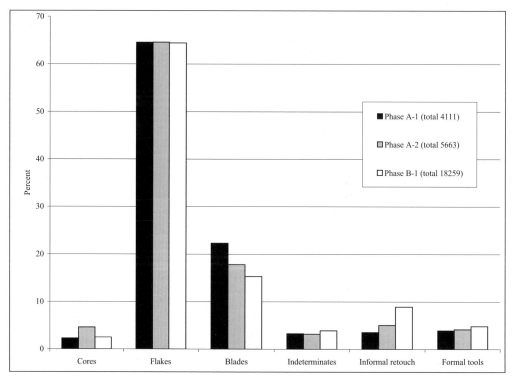

Figure 10.5. Bar chart showing the composition of the flint industry at Domuztepe, by phase.

obtained mostly in the form of semi-prepared cores. The technologies of the flint and obsidian industries seem to be different as are the products which were made. This will be discussed in more detail below.

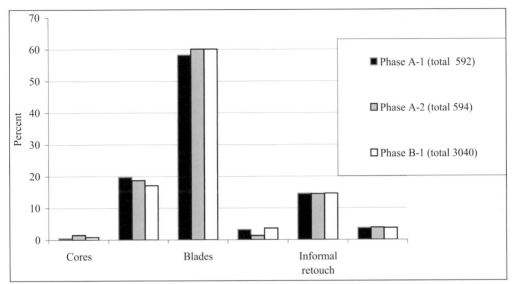

Figure 10.6. Bar chart showing the composition of the obsidian industry at Domuztepe, by phase. (The unlabelled categories are as in Figure 10.5).

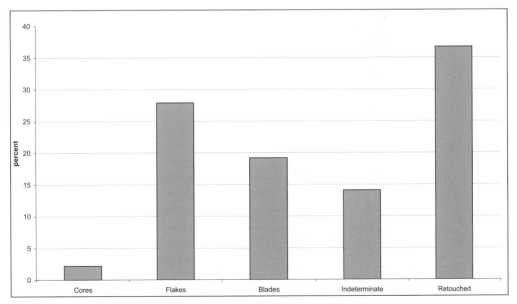

Figure 10.7. Bar chart showing the composition of the flint industry from Tell Kurdu (n= 1963).

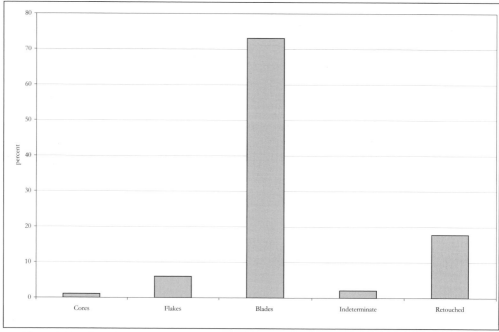

Figure 10.8. Bar chart showing the composition of the obsidian industry from Tell Kurdu (n=584).

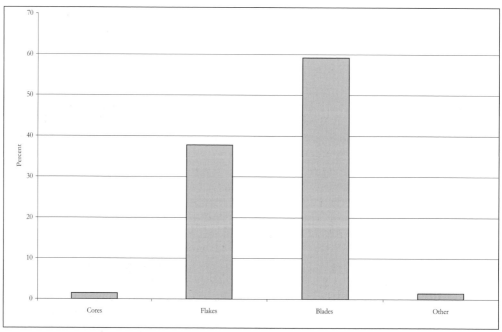

Figure 10.9. Bar chart showing the composition of the obsidian industry from Tell Arpachiyah (n=1905).

Raw materials

At Domuztepe the flint is likely, at least for the most part, to have been obtained locally in the limestone hills surrounding the valley, but the nearest obsidian sources are over 250 km to the north-west or 500 km to the north-east as the crow flies, and themselves some 600 km apart. Because of the location of Domuztepe we expected that obsidian would have been obtained from both areas. Obsidian accounts for between 6 and 19 per cent of the raw materials depending on phase and context. At Tell Kurdu obsidian (also an exotic raw material) accounted for 23 per cent of the raw materials overall, although there was a marked difference in the density of artefacts between streets and rooms – one house had as much as 42 per cent (Özbal *et al.* 2004, table 9). At Tell Arpachiyah obsidian apparently comprises about 50 per cent of the raw materials (Mallowan and Rose 1935, 102) even though the nearest sources are at least 250 km away.

In order to be able to identify where the obsidian was acquired from and the relative proportions from each source, as well as to establish how the different obsidians were worked and used, the artefacts from Domuztepe were initially separated into groups on the basis of macroscopic characteristics of the obsidian (Healey 2000, 106ff; see also Skinner 2008), and then these groups were sub-sampled for geochemical analysis. This process was repeated at Tell Kurdu and Tell Arpachiyah. The results of the analyses of the obsidians from Domuztepe (by Dr J.-L. Poidevin at Clermont-Ferrand) and from Tell Kurdu (by Dr G. Poupeau in Bordeaux) established that obsidians from far more sources were present than had been expected. For Domuztepe the sources involved are in three different geographic areas: i) Göllüdağ-east and Nenezi Dağ in Cappadocia, ii) Bingöl per-alkaline and calc-alkaline, Meydan Dağ in south-eastern Anatolia and iii) Pasinler, and Arteni in northeastern Anatolia and Armenia (Figure 10.1) as well as from two unknown sources. The Tell Kurdu obsidians also include Göllüdağ-east, Bingöl/Nemrut Dağ per-alkaline and Bingöl calc-alkaline sources as well as obsidian from Sarıkamış in N.E. Anatolia (Poupeau pers. comm.). Amongst the obsidians at Arpachiyah there is material from the Bingöl calc-alkaline sources, the Bingöl/Nemrut Dağ per-alkaline sources and Meydan Dağ (Renfrew *et al.* 1966, table 2, nos: 46, 47, 78, 79 and 80).

Blind tests demonstrated that there was a strong statistical correlation between the macroscopic characteristics and the geochemical analysis (Healey and Campbell 2009) enabling us to apportion the entire assemblage both at Domuztepe and at Tell Kurdu to various sources with some confidence. In brief, and with at least 75 per cent certainty, it is possible to suggest that the translucent grey obsidians at Domuztepe and Tell Kurdu come from Cappadocia, the translucent dark/olive green obsidians come from the per-alkaline sources of Bingöl and/or Nemrut Dağ (cf. Francavigilia 1990), the black and translucent brown obsidians probably come from the calc-alkaline source at Bingöl or possibly Meydan Dağ, the rarer translucent reddy-brown with black stripes from Arteni, and the red-brown and some striped translucent greys from Pasinler. Our estimate on the basis of these visual attributions is that just over a third of the obsidians at Domuztepe can be attributed to sources in Cappadocia and the rest to eastern Anatolian sources. The preferred source, at least in Phase A-1, seems to have been the per-alkaline source of Bingöl/Nemrut Dağ which supplied some 38 per cent of the obsidian (Figure 10.10). Although the results should be regarded as preliminary, we were also able to demonstrate a reduction in the use of the per-alkaline obsidians through time, although obsidian from eastern sources remains predominant. At Tell Kurdu (Figure 10.11) the green per-alkaline obsidians predominated, which is broadly consistent with the higher levels of green obsidians in the earlier phases at Domuztepe and with the eastern connections seen in the ceramics.

At Arpachiyah the five samples analysed by Renfrew were also described by colour, so the bulk of the assemblage could be retrospectively grouped according to its visual characteristics. Renfrew identified two pieces from the Bingöl/Nemrut Dağ per-alkaline source (his 4c), which he described as being translucent green, two from the Meydan Dağ (his 3a) source, which were grey (one almost opaque and the other translucent), and one

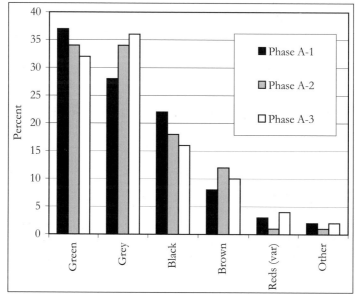

Figure 10.10. Bar chart showing variation in different types of obsidian at Domuztepe, by phase.

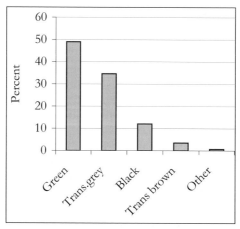

Figure 10.11. Bar chart showing the proportions of the different obsidians present at Tell Kurdu.

from the Bingöl calc-alkaline source (his group 1g), which was an opaque greenish-brown colour. Of the material examined by me about 75 per cent of the obsidians were green, 15 per cent grey, and the rest includes uncertain examples and low numbers of black, brown, and red colours not analysed by Renfrew (Figure 10.12 and Healey 2000, 147). Thus all the obsidians from Arpachiyah are attributable to eastern sources, as one might expect from its geographic location, with the Bingöl/Nemrut Dağ source being predominant , though a number of others sources appear to be involved too. In general the presence of obsidian from the Meydan Dağ source at both Arpachiyah and particularly at Domuztepe might indicate that the per-alkaline obsidians came from Nemrut Dağ rather than the Bingöl region as the two seem to occur together (Chataigner 1998, 313).

Although the results should still be regarded as preliminary (there are now another 4000 obsidian artefacts from Domuztepe awaiting analysis), it seems that visual characteristics coupled with sub-sampling for elemental analysis can enable us to attribute the obsidians to different source areas with a reasonable degree of certainty and thus to demonstrate preferences for certain sources as well as the strength of the connections both between sites and between sources (see also Maeda 2003,176; Tykot and Ammerman 1997). When coupled with technological and typological analysis interesting results begin to emerge.

Technology

From the composition of the assemblages it is clear that there is a difference in the reduction trajectories of flint and obsidian (Figures 10.5 and 10.6). For example, the flint assemblage at Domuztepe is largely flake-based whereas obsidian is predominantly blade-based. Furthermore, the technique of blade production for flint and obsidian appears to be different (Healey in prep.). The flint blade-cores are fairly standardized in form, though showing some size variation. They are shaped by flaking on the sides and

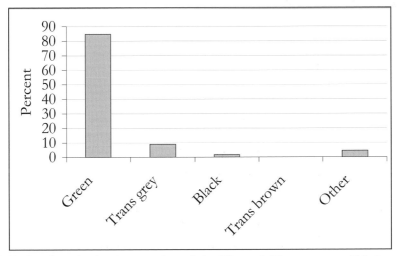

Figure 10.12. Bar chart showing the proportions of the different obsidians present at Tell Arpachiyah.

sometimes on the back, though this may be left unworked. They are uni-directional and have markedly oblique, plain striking-platforms and were probably worked using soft hammer percussion.

By contrast, the obsidian technology was geared towards blade production using pressure (Figure 10.13). It is difficult to relate all the cores to sources using visual characteristics because their thickness masks some of their characteristics, though cores of translucent grey and translucent brown obsidians are present, cores of green obsidian appear to be uncommon, and no cores of red obsidian were recovered. Most of the cores seem to have reached the site in a semi-prepared form as removals with cortex and early stage pieces are rare. Cores are for the most part uni-directional though two opposed-platform cores and a flake with an opposed striking-platform remnant on its distal end were recorded (Figure 10.13:7 and 11). They are prepared and maintained by cresting and flaking on the side (Figure 10.13:1 and 8); generally blades are detached from one face only and many have straight ends; pyramidal cores are not found. The core striking platforms are ground and mostly at 90 degrees to the core face (Figure 10.13:4 and 6). The cores are small, measuring between 25 and 54 mm in length with an average weight of just over 6 grams. However, the largest reconstructable blade measures about 80 mm in length (Figure 10.13:16). There are also portions of larger and more robust blades (usually of black obsidian), measuring over 90 mm and between 33 and 43 mm in width (Figure 10.13:13), which may have been acquired as blades rather than produced on site, though this remains to be confirmed. The blades usually (more than 70%) have ground striking-platform remnants thus correlating with the cores (flakes do not have ground platform remnants). The parallel sides, regular thickness and pointed or square and slightly hooked distal ends of the blades (e.g. Figure 10.13:14) are consistent with reduction by pressure using some sort of block or holding-device (Inizan and Lechevallier 1994, 27; Wilke 1996, 300). Similar blades were recovered from Tell Kurdu (Healey 2004, 57).

In order to see if there was a difference in technology between the different obsidians we ran some statistical tests on the technological features of the blades from Domuztepe. The results demonstrated that blades of green obsidian had more ground platforms than expected; that the blades of green and grey obsidians were narrower and thinner than the black; and both green and grey tend to have quadrilateral (prismatic) cross-sections (Figure 10.13:14 and 15). Black obsidians on the other hand were thicker, and generally had un-ground platforms and triangular cross-sections (Figure 10.13:13 and Healey 2000, 137–138 and appendix 2), perhaps suggesting a different reduction technique or perhaps acquisition as blades, as many are considerably bigger than the surviving cores. Some of the rarer obsidians, especially the reds, are present only as blades and flakes. On the basis of our macroscopic groupings these correspond to the obsidians linked to the Pasinler and Armenian sources which are considerably further away and so their rarity may be a factor of distance. This does, however, require further investigation.

At Arpachiyah the cores (the majority of green obsidian) are much larger than the Domuztepe cores, weighing up to 53 grams and measuring between 32 and 72 mm in length, and they are reduced differently, most having plain or occasionally faceted, oblique striking-platforms and pointed distal ends (Figure 10.14:1). Some are worked around the entire circumference (Figure 10.14:3), others have flat backs often formed by a natural surface (Figure 10.14:2 and 4). Green obsidians also dominate in the assemblage both

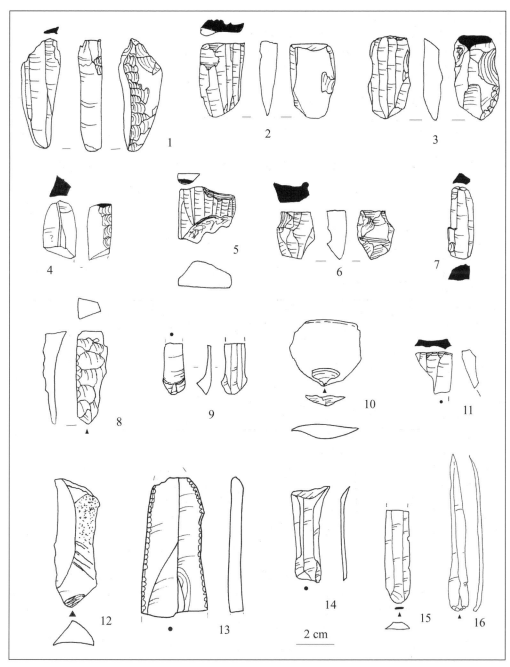

Figure 10.13. Obsidian technology at Domuztepe: 1–7: cores; 8: half crested blade; 9: plunging blade; 10: flake; 11: blade struck from an opposed platform core; 12: flake with cortex; 13: large wide blade of black obsidian with prismatic cross-section:, 14: distal end of blade; 15: proximal end of prismatic blade; 16: complete blade.

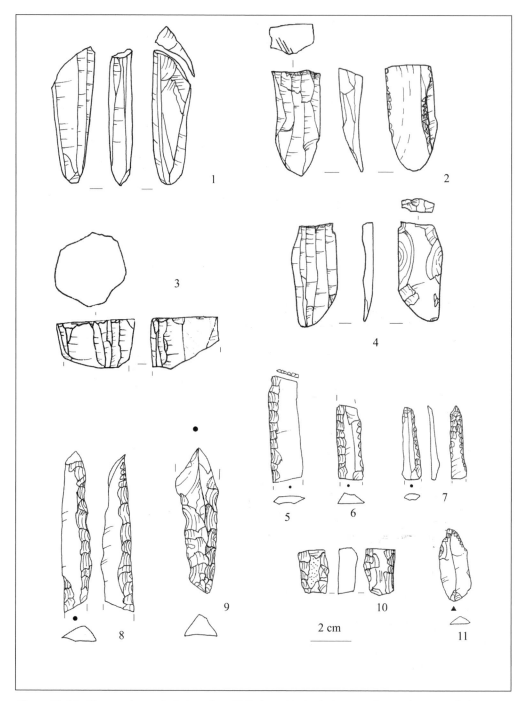

Figure 10.14. Cores and retouched pieces from Tell Arpachiyah: 1–4: cores; 5, 6 and 8: retouched pieces; 7 and 11: piercers; 9: tanged piece; 10: retouched fragment.

numerically and by weight – there is about nine times the amount of green obsidian to grey when compared by weight, though only about five times numerically. Also there are more flakes of the green obsidian than any other obsidian and a number of them had cortex on their dorsal surfaces (Figure 10.13:12, a feature noted on only a few pieces at Domuztepe and Tell Kurdu); a higher proportion of preparation pieces in green obsidian was also noted (Figure 10.15; Campbell 1992, 154; Healey 2000, 147ff.). By whatever method the occupants of Arpachiyah obtained their green obsidians it seemed that they were acquired in a less prepared state than the grey. It is possible that this, together with a high incidence of cortex, reflects the nature of the raw obsidian as much as the acquisition method – indeed the obsidian at the Çavuslar per-alkaline source at Bingöl is described as being grey to green in colour, in rounded to spherical blocks between 100 and 250 mm in diameter in an argillaceous matrix and probably a secondary deposit (Cauvin *et al.* 1986, 89–91). It is not certain that this was the source used and there is now some evidence to suggest that the Nemrut Dağ source supplied at least some of the obsidian. While these studies only hint at the method of acquisition of the obsidian and the form in which it was acquired, it may be noted that no caches of blades, similar to that from Damishliyya, have been found at any of the Halaf sites although we may note in cases where obsidian is rare, suggestions that the obsidian was imported in the form of blades. However, there is evidence for at least some blade production at each site studied, perhaps indicating direct or localized connections with the sources or other distribution centres. Clearly in view of the results now coming from the workshops at Göllüdağ east source (see above), there are compelling reasons to investigate systematically the sources and technologies at associated workshops at Bingöl, Nemrut Dağ and other eastern sources.

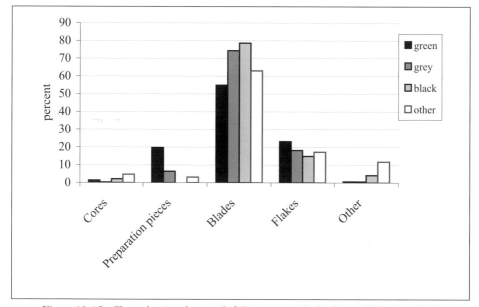

Figure 10.15. Chart showing the use of different types of obsidian at Tell Arpachiyah.

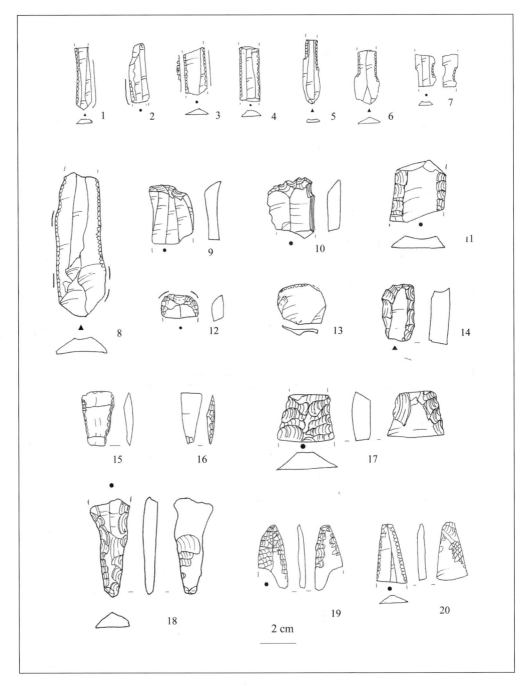

Figure 10.16. Retouched pieces from Domuztepe: 1–3 and 8: edge retouch with heavy wear as indicated; 3–7: edge retouched blades; 9,10 and 12: scrapers; 13: edge retouched flake; 11 and 14: more extensively retouched pieces; 15 and 16: transverse arrowheads; 17, 19 and 20: pieces with invasive retouch; 18: tanged piece.

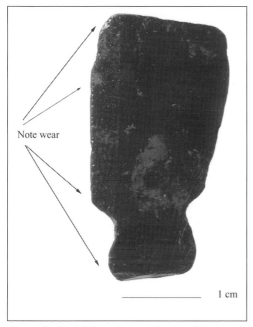

Note wear

1 cm

Figure 10.17. Blade with worn edge from Domuztepe.

Modification

Only 14 per cent of the obsidian blades from Domuztepe are retouched or show some chipping on the edges, whereas 33 per cent of the flint blades were retouched; a similar situation pertains at Tell Kurdu (Figures 10.5 and 10.8; Healey 2004, table 5) suggesting that, at least in some situations, a sharp fresh edge was the intended product. Details were not collected for Arpachiyah because of the condition of the assemblage. Heavy wear or rounding is also apparent on a number of the blades (Figure 10.16:1–3, 8 and 12) at least one of which, from Domuztepe (Figure 17), appears to have been used to work stone (Lemorini pers. comm.), but full functional analysis has not yet been undertaken.

Both flint and obsidian are retouched into more standardized tool forms including transverse and bifacially flaked arrowheads, tanged pieces, sickle blades (flint only), backed and/or truncated pieces, piercers, scrapers, knives, denticulates and so on. There are few formally retouched pieces from Tell Kurdu, perhaps reflecting the different type of contexts there. A range of obsidian artefacts is illustrated in Figures 10.14 and 10.16.

Ground and polished items

In addition to the regular tools, obsidian is also made into non-utilitarian items which are often finished to a high standard by grinding and polishing. Some partially finished pieces were found both at Domuztepe and at Arpachiyah, suggesting that at least some were made on site. Flint is also ground and polished but made into tools rather than items of adornment. At Domuztepe most of the ground and polished objects are made of translucent grey and translucent brown obsidians, green being rarely used. Round, barrel or biconical beads (Figure 10.18), flat spacer-beads (lozenge, crescentic, oval and flanged) are the most common forms (Figure 10.19). There is a pendant from phase A-1 which is only minimally ground on the sides (Figure 10.20). The pendant shown in Figure 21 measures only 17 mm in length and is on a small flake, the upper surface of which has been ground and decorated with an incised geometric pattern similar to that found on the stamp-seals made on local raw materials. It seems to have broken across the original perforation and to have been remade and perhaps reshaped, suggesting that it was of some value to its owner. There are a number of flat disc-like objects or 'mirrors' with one flat highly polished surface, some of which are decorated around the circumference with concentric grooves and one has a strap or loop handle (Figure 10.22:1 and 2). There are also fragments of at least 19 vessels, most of which are of grey obsidian, but three

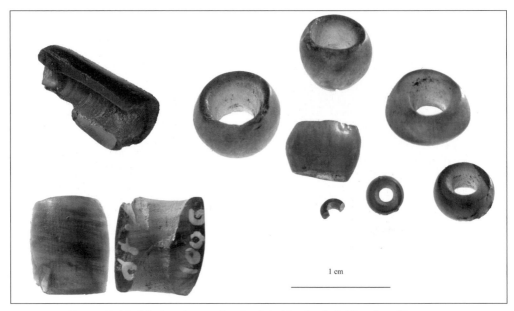

Figure 10.18. Selection of ground and polished beads of obsidian from Domuztepe.

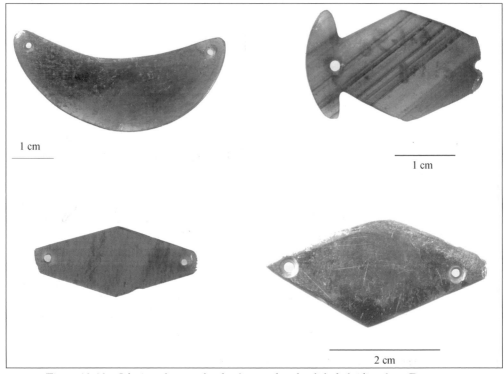

Figure 10.19. Selection of spacer beads of ground and polished obsidian from Domuztepe..

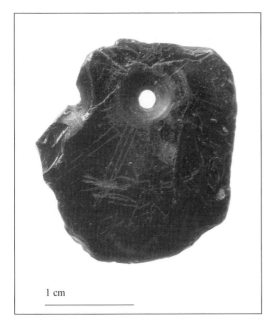

Figure 10.20. Pendant ground on the edges and with two perforations (one broken) from Domuztepe..

Figure 10.21. Pendant from Domuztepe made on a flake of semi-translucent grey obsidian. The dorsal surface is ground-and-polished and with incised geometric decoration similar to that on the stamp-seals.

are of reddy-brown obsidian consistent with the obsidians sourced to the Pasinler area (Figure 10.23). Additionally there are some tranchet objects (superficially similar to, but larger than, the transverse arrowheads) made on segments of large blades, the sides of which have been ground and polished and sometimes also the blade (Figure 10.24:1) There is also a miniature 'axehead' with marks from binding around the circumference just above mid-point (Figure 10.24:2). Different degrees of finish are noted particularly among pendants, some of which are only cursorily shaped (Figure 10.20), the mirrors and vessels where we can contrast the majority with very thin walls with others which are thicker and have less finished surfaces.

At Tell Kurdu ground and polished items are rare in the Halaf levels, but include beads (Figure 10.25:1 and 2), two of which came from room deposits, and there is a spacer-bead from the floor of Room 28 (Figure 10.25:3) made on a flake of obsidian which has been chipped to make it into a symmetric oval shape and perforated at both ends, although there is no evidence of grinding. This perfunctory treatment is similar to the pendant from the early A-1 levels of Domuztepe (Figure 10.20). We might also note that in the later Chalcolithic levels beads are made on rudimentarily shaped and minimally ground blanks, but there are also some more finely finished objects (Yener *et al.* 2000, 72–73).

At Arpachiyah there are also considerable numbers of ground and polished items, which were found in the Burnt House (details in Healey 2000, 152–155; cf. Campbell 2000, 29–31).

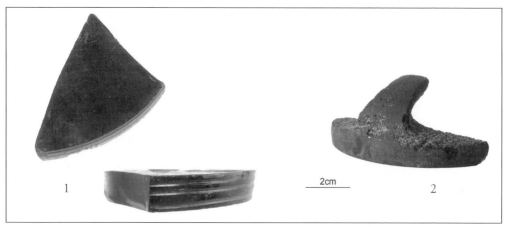

Figure 10.22. Mirrors from Domuztepe. 1: disc mirror with highly polished upper surface and less well finished lower surface and with three concentric groves around the thickness of the mirror; 2: mirror with strap handle. The mirror surface is highly polished, but the back is only pecked.

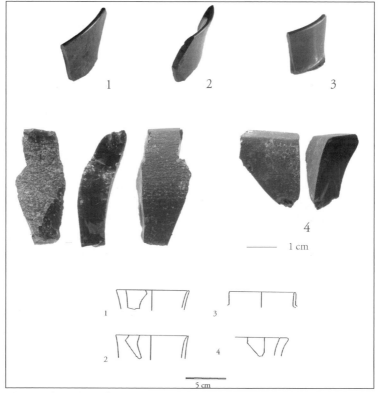

Figure 10.23. A range of vessels made of ground and polished obsidian from Domuztepe. The exterior surfaces are generally more highly polished than the interior. 1–3: have thin walls and no.3 has broken on the carination; 4 and 5 are much thicker and cruder.

This includes at least 36 rectangular links made on largish blades (80% green obsidian), some measuring up to 90 mm in length, which have been ground and polished on their dorsal surfaces and perforated at both ends (Figure 10.26). There is also a series of six oval and lozenge-shaped links (Figure 10.27) made on flakes of green obsidian which have been regularized by chipping and then ground and polished. These have been reconstructed as a necklace by Mallowan, apparently 'in the order found' and interspersed with cowrie shells and a bead of grey stone (Mallowan and Rose 1935, 97, pl.XI; cf. Healey 2000, 132–133). A jar or vase made of obsidian, now broken but originally 160 mm in height and 85 mm in diameter, and ranging in thickness from 12 mm at the rim to 35 mm on the shoulder and 43 mm at the base, was also recovered from the Burnt House. The rim is ground smooth but its outer surface is pecked rather than ground and it may be unfinished or broken in manufacture (Mallowan and Rose 1935, 76, fig. 44: 15 and pl.Vc; but see Campbell 1992, 290; 2000, 12). Among the collections in the Institute of Archaeology there are also some small flattened disc-shaped objects which have some grinding on their surfaces and are probably bead blanks (Figure 10.25: 4–8).

Spatial distribution and context

The full contextual details of the Domuztepe material have yet to be finalized, but preliminary results suggest that the stone vessels and mirrors show a restricted distribution (Campbell pers.comm.). A number of obsidian bead-blanks of translucent grey-brown obsidian were found in the 2005 excavations in a restricted area adjacent to a burnt

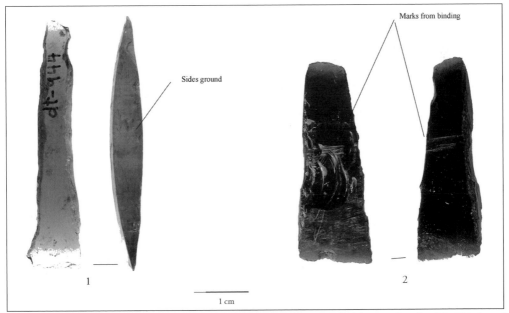

Figure 10.24. 1: tranchet-like object with ground sides; 2: small axehead with ground and polished blade and marks from binding at the mid point. Both from Domuztepe.

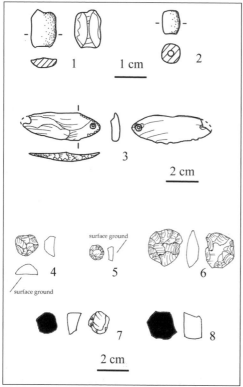

Figure 10.25. 1–2: biconically perforated beads of ground and polished obsidian, from Tell Kurdu; 3: a spacer-bead made on a flake of obsidian which has been chipped into shape, from Tell Kurdu; 4–8: possible bead blanks, from Tell Arpachiyah.

house which has tentatively been identified as a possible workshop (Campbell 2005, 15). At Tell Kurdu, where house-by-house information is available, it is clear that some houses had considerably higher proportions of obsidian than others (Özbal *et al.* 2004, 86, table 9). At Arpachiyah the majority of the obsidian, and particularly the ground and polished material, was found in the Burnt House, which may have been a workshop, store, or redistribution centre (Campbell 1992, 202; 2000, 23–25; Healey 2000, 145–146, 155–157; Healey 2007, 181).

THE WIDER PICTURE

The data from other Halaf obsidian assemblages are discussed in Healey (2000: chap. 8 and appendix 5). In general these lithic assemblages are not well researched (Cauvin and Chataigner 1998, 345), partly because many of them date from excavations in the first half of the twentieth century. Mallowan, for example, excused what he described as 'a somewhat cavalier treatment of a monotonous series of flint and obsidian blades', saying 'I have no great hopes that a more detailed examination of the flints and obsidian will prove of any great value, but this task I am reserving for a sedentary old age, by which time, perhaps, the much more important material from one or two other yet unpublished western Asiatic sites will have been properly dealt with' (Mallowan 1947, 245). Many assemblages are still not yet fully published and Halaf industries are still accused of being 'impoverished' or 'banal' (Akkermans 1993, 272; Copeland 1996, 248, 267); however, the more integrated approach of raw material studies and technology used for assemblages from Domuztepe, Tell Kurdu, and Arpachiyah suggests that stone assemblages may be what Edens describes as 'passive markers of identity' (Edens 2000, 24). The following brief overview discusses some of the variations present and the potential for future analysis.

Sources of obsidian used and scale of consumption in the Halaf culture

The majority of sites obtain their obsidians from the eastern sources (Figure 10.1), although sites in the Levant and Euphrates, such as Halula, Domuztepe and Tell Kurdu have obsidians from both source areas, and in the Rouj basin the use of obsidian from eastern sources increases in the Halaf period (Maeda 2003, 181). An unlocated source which is distinguished by a high proportion of rubidium (Renfrew's 3d) is used more than in earlier times (Chataigner 1998, 317, figs 18a and b). New sources are also exploited. For example the Meydan Dağ source begins to have a widespread distribution (Chataigner 1998, 313, figs 17a and b). Also the results of the recent analysis of the obsidians from Domuztepe and Tell Kurdu show that obsidian from Pasinler is present at Domuztepe (Poidevin pers. comm.) and from Sarıkamış at Tell Kurdu (Poupeau pers. comm.), both sources in NE Anatolia. Some of the obsidian from Banahilk may also have come from this area (Watson 1983, 572). Additionally, Armenian obsidian from Arteni is found at Domuztepe (Poidevin pers. comm.). However, more comprehensive analysis of obsidians from other sites may also demonstrate use of obsidians from similar sources and it is something that we should be aware of when considering distributions and targeting assemblages for analysis.

The quantity of obsidian circulating during the Halaf period is generally less than in previous periods and there is a change in emphasis of concentration (Cauvin and Chataigner 1998, 345). The amount and proportion of obsidian in an assemblage may, of course, be affected by its distance from source (see for example Renfrew 1975; 1977; cf. Bostyn 1997), geographic and environmental situation, social characteristics – including the nature and size of the settlement, and the availability of other raw materials, as well as the method

Figure 10.26. Rectangular spacer-beads from Tell Arpachiyah.

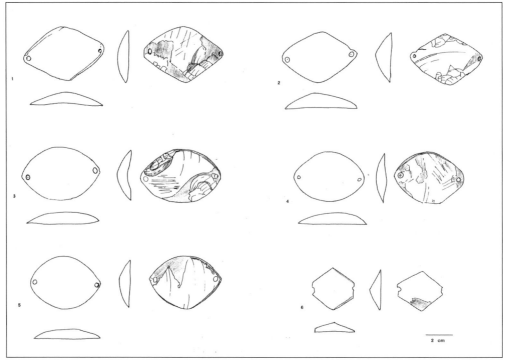

Figure 10.27. Oval and lozenge spacer-beads from the necklace at Tell Arpachiyah.

of excavation, the area excavated and other factors. For example, it has been suggested that the reason that PPNB sites in the Upper Euphrates region had little or no obsidian was because good flint is readily available there (Cauvin and Chataigner 1998, 337) and that the relatively high proportion of obsidian in the Khabur area is because flint in this area is of 'rather poor quality' (Davidson and Watkins 1981, 11), but it is likely that other factors come into play as well. Girikihaciyan, located only about 100 km south of the Bingöl sources (although the obsidian form Girikihaciyan is unprovenanced) and at the northern limits of the Halaf area, has about 30 per cent obsidian (1505 pieces, but only amounting to 15% of the chipped stone by weight), despite the fact that flint is poor in this area (Watson and le Blanc 1990, 86). Cores are present and a number of 'waste flakes' but it is not clear whether they were imported in a semi-prepared state or whether obsidian was acquired in a raw state; blades predominate (Watson and le Blanc 1990, 81). At Kazane, on the Harran plain, obsidian formed only 3 per cent (33 pieces) of the chipped-stone assemblage from the Halaf levels, which was otherwise mainly made from local cherts (Bernbeck *et al.* 1999, 122, table 8).

In upper Mesopotamia (the main Halaf area), sites have a much higher proportion of obsidian – Aqab has about 80 per cent obsidian (no count given), but raw blocks, cores, and debitage are present (Davidson and Watkins 1981, 10–11). At Chagar Bazar obsidian constituted 73.4 per cent of the lithic assemblage from area E although only 220 lithic artefacts were recovered; it reached the site in the form of cores ready for pressure flaking. The obsidian has not yet been sourced (Ferrer 2006, 95–101) although the pendant (see below) is described as translucent black (Cruells 2006, 87). Umm Qseir has 36.4 per cent obsidian (304 pieces), cores are rare, and the assemblage consists mostly of blades. The technology is different from that employed for the flint from the local gravels (Maeda 1998, 105). The obsidians are greenish-black and grey in colour and originated from the eastern sources (Maeda 1998, 89, 102–105; 2003, 184). The chipped-stone industry at Tell Halaf is described as being present 'in great quantity' and the obsidian as 'especially numerous' (von Oppenheim 1919, 203). Unworked blocks of obsidian are mentioned as being present, but blades predominate. Obsidians of various colours are described, including opaque shiny black, spotted duller grey and a shiny brown obsidian with black flecks (von Oppenheim and Schmidt 1943, 107) and a transparent grey-green (von Oppenheim 1933, 203). Characterized pieces come from Meydan Dağ and the unidentified source strong in rubidium (Chataigner 1998, 317). In amounts present and sources exploited these sites compare with the material from Arpachiyah already discussed.

A little further south in the Sinjar, at Yarim Tepe II obsidian accounts for about 34 per cent (180 pieces) of the lithic assemblage and is present almost entirely as blades (Merpert and Munchaev 1993a, 146). Blades are also present at Yarim Tepe III, though no numbers are given (Merpert and Munchaev 1993b, 178, 195). At the eastern edge of the Halaf region Banahilk has about 30 per cent obsidian although this only amounts to 554 pieces; there are no cores but a high percentage of waste flakes may indicate obsidian working there (Watson 1983, 572–573; Watson and Le Blanc 1990, 83, table 6.2).

To the west on the Balikh river at Sabi Abyad I (levels 1–3) the proportion of obsidian (19.5%) shows a slight increase from earlier periods but only comprises 167 artefacts; technologies used in early periods are still used (Copeland 1996, 261, table VIII). Two groups of obsidian are present, one almost certainly from Bingöl and the other – a coarse grained one – Suphan Dağ, just north of Nemrut Dağ on Lake Van is the suggested source (Copeland 1996, 268 and appendix B). Sites in the middle Euphrates such as Shams ed-Din have only limited amounts of obsidian (11% or 473 pieces); there are no cores and few flakes, but the presence of crested blades suggests obsidian working. The assemblage is predominantly blade-based and it is suggested that the blades were probably detached by pressure (Azoury and Bergman 1980). Halula, on the middle Euphrates, is interesting because, like Tell Kurdu and Domzutepe, it has obsidian from the Bingöl/Nemrut Dağ per-alkaline sources and from Göllüdağ-east but it also has side-blow blade flakes and corner-thinned blades, which may be derived from earlier contexts (Pernicka *et al.* 1997, 117). Arjoune, on the Orontes, has only seven pieces of obsidian but it is of different colours – grey, green, black and brown – perhaps indicating different sources (Copeland 2003, 72, 118). At Ras Shamra IVC / IVB, obsidian increases from the previous period to between 8.5 and 14 per cent (107 and 249 artefacts respectively). A few cores are present but the assemblage mainly consists of blades (de Contenson 1992, 71–82); the only pieces sourced from these levels come from Göllüdağ-east (Chataigner 1998, table 7a). In the Rouj basin obsidian use increases and the Halaf period marks a change of source from Cappadocian sources to eastern sources (Maeda 2003, 182). At Mersin, to the west of the Halaf area, obsidian (from Cappadocian sources) seems to decline after the Halaf period (Renfrew *et al.* 1966, 48).

When considering patterns of distribution based on percentages it is easy to be seduced by apparent high proportions without knowing the precise context and the composition and nature of the assemblage or indeed the size and weight of the material let alone the relative proportion of different sources present. Indeed, even the apparently substantial numbers of obsidian artefacts at Domuztepe may amount to little more than 25 blades (perhaps amounting to 150–200 grams of obsidian in total) per household per year (based on figures in Healey 2000, 141–142), thus comparing quite closely to the Kurdu households some of which have as many as 27 artefacts (and there are more in the courtyards and streets: Özbal *et al.* 2004, table 9). Arpachiyah seems to have used more obsidian and to have had larger cores, but most of that studied seems to have come from the Burnt House which may be an exceptional context (see above). The quantities should perhaps be contrasted with those from Çatalhöyük, earlier in the Neolithic, where obsidian is used almost exclusively and it has been calculated that a minimum of 116–318 kilograms per person per year was involved (i.e. more than several hundred times the amount at Domuztepe)(Cessford and Carter 2005, 310).

The technologies evident in the PPNB and earlier Pottery Neolithic, such as the naviform core technology associated with the Kaletepe workshop on Göllüdağ-east (see above) and other industries described for Çatalhöyük (Carter *et al.* 2006a; 2006b), are no longer to be seen (Cauvin and Chataigner 1998, 345). Similarly, certain forms such as side-blow blade-flakes and corner-thinned blades, which are considered to be related to obsidian from the eastern sources (Nishiaki 1993), die out, lingering in only a few places which have had them in earlier occupations, for example Sabi Abyad and Halula (Copeland 1996; Molist and Ferrer 1996). In the Rouj basin, where also there is earlier occupation, the Halaf period marks a change in the supply of obsidian and an increased reliance on eastern sources, though the technology does not change (Maeda 2003, 182), despite the fact that in earlier periods there is evidence of the presence of eastern traditions of working some obsidian (Maeda 2003, 184, note 15). Nevertheless, the evidence from Domuztepe and Arpachiyah implies that some blade manufacturing techniques may have been source-related or at least determined by the form in which the obsidian was acquired, whether as semi-prepared cores or in a less prepared state of the pre-cores. Although the use of obsidian from distant sources was well-established long before the Halaf period, it is indicative of the wide-spread contacts at that time and the exploitation of new sources demonstrates this too; different communities seem to have participated in different ways and to different degrees (cf. Ammerman and Andrefsky 1982; Ammerman and Polgaze 1993). Any such patterns can only be elucidated by detailed analysis of both sources and technologies within each context.

Non-utilitarian items

In the Halaf culture the non-tool use of obsidian increases in the number of sites, quantity and in range of forms (Figure 10.28), although the background to the distribution of these non-utilitarian items at the moment is not fully clear; some sites have considerably higher numbers and a more varied range of items than others (see review in Healey 2000, appendix 4c). This needs to be correlated with type of site and other factors (Healey in preparation). Evidence for the manufacture on site of non-utilitarian obsidian items is ambivalent, though the less well-finished forms present suggest that local fabrication may be the case at

Domuztepe (where bead-blanks were also found), at Tell Kurdu and at Arpachiyah, perhaps also at Tell Halaf (von Oppenheim and Schmidt 1943, 114, pl.XXXVII and pl.CXIII: 4) and at Ras Shamra, where there are what seem to be pre-forms (de Contenson 1992, 11, fig. 115:17, 18).

In general the more finely finished objects include barrel and bi-conical beads, which continue from earlier periods, as do pendants (see Figure 10.28 for an overview). Spacer-beads are a new form in the Halaf culture and here regional differences seem to be present. For example, the rectangular form of links are found at Arpachiyah (above), Gawra (Tobler 1950, pl.CLXXV: 71), Banahilk (Watson 1983, fig. 210: 4), and possibly Kazane (Bernbeck *et al.* 1999, 124, fig. 17c), and the large oval to lozenge shaped (or rhomboidal) spacer-beads found in the necklace at Tell Arpachiyah (above) are also found at Gawra (Tobler 1950, pl.CLXXV: 70, pl.XCII: C2), Aqab (Davidson and Watkins 1981, 10), Yarim Tepe II (Campbell 2000, 12), YarimTepe III (Merpert and Munchaev 1993b, fig. 9.22:4; fig. 9.23), and possibly Banahilk (Watson 1983, 573) and Ras Shamra IVB (de Contenson 1992, pl.XCVIII: 5). Apart from the one from Ras Shamra, these forms appear to have an eastern distribution. Mirrors of flat discoidal type – and so of different form from the ones in earlier contexts at Çatalhöyük (Conolly 1999, 42–43) – are found only at Domuztepe, though one with a strap-handle and grooves (cf. Figure 10.22 from Domuztepe) was found at Kabri in Israel as a surface find, but it may be of approximately the same date (Prausnitz 1969, pl.37). Smaller discs, measuring about 40 mm in diameter are present at Tell Halaf (von Oppenheim and Schmidt 1943) and Ras Shamra (de Contenson 1992) and other sites. Vessels are rare in the Halaf period, so far identified at Domuztepe, Arpachiyah and Banahilk (Watson 1983, 576, table 490); a surface find from Kurdu, described as being of brown rhyolitic obsidian, and perhaps similar to one from Domuztepe, may also belong to this period (Braidwood and Braidwood 1960, 172, pl.134:7), although they become more frequent during the Ubaid period and later. A probable parallel for the miniature axehead from Domuztepe (Figure 10.24:2) has been noted at Sabi Abyad (Copeland 1996, 305–306) and what appear to be similar objects to the tranchet tools from Domuztepe (Figure 10.24:1) are found at Ras Shamra (de Contenson 1992, 80, fig. 115: 3 and 4) and Ras al Amiya (Stronach 1961, 106, pl.XLIII:13). Incised pendants with patterns similar to those found on seals (Figure 10.21) are found at Domuztepe,Chagar Bazar (Cruells 2006, 87–88, pl.4.1: b and pl.4.4: CB1369.), a little later at Tepe Gawra XV (Tobler 1950, pl.CLXXII: 22 and 29, and at Tell Judaidah (Braidwood and Braidwood 1960, 327–8, fig. 252:29).

The use of obsidian for such items as those just listed is relatively rare compared to tool-use and is by no means universal, although it increases markedly in the Halaf period (Figure 10.28). Similar objects are more frequently made of other stone including exotic and local raw materials, but flint does not seem to have been used in this way. The increasing use of obsidian for non-tool items in an emerging complex society is a good example of how raw materials and their use are bound up with and are manipulated within communities in response to various situations (Edmonds 1995, 56–59, 120, 129ff). To understand how such objects functioned within a particular society and whether they were bound up with identity, or even with ownership and accountability, the type and range of objects made needs to be interrogated in terms of origins and choice of the raw materials and who made and used them in the framework of that community and the rest of its material culture (Healey in prep.).

	Beads	Pendants	Spacer beads (large rectangular)	Spacer-beads (large oval)	Spacer beads (other)	Discs and Buttons	Mirrors	Vessels	Axeheads	Tranchet	Inlays	Other
Pre-Halaf	Aswad Catalhoyuk Hacilar Halula Judaidah Ramad Ras Shamra Yarim Tepe I	Aswad Catalhoyuk El Kowm Hacilar Hassuna Jarmo ? Magzaliyah Qdeir Ramad Ras Shamra				Aswad ?	Catalhoyuk				Hacilar Bouqras	Archaq (frag) Askili (bracelet) Nineveh (nail) Sawwan (nail) Shimshara (stud)
Halaf and related	Domuztepe Gawra Halula Judaidah Kurdu Ras Shamra Sabi Abyad Yarim Tepe II	Domuztepe Chagar Bazar Gawra Kurdu Ras Shamra Sabi Abyad	Arpachiyah Banahilk Kazane ?	Aqab Arpachiyah Banahilk Gawra Chagar Bazar Ras Shamra Yarim Tepe III	Banahilk Domuztepe Gawra Halaf Kurdu Ras Shamra Yarim Tepe II ? Yarim Tepe III	Arpachiyah Halaf Ras Shamra	Domuztepe Kabri	Arpachiyah Banahilk Domuztepe Kurdu ? Sabi Abyad ? (palette) Yarim Tepe III (palettes)	Domuztepe Sabi Abyad	Domuztepe Ras Al'Amiya ? Ras Shamra ?	Chagar Bazar	Banahilk (bracelet?) Sabi Abyad (frags) Ras Shamra (stick) Yarim Tepe II
Post-Halaf	Gawra Judaidah Kurdu Malyan Ras Shamra	Byblos Gawra Judaidah Kurdu Ras Shamra Tulintepe	Gawra	Choga Mami	Yarim Tepe III	Arpachiyah Ras Shamra Kurdu		Alalakh Acem Brak Gawra tomb Kenan Kultepe Malyan Ras Shamra Tulintepe Ur Uruk			Yanik Tepe	Gawra (seals/weight) Judaidah Ouelli (stud) Tulintepe (stud) Dorak Treasure

Figure 10.28. Chart summarizing the main occurrences of ground and polished objects of obsidian.

CONCLUSIONS

Comprehensive sourcing and studies of technology and artefact types suggest that the reasons for the use of obsidian are complex, as for other raw materials in Europe. In the Halaf period obsidian continues as a 'must have', but there is a marked change in what is done with it. Its dual nature, outlined by Chataigner *et al.* (1998, 517–518) and discussed by Cauvin (1998), is emphasized and the use of new sources may reflect increasingly widespread contacts.

Lithic artefacts have tended to be treated as utilitarian items and the acquisition of exotic raw materials considered from an economic standpoint, even though their social nature has been explored (e.g. Campbell 2000; Edmonds 1995; Gero 1989; Nassaney 1996, 184). Goring-Morris and Belfer-Cohen (2001, 257) have suggested that we should pay more attention to the symbolic significance of lithic artefacts. It is difficult to uncover such nuances in archaeological data, but obsidian clearly has a fascination beyond the purely utilitarian. For all intents and purposes it seems to be used for everyday tools although it is rarely an essential raw material, and practical uses could be, and were, covered by other materials, such as flint, but obsidian is also used for non-practical purposes. A number of factors could be involved, not least because of the aesthetically pleasing quality of obsidian. There is strong evidence that rocks and minerals have special qualities. In Assyrian texts and classical *Lapidaries* obsidian is regarded as precious with magical, apotropaic, and medicinal qualities (Coqueugniot 1998; Decourt 1998). Flakes of obsidian are used, for example, to represent eyes at Hacilar (Mellart 1970, 103, pl.XV: 9–5) and Yanik Tepe (Burney 1962, 138, pl.XLIII: 12), where they are inserted in the wall of pots, or as inlays in the eyes of a stylised human face at Bouqras (Akkermans *et al.* 1983, 346), as they are elsewhere in the world, for example in Egypt, Easter Island, and so on (Coqueugniot 1998, 356). Exotic materials *per se* have always held a fascination and have inherent meanings and values simply because of their 'foreignness'. Sometimes this characteristic is transferred to the people who acquire them because of their possession of special esoteric knowledge (Helms 1988, 131–171). Indeed, it has been suggested that the acquisition of obsidian in the Levant during the pre-pottery Neolithic is 'dictated by behaviours linked by social honour and show off [sic] in a context marked by the development of social complexity and craft specialization' (Binder and Balkan-Atlı 2001, 15). Could it be that as society becomes increasingly complex, as in the Halaf period, materials which once may have been used for practical purposes, while perhaps carrying information of distant connections and relations, were transformed into items of personal adornment which project information not only about their origins but also about the maker and owner in their particular milieu (Edmonds 1995, 147, 153; cf. for example Sinclair 2000)? Towards the end of the Neolithic period in Europe, Sherratt (1987, 204) has noted a move away from everyday items to a concentration on types and materials with explicit symbolism (though obsidian does not fall into this category in central Europe). We may note an increase in the production of non-utilitarian items in everyday materials, for example the obsidian 'medallion' with a hunting scene in Croatia (Tripković 2003, 122), the finely executed objects made in flint, including daggers and arrowheads such as those from various locations illustrated in the catalogue *Symbols of Power* (Clarke *et al.* 1985), the arrowheads from Breach Farm Down, Wales (Grimes 1938, 115, fig. 6), or the thin, highly polished knife from Burial 6 at Duggleby Howe, Yorkshire, England (Kinnes *et al.* 1983, 86, 98).

It is to be hoped that a more integrated approach to the study of obsidian, together with studies in other areas, will in future allow us to tease out some of these themes within the framework of the raw materials, practices, ideologies and cosmologies of Halaf society.

ACKNOWLEDGEMENTS

I am grateful to Dr Stuart Campbell and Professor Elizabeth Carter and to Rana Özbal for inviting me to study the lithic assemblages from Domuztepe and Tell Kurdu respectively and to use the obsidian data before full publication of the sites. To Dr Harriet Crawford, Institute of Archaeology, University College London, for making the Arpachiyah material available to me and to Dr John Curtis in the British Museum for permission to examine the artefacts there, and to Sarah Collins for assisting me. The photographs were taken by Stuart Campbell and I am grateful to him for allowing me to use them in this publication. The obsidians from Domuztepe were analysed by J.-L. Poidevin in Clermont-Ferrand and those from Tell Kurdu by Gerard Poupeau in Bordeaux. This chapter was initially submitted in 2006 and updated in November 2008.

BIBLIOGRAPHY

Akkermans, P. P. M., 1993, *Villages in the Steppe. Later Neolithic Settlement and Subsistence in the Balikh Valley, N. Syria*. Ann Arbor, Michigan: International Monographs in Prehistory.

Ammerman, A. J. and Andrefsky, W., 1982, Reduction sequences and the exchange of obsidian in Neolithic Calabria. In J. E. Ericson and T. K. Earle (eds), *Contexts for Prehistoric Exchange*, 149–172. New York: Academic Press.

Ammerman, A. J. and Polgaze, C., 1993, New evidence on the exchange of obsidian in Italy. In C. Scarre and F. Healy (eds), *Trade and Exchange in Prehistoric Europe*, 101–107. Oxford: Oxbow Monograph 33.

Andrefsky, W. Jr., 1994, Raw-material availability and the organization of technology. *American Antiquity* 59(1), 21–34.

Astruc, L., Gratuze, B., Pelelgrin, J. and Akkermans, P., 2007, From production to use: a parcel of obsidian bladelets at Sabi Abyad II. In L. Astruc, D. Binder and F. Brios (eds), *Systèmes techniques et communautès du Néolithique précéramique au Proche-Orient. Technical Systems and Near Eastern PPN Communities*, 327–341. Antibes: Éditions APDCA.

Azoury, I. and Bergman, C., 1980, The Halafian lithic assemblage of Shams ed-Din Tannira. *Berytus* 28, 127–143.

Baird, D., 2006, The epipalaeolithic of central Anatolia; the emergence of central Anatolian identities. Unpublished paper given at the '*Trans-Anatolia: bridging the gap between east and west in the archaeology of ancient Anatolia*' conference, British Museum, London, March 2006.

Balkan-Atlı, N. and Der Aprahamian, G., 1998, Les nucléus de Kaletepe et deux ateliers de taille en Cappadoce. In M.-C. Cauvin, A. Gourgaud, B.Gratuze, N. Arnaud, G. Poupeau, J.-L. Poidevin and C. Chataigner (eds), *L'Obsidienne au Proche et Moyen Orient. Du Volcan á L'Outil*, 241–258. Oxford: Maison de L'Orient Méditerranéen/British Archaeological Reports (International Series 738).

Balkan-Atlı, N., Binder, D. and Cauvin, M.-C., 1999, Obsidian: sources, workshops and trade in central Anatolia. In M. Özdoğan and N. Başgelen (eds), *Neolithic in Turkey. The Cradle of Civilisation. New Discoveries*, 133–146. Istanbul: Arkeoloji ve Sanat Yayınları.

Barber, M., Field, D. and Topping P., 1999, *The Neolithic Flint Mines of England*. Swindon: English Heritage.

Bernbeck, R., Pollock, S. and Coursey, C., 1999, The Halaf Settlement at Kazane Hoyuk. Preliminary report on the 1996 and 1997 seasons. *Anatolica* 25, 109–147.

Binder, D., 2002, Stones making sense: what obsidian could tell us about the origins of the central Anatolian Neolithic. In F. Gérard and L. Thissen (eds), *The Neolithic of Central Anatolia. Internal Developments and External Relations During the 9th–6th Millennia cal BC*, 79–90. Istanbul: Ege Yayınları.

Binder, D. and Balkan-Atlı, N., 2001, Obsidian exploitation and blade technology at Kömürcü-Kaletepe (Cappadocia, Turkey). In I. Caneva, C. Lemorini, D. Zampetti and P. Biagi (eds), *Beyond Tools: Redefining the PPN Lithic Assemblages of the Levant. Proceedings of the Third Workshop of PPN Chipped Lithic Industries, Venice 1998*, 1–16. Berlin: ex oriente (Studies in Early Near Eastern Production, Subsistence, and Environment).

Blackman, J., 1984, Provenance studies of Middle Eastern obsidian from sites in Highland Iran. ACS: advances in chemistry, series III. *Archaeological Chemistry* 3, 19–50.

Bostyn, F., 1997, Characterization of flint production and distribution of the tabular Bartonian flint during the early Neolithic (Villeneuve-Saint-Germain period) in France. In R. Schild and Z. Sulgostowska (eds), *Man and Flint*, 171–183. Warsaw: Polish Academy of Sciences (Institute of Archaeology and Ethnology).

Bradley, R. and Edmonds, M., 1993, *Interpreting the Axe Trade. Production and Exchange in Neolithic Britain*. Cambridge: Cambridge University Press.

Braidwood, R. and Braidwood, L., 1960, *Excavation in the Plain of Antioch I. The Earlier Assemblages A-J*. Chicago: University of Chicago Press (Oriental Institute Publication 61).

Breniquet, C., 1996, *La disparition de la Culture de Halaf. Les Origines de la Culture de l'Obeid et le Nord de la Mésopotamie*. Paris: Editions Recherche sur les Civilisations.

Brennan, P., 2000, Obsidian from volcanic sequences and recent alluvial deposits, Erzurum district, north-eastern Anatolia: chemical characterisation and archaeological implications. *Ancient Near Eastern Studies* 37, 128–152.

Burney, C., 1962, Excavations at Yanik Tepe, Azerbijan 1961 – second preliminary report. *Iraq* 24, 134–153.

Campbell, S., 1992, Culture, Chronology and Change in the Later Neolithic of Northern Mesopotamia. Unpublished PhD thesis, University of Edinburgh, Scotland, UK.

Campbell, S., 1997, Problems of definition: the origins of the Halaf in North Iraq. *Suartu* 4(1), 39–52.

Campbell, S., 1999, Archaeological constructs and past reality on the Upper Euphrates. In G. del Olmo Lete and J. Montero Feneollós (eds), *Archaeology of the Upper Syrian Euphrates: The Tishrin Dam Area*, 573–583. Barcelona: Editorial Ausa.

Campbell, S., 2000, The Burnt House at Arpachiyah: a re-examination. *Bulletin of the American Schools of Oriental Research* 318, 1–40.

Campbell, S., 2005, Domuztepe 2005. *Anatolian Archaeology* 11, 13–15.

Campbell, S., Carter, E., Healey, E., Anderson, S., Kennedy, A., Whitcher S. 1999, Emerging complexity on the Kahramanmaraş plain, Turkey: the Domuztepe project 1995–1997. *American Journal of Archaeology* 103, 395–418.

Caneva, I., Conti, A.-M., Lemorini, C. and Zampetti, D., 1994, The lithic production at Çayönü: a preliminary overview of the aceramic sequence. In H. G. Gebel and S. K Kosłowski (eds), *Neolithic Chipped Stone Industries of the Fertile Crescent*, 253–266. Berlin: ex oriente (Studies in Early Near Eastern Production, Subsistence and Environment 1).

Carter, T., Conolly, J. and Spasojević, A., 2006a, The chipped stone. In I. Hodder (ed.), *Changing Materialities at Çatalhöyük: Reports from the 1995–1999 Seasons*. Cambridge: McDonald Institute Monographs/British Institute of Archaeology at Ankara Monograph.

Carter, T., Poupeau, G., Bressy, C. and Pearce, N. J. G., 2006b, A new programme of obsidian characterization at Çatalhöyük, Turkey. *Journal of Archaeological Science* 33 (7), 893–909.

Cauvin, J., 1998, La signification symbolique de l'obsidienne. In M.-C. Cauvin, A. A. Gourgaud, B. Gratuze, N. Arnaud, G. Poupeau, J.-L. Poidevin and C. Chataigner (eds), *L'Obsidienne au Proche et Moyen Orient. Du Volcan á L'Outil*, 379–382. Oxford: Maison de L'Orient Méditerranéen/British Archaeological Reports (International Series 738).

Cauvin, J., 2000, (translated by T. Watkins), *The Birth of the Gods and the Origins of Agriculture*. Cambridge: Cambridge University Press.

Cauvin, M.-C., 1998, L'obsidienne: données récentes provenant de sites-habitats néolithiques. In M.-C. Cauvin, A. A. Gourgaud, B. Gratuze, N. Arnaud, G. Poupeau, J.-L. Poidevin and C. Chataigner (eds), *L'Obsidienne au Proche et Moyen Orient. Du Volcan á L'Outil*, 259–272. Oxford: Maison de L'Orient Méditerranéen/British Archaeological Reports (International Series 738).

Cauvin, M.-C., Balkan, N., Besnus, Y. and Şaroğlu, F., 1986, Origine de l'obsidienne de Cafer Höyük (Turquie): premiers résultats. *Paléorient* 12(2), 89–97.

Cauvin, M.-C. and Chataigner, C., 1998, Distribution de l'obsidienne dans les sites archéologiques du Proche et Moyen Orient. In M.-C. Cauvin, A. Gourgaud, B. Gratuze, N. Arnaud, G. Poupeau, J.-L. Poidevin and C. Chataigner (eds), *L'Obsidienne au Proche et Moyen Orient. Du Volcan á L'Outil*, 325–350. Oxford: Maison de L'Orient Méditerranéen/British Archaeological Reports (International Series 738).

Cauvin, M.-C., Gourgaud A., Gratuze, B., Arnaud, N., Poupeau G., Poidevin J.-L. and Chataigner, C. (eds), 1998, *L'Obsidienne au Proche et Moyen Orient. Du Volcan á L'Outil*. Oxford: Maison de L'Orient Méditerranéen/British Archaeological Reports (International Series 738).

Cessford, C. and Carter, C., 2005, Quantifying the consumption of obsidian at Neolithic Çatalhöyük, Turkey. *Journal of Field Archaeology* 30, 305–315.

Chataigner, C., 1998, Sources des artefacts du Proche Orient d'après leur caractérisation géochimique. In M.-C. Cauvin, A. Gourgaud, B. Gratuze, N. Arnaud, G. Poupeau, J.-L. Poidevin and C. Chataigner (eds), *L'Obsidienne au Proche et Moyen Orient. Du Volcan á L'Outil*, 273–324. Oxford: Maison de L'Orient Méditerranéen/British Archaeological Reports (International Series 738).

Chataigner, C., Poidevin, J.-L. and Arnaud, N. O., 1998, Turkish occurrences of obsidian and use by prehistoric people in the Near East from 14,000 to 6000 BP. *Journal of Volcanology and Geothermal Research* 85, 517–537.

Clarke, D. V., Cowie. T. G. and Foxon, A., 1985, *Symbols of Power at the Time of Stonehenge*. Edinburgh: HMSO.

Conolly, J., 1999, *The Çatalhöyük Flint and Obsidian Industry: Technology and Typology in Context*. Oxford: British Archaeological Reports (International Series 787).

Copeland, L., 1996, The flint and obsidian industries. In P. M. M. Akkermans (ed.), *Tell Sabi Abyad. The Late Neolithic Settlement. Report on the Excavations of the University of Amsterdam (1988)*, 285–338. Istanbul: Nederlands Historisch-Archaeologisch Instituut te Istanbul.

Coqueugniot, E., 1998, L'obsidienne en Méditerrané orientale aux époques post-néolithiques. In M.-C. Cauvin, A. Gourgaud, B. Gratuze, N. Arnaud, G. Poupeau, J.-L. Poidevin and C. Chataigner (eds), *L'Obsidienne au Proche et Moyen Orient. Du Volcan á L'Outil*, 351–362. Oxford: Maison de L'Orient Méditerranéen/British Archaeological Reports (International Series 738).

Davidson, T. E. and Watkins, T., 1981, Two seasons of excavation at Tell Aqab in the Jezireh, north-east Syria. *Iraq* 43, 1–18.

de Contenson, H., 1992, *Préhistoire de Ras Shamra. Les Sondages Stratigraphiques de 1955 à 1976*. Paris: Éditions Recherché sur les Civilisations.

Cruells, W. , 2006, Les Objets. In Ö. Tunca and A. M. Baghdo (eds) *Chagar Bazar (Syrie) 1. Les Sondages Préhistoriques (1999–2001)*, 81–94. Louvain Paris and Dudley (MA) Peeters: APHAO. Publications de la Mission archéologique de l'Université de Liège en Syrie.

Decourt, J., 1998, L'obsidienne dans les sources anciennes. Notes sur l'histoire du mot et l'utilisation de la roche dans l'antiquité. In M.-C.Cauvin, A. Gourgaud, B. Gratuze, N. Arnaud, G. Poupeau,

J.-L. Poidevin and C. Chataigner (eds), *L'Obsidienne au Proche et Moyen Orient. Du Volcan á L'Outil*, 363–378. Oxford: Maison de L'Orient Méditerranéen/British Archaeological Reports (International Series 738).

Diebold, B. E., 2004, Excavations at Tell Kurdu, 2001: the pottery. In R. Özbal, F. Gerritsen, B. Diebold, E. Healey, N. Aydın, M. Loyet, F. Nardulli, D. Reese, H. Ekstrom, S. Sholts, N. Mekel-Bobrov and B. Lahn, Tell Kurdu Exavations 2001. *Anatolica* 30, 52–54.

Edens, C., 2000, The chipped stone industry at Hacinebi: technological styles and social identity. *Paléorient* 25(1), 23–33.

Edmonds, M, 1995, *Stone Tools and Society*. London: Batsford.

Ferrer, A., 2006, Chantier E. L'industrie lithique. In Ö. Tunca and A. M. Baghdo *(eds) Chagar Bazar (Syrie) 1. Les Sondages Préhistoriques (1999–2001)*, 95–101. Louvain Paris and Dudley (MA) Peeters: APHAO. Publications de la Mission archéologique de l'Université de Liège en Syrie.

Francaviglia, V., 1990, Les gisements d'obsidienne hyperalcaline dans l'ancien monde: étude comparative. *Revue d'Archéometrie* 14, 43–64.

Gero, J., 1989, Assessing social information in material objects: how well do lithics measure up? In R. Torrence (ed.), *Time, Energy and Stone Tools*: 92–105. Cambridge: Cambridge University Press.

Goring-Morris, N and Belfer-Cohen, A., 2001, The symbolic realms of utilitarian material culture: the role of lithics. In I. Caneva, C. Lemorini, D. Zampetti and P. Biagi (eds), *Beyond Tools: Redefining the PPN Lithic Assemblages of the Levant*, 257–273. Berlin: ex oriente (Studies in Early Near Eastern Production, Subsistence and Environment 9).

Grimes, W. F., 1938, A barrow on Breach Farm, Llanbleddian, Glamorgan. *Proceedings of the Prehistoric Society* 4(1), 107–121.

Healey, E., 2000, The Role of Obsidian in the Late Halaf. Unpublished PhD thesis, University of Manchester, England, UK.

Healey, E., 2004, Tell Kurdu 2001: chipped stone. In R. Özbal, F. Gerritsen, B. Diebold, E. Healey, N. Aydın, M. Loyet, F. Nardulli, D. Reese, H. Ekstrom, S. Sholts, N. Mekel-Bobrov, B. Lahn, Tell Kurdu Excavations 2001. *Anatolica* 30, 56–60.

Healey, E., 2007, Obsidian as an indicator of inter-regional contacts and exchange: three case-studies from the Halaf period. *Anatolian Studies* 57, 171–189.

Healey, E. and Campbell, S., 2009, The challenge of characterizing large assemblages of exotic materials: a case study of the obsidian from Domuztepe, S.E. Turkey. *Internet Archaeology* 26 (http://intarch.ac.uk/journal/issue26/healy_index.html).

Helms, M. W., 1988, *Ulysses' Sail: An Ethnographic Odyssey of Power, Knowledge and Geographical Distance*. Princeton: Princeton University Press.

Inizan, M.-L. and Lechevallier, M., 1994, L'adoption du débitage laminaire par pression au Proche-Orient. In H. G. Gebel and S. K Kosłowski (eds), *Neolithic Chipped Stone Industries of the Fertile Crescent*, 23–30. Berlin: ex oriente (Studies in Early Near Eastern Production, Subsistence and Environment 1).

Kinnes, I., Schadla-Hall, T., Chadwick, P. and Dean, P., 1983, Duggleby Howe reconsidered. *Archaeological Journal* 140, 83–108.

Kobayashi, K. and Sagona, A., 2007, A survey of obsidian sources in the provinces of Erzurum, Erzincan, Rize and Bitlis, 2006. In *25. Araştırma Sonuçları Toplantısı 2. Cilt. (29 Mayıs –01 Haziran 2007)*, 185–196. Kocaeli: T.C. Kültür ve Turizm Bakanlığı. Kültür Varlıkları ve Müzeler Genel Müdürlüğü.

Maeda, O., 1998, Chipped and ground stone artefacts. In A. Tsuneki and Y. Miyake (eds), *Excavations at Tell Umm Qseir in Middle Khabur Valley, North Syria. Report of the 1996 season*: 86–107 and 189–196. Tsukuba: University of Tsukuba (Studies for West Asian Archaeology: Al-Shark 1).

Maeda, O., 2003, Prehistoric obsidian distribution in the Rouj basin. In T. Iwasaki and A. Tsuneki (eds), *Archaeology of the Rouj Basin. A Regional Study of the Transition from Village to City in Northwest Syria. Vol.1*, 167–186. Tsukuba: University of Tsukuba (Studies for West Asian Archaeology: Al-Shark 2).

Mallowan, M., 1947, Excavations at Brak and Chagar Bazar. *Iraq* 9, 1–266.

Mallowan, M and Rose, J. C., 1935, Excavations at Tell Arpachiyah 1933. *Iraq* 2, 1–178.

Mellaart, J., 1970, *Excavations at Hacilar*. Edinburgh: Edinburgh University Press.

Merpert, N. Ya. and Munchaev, R. M., 1993a, Yarim Tepe II: the Halaf levels. In N. Yoffe and J. J. Clark (eds), *Early Stages in the Evolution of Mesopotamian Civilisation. Soviet Excavations in Northern Iraq*, 128–162. Tucson and London: University of Arizona Press.

Merpert, N. Ya. and Munchaev, R. M., 1993b, Yarim Tepe III: the Halaf levels. In N. Yoffe and J. J. Clark (eds), *Early Stages in the Evolution of Mesopotamian Civilisation. Soviet Excavations in Northern Iraq*, 163–206. Tucson and London: University of Arizona Press.

Molist, M. and Ferrer, A., 1996, Industries lithiques de la période 8000–7500 B.P. à Tell Halula (Moyen Euphrate Syrien). In S. K. Kosłowski and H. G. Gebel (eds), *Neolithic Chipped Stone Industries of the Fertile Crescent and their Contemporaries in Adjacent Regions*, 431–441. Berlin: ex oriente (Studies in Near Eastern Production, Subsistence and Environment 3).

Nassaney, M. S., 1996, The role of chipped stone in the political economy of social ranking. In G. H. Odell (ed.), *Stone Tools. Theoretical Insights into Human Prehistory*, 181–228. New York and London: Plenum Press.

Nishiaki, Y., 1993, Anatolian obsidian and Neolithic obsidian industries of north Syria: a preliminary review. *Essays on Anatolian Archaeology* 7, 140–160.

Özbal, R., Gerritsen, F., Özbal, R., Gerritsen, F., Diebold, B., Healey, E., Aydın, N., Loyet, M., Nardulli, F., Reese, D., Ekstrom, H., Sholts, S., Mekel-Bobrov, N., Lahn, B., 2004, Tell Kurdu Exavations 2001. *Anatolica* 30, 37–107.

Pernika, E., Keller, J. and Cauvin, M.-C., 1997, Obsidian from Anatolian sources in the Neolithic of the middle Euphrates region, Syria. *Paléorient* 23(1), 113–122.

Pétrequin, P., Pétrequin, A.-M., Jeudy, F., Jeuness, C., Monnier, J-L., Pelegrin, J. and Praud, I., 1998, From the raw material to the Neolithic stone axe. Production processes and social context. In M. Edmonds and C. Richards (eds), *Understanding the Neolithic of North-Western Europe*, 277–311. Glasgow: Cruithne Press.

Poidevin, J.-L., 1998, Les gisements d'obsidienne de Turquie et de Tanscaucadie: géologie, géochemie et chronométrie. In M.-C. Cauvin, A. Gourgaud, B. Gratuze, N. Arnaud, G. Poupeau, J.-L. Poidevin and C. Chataigner (eds), *L'Obsidienne au Proche et Moyen Orient. Du Volcan á L'Outil*, 105–404. Oxford: Maison de L'Orient Méditerranéen/British Archaeological Reports (International Series 738).

Poupeau, G., Delerue, S., Carter, T., Pereira, C. E. de B., Miekeley, N. and Bellot-Gurlet, L., 2005, How homogeneneous is the "East Golludag" (Cappadocia, Turkey) obsidian "source" composition? *International Association of Obsidian Studies Bulletin* 32, 3–8.

Prauzsnitz, M. W., 1969, The excavations at Kabri. *Erezt̄ Israel* 9, 122–129 (in Hebrew; English summary on p.137).

Renfrew, C., 1975, Trade as an action of distance: questions of integrations and communication. In J. A. Sabloff and C. C. Lamberg-Karlovsky (eds), *Ancient Civilisation and Trade*, 3–59. Albuquerque: University of New Mexico Press.

Renfrew, C., 1977, Alternative models for exchange and spatial distribution. In T. K. Earle and J. E. Ericson (eds), *Exchange Systems in Prehistory*, 71–90. London and New York: Academic Press.

Renfrew, C., Dixon, J. E. and Cann, J., 1966, Obsidian and early cultural contact in the Near East. *Proceedings of the Prehistoric Society* 32, 30–72.

Renfrew, C., Dixon, J. E. and Cann, J., 1968, Further analysis of Near Eastern obsidians. *Proceedings of the Prehistoric Society* 34, 319–331.

Renfrew, C. and Dixon, J. E., 1976, Obsidian in western Asia: a review. In G. de G. Sieveking, I. H. Longworth and K. E. Wilson (eds), *Problems in Economic and Social Archaeology*, 137–150. London: Duckworth.

Rosenberg, M., 1994, Preliminary description of lithic industry from Hallan Çemi. In H. G. Gebel and S. K Kosłowski (eds), *Neolithic Chipped Stone Industries of the Fertile Crescent*, 223–238. Berlin: ex oriente (Studies in Early Near Eastern Production, Subsistence and Environment 1).

Rosenberg, M., 1999, Hallan Çemi. In M. Özdoğan and N. Başgelen (eds), *Neolithic in Turkey. The Cradle of Civilisation. New Discoveries*, 25–33. Istanbul: Arkeoloji ve Sanat Yayınları.

Sherratt, A., 1987, Neolithic exchange systems in central Europe 5000–3000 BC. In G. de G. Sieveking and M. H. Newcomer (eds), *The Human Uses of Flint and Chert. Proceedings of the Fourth International Flint Symposium held at Brighton Polytechnic 10–15 April 1983*, 193–204. Cambridge: Cambridge University Press.

Sinclair, A., 2000, Constellations of knowledge. Human agency and material affordance in lithic technology. In M.-A. Dobres and J. Robb (eds), *Agency in Archaeology*, 196–212. London and New York: Routledge.

Skinner, C. E., 2008, *Obsidian Terminology*. (accessed 4 October 2008) http://www.obsidianlab. com/terminology.html

Stronach, D., 1961, Excavations at Ras Al'Amiya. *Iraq* 23, 95–137.

Tobler, A. J., 1950, *Excavations at Tepe Gawra*. Philadelphia: University of Pennsylvania Press.

Tripković, B., 2003, The quality and value in Neolithic Europe: an alternative view on obsidian artefacts. In Ts. Tsonev and E. M. Kokelj (eds), *The Humanised Mineral World. Towards Social and Symbolic Evaluation of Prehistoric Technologies in South Eastern Europe*, 119–123. Liége-Sofia: Études et Recherches Archéologique de l'Université de Liége 103.

Tykot, R. H. and Ammerman, A. J., 1997, New directions in central Mediterranean obsidian studies. *Antiquity* 71, 1000–1006.

von Oppenheim, M., 1933, *Tell Halaf. A New Culture in Oldest Mesopotamia*. London and New York: G. P. Putnam's Sons.

von Oppenheim, M. and Schmidt, H., 1943, *Tell Halaf I: Die Prähistorichen Funde*. Berlin: Walter de Gruter and Co.

Watson, P. J., 1983, The soundings at Banahilk. In L. Braidwood, R. Braidwood, B. Howe, C. Reed and P. Watson (eds), *Prehistoric Archaeology along the Zagros Flanks*, 545–613. Chicago: Oriental Institute (Oriental Institute Publications 105).

Watson, P. J. and Leblanc, S. A., 1990, *Girikihaciyan. A Halafian Site in Southeastern Turkey*. Los Angeles: University of California (Institute of Archaeology, Monograph 33).

Wilke, P. J., 1996, Bullet-shaped micro-blade cores of the near Eastern Neolithic: experimental replicative studies. In S. K. Kosłowski and H. G. Gebel (eds), *Neolithic Chipped Stone Industries of the Fertile Crescent and their Contemporaries in Adjacent Regions*, 289–310. Berlin: ex oriente (Studies in Near Eastern Production, Subsistence and Environment 3).

Yalçinkaya, I., 1998, Découvres paléolithiques en obsidenne en Anatolie orientale. In M.-C. Cauvin, A. Gourgaud, B. Gratuze, N. Arnaud, G. Poupeau, J.-L. Poidevin and C. Chataigner (eds), *L'Obsidienne au Proche et Moyen Orient. Du Volcan á L'Outil*, 235–240. Oxford: Maison de L'Orient Méditerranéen/British Archaeological Reports (International Series 738).

Yener, K. A., Edens, C., Cassana, J., Diebold, B., Ekstrom, H. Loye, M. and Özbal, R., 2000, Tell Kurdu Excavations 1999. *Anatolica* 26, 31–117.

Chapter 11

Polished rectangular flint knives – elaboration or replication?

Roy Loveday

INTRODUCTION

The terms 'prestige' and 'elaborate' have been applied to a range of Later Neolithic artefacts in Britain (Edmonds 1995; 1998; Kinnes 1979; Manby 1974) but none appear more deserving of the title than polished rectangular flint knives. Only waisted, edge-polished axeheads of the Seamer and Duggleby series approach their quality, yet neither so exceptionally strain the boundaries of flint technology. Polished rectangular flint knives are quite simply virtuoso products combining extravagant flake size and precise shaping with exceptional thinness and often exquisite finish. No simple functional criterion appears to explain these features; the parallel-sided form coupled with considerable breadth would appear to have rendered the implements extremely awkward to use, as would the fragility of the finest pieces. Moreover, as Saville (1981, 56) has emphasized, polish may enhance the resilience or precision of an edge but its application to the entire surface of an implement of this type rendered no advantage. Purely aesthetic factors it seems must be accorded primacy.

But what underlay these aesthetic factors? Familiar arguments emphasize prestige elaboration of male accoutrements, either as individual identifying artefacts or as elements of a fully-fledged prestige goods system, but the morphological choices made in this process are rarely questioned. If we can begin to understand their basis we might better grasp the motors driving change in the Mid–Late Neolithic period.

CLASSIFICATION AND ITS PROBLEMS

Polished rectangular flint knives in Britain are of two distinct types: flake knives and so-called 'discoidal' knives. The former, as their name suggests, are generally smaller, thinner, 'finer', and more fragile than the discoidal knife type. In Manby's corpus of polished knives and related Later Neolithic artefacts in northern England the wholly polished flake knives were classified as type 1 (Manby 1974, 113). This is an extremely rare form; only four were recorded in a total of 63 polished flake knives (Manby 1974, 113–115). They occurred with burials at Duggleby Howe (burial D)[1] and Aldro C75, Yorkshire (Manby 1974, fig. 36:1–2; Mortimer 1905, figs 58 & 160), and as stray finds at Goathland, Yorkshire (Manby 1974, fig. 36:3), and Elton Moor, Derbyshire (Radley and Cooper 1968, fig. 3:23); the latter, however, is broken and has a somewhat tapering form.

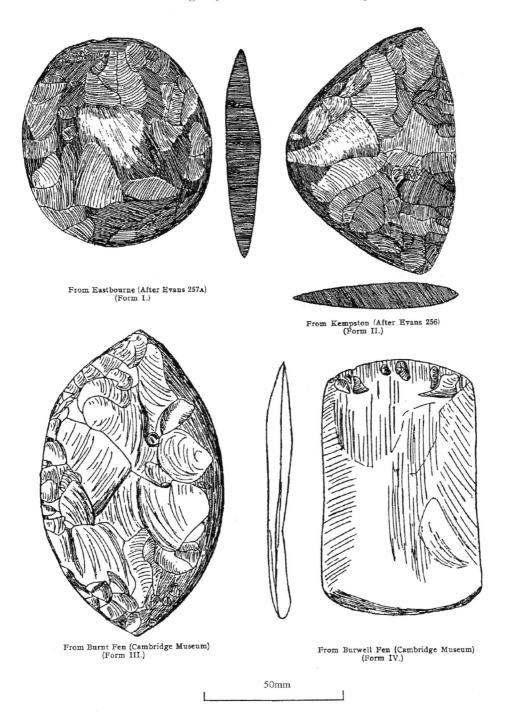

From Eastbourne (After Evans 257A)
(Form I.)

From Kempston (After Evans 256)
(Form II.)

From Burnt Fen (Cambridge Museum)
(Form III.)

From Burwell Fen (Cambridge Museum)
(Form IV.)

50mm

Figure 11.1. Discoidal knife types (after Clark 1928).

Polished rectangular 'discoidal' knives are larger, heavier and thicker than Manby's type 1 polished flake knives. Clark (1928) linked the rectangular examples (his type IV) to a series of other knives exemplified by the circular-horseshoe form (type I) – hence the discoidal label. He recognized a series ranging through sub-triangular/fan (type II) and lozenge shapes (type III) and implied that the rectangular form (type IV) represented the final refinement of the type (Figure 11.1), significantly remarking that: '[i]n this form ... it is impossible to trace any transitional forms' (Clark 1928, 44). It is that point which I will concentrate on here – the lack of fit of type IV knives in the discoidal series. Flake knife forms are not discussed in view of the extreme rarity of fully polished forms; all classification hereafter relates to Clark's 1928 paper. Clark linked implements in his discoidal series to edge-polished scrapers rather than knives, since he considered their bluntly bevelled edges to have been distinctly poor for cutting. But, as Saville (1981, 56) has emphasized in the Grimes Graves report, while scrapers and type I knives may share general form, their edges and extent of grinding and polishing are very different. Nevertheless, seeking instead an origin in the knife series is equally problematic. Although Clark's type I (D-shape discoidal variant) roughly resembles the simple backed knife, the 'business' edges are *reversed*; the curved edge here is for cutting and the straight edge blunted. Equally, parallel-sided flake knives are generally longer and far narrower than type IV discoidal knives (proportions of 1:5/6 as against 1:2). Nor is the distinctive overall polish commonly encountered.

Type III discoidal knives – largely restricted to East Anglia – do, however, bear more than a passing resemblance to earlier laurel leaves. They are similarly bifacially worked, slightly asymmetric, have a convex cutting edge opposed to a more irregular, partially blunted edge, and lack clear points. Laurel leaves were noted as being of both leaf and sub-triangular shape at the Staines, Surrey, causewayed enclosure (Robertson Mackay 1987, 101), and an example from the upper levels at Windmill Hill, Wiltshire, displays evidence of polishing at points along its edges and across adjacent flake scars (Smith 1965, 99–100). Significantly perhaps, grinding and polishing on type III lozenge-shaped discoidal knives are frequently restricted to one curved edge, and are certainly less extensive than on many type I knives – Clark's favoured progenitors. Continued emphasis on such a long curved cutting-edge (perhaps for flaying purposes) might explain the 'spearheads/ovates/knife blanks/laurel leaves' found in Later Neolithic contexts at, amongst other places, Liffs Lowe, Derbyshire (Bateman 1848, 4–43), and in the York hoard (Clarke *et al.* 1985, 172, fig. 5.9). Leaf and triangular forms might then be conceived as leading, via the impetus to elaboration, to D-shaped and round forms – the latter perhaps influenced by scraper morphology rather than technology. But where would type IV knives fit into such a development?

ELABORATION? FORM AND SEQUENCE

A few sub-rectangular polished discoidal knives appear intermediate between types I and IV, exhibiting something of the curved edge along one side (Clay 1929). This is, however, entirely missing from the finest specimens, which are characterized by parallel sides and by ends that vary from flat to convex. In several examples, one or both of these ends represent the only real cutting edges; as Clark remarked regarding the highly polished examples from Burwell and Quy in East Anglia: '... the two ends are sharp, the sides relatively blunt' (Clark

1928, 44). This is even evident in the short, minimally polished example from a swallow hole on Carnaby Top, near Rudston, Yorkshire (Site 12: Manby 1974, 26–28, 86). Importantly, the Grooved Ware/Beaker context of the Carnaby Top find considerably pre-dates the Middle Bronze Age context of an unpolished, sub-rectangular specimen from the 1972 shaft at Grimes Graves (Saville 1981, 21, 56, fig. 51). This suggests that the sub-rectangular type, rather than being intermediate in a process that witnessed the cutting edge diminish and migrate from side to ends, *could* be later; perhaps a response to – rather than a step towards – the novel form of type IV rectangular knives.

Clearly much here depends on dating evidence and that is sadly lacking. Discoidal knives were not selected as grave goods and the numerous surface finds of type IV knives from North Dale in Grindale, Yorkshire, 10 km to the east of Rudston, emanated from a huge multi-period flint scatter (Durden 1995). A broken fragment of a type IV knife came from the lower of two surfaces producing Grooved Ware at Honington in Suffolk, but that same surface also produced 16 chisel arrowheads, a type more usually associated with Peterborough Ware (Green 1980), and this ceramic was found on the edge of the 20 m wide area being investigated (Fell 1951, 33–34). The most that can be currently said is that much of the output of Grooved Ware activity at Grimes Graves appears to have been directed toward the production of discoidal knives, although probably primarily of type I and II forms, and that an example of the former (D shaped) has been recovered from the sealed context of a pit (703) containing Grooved Ware at Abbey Quarry, Doulting, Somerset (Lewis 2005, 108–110).[2]

It is of course possible that there was no simple developmental sequence. The type IV knife shape could have been opportunistically triggered by an equation drawn between fortuitously parallel-sided 'Levalloisoid' flakes and narrow blade knives. Durden (1995, 430) has argued from the lower than predicted incidence of tortoise cores on a production site at North Dale, Yorkshire, and the evidence of bifacial working (unnecessary on the ventral face of a flake to be polished), that tortoise cores were being recycled for knife production. This has much to recommend it, yet fails to furnish a *raison d'être* for the severely rectangular form that characterizes the output of knives from the site – tortoise cores being essentially polygonal (Durden 1995, fig. 4).

Form certainly appears to have been of central importance; whether from Wales or Wiltshire, the Yorkshire Wolds or the Fen edge, type IV knives cluster markedly at around 90 mm in length and 55 mm in breadth. With few examples below 80 × 50 mm this virtual standardization is striking. It belies the notion that they were merely the upper, prestige, end of a broad flake knife continuum. If that were so a significant number of smaller examples could be predicted.

Extravagant care was also lavished on their finish (Figures 11.2–11.3). Grinding and polishing to remove *all* signs of flake scars across the entire body of the implement – unique it seems to type IV knives – can have had no functional basis. It has additionally reduced many to a level of fragility that precludes effective use, and compounds the handling difficulties of instruments too wide to easily cup in the hand and, bizarrely, often sharpened at both ends (Clark 1928, 44; Clay 1929; Evans 1897, 339–342). A wide parallel-sided knife would be difficult to use; one where the cutting edges lay at the ends, ridiculously so. Handling problems akin to those encountered using the ends of a comparably sized modern credit card (85 × 55 mm) for cutting suggests that functional development from within the discoidal series is improbable.

Prestige elaboration may of course pay scant regard to function and the distinctive nature of these type IV knives is emphasized by their distribution within Yorkshire. Manby's (1974, 111–115) invaluable corpus reveals that, with only a couple of examples of Clark's type II–III discoidal knives from the county, types I and IV dominate. Numerically they are closely comparable, but in distribution, *totally different*. Whereas type I knives are widely spread, 75 per cent of the type IV specimens come from the Grindale and abutting Bridlington areas; some 86 per cent if we include material subsequently recorded by Martin Green (pers. comm.) and Earnshaw (1995). More importantly, none has been certainly provenanced beyond 15 km of that centre. The Grindale region would appear to have been *both* production and consumption area. Similarly in the Peak District of Derbyshire, type IV knives are clustered at, and within 2 km of, the Arbor Low henge monument (Burl 2000, 288–291; Manby 1974, 111). The prestige implications of this are greater if we suppose types I and IV to have been in contemporary use, but either way a picture of restriction emerges.

Apparent concentration of production at Grindale supports this. Within a very extensive spread of Later Neolithic flint-working debris at least 14 type IV knives have been recorded, mostly from a single area within one field (Earnshaw 1995; Lewis 1987; Martin Green pers. comm). In addition to three complete specimens (Figures 11.2–11.3; Earnshaw 1995, fig. 7), eleven fragments display characteristic straight sides, slightly oblique corners, or gently convex ends. Most of these have been reworked but in a very clumsy manner and others appear to have been deliberately smashed and even 'butchered' – percussion points being

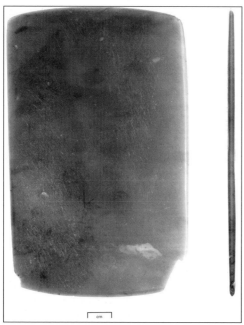

Figure 11.2. Polished rectangular knife 1 from North Dale, Yorkshire (Martin Green collection). (Photo: David Cousins).

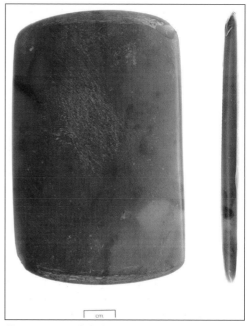

Figure 11.3. Polished rectangular knife 2 from North Dale, Yorkshire (Martin Green collection). (Photo: David Cousins).

clearly visible on one fragment (Martin Green pers. comm.). Exhaustive analysis of the background debitage suggests they emanated principally from an extensive domestic scatter that contrasted with a specialist knapping area some 400 metres away, where skilled primary shaping was probably undertaken (Durden 1995, 416–417, fig. 4.3; Lewis 1987). Breakage, and attendant frustration, during final polishing on a production site, rather than ritual destruction, seems probable. Interestingly, production on the site seems very rarely to have included the more common discoidal knife forms. The fact that the only closely provenanced type I knife (Earnshaw 1995, fig. 7.6) comes from a field wholly peripheral to the type IV scatter supports detachment of the distinctive polished rectangular implements from the series. The fact that the polished discoidal knife types found in Scotland appear, from Clark's (1928) corpus, to have been exclusively of type I and IV, accords with other evidence for prestige artefact exchange between communities there and in eastern Yorkshire (Sheridan 1992, 206–207). A similar picture emerges from Derbyshire. By contrast, in southern England the dominant forms are types I and II, whilst in the spread of implements along the eastern Fen edge all types are represented. Genesis of the discoidal series – perhaps through the development and elaboration of laurel leaves to type II/III knives – may well have occurred in the latter area but there is no sign there of the close grouping of type IV implements that mark out eastern Yorkshire. Polished rectangular flint knives appear rather to have been tightly controlled northern prestige artefacts, produced in isolation and circulating along the North Sea coast from the Fens to the Borders, with just a few outliers beyond those limits.

Yet, even viewed as non-functional prestige artefacts, type IV knives do present problems. Unlike most of the other items in the prestige repertoire – axeheads, maceheads, belt sliders – they appear to have had little apparent display potential. Backed examples, like that from Frisby in Leicestershire (Graf and Pirie 1986), might conceivably have been hafted, but the quality of the all-over polishing applied to the finest specimens makes this far less likely in their case. Split hafting is practical but implausible; why go to such lengths to produce an extravagantly broad implement when two smaller blades set on opposing side of a haft would produce the same visual effect? With no apparent means of hanging or mounting, display would presumably have been limited to a small group. Why then was this type IV template, that displays a distinct lack of fit with the rest of the discoidal knife series, chosen for such extravagant shaping and polishing rather than equally impressive, but developmentally cohesive, types I–III? Since these exquisite polished rectangular knives appear neither to offer functional advantage nor very obvious display potential, should we seek a *raison d'être* for them outwith the series altogether?

REPLICATION? PROTOTYPES AND STIMULI

Replication in flint of a quite different artefact type would necessarily have drawn on common, specialized 'Levalloisoid' core technology and on grinding expertise. In the case of type IV knives, however, this is pushed to its limits. Extreme difficulty of production, lavish attention to polishing, and lack of very obvious display potential, all argue for a compelling prototype.

Orcadian stone tools have been advanced as prototypes for the classic type I discoidal knives (Saville 1994). A decorated knife from the early phase settlement at Skara Brae was manufactured from a thin sandstone pebble, given a bifacially bevelled cutting edge on its broad side and blunted on the other, and decorated with shallow incisions. To judge from its overall polish (from use or curation in a leather pouch) it was a valued item, unlike the expediently produced, disposable Skaill knives that it resembles; one such was, however, found with comparable decoration. These items might, if transferred to a different milieu, attain enhanced significance – in their own right or by association – and thus furnish prototypes for the main discoidal series. But only two artefacts from this northern source have much in common with type IV rectangular knives. One is a small (52 × 46 mm) thin, sub-square piece of sandstone with a bifacially ground edge from the early phase settlement at Skara Brae (Clarke 1976, fig. 5.2); the other is the blade end fragment of an unusually narrow (13 mm) parallel-sided polished axehead from Barnhouse (Clarke 2005, 331, fig. 14.1c). The former is square rather than rectangular and rather undistinguished as a possible prototype form; the latter, being incomplete, is unknowable.

A potentially closer northern prototype exists in the Shetland felsite knife (Varndell 2004, 120). These were flaked and then ground on opposing sides to produce highly polished ovate plates sometimes as little as 4 mm thick. Their large size (150–200 mm – twice the size of type IV discoidal knives) makes then ideal prestige artefacts and hoards of stacked or arranged knives suggest special deposits. Others have been re-sharpened and obviously used. Like type I discoidal knives their sharpened edge encircles the implement with the exception of one blunted side. This is quite unlike the sharpened ends of type IV knives, however, and Shetland knives remain unknown outside Shetland, with the possible exception of a stray find from Lanarkshire (Fojut 1993, 28–29).

The almost standardized form of type IV knives suggests careful replication of a more precise, noteworthy prototype. Casting the net wider furnishes a strikingly close parallel in another type of raw material – the copper rectangular flat axehead. This copper artefact type is rare in the West but widespread in central and south-eastern Europe: Type Vinča and Type Bytyń (variant B) in Poland (Szpunar 1987); Type Altheim in Slovakia (Novotná 1970); Group VII in Moravia (Říhovský 1992); and Type Vinča in Austria (Mayer 1977). It has also been recorded in Denmark (Vandkilde 1996, 55–57). Although it occurs in two basic forms – with and without the cutting edge slightly expanded to form points – this is only recognized as a basis for typological distinction in Poland (Szpunar 1987, 14–18). It is possible that the form lacking points (Bytyń variant B) results from frequent resharpening of Type Vinča implements by grinding (subsequently at both ends), and the use of such worn specimens as mould prototypes by south-eastern TRB copper working groups (Midgely 1992, 295–296). Equally, lateral expansion of the cutting edge might result from periodic hammer sharpening and annealing (Stuart Needham pers. comm.). A further distinction can be drawn over the thickness of the artefacts; those few known from western contexts are fairly substantial (Type Ete: Kibbert 1980, Taf. 6), whilst many of those from central and eastern Europe 'have the appearance of sheet metal' (Novotná 1970, 18–19). Their functional value might therefore be questioned, but that is not our purpose here; our concern is with their morphological, geographical, and temporal potential to fulfil the role of polished rectangular flint knife prototypes (albeit archaeologically invisible ones). As parallels they are remarkably close (Figure 11.4, with some type Vinča implements included to illustrate that form). Clark's observation that '[i]n the case of both the Burwell and the Quy specimens the two ends are sharp, the sides being relatively blunt' is particularly

Figure 11.4. Continental European rectangular copper flat axeheads and British polished rectangular flint knives – morphology. Row 1: *Poland (Szpunar 1987, 61, 62, 24, 59, 60).* Row 2: *Slovakia and Moravia (Novotná 1970, 71a, 70, 69, 67; Říhovský 1992, 133).* Row 3: *Austria (Mayer 1977, 181, 173, 180, 175).* Row 4: *Britain: Aldro C75, Duggleby Howe, Arbor Low, North Dale (2) (Durden 1995, fig.1; Manby 1974, figs 34 and 36).*

pertinent and he recognized that the fine polishing technique 'may have been suggested … by a knowledge of metal' (1928, 44–45).

Currency of both Type Vinča and Type Bytyń variant B in Poland *c.* 3400–2900 cal BC can be established by their association in the Krietrz hoard with trapezoidal Bytyń variant A axeheads – a type recovered with later TRB ceramics on a settlement site at Kornice, Silesia (Mayer 1977, 17). In Denmark, similar Bytyn A trapezoidal axeheads have been dated to the earlier Volling phase (*c.* 3800–3500 cal BC) from the pot containing the Bygholm hoard

(Mayer 1977, 18; Randsborg 1978). That rectangular flat axeheads were current in the same period may be indicated by the presence of rare chevron decoration on the butt ends of the sole Danish example of a Bytyń B type ('Oddens Gamle Teglvaerk'; Vandkilde 1996, 55) and on one of the trapezoidal Bygholm axeheads (Brønsted 1957, 188). The presence of copper artefacts in the north is not, however, restricted by the apparent chronological horizons of that hoard (Shennan 1993); the broken pot containing it may have been selected from an offering context because of its age and ancestry, and, as Midgley has pointed out (1992, 301), axehead pendants of amber in Danish passage graves (clearly mimicking copper) confirm later familiarity – only depositional practices had changed. Most importantly, the arsenical low impurity copper of the axeheads contrasts with the non-arsenical copper of western TRB artefacts but is well paralleled in metalwork of the Mondsee Group (Vandkilde 1996, 19, 178), where such rectangular flat axeheads occur as one product of a briefly metal-rich artefact assemblage datable to *c.* 3500–3000 cal BC (Shennan 1993). Similarities of material culture and the use of Swabian flint support the idea that Bohemian TRB groups were in contact with Altheim-Mondsee communities (Midgley 1992, 296), and so could represent the first link in the elongated exchange chain taking copper axeheads along the Oder to the northern periphery.

But could a further link in this greatly extended chain be envisaged that would have brought examples to Britain? Support for the idea is to be found in three other artefact types. The first are long, highly polished axeheads of 'agate' flint exemplified by those from Smerrick in north-east Scotland (Clarke *et al.* 1985, 173, fig. 5.10). Their raw material, at least, seems certain to have originated in Denmark, a point supported by their predominantly east coast distribution (Sheridan 1992, 209; Saville 1999; 2004). The often considerable size and fine polish of such axeheads leaves no doubt that they were regarded as prized exotic imports.

The other two artefact types – Seamer axeheads and Duggleby adzeheads – belong in the insular 'prestige package'. Until Piggott (1954, 355) dated them to the Later Neolithic, these waisted implements had long been regarded as copies of metal prototypes. Broad similarity to Bytyn variant A/Byholm copper trapezoidal axeheads is, nevertheless, clear (Figure 11.5) and could explain the selection of adzehead form; whilst unusual amongst earlier flint and stone axes, copper casting in an open mould not infrequently resulted in an asymmetric profile (cf. Vandkilde 1996, 45, 56). It might also explain the choice of red, yellow, pink, orange and mottled flint for their production (Manby 1974, 98). Both form and colour appear to reference copper. Lack of concern to replicate the flat sides and thick butt of trapezoidal axeheads, and the restriction of polishing to the blade area, appear obstacles to such an equation, yet may furnish valuable circumstantial evidence; copper trapezoidal implements hafted in the manner of the Iceman's axehead (Barfield 1994) would reveal only the blade.

If, several centuries before the advent of Beaker metallurgy, a very few copper axeheads reached Britain they may well have been regarded as 'gifts from the gods' and therefore have occasioned veneration rather than investigation. Adoption as symbols of power in eastern Yorkshire (Loveday 2009) could, in view of their extreme rarity, be predicted to lead to replication, but only of their visible features – hafted in the case of trapezoidal axeheads; unhafted in the case of rectangular specimens. Existing 'Levalloisoid' core technology would necessarily be drawn upon to produce imitations of thin Altheim–Vinca axeheads,

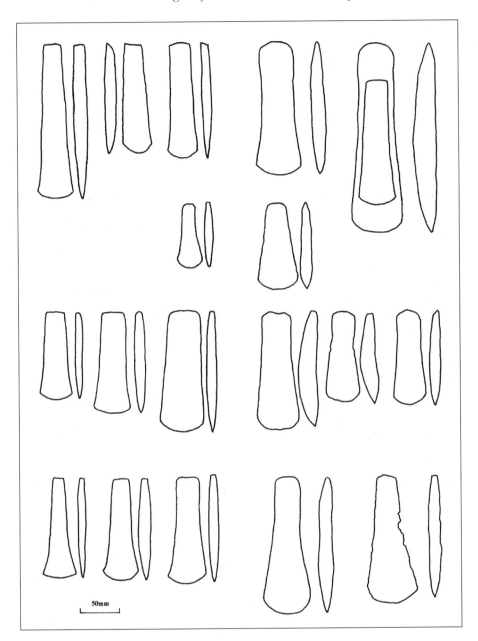

Figure 11.5. Continental European trapezoidal copper flat axeheads (left) and Seamer/Duggleby flint axeheads/adzeheads (right) – morphology. Row 1: S12, M90, S11, York, Duggleby Howe (with P55 imposed). Row 2: P35, Seamer Moor. Row 3: P45, M119, M114, Potter Brompton, Willerby Carr, Biggar (South Lanarkshire). Row 4: P6, M86, P44A, Kingston Upon Thames, Harrowgate. [P: Poland (Szpunar 1987); M: Moravia (Říhovský 1992); S: Slovakia (Novotná 1970); flint axeheads (Adkins and Jackson 1978, 185; Ashbee 1970, fig. 41; Kent 1937; Kinnes et al. 1983; Manby 1974, fig. 42; Sheridan 1992, fig. 15.4)].

hence the broad similarities that cut across what is best regarded as a multi-linear discoidal series. Proof, in the form of the hypothesized copper prototypes for type IV knives, may always remain elusive given that elevation to relic status would inhibit deposition. To dismiss the circumstantial evidence of form and finish would, however, be a mistake, since, even in continental Europe, copper's '... rarity is indicated not just by the small numbers of metal objects in archaeological contexts ... but by the imitations of copper items which are widespread' (Shennan 1993).

ACKNOWLEDGEMENTS

I am very grateful to Terry Manby for advice and encouragement; without his invaluable 1974 corpus this chapter would not have been possible. Thanks are also due to Stuart Needham and Mike Parker Pearson for generously giving their time and critical advice; they are not of course implicated in the conclusions drawn here. Particular thanks go to Martin Green for placing his superb examples of polished rectangular knives in my hands and starting this train of thought. His assistance and advice over the Grindale material has been invaluable. I am also very grateful to David Cousins for his skilful photography.

NOTES

1. A date of 3090–2900 cal. BC (OxA 16747: 4344 ± 33 BP) has recently been obtained from burial D at Duggleby Howe in association with a polished flake knife of Manby's type 1 (Gibson and Bayliss 2009, 64).
2. A burnt fragment of a sub-square/rectangular polished flint knife has recently been reported from a pit at Kingsmead Quarry, Horton, Berkshire, which also contained Grooved Ware sherds and a large fragment of Peterborough Ware. Residue dating suggests the latter had been curated. (Reported by Gareth Chaffey at the Neolithic Studies Group meeting on 9 November 2009.)

BIBLIOGRAPHY

Ashbee, P., 1970, *The Earthen Long Barrow in Britain*. London: Dent.

Adkins, R. and Jackson, R., 1978, *Stone and Flint Axes from the River Thames*. London: British Museum.

Barfield, L., 1994, The Iceman reviewed. *Antiquity* 68, 10–26.

Bateman, T., 1848, *Vestiges of the Antiquities of Derbyshire*. London: J. R. Smith.

Brønsted, J., 1957, *Danmarks Oldtid I: Stenalderen*. Copenhagen: Gyldendal.

Burl, A., 2000, *The Stone Circles of Britain, Ireland and Brittany*. New Haven and London: Yale University Press.

Clark, J. G. D., 1928, Discoidal polished flint knives, their typology and distribution. *Proceedings of the Prehistoric Society of East Anglia* 6(1), 41–54.

Clarke, A., 2005, The stone tool assemblage. In C. Richards (ed.), *Dwelling Among the Monuments: the Neolithic Village of Barnhouse, Maeshowe Passage Grave and Surrounding Monuments at Stenness, Orkney*, 323–334. Cambridge: McDonald Institute.

Clarke, D. V., 1976, *The Neolithic Village at Skara Brae, Orkney: 1972–3 Excavations: an Interim Report*. Edinburgh: HMSO.

Clarke, D. V., Cowie, T. G. and Foxon, A., 1985, *Symbols of Power at the Time of Stonehenge*. Edinburgh: HMSO.

Clay, R. C. C., 1929, Polished flint knives, with particular reference to one recently found at Durrington. *Wiltshire Archaeological and Natural History Magazine* 44, 97–100.

Durden, T., 1995, The production of specialised flintwork in the later Neolithic: a case study from the Yorkshire Wolds. *Proceedings of the Prehistoric Society* 61, 409–432.

Earnshaw, J. R., 1995, A Neolithic flint industry site at Grindale, near Bridlington. *Yorkshire Archaeological Society: Prehistory Research Section Bulletin* 32, 1–22.

Edmonds, M., 1995, *Stone Tools and Society*. London: Batsford.

Edmonds, M., 1998, Sermons in stone: identity, value, and stone tools in later Neolithic Britain. In M. Edmonds and C. Richards (eds), *Understanding the Neolithic of North-Western Europe*, 248–276. Glasgow: Cruithne Press.

Evans, J., 1897, *The Ancient Stone Implements, Weapons and Ornaments of Great Britain* (2nd edition). London: Longmans, Green & Co.

Fell, C. I., 1951, A Late Bonze Age urnfield and Grooved Ware occupation at Honington, Suffolk. *Proceedings of the Cambridgeshire Antiquarian Society* 45, 34–40.

Fojut, N., 1993, *A Guide to Prehistoric and Viking Shetland*. Lerwick: Shetland Times.

Gibson, A. and Bayliss, A., 2009, Recent research at Duggleby Howe, North Yorkshire. *Archaeological Journal* 166, 39–74.

Graf, A. and Pirie, V., 1986, A polished flint knife from Frisby on the Wreake. *Transactions of the Leicestershire Archaeological and Historical Society* 60, 82–84.

Green, H. S., 1980, *The Flint Arrowheads of the British Isles*. Oxford: British Archaeological Reports (British Series 75).

Kent, B. W. J., 1937, A polished flint axe from Harrowgate. *Yorkshire Archaeological Journal* 33, 116–117.

Kibbert, K., 1980, *Die Äxte und Beile im mittleren Westdeutschland I*. München: C. H. Beck (Prähistorische Bronzefunde, Abteilung IX, Band 15).

Kinnes, I., 1979, *Round Barrows and Ring-Ditches in the British Neolithic*. London: British Museum (Occasional Paper 7).

Kinnes, I., Schadla-Hall, T., Chadwick, P., and Dean, P., 1983, Duggleby Howe reconsidered. *Archaeological Journal* 140, 83–108.

Lewis, B., 1987, The Martin Green Collection of Lithic Artefacts from North Dale, Parish of Grindale, Humberside. Unpublished typescript: Martin Green Collection, Down Farm, Woodcutts, Dorset.

Lewis, J., 2005, *Monuments, Ritual and Regionalty: The Neolithic of Northern Somerset*. Oxford: British Archaeological Reports (British Series 401).

Loveday, R., 2009, From ritual to riches – the route to individual power in later Neolithic Eastern Yorkshire. In G. Barclay and K. Brophy (eds), *Defining a Regional Neolithic: The Evidence from Britain and Ireland*, 35–52. Oxford: Oxbow Books (Neolithic Studies Group Seminar Papers 9).

Manby, T. G., 1974, *Grooved Ware Sites in Yorkshire and the North of England*. Oxford: British Archaeological Reports (British Series 9).

Mayer, E. F., 1977, *Die Äxte und Beile in Österreich*. München: C. H. Beck (Prähistorische Bronzefunde, Abteilung IX, Band 9).

Mortimer, J. R., 1905, *Forty Years' Researches in British and Saxon Burial Mounds of East Yorkshire*. London: A. Brown & Sons.

Midgley, M. S., 1992, *TRB Culture: The First Farmers of the North European Plain*. Edinburgh: Edinburgh University Press.

Novotná, M., 1970, *Die Äxte und Beile in der Slowakei*. München: C. H. Beck (Prähistorische Bronzefunde, Abteilung IX, Band 3).

Piggott, S., 1954, *The Neolithic Cultures of the British Isles*. Cambridge: Cambridge University Press.

Radley, J. and Cooper, L., 1968, A Neolithic site at Elton, an experiment in field recording. *Derbyshire Archaeological Journal*, 88, 37–46.

Randsborg, K., 1979, Resource, distribution and the function of copper in early Neolithic Denmark. In M. Ryan (ed.), *The Origins of Metallurgy in Atlantic Europe. Proceedings of the 5th Atlantic Colloquium*, 303–318. Dublin: Stationary Office.

Říhovský, J., 1992, *Die Äxte, Beile, Meisel und Hämmer in Mähren*. Stuttgart: Franz Steiner Verlag (Prähistorische Bronzefunde, Abteilung IX, Band 17).

Robertson-Mackay, R., 1987, The Neolithic causewayed enclosure at Staines, Surrey: excavations 1961–63. *Proceedings of the Prehistoric Society* 53, 23–128.

Saville, A., 1981, *Grimes Graves, Norfolk, Excavations 1971–72. Volume II: The Flint Assemblage*. London: HMSO (Department of the Environment Archaeological Reports No.11).

Saville, A., 1994, A decorated Skaill knife from Skara Brae, Orkney. *Proceedings of the Society of Antiquaries Scotland* 124, 103–111.

Saville, A., 1999, An exceptional polished flint axe-head from Bolshan Hill, near Montrose, Angus. *Tayside and Fife Archaeological Journal* 5, 1–6.

Saville, A., 2004, A polished flint axehead from near Haycastle, Pembrokeshire, Wales, and its typological context. In R. Cleal and J. Pollard (eds), *Monuments and Material Culture. Papers in Honour of an Avebury Archaeologist: Isobel Smith*, 225–230. Salisbury: Hobnob Press.

Shennan, S., 1993, Commodities, transactions, and growth in the central European Early Bronze Age. *Journal of European Archaeology* 1(2), 59–72.

Sheridan, A., 1992, Scottish stone axeheads: some new work and recent discoveries. In N. Sharples and A. Sheridan (eds), *Vessels for the Ancestors: Essays on the Neolithic of Britain and Ireland in Honour of Audrey Henshall*, 194–212. Edinburgh: Edinburgh University Press.

Smith, I. F., 1965, *Windmill Hill and Avebury: Excavations by Alexander Keiller 1925–1939*. Oxford: Clarendon Press.

Szpunar, A., 1987, *Die Beile in Polen I (Flachbeile, Randleistenbeile, Randeistenmeisel)*. München: C. H. Beck (Prähistorische Bronzefunde, Abteilung IX, Band 16).

Varndell, G., 2004, The Great Baddow hoard and discoidal knives: more questions than answers. In A. Gibson and A. Sheridan (eds), *From Sickles to Circles: Britain and Ireland at the Time of Stonehenge*, 116–122. Stroud: Tempus.

Vandkilde, H., 1996, *From Stone to Bronze: The Metalwork of the Late Neolithic and Early Bronze Age in Denmark*. Aarhus: Jutland Archaeological Society Publications 32.

Chapter 12

Burning issues: fire and the manufacture of stone tools in Neolithic Britain

Amelia Pannett

Analysis of numerous lithic assemblages from Neolithic sites in Britain has revealed that the heat treatment or burning of raw materials was common practice. Traditional explanations for the use of fire in the working of lithic materials have suggested a functional role, namely to compound the structure of the raw material to make it easier to knap. While this idea may hold some weight, with a number of studies demonstrating that the heating of material may have proved advantageous to knappers, it fails to account fully for the quantity of burnt lithic material found on sites, particularly those in areas where the lithic resource is abundant and/or of high quality. The application of heat causes a variety of physical alterations to stone: colour change, crazing of the surface and, ultimately, shattering. Could the alteration of stone through the use of fire have had a more complex role in lithic technologies than simply easing the process of manufacture? Was the transformation of the raw material through the application of heat considered significant? Were people choosing to deliberately heat lithic materials as a means of expression? Was the potency of tools heightened through the use of burnt lithic materials? This chapter will examine the role fire could have played in the manufacture of stone tools, both as a functional tool, and a means of transformation and social expression.

INTRODUCTION

The issue of burnt flint is rarely dealt with in any detail in lithic reports, with quantities of such material noted but little, if any, discussion of the significance of its presence within an assemblage. The relative paucity of analysis of such material stems, I suggest, from our lack of understanding of *why* this material occurs in assemblages, and the processes involved in its production. Traditional explanations for the burning of flint, and other siliceous materials, focus on the use of heat treatment to compound the structure of the material and improve its fracturing characteristics (Schindler *et al.* 1982). However, although this may hold some weight in areas such as Scotland, where the primary lithic raw material is often flawed, poor quality beach pebbles, it does not account for the occurrence of burnt material in assemblages from, say, Wessex, where high quality flint is in abundance. In this chapter I will:

- explore burnt lithic material from a number of sites, to investigate whether this material played a more complex role in the lithic technologies than previously assumed;

- speculate on the idea that the use of fire in lithic technologies provided a means for transformation, expression and consumption;
- and attempt to steer debate away from purely functional explanations towards an idea of fire, and the burning of lithic material and artefacts as an integral part of the *chaîne opératoire*.

The term *chaîne opératoire* is used here not simply as a means of discussing the process of manufacture, but in relation to the 'development of social relations at different points along it and through it' (Evans 2003, 35).

FIRE AS A FUNCTIONAL TOOL

Experiments carried out on a variety of siliceous materials have demonstrated that the controlled application of heat can alter the structure of the stone, decreasing its resistance to fracture, and making it easier to knap (Schindler *et al.* 1982). The experimental heat treatment of jasper from a site in Pennsylvania, USA, sought to examine why the lithic material became less resistant to fracture following the application of varying degrees of heat (Schindler *et al.* 1982). Following the controlled exposure of jasper to temperatures ranging from 100°C to 700°C, it was determined that goethite within the structure of the stone started to decompose, leaving voids or 'channels' (Schindler *et al.* 1982, 535). These voids ran through the stone, leaving micro cracks, which weakened the jasper, decreasing its resistance to fracture (Schindler *et al.* 1982, 535). However, it became clear that above 500°C the stone suffered extensive cracking, shattering easily and becoming unworkable. Clearly then, the application of heat had to be carefully controlled if the desired outcome was a more easily workable lithic resource.

The jasper experiments demonstrated a further consequence of the application of heat to lithic material – a distinct change in colour from the yellow (characteristic of fresh jasper at this particular source) to red (Schindler *et al.* 1982, 529). The actual colour achieved, and the depth of the surface reddening was, however, dependent on the temperature to which the stone had been subjected, and the length of time it was exposed. The colour change resulted from the decomposition of iron within the structure of the material, and occurs in a number of siliceous materials when heated. Indeed, the occurrence of a red surface has been noted on flint displaying other signs of heat treatment in assemblages from my own area of research, Caithness in northern Scotland.

Apart from a distinct colour change, other characteristics of burnt flint include a crazing or cracking of the surface of the material, and a glossy, lustrous sheen across fracture faces (Schindler *et al.* 1982, 535). However, as experiments have demonstrated, these physical alterations are highly varied, dependent on the specific material being heated (Collins 1973, 462), and often occur only on the most heavily burnt material (C. R. Wickham-Jones pers. comm.). As the investigations on jasper have demonstrated, lithic material is prone to cracking above 500°C, or after prolonged exposure to moderate heat (Schindler *et al.* 1982). By contrast, colour change can readily occur during exposure of material to temperatures between 100°C and 400°C for a relatively short length of time (around three hours; Schindler *et al.* 1982) – a temperature range easily achievable in a small fire.

Collins (1973) cites several examples of lithic pieces where heat treatment formed an integral part of their production. He follows Bordes (1969) in discussing the Solutrean site of Laugerie Haute in France, where the intentional heat alteration of materials appears to have been used to facilitate flaking (Collins 1973, 461). He notes the presence of a 'high lustre' on some pieces, and the occurrence of partial surface reddening (Collins 1973, 462). Collins suggests that, in the case of Laugerie Haute, flakes were struck from a core, heated and subsequently pressure flaked (Collins 1973, 462). Here, the intentional heating of lithic materials was clearly central to the technology, but can we be certain that it was undertaken for purely functional reasons?

LITHIC BURNING IN THE NEOLITHIC

The idea that the primary reason for heat treating lithic material was to facilitate knapping clearly holds some weight, as the experiments on jasper and the Solutrean material have demonstrated. However, the physical changes to material subjected to low temperatures are generally difficult to identify at a macroscopic level (Finlayson 1990), with the exception of the sheen and colour change. It is possible, therefore, that the majority of pieces identified as burnt in lithic assemblages only represent a small proportion of those actually exposed to heat – those pieces that were subjected to prolonged heat or high temperatures. Perhaps what we are seeing are pieces that were accidentally or deliberately left in the fire long after they would have become unworkable.

In her report on the lithic assemblages from the Neolithic enclosure at Donegore Hill, Northern Ireland, Eiméar Nellis comments on the high proportion of burnt flint material recovered during survey and excavation, noting that much of this material could only be classified as shatter (Nellis 2003, 205). She does note, however, that 'it is probable that this material represents the remains of damaged flakes, blades, cores and modified tools' (Nellis 2003, 208). At North Yarrows, in Caithness, a large, discrete lithic scatter with material diagnostic of the Late Mesolithic, Neolithic and Early Bronze Age was identified during fieldwalking (Pannett in preparation). Of this material, around 10 per cent displayed characteristic signs of having been burnt. Much of the material had shattered, with crazing evident on worked surfaces and reddening also identifiable, but it was possible to discern that a large proportion of the assemblage had been worked prior to its exposure to heat. The burnt assemblage comprised flakes and blades, a number of cores, and retouched tools, including a broken leaf-shaped arrowhead. Clearly, the possibility that the material had been heat treated in order to facilitate knapping can be excluded; but why was this material burnt? What purpose did burning struck tools and cores beyond recognition and use serve?

I want to turn briefly to the Mesolithic site of Rock Common in Sussex to explore one of the traditional explanations for the presence of burnt flint on sites, that is as representative of the location of hearths. At Rock Common, dense clusters of apparently unworked, burnt material were identified in association with discrete spreads of worked lithics and tools (Harding 2000). The apparently unworked burnt material is given short shrift in the excavation report; none of it was analysed in any detail, with only the total number of pieces and the total weight per square metre recorded (Harding 2000, 33). Whilst the time constraints imposed on developer-funded archaeology such as the Rock

Common excavation clearly influenced the way in which the material was prioritized for analysis, overlooking burnt material leaves a gap in our understanding of the site and the activities undertaken there. In lieu of detailed analysis of the burnt material, the excavator has interpreted the clusters of burnt material as representative of the location of hearths, around which knapping activities were focused (Harding 2000, 43). Surely, however, in order for these clusters to be representative of hearths, it must be assumed that it was common practice to put (I hesitate to use the word 'discard') lithic material into the fire in the first place?

The tradition of knapping close to hearths extends into the Neolithic period, although the number of documented associations between lithic assemblages and hearths is relatively limited. At the settlement of Links of Noltland in Orkney, an assemblage of lithic material, including a number of burnt pieces, was found in a discrete area to the northwest of a hearth (C. R. Wickham-Jones pers. comm.). The excavators suggested that the material represented the location of a knapping floor (C. R. Wickham-Jones pers. comm.). Interestingly, no lithic material was found within the hearth itself, and the excavator suggested that this may indicate the clearing out of the hearth, with ash and other material deposited elsewhere (C. R. Wickham-Jones pers. comm.). It is possible that the burnt material identified in the main lithic scatter may represent pieces swept from the hearth and incorporated into the general spread of lithic material (C. R. Wickham-Jones pers. comm.). The association between hearths and knapping activities is logical; people would have sat around fires, manufacturing tools, discarding unsuitable or unwanted material and tools. But was the discard of material in fires simply a prosaic means of disposing of 'rubbish', or were there social connotations?

TRANSFORMATION AND CONSUMPTION

The examples discussed above suggest the use of fire in lithic technologies for more than functional purposes. Indeed, it highlights that whilst fire may have been used to facilitate knapping, it is only those pieces that have been burnt beyond the point of being usable that are generally recognized. Rather, it would seem that fires themselves formed an integral part of the *chaîne opératoire*, providing a suitable context for the disposal of material that had already been knapped. I suggest that our preoccupation with the idea that the burning of flint was for purely functional or prosaic reasons is predicated on the way in which lithic artefacts are studied in general in archaeology. Functionality forms the basis for all lithic studies; indeed it is only in recent years that the idea of sociality has started to emerge in interpretations of lithic technologies (e.g. Finlay 2000). That is not to say that the way we interpret the *context* of the assemblages is flawed, merely that the way we study the materials in the first place has not kept pace with developments in theory and interpretation. It is for precisely this reason that burnt flint has remained problematic; it does not fit into the clearly bounded typological categories that we have created. We simply don't know what to do with it.

Edmonds has commented that the knapping debris and tools we find would have been entrenched in a world of social practice (Edmonds 1995, 11). In this sense, all material produced during a knapping episode would have been culturally significant. The burning of flint, even pieces we would regard as waste, should therefore be attributed similar levels of importance in our schemes of analysis as, say, the production of an arrowhead or the crafting of a blade core.

I suggest that a consideration of the burnt flint we encounter in terms of the *act* of burning could provide a means for comprehending its role within the lithic technologies. It would be easy to stamp a 'ritual' label on to the practise of burning lithic material, as an act that is not adequately explained by functionality (Brück 1999, 317). However, I do not believe that this would bring us any closer to understanding the particularities of the practice. People were actively choosing to burn lithic material, perhaps selecting particular tools or nodules to consign to the fire. But why? What purpose did the deliberate destruction of material serve, and what was being expressed through this act?

The use and significance of fire is well documented for the Neolithic in Britain. Fire was used in the deliberate destruction of buildings and other wooden structures; acts which have been generally regarded as motivated by 'ritual' (e.g. Thomas 2000, 80). The hearth has been seen as playing a central role in Neolithic life, both in functional and symbolic terms (Cooney 2000, 61; Richards 1990, 116). In Neolithic Orkney it formed the focus for both domestic and more formal activities, occupying the central space in houses, and also at monumental structures such as the Stones of Stenness henge (Ritchie 1985). It would have been a place for gathering together, for cooking, for eating, and for undertaking a range of practical activities. In this sense the hearth would have provided the focus for life in the Neolithic, and is likely to have been integral to the formation and maintenance of social relations, and for the passing on of knowledge and ideas.

That flint knapping occurred around fires and hearths is clear, as the evidence from Links of Noltland and Rock Common demonstrates. People would have sat, enjoying the warmth it provided and making use of the light. Anyone who has sat near a fire will have experienced the hypnotic dancing of the flames and the comforting crackle of wood as it burns, and we can imagine that it would have been no different for people in prehistory. In this hearthside environment, tools would have been made and repaired, stories would have been told, and through those stories techniques and skills would probably have been taught. Perhaps, in the context of inculcating necessary skills, some of the burnt flint we find would have been created; pieces that were left too long by novices not yet adept at the subtle art of controlled heat treatment. Yet this explanation can only account for a tiny proportion of the material that we find, unless we envisage a situation where the accidental destruction of nodules was a common occurrence. Perhaps we should consider instead the deliberate addition of nodules to the fire, nodules which were designed to be burnt beyond the point of being workable.

When lithic material is heated it retains heat for a considerable period of time after it has been removed from the fire – as the evidence for stone being used as potboilers attests. It is possible that this practice was occurring, although why then do we find little evidence for the heating of other types of stone? Why would siliceous material be favoured over other, perhaps more locally available material? I suggest that instead of the stones themselves being the intended outcome, the heating of the stone may have been the intended act; '... the creative act, rather than a product, ... was the object of attention' (Edmonds 1999, 117). The glow of flint nodules in the fire would have contributed to the visuality of the hearthside environment; the sound of the stones cracking as they passed the 500°C point would have heightened the acoustic experience of those in the vicinity, and the possibility that a nodule could explode at any minute would have added a degree of thrill and entertainment to the proceedings. Whilst these suggestions may seem rather banal, I feel it is important to remember that people were living an essentially ordinary life, a fact that it often lost in our accounts of the Neolithic.

Nevertheless, the material remains do demonstrate the occurrence of more formal routines of activity in the burning of flint. The deposition of worked material, including apparently usable tools, in a fire may hint at the idea of consumption – the deliberate removal of pieces from circulation. In his discussion of burnt flint axeheads and other tools from sites in southern Sweden, Larsson (2000, 609) suggests that such an act of burning and destruction could have provided a means of expressing wealth and prestige. He cites the sites of Kverrested and Svartskylle in Scania as providing pertinent examples of conspicuous consumption designed solely for the achievement of social prestige. At these sites large numbers of flint tools and axeheads appear to have been destroyed through fire in single, evidently spectacular, events. The drama of these episodes of destruction would, he suggests, have been designed to send a message to both the human and metaphysical onlookers about the power and wealth of the community (Larsson 2000, 609). On a smaller scale, but nevertheless following the theme of consumption, Thomas (1999, 66) cites several examples of deposits containing lithic tools that have been deliberately broken prior to their deposition in pits. Although the context of deposition clearly differs, I suggest that the deposition of material in a fire served a similar, albeit more immediate and, as evidenced by the Swedish sites, dramatic means of removing lithic artefacts and nodules from circulation. Thomas suggests that such activities may have been dictated by conceptions of pollution, with particular materials considered as no longer appropriate for use (Thomas 1999, 66). In his discussion of pit deposits he notes that '[s]ome of the artefacts … may have been made for the purpose of deposition, and others were fine goods which had been in circulation for some while … [b]ut a large proportion of the objects … was more mundane …' (Thomas 1999, 87). I suggest that this is also true of the materials deposited in fires. At Donegore Hill, the suggestion that items such as cores and tools were 'damaged' before being burnt (Nellis 2003, 208) follows our assumptions that burnt material simply reflects waste. I further suggest that it would be apposite to reconsider such artefacts instead in terms of the relationship between the material and those engaged in its destruction. The material deposited in fires would have undergone several different stages of interpretation and reinterpretation relating to the context in which it was being used prior to its eventual destruction. The source of the material, and the process of acquisition, would have held social connotations for those engaged in such activities. The process of working the stone, transforming an irregular nodule into a precisely engineered core suitable for the production of blades and flakes, would have imbued different symbolic meaning to the material, while the actual act of tool manufacture would have added a further level of social complexity. In a sense, each piece found in a lithic assemblage will have been through a distinct life cycle, from source to discard (Cooney 2000, 210). Through the deposition in a fiery context of certain materials, whether finished tools or unworked nodules, people may have been symbolically returning them to source. Through such acts connections may have been maintained between the land and those who relied on its resources. Through the destruction of finely made tools, as well as more mundane pieces, Neolithic people were perhaps recognizing the role this material played in their lives, and militating against circumstances that could lead to its depletion.

The burning of lithic material, both worked and unworked pieces, also hints at the idea of transformation – the alteration of usable, functional pieces into an unusable material form. This can be regarded as a culturally specific process, one that embodied concepts of sociality, and which fulfilled a symbolic function within the routines of lithic procurement and working. The heating of flint, and the consequent physical changes that would have occurred, may have provided a means of expression for Neolithic flint-workers; the considered transformation of a 'natural' resource into a humanly altered material. The burning of flint may have symbolized the ability of the knapper to control and manipulate the stone beyond the relational process of knapping itself. As Tilley notes '[p]roduction is, above all, the transformation of matter and human intervention in nature ... people are facilitators in a process inherent in the materials themselves ...' (Tilley 1996, 323). The deliberate burning of flint clearly opposes this process, and may have symbolized control of the natural resources.

While symbolism may have been imbued in the burning of flint, forming an integral part of the *chaîne operatoire*, it is possible that the act of throwing nodules or knapped pieces may have served a more emotive purpose. The act of sitting around a fire, knapping, and perhaps engaging in activities such as story telling, would have created a social context within which people would have interacted and, undoubtedly, had fun. I recently carried out an experiment designed to assess the atmosphere of the hearthside, particularly in the context of burning flint. I hasten to add that this was not a scientific experiment in the strictest sense, the intention being to experience the hearthside environment rather than measure the effects of fire on lithics. A small fire was constructed, using wood as the primary fuel, and flint was added at various points during the burning. The inclusion of flint added considerably to the visuality of the hearthside environment – pieces glowed as they heated up, and appeared to dance in the flames as they began to fragment. The heat given off by the fire also appeared to increase as more flint was added.

It was the shattering of the stone that proved to be the most dramatic and surprising aspect of the burning process. As pieces danced in the flames they began to break up, with small shards of flint flying out of the fire at high speed. These small pieces were incredibly hot and sharp, and in some instances travelled a good 5m from the fire, ricocheting off anything in the way. The hearthside was a dangerous place to be while the flint was breaking up, but perhaps that was all part of the experience; the possibility of being struck by a piece of red hot flint added a degree of thrill and excitement to the proceedings. The sound created by the shattering flint added to the acoustic experience, emitting a series of sharp crackles and pops distinct from those of the burning wood. At the same time, streams of sparks would fly out of the fire. Each shatter event would last only a short time, dying down as quickly as it had started. What was interesting though was the unpredictability of the materials – some pieces would start to shatter almost as soon as they were put into the fire, while others would lie dormant for several minutes before the pops and crackles signalling the start of the show would commence. Although what I witnessed in the fire is easily explained by modern science, it was nevertheless an exciting and addictive experience. Each shatter event was akin to a primitive firework display, evoking similar emotional responses from those participating as caused by the firing of a rocket on bonfire night. I believe such emotive responses are an important consideration in our understanding of why people in the Neolithic burnt flint. Essentially, it was fun! This does not detract from the ideas discussed earlier in relation to consumption and transformation but, rather, I would like to suggest that the two types of practice were not mutually exclusive. Emotion would have pervaded every aspect of formal practice, heightening the experience of those involved. The drama and thrill of depositing lithic pieces into a fire would have engaged all those in the vicinity of the hearth, and would perhaps have provided a means for expressing the symbolism imbued in such acts.

CONCLUSIONS: SPECULATIONS ON BURNING

The discussions above have presented a number of possible explanations for the discovery of burnt lithic material in archaeological contexts. The aim here was to be speculative; my intention was not to present one clear-cut reason for why people were burning flint in the Neolithic, but to open up debate on the subject. The idea of consumption follows well-established ideas proposed for numerous contexts of deposition recognised in Neolithic Britain, but I feel that it is one that is relevant to the issue under discussion. That people were deliberately destroying usable tools and raw materials is not questioned in the context of pit deposits, or ditch fills, but has never been considered in a lithic context. It stands to reason that if Neolithic ideology included the symbolic destruction and removal of artefacts from circulation, such practices could have been undertaken at home, around the hearth, as well as in a more formal setting. It is possible that the motivation for such actions could lie in the desire to symbolize the relationship between the knapper and the material resource, be that in terms of cohesion or, conversely, control.

ACKNOWLEDGEMENTS

This chapter was originally presented at 'Firey Theory', a session organized by Dr Cole Henley and myself at TAG 2004 in Glasgow. I extend my thanks to all those who participated in this session, and to Cole for his comments on earlier drafts. Thanks to the late John Evans for various inspiring discussions about lithics. Particular thanks go to Dr Steve Mills, who was instrumental in the organization of the flint burning experiment, created the sound backtrack for my TAG presentation, and commented on various drafts of the chapter. Thanks also to my parents for allowing us to set fire to a small patch of their garden, in the name of archaeological experimentation!

BIBLIOGRAPHY

Bordes, F., 1969, Traitement thermique du silex au Solutréen. *Bulletin de la Société Préhistorique Française* 66, 197 (*Compte Rendu des séances mensuelles de la Société Préhistorique Française*, 7).
Brück, J., 1999, Ritual and rationality: some problems of interpretation in European archaeology. *European Journal of Archaeology* 2(3), 313–344.

Collins, M. B., 1973, Observations on the thermal treatment of chert in the Solutrean of Laugerie Haute, France. *Proceedings of the Prehistoric Society* 39, 461–466.

Cooney, G., 2000, *Landscapes of Neolithic Ireland*. London: Routledge.

Edmonds, M., 1995, *Stone Tools and Society*. London: Batsford.

Edmonds, M., 1999, *Ancestral Geographies of the Neolithic: Landscape, Monuments and Memory*. London: Routledge.

Evans, J. G., 2003, *Environmental Archaeology and the Social Order*. London: Routledge.

Finlay, N., 2000, Microliths in the making. In R.Young (ed.), *Mesolithic Lifeways. Current Research from Britain and Ireland*, 23–31. Leicester: University of Leicester (School of Archaeological Studies, Leicester Archaeology Monograph 7).

Finlayson, B., 1990, The examination of surface alteration. In C. R. Wickham-Jones, *Rhum, Mesolithic and Later Sites at Kinloch: Excavations 1984–86*, 53. Edinburgh: Society of Antiquaries of Scotland (Monograph Series No. 7).

Harding, P., 2000, A Mesolithic site at Rock Common, Washington, West Sussex. *Sussex Archaeological Collections* 138, 29–48.

Larsson, L., 2000, Fire transformation of flint objects in the Neolithic of Southern Sweden. *Antiquity* 74, 602–610.

Nellis, E., 2003, Donegore Hill and Lyles Hill, Neolithic enclosed sites in Co. Antrim: the lithic assemblages. In I. Armit, E. Murphy, E. Nellis and D. Simpson (eds), *Neolithic Settlement in Ireland and Western Britain*, 203–217. Oxford: Oxbow Books.

Pannett, A., in preparation, The Caithness Fieldwalking Project 2000–2004.

Richards, C., 1990, The late Neolithic house in Orkney. In R. Samson (ed.), *The Social Archaeology of Houses*, 111–124. Edinburgh: Edinburgh University Press.

Ritchie, G., 1985, Ritual monuments. In C. Renfrew (ed.), *The Prehistory of Orkney*, 118–130. Edinburgh: Edinburgh University Press.

Schindler, D. L., Hatch, J. W., Hay, C. A. and Bradt, R. C., 1982, Aboriginal thermal alteration of a central Pennsylvania jasper: analytical and behavioral implications. *American Antiquity* 47(3), 526–544.

Tilley, C., 1996, *An Ethnography of the Neolithic: Early Prehistoric Societies in Southern Scandinavia*. Cambridge: Cambridge University Press.

Thomas, J., 1999, *Understanding the Neolithic*. London: Routledge.

Thomas, J., 2000, The identity of place in Neolithic Britain: examples from southwest Scotland. In A. Ritchie (ed.), *Neolithic Orkney in its European Context*, 79–87. Cambridge: McDonald Institute Monograph.

Chapter 13

A Shot in the Dark? Interpreting Evidence for Prehistoric Conflict

Martin Smith, Megan Brickley, and Stephany Leach

INTRODUCTION

Unlike some others in this volume, this chapter is not so much about flint itself as about what it does, specifically when it comes into sudden contact with bone. The versatility of stone, and particularly flint, technologies, means that lithic artefacts can serve a multitude of practical functions, from carpentry to clothing manufacture, as well as a wide range of uses connected to the acquisition and preparation of food. Whilst many such applications of flint have been the subject of intensive and detailed study (for example Anderson 1980; Clemente and Gibaja 1998), the use of stone artefacts for acts of aggression is an area which has until very recently received relatively little attention. Studies of lithic objects which can be classified as weapons can be argued to have lagged behind those of more mundane artefacts, possibly due to the previous dominance of 'pacified' views of the later prehistoric past (Keeley 1996). Where specific attention has been given to projectiles and axeheads, earlier publications (Green 1980, Smith 1927; Tyler 1976), tended to be chiefly, and perhaps necessarily, typological. However, although more recent studies have largely broken out of this mould, few have concerned themselves with the actual offensive uses of such implements.

Instead, researches concerned with axeheads and arrowheads have tended to focus upon broader issues such as production (Mandal *et al.* 1997), distribution and exchange (Bradley and Edmonds 1993; Cooney and Mandal 1998), or the extent to which such artefacts were objects of prestige (Edmonds 1995, 102–114; Taylor 1996). A recent exception is the study of Neolithic cranial trauma by Schulting and Wysocki (2005), which investigates the offensive use of flint by looking at the incidence of traumatic bony injuries consistent with the use of such weapons. Schulting and Wysocki (2005) pay careful attention to examining skeletal material first hand rather than simply accepting older published observations of alleged injuries. Although noting that many such older identifications are inaccurate, they also demonstrate that an equally large, if not larger, quantity of weapon-related injuries from the Neolithic have been missed by earlier investigators.

Whilst Schulting and Wysocki's (2005) work focuses mainly upon damage wrought by hand-held weapons, the current chapter specifically examines skeletal trauma caused by flint-tipped projectiles. In the wider context of osteology much attention has recently been given to the identification and interpretation of violence-related injuries and particularly to discerning such trauma from other phenomena such as taphonomic damage. However, the vast majority of such work has focused upon bladed implements and blunt trauma with relatively little attention given to injuries caused by projectiles. Where mentions of projectile wounds exist in the archaeological literature these were found by the present authors to be based upon limited quantities of, generally secondary, data. Consequently it was decided to obtain fresh data by experimentation, with a view to facilitating future identifications of this type of injury. This chapter discusses the context and results of the respective experiments in relation to bone, and some observations are also made concerning the effects of such impacts upon the projectiles themselves.

BRITISH EVIDENCE FOR THE USE OF FLINT-TIPPED PROJECTILES

The majority of human skeletal material surviving from Neolithic Britain has been excavated from collective funerary monuments. Clearly, this sample can represent only a fraction of the total population that lived during the period, and a prominent question concerning these assemblages is by what criteria people qualified for burial within monuments? A point which has become increasingly apparent during recent years is that a proportion of the people interred in monuments exhibit injuries consistent with interpersonal violence either due to blunt trauma or through injury by flint projectiles. Probably the best known examples of the latter are the skeleton from West Kennet, Wiltshire, with an arrowhead positioned in the region of its throat (Piggott 1962, 25), the projectile point embedded in a lumbar vertebra from Ascott-under-Wychwood, Oxfordshire (Knüsel 2007), and the point embedded in a rib from Penywyrlod, Brecknock (Wysocki and Whittle 2000, 599–600). Other possible examples include a further arrowhead, beneath a rib at Ascott-under-Wychwood, which has been suggested to have arrived within, rather than with the respective body (Mercer 1999, 149) and also three arrowheads from Wayland's Smithy, Oxfordshire. These arrowheads were each found in contact with pelvic bones. They may therefore have been lodged in the adjacent soft tissues (Whittle 1991, 70). In addition, Thorpe's (2006) recent review of published evidence for violence in British prehistory lists two further embedded projectiles and two possible projectile wounds from earlier Neolithic sites. Other examples of arrowheads found in close association with human remains include a Neolithic burial at Fengate, Peterborough (Pryor 1976, 232–233), and also a skeleton from the ditch at Hambledon Hill, Dorset (Mercer 1980, 50), both with arrowheads apparently lodged in their thoracic cavities.

However, despite the growing number of recognized examples of such trauma, the actual frequency of physical aggression within Neolithic communities remains difficult to discern. It is possible that death by violence may have been a criterion for burial within monuments, with the respective individuals qualifying for special funerary treatment. If so the skeletal remains with weapon injuries would constitute a biased sample, with the possibility that violence may actually have been relatively uncommon. However, such a view may be countered by the evidence noted at several enclosure sites which appear to have been attacked by large numbers of archers. These include: Hambledon Hill, Dorset; Crickley Hill, Gloucestershire; Carn Brea, Cornwall; and Hembury, Devon (Mercer 1980, 65; 1999, 151); and Thorpe (2006) also suggests Helman Tor, Cornwall, and Maiden Castle, Dorset. On a smaller scale, Moore (2004) cites several domestic sites in Ireland where houses or small settlements appear to have been attacked with arrows. When such 'site based' observations are considered in conjunction with the osteological data, these two strands of evidence certainly appear to indicate repeated instances of inter-group conflict, perhaps at varying scales.

The high frequency of arrowheads in Neolithic monuments was first commented upon by Thurnam (1857, 165). Whereas such inclusions were once thought of only as grave goods, a number of authors have since suggested that they may often represent the cause of death (Mercer 1999, 150; Saville 1990, 264; Woodward 2000, 34). Certainly, the likelihood of archaic projectile points remaining within the body is supported by modern ballistic studies. De la Grandmaison's (2001) study of gunshot wounds noted that 91 of 130 bullets (70%) remained lodged within the bodies of the victims studied. Even in cases of cranial gunshot wounds Quatrehomme and İşcan (1999) found that bullets failed to exit in 9 of 21 cases studied (43%). Given that bullets travel considerably faster and have much greater kinetic energy available than arrows, the likelihood of archaic projectile points remaining within a body is high.

On the other hand, examples also exist which may be more consistent with deliberate deposition than violent death. For example, the 12 complete and 12 broken arrowheads at Gwernvale, Brecknock (Britnell and Savory 1984, 126–127), suggest such items to be grave goods in at least some instances. Arrowheads are also often included in other, clearly deliberate, depositional contexts such as flint mines (Topping 2004, 184). Consequently, it may be safer to view arrowheads in monuments as a mixture of 'embedded' points and at least some deliberate deposition, which prompts the question of how these two phenomena can be differentiated?

EARLIER RESEARCHES INTO PROJECTILE–RELATED TRAUMA

One possible avenue of enquiry is the examination of projectile points found in contexts where human remains are present. A number of experimental studies have documented patterns of fracture and microwear produced when flint projectile points are subjected to impacts (examples include Ahler 1971; Barton and Bergman 1982; Fischer 1985; Odell and Cowan 1986; Shea 2001). However, although such observations might demonstrate that a projectile point has been used, they cannot discern the nature of the target and in particular whether projectiles were shot at humans or animals. Such distinctions are only possible through recognition of the resultant defects on bone where projectiles have come into contact with the skeleton. Secure, experimentally observed signatures for such trauma need to be established if trauma inflicted in this way is to be detected in archaeological samples.

As noted by Lambert (1997, 91), identifications of projectile trauma in skeletal material generally fall into three categories. These are: embedded projectile points; 'associated' projectile points (as in the aforementioned examples from West Kennet etc.); and finally defects in bone which are interpreted as penetrative injuries on the basis of their form and position. Both Lambert's (1997) work and a further study by the present authors (Smith *et al.* 2007) indicate the vast majority of projectile wound identifications to be based upon embedded points. Relatively few identifications relate to associated points, with less than 10 per cent being based upon 'wound' morphology alone. Many examples of such injuries may have been missed in the past simply because they have not been recognized, with only the most obvious examples (i.e. embedded projectiles) generally being noted.

Most osteoarchaeological examinations of weapon trauma have been largely concerned with blunt injuries and bladed weapon injuries. Mentions of projectile trauma tend to be brief and to contain very little primary data, generally relying upon extrapolating data derived from modern gunshot wounds rather than any experimental or direct observation of injuries caused by archaic projectiles. Most experiments which have been conducted with archaic projectiles have focused upon the implements themselves, whilst those that have examined the effects of such weapons upon their targets have largely been concerned with soft tissue (for example Fischer 1985; Pope 1918). Those that have involved bone have tended only to consider the depth of penetration (Karger *et al.* 1998; Karlsson and Stahling 2000), while offering limited insight as to how such injuries might be recognized archaeologically.

EXPERIMENTING WITH FLINT-TIPPED ARROWS

Methods

Two methods were used to obtain empirical data regarding flint projectile trauma. The first of these simply involved using a bow to shoot replica arrows at bone targets. The arrows were constructed similarly to known archaeological examples (Barton and Bergman 1982, 238–239; Bergman *et al.* 1988, 668; Mercer 1999, 147; Spindler 1994, 123) and the majority were tipped with 'leaf-shaped' arrowheads of the style distinct to the British Neolithic, although a selection of 'Beaker' style barbed-and-tanged arrowheads were also used. The bow was a single stave made from yew, to the basic longbow design, which varied little between prehistory and the Middle Ages (Hardy 1975, 16–18; Spindler 1994, 86–87). This was D-shaped in profile rather than being a 'flat bow' of Meare Heath type (Clark 1963, 56–58) and measured 1.81 m, with a pull of approximately 50 pounds (23 kg). The arrowheads were hafted using pine resin and linen thread. Seventeen of the shafts were made from ash and 15 from pine. No modern materials were used in either the bow or the arrows and the bow was found to perform comparably to published examples of other experimental long bows. Arrows were shot into fresh cattle and pig scapulae (Figure 13.1).

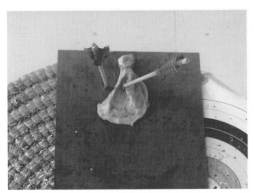 

Figure 13.1. Views of arrows shot at a fresh pig scapula, illustrating the potential for such weapons to penetrate bone and also the fact that experimentation of this kind can be a 'hit-and-miss' affair, requiring a degree of patience.

The second type of test involved using a 'charpy' impact-testing machine (Abrate 1998). This is a fairly simple device used to test the impact toughness of various materials, consisting of a pendulum arm which falls at a constant rate (and therefore with constant kinetic energy) to strike a sample in order to test its resistance to impacts. The main reason for using this machine is that it offers a high degree of precision, whereas using a bow is, quite literally, a hit-and-miss affair. The machine was adapted in order to hold arrowheads hafted to short shafts identical to the 'full-sized' arrows.

Impact energies were calculated according to the principle that if the speed at which an object is travelling is known, in addition to its weight, it is possible to calculate how much energy it imparts when it strikes a target (using the formula: $KE = MV^2/2$, where $KE=$ kinetic energy, $M=$ mass and $V=$ velocity). Each arrow was weighed and the velocities were calculated by averaging the speeds achieved in other published experiments using bows of similar size (Bergman *et al.* 1988; Karger *et al.* 1998; Miller *et al.* 1986).

The present study was based upon the premise that not only do flat areas of bone respond similarly to localized trauma in humans, but that this is also the case for other large mammals. Consequently, the use of cattle scapulae as a mimic for human crania is advocated in a recent report by the Northern Ireland Office (Patten Report 2004) for testing projectiles such as plastic bullets. Certainly, it was felt that these were the closest available alternative and that the response of these elements to impact by a missile is unlikely to differ widely from that seen in flat areas of bone in humans. Although soft tissues were considered, these have been shown in prior experiments (Fischer 1985, 37; Knight 1975, 253) to offer little resistance to stone-tipped projectiles. Furthermore, in the case of cranial trauma there is very little soft tissue covering a human skull and the lack of soft tissue in these experiments was felt unlikely to substantially affect the outcome. In addition to gross examination the samples were analysed using a light microscope and, where appropriate, by a scanning electron microscope (SEM).

Results

Various types of damage were observed to have been produced and are listed below.

1. INTERNAL BEVELLING. As stated, most ideas concerning projectile trauma have simply been drawn from observation of gunshot wounds. A large proportion of gunshot entry wounds have been noted to display internal bevelling (Berryman and Symes 1998, 344; Quatrehomme and İşcan 1999; Smith *et al.* 2003), where the internal dimensions of the wound are greater than its external dimensions. This is not exclusive to the skull, but also occurs on other flat areas of bone such as the mandible and the pelvic bones. Several of the experimental impacts punctured the respective bones entirely (7 of 32; 22%). The form of these punctures confirmed that arrow wounds to areas of flat bone can indeed exhibit internal bevelling, similar to that produced in gunshot wounds. With arrow wounds the entrance defects were elliptical rather than round as in bullet wounds (Figure 13.2). One observation noted concerning these full thickness punctures was that all such defects produced in the experiments involved larger, more robust arrowheads, with smaller arrowheads being more likely to break at the tip, often leaving small fragments embedded.

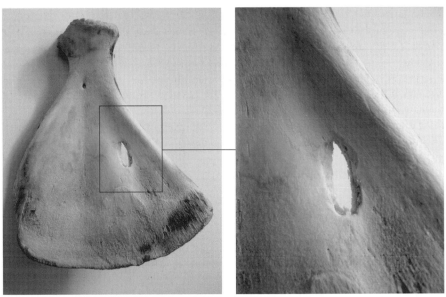

Figure 13.2. 'Internal' views of a full thickness puncture in a pig scapula (shown in Figure 13.1), showing a 'punched out' or bevelled area of bone opposite the point of impact.

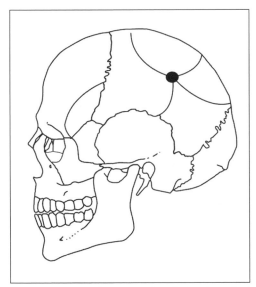

Figure 13.3. An illustration of radiating (or stellate) fractures produced by a modern high velocity bullet wound to the skull. These are secondary fractures which spread out from the initial point of impact; such fractures may also be produced when the skull is impacted by larger objects travelling at low velocities.

A feature common to modern gunshot wounds that is unlikely to have been produced by archaic projectiles is radiating (or stellate) fractures (Figure 13.3). Such fractures are produced by the rapid transfer of large amounts of kinetic energy through the skull. Sufficient forces to achieve this can be constituted either when the skull is impacted by a massive object, such as a club or mace, or by a small object such as a bullet, travelling at high velocity. Radiating fractures tend to be produced by firearms only when the bullet is travelling at speeds exceeding the speed of sound (*c.* 340 m/s). At lower velocities, small projectiles simply core out a track in the area struck with minimal displacement of surrounding tissues (a concise explanation of why this is so is given by Owen Smith 1981, 15–41). Experiments with a variety of different styles of bow have shown none to achieve arrow velocities of more than 55 m/s (Bergman *et al.* 1988, 667). Archaic projectiles are therefore unlikely to cause radiating fractures.

2. EMBEDDED FRAGMENTS. Embedded fragments appear to be very frequent when flint projectile points strike bone, with 14 of 25 impacts (56%) which didn't puncture the bone completely leaving some quantity of embedded flint. In several cases such fragments were obvious, and could clearly be seen protruding above the cortical surface of the bone. However, there were also repeated instances where microscopic examination revealed small embedded fragments in defects where they weren't obvious macroscopically. Where protruding fragments were visible attempts were made to manually remove these, primarily to ascertain how much force would be required to do so. Interestingly, each time this was attempted a smaller fragment was noted to remain deep within the respective defect (Figure 13.4). Consequently, it is unclear at which point this fracturing of flint projectile points occurs, with the possibility that at least some may occur on impact.

3. MICRO-STRIATIONS. Incised cut-marks made with flint on bone can be identified microscopically by the presence of multiple, parallel internal striations, which derive from surface irregularities in the cutting edge of the flint. Such features are consequently not seen in slicing marks made with metal tools (Figure 13.5). For obvious reasons the cutting edges of a projectile point are subject to the greatest amount of working and consequently have a greater concentration of facets and edges. Where the arrowheads used in the experiments had struck bone at a tangent the consequent marks proved indistinguishable from cut-marks made using a flint blade, and were visible at relatively low magnifications (× 30–40). However, where the faces of arrowheads had come into contact with bone in perpendicular impacts, the resultant internal striations proved much less dramatic (Figure 13.5), only being visible at higher magnifications (>×150).

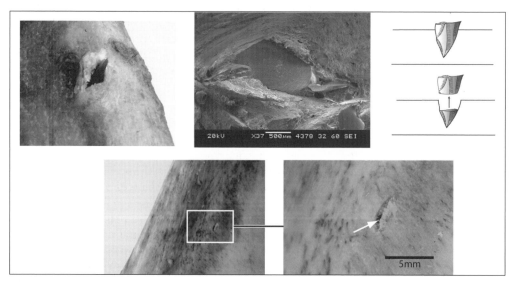

Figure 13.4. Fragments of flint are commonly left embedded in bone samples following projectile impacts. The electron micrograph (upper middle) shows a further fragment which remained deeply embedded after the fragment shown upper left was removed. The two lower views illustrate the use of light microscopy in identifying small embedded fragments which may not be obvious macroscopically.

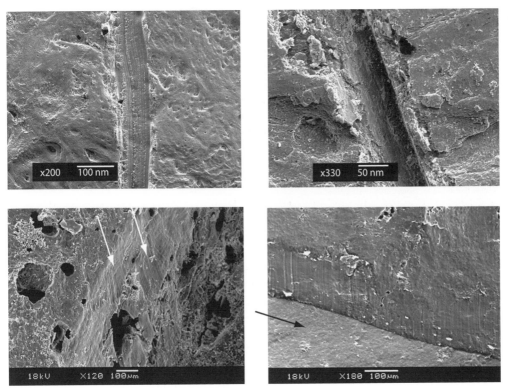

Figure 13.5. Electron micrographs illustrating the microscopic effects of flint projectiles on bone. Upper left: experimental cutmark made on fresh sheep femur using a flint blade, showing internal longitudinal striations; upper right: experimental cutmark made on fresh sheep femur using a steel blade, internal striations are absent. Lower left and right: internal views of defects produced in bone by impact with flint-tipped arrows, showing striations running 'down' into each defect in the direction of impact (arrowed in white). In the lower right image a fragment of embedded flint is also visible (arrowed).

Comparison with archaeological examples

An obvious criticism of the above experiments would be the question of whether the features noted would survive in a recognizable state in archaeological material. Through comparison of the experimental results with archaeological examples of suspected arrow wounds it was concluded that such evidence can indeed be recognized, although the potential for this is to an extent dependent upon preservational factors. Firstly, Figure 13.6 illustrates a Neolithic skull with a full thickness perimortem defect, which the present authors had previously considered to be a possible projectile wound due to its ovoid form and internal bevelling. A further example noted from West Tump long barrow, Gloucestershire, was felt to particularly resemble some of the elliptical, internally bevelled defects produced in the experiments (illustrated in Smith *et al.*, 2007). Secondly, whilst it is already clear that embedded projectile points are often seen in archaeological bone, an example from Durrington Walls, Wiltshire, demonstrated that small, deeply embedded fragments of the

Figure 13.6. A human skull from the Cotswold-Severn chambered monument at Littleton Drew, Gloucestershire, with a probable projectile wound. The full thickness puncture exhibits similar internal bevelling to those produced experimentally, with no sign of bone remodelling, indicating the individual did not survive this injury.

kind noted experimentally may also be identified in archaeological material. Amongst the large animal bone assemblage excavated from Durrington Walls were four cattle and pig limb bones with embedded lithic fragments, identified as the tips of projectile points (Albarella and Serjeantson 2002, 43–44). In the case of one of these, a pig humerus, the respective fragment was loose, permitting examination of the defect in which it had been situated. Microscopic examination of this defect by the present authors revealed a further flint fragment embedded more deeply, similar to those observed experimentally. Such fragments can generally be observed using a light microscope, which is both rapid and inexpensive and may contribute significantly to the number of such injuries which are identified.

Finally, re-examination of a previously excavated skeleton from Feizor Nick Cave, Yorkshire, revealed that micro-striations relating to injury from flint-tipped projectiles are also observable in archaeological material. Figure 13.7 shows a lozenge shaped, perimortem defect visible on the skeleton's 12th thoracic vertebra. When this defect was examined using a SEM, a series of parallel striations consistent with damage inflicted by a flint implement were observed running parallel to the longitudinal axis of the defect. The gross morphology of the defect is consistent with a pointed implement rather than a blade. When considered in relation to the anatomical location of the defect, the gross and microscopic features are consistent with a perimortem penetrating injury produced by a flint-tipped projectile. These findings caused the authors to discard initial feelings that this skeleton may be relatively late (possibly Anglo-Saxon), instead suggesting the individual to be of prehistoric date. This was subsequently confirmed by radiocarbon dating when the skeleton was found to date from 3720±30 BP (OxA-14263; 2210–2030 cal BC at 2 s.d. using OxCal v.3.10).

It is not possible to discern whether the implement responsible was a thrusting weapon (such as a spear) or a projectile (such as an arrow) but, given the radiocarbon date, the latter possibility seems more likely. By the early second millennium BC flint was declining as a material for incorporation in hand-to-hand weapons, being gradually superseded by metals. However, the use of flint arrowheads persisted for several centuries with the leaf-shaped

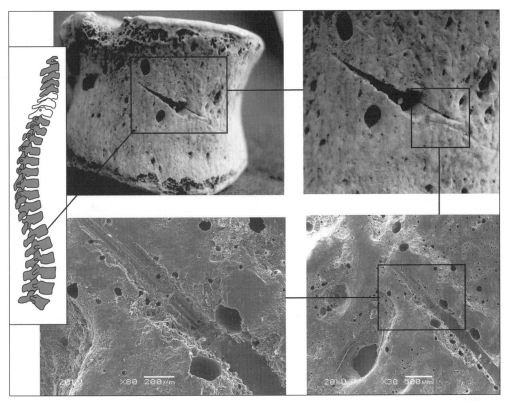

Figure 13.7. A vertebra from Feizor Nick Cave, Yorkshire, with a perimortem defect on its anterior surface. The two lower views are electron micrographs which show striations at the margin of the defect consistent with the damage having been produced by a flint implement.

points of the Neolithic being replaced by barbed-and-tanged arrowheads. It is argued that such a projectile point is the most likely candidate to have caused the injury in question.

RESILIENCE AND REUSABILITY: THE EFFECTS OF IMPACT UPON PROJECTILES

Several observations were also made regarding the gross effects of impact upon the arrowheads and their haftings (Table 13.1). As already indicated by the number of flint fragments left embedded, the arrowheads themselves were prone to break upon striking bone. However, the majority of arrowheads from both types of test were not beyond repair with 8 of 14 (57%) broken points from the bow tests and 7 of 13 (54%) from the 'charpy' tests being potentially reusable after retouching. The breakages observed were noted to resemble other experimental examples (Barton and Bergman 1982, 239; Dockall 1997; Fischer 1985, 31; Odell and Cowan 1986, 200–201).The experimental samples also resembled proposed archaeological instances of impact-damaged flint arrowheads (Barton and Bergman 1982, 239; Dockall 1997; Odell 1988, 344).

Arrow No.	Experiment Type	Arrowhead type	Shaft	Target	Point Breakage	Point Reusability	Hafting
1	Bow	Leaf	Ash	Ox Scapula	Yes	Yes*	Intact
2	Bow	Leaf	Ash	Ox Scapula	Yes	No	Intact
3	Bow	Leaf	Ash	Pig Scapula	No	Yes	Intact
4	Bow	Leaf	Ash	Ox Scapula	Yes	Yes*	Failed
5	Bow	Leaf	Ash	Ox Scapula	Yes	No	Intact
6	Bow	Leaf	Ash	Ox Scapula	Yes	No	Failed
7	Bow	Leaf	Ash	Pig Scapula	Yes	No	Intact
8	Bow	Leaf	Pine	Ox Scapula	No	No	Failed **
9	Bow	Leaf	Pine	Ox Scapula	Yes	Yes*	Failed **
10	Bow	Barb & Tang	Pine	Ox Scapula	Yes	Yes*	Failed **
11	Bow	Barb & Tang	Pine	Cattle Ribs	Yes	Yes*	Failed **
12	Bow	Leaf	Pine	Cattle Ribs	Yes	Yes*	Failed **
13	Bow	Barb & Tang	Pine	Cattle Ribs	Yes	Yes*	Failed
14	Bow	Leaf	Ash	Pig Scapula	No	Yes	Intact
15	Bow	Leaf	Pine	Pig Scapula	Yes	Yes*	Failed **
16	Bow	Leaf	Ash	Pig Scapula	Yes	No	Intact
17	Charpy	Leaf	Ash	Ox Scapula	Yes	Yes*	Failed
18	Charpy	Leaf	Ash	Ox Scapula	No	Yes	Failed
19	Charpy	Leaf	Ash	Ox Scapula	Yes	Yes*	Intact
20	Charpy	Leaf	Ash	Ox Scapula	Yes	Yes*	Intact
21	Charpy	Leaf	Ash	Ox Scapula	Yes	Yes*	Intact
22	Charpy	Leaf	Ash	Ox Scapula	Yes	Yes*	Intact
23	Charpy	Leaf	Ash	Ox Scapula	Yes	No	Failed**
24	Charpy	Leaf	Ash	Ox Scapula	Yes	Yes*	Intact
25	Charpy	Leaf	Pine	Ox Rib	Yes	No	Failed **
26	Charpy	Leaf	Pine	Ox Scapula	Yes	Yes	Failed **
27	Charpy	Barb & Tang	Pine	Ox Scapula	No	Yes	Failed
28	Charpy	Barb & Tang	Pine	Ox Scapula	Yes	Yes*	Failed
29	Charpy	Leaf	Pine	Ox Rib	Yes	No	Failed
30	Charpy	Leaf	Pine	Ox Scapula	Yes	No	Failed
31	Charpy	Leaf	Pine	Ox Rib	Yes	No	Failed **
32	Charpy	Leaf	Pine	Ox Rib	Yes	No	Failed **

* Point reusable with retouch
** Shaft split

Table 13.1. Effects of impacts on arrowheads and haftings.

The apparent high frequency with which point breakage occurs may in fact have been advantageous to stone projectile-using communities in so far as the majority of points which fractured in the present study were noted to need only minor retouching to be reusable. Similarly, the tendency for haftings to break upon impact may also have been viewed as desirable by prehistoric hunters. In terms of the time invested in manufacture, the shaft of an arrow is much more costly than the head (Keeley 1982, 800). Where arrowshafts became detached from their points on striking prey they could be recovered and re-used. Such potential for reuse is likely to have influenced the choice of material from which arrowshafts were made, for example the greater propensity for the ash shafts used in the present study to resist impact (see Table 13.2) would be consistent with the choice of ash and other harder woods for arrowshafts in prehistory (Mercer 1999, 147; Spindler 1994, 123). This contradicts Green's (1980, 182) assertion that arrowshafts were simply manufactured from whichever type of wood was available locally with no element of deliberate selection.

Arrowshaft material	N. Failed Haftings	N. Split Shafts
Pine:	11/15 (73.3%)	10/15 (66.7%)
Ash:	5/17 (29.4%)	1/17 (5.9%)

Table 13.2. Effects of using two different types of wood on the reusability of arrowshafts following impacts with bone.

CONCLUSION

Sound middle-range theory based upon empirically derived signatures is essential in the interpretation of past socio-cultural practices. As such, experimental studies of the kind presented may have the potential to significantly enhance the recognition of evidence for conflict during the Neolithic and Early Bronze Age. Several major conclusions were produced during this study, particularly in regard to interactions between flint and bone. Firstly, full thickness punctures of flat bones caused by flint projectiles have distinctive features, which can be recognized macroscopically. Secondly, when flint projectile points strike bone, small fragments of flint are commonly retained. Whilst such fragments may often be missed on gross examination, these can be identified through light microscopy. Thirdly, and perhaps most importantly, it has been established that by analysis using a SEM, flint projectile trauma can be identified even in cases where the 'murder weapon' is absent. In particular, the present authors would recommend careful examination of human bone from Neolithic contexts for the features discussed above. Such attention is particularly warranted where arrowheads have been found in association with human remains, in order to shed further light on the extent to which such artefacts may have arrived 'in', rather than 'with', the respective bodies.

ACKNOWLEDGEMENTS

The research presented was funded by the Leverhulme Trust (Grant No: F/00 094/AJ). The authors would like to thank Will Lord for manufacturing the bow, arrowheads and finished arrows used in this study. We are particularly grateful to Mick Cunningham and Avril Rogers of the Department of Metallurgy and Materials, School of Engineering, University of Birmingham, for their advice and assistance with the impact tests. We would also like to thank Leslie Tomkins and Paul Stanley of the Centre for Electron Microscopy, University of Birmingham, and are additionally grateful to T. Hands and staff and A. Holder for supplying the animal bones used in the experiments. This chapter was initially submitted in 2006 and updated in November 2008.

BIBLIOGRAPHY

Abrate, S., 1998, *Impact On Composite Structures*. Cambridge: Cambridge University Press.

Ahler, S., 1971, *Projectile Point Form and Function at Rogers Shelter, Missouri*. Missouri: Missouri Archaeological Society Research Series 8.

Albarella, U. and Serjeantson, D., 2002, A passion for pork: meat consumption at the British late Neolithic site of Durrington Walls. In P. Miracle and N. Milner (eds), *Consuming Passions and Patterns of Consumption*, 33–49. Cambridge: McDonald Institute Monographs.

Anderson, P. C., 1980, A testimony of prehistoric tasks: diagnostic residues on stone tool working edges. *World Archaeology* 12, 181–194.

Barton, R. N. E. and Bergman, C. A., 1982, Hunters at Hengistbury: some evidence from experimental archaeology. *World Archaeology* 14, 237–248.

Bergman, C. A., McEwen, E. and Miller, R., 1988, Experimental archery: projectile velocities and comparison of bow performances. *Antiquity* 62, 658–670.

Berryman, H. E. and Symes, S. A., 1998, Recognising gunshot and blunt cranial trauma through fracture interpretations. In K. J. Reichs (ed.), *Forensic Osteology: Advances in the Identification of Human Remains*, 333–352. Illinois: Charles C. Thomas.

Bradley, R. and Edmonds, M., 1993, *Interpreting the Axe Trade*. Cambridge: Cambridge University Press.

Britnell, W. J. and Savory, H. N., 1984, *Gwernvale and Penywyrlod: Two Neolithic Long Cairns in Brecknockshire*. Cardiff: Cambrian Archaeological Association.

Clemente, I. and Gibaja, J. F., 1998, Working processes on cereals: an approach through microwear analysis. *Journal of Archaeological Science* 25, 457–464.

Clark, J. G. D., 1963, Neolithic bows from Somerset, England, and the prehistory of archery in north-western Europe. *Proceedings of the Prehistoric Society* 29, 50–98.

Cooney, G. and Mandal, S., 1998, *The Irish Stone Axe Project: Monograph I*. Bray: Wordwell.

De la Grandmaison, G. L., 2001, Frequency of bone lesions: an inadequate criterion for gunshot wound diagnosis in skeletal remains. *Journal of Forensic Sciences* 46, 593–595.

Dockall, J. E., 1997, Wear traces and projectile impact: a review of the experimental and archaeological evidence. *Journal of Field Archaeology* 24, 321–331.

Edmonds, M., 1995, *Stone Tools and Society*. London: Batsford.

Fischer, A., 1985, Hunting with flint tipped arrows: results and experiences from practical experiments. In C. Bonsall (ed.), *The Mesolithic in Europe, Papers Presented at the Third International Symposium, Edinburgh 1985*, 29–39. Edinburgh: John Donald.

Green, H. S., 1980, *The Flint Arrowheads of the British Isles: a Detailed Study of Material from England and Wales with Comparanda from Scotland and Ireland*. Oxford: British Archaeological Reports (British Series 75).

Hardy, R., 1975, *Longbow: a Social and Military History*. Cambridge: Patrick Stephens.

Karger, B., Sudhues, H., Kneubuehl, P. and Brinkmann, B., 1998, Experimental arrow wounds: ballistics and traumatology. *Journal of Trauma* 45, 495–501.

Karlsson, T. and Stahling, S., 2000, Experimental blowgun injuries: ballistic aspects of modern blowguns. *Forensic Science International* 112, 59–64.

Keeley, L. H., 1982, Hafting and retooling: effects on the archaeological record. *American Antiquity* 47, 798–809.

Keeley L. H., 1996, *War before Civilization: the Myth of the Peaceful Savage*. Oxford: Oxford University Press.

Knight, B., 1975, The dynamics of stab wounds. *Forensic Science* 6, 249–255.

Knüsel, C., 2007, The arrowhead injury to Individual B2. In D. Benson and A. Whittle (eds), *Building Memories: the Neolithic Cotswold Long Barrow at Ascott-under-Wychwood, Oxfordshire*, 218–220. Oxford: Oxbow Books.

Lambert, P. M., 1997, Patterns of violence in prehistoric hunter-gatherer societies of coastal southern California. In D. L. Martin and D. W. Frayer (eds), *Troubled Times: Violence and Warfare in the Past*, 77–109. New York: Gordon and Breach.

Mandal, S., Cooney, G., Meighan, I. G. and Jamison, D. D., 1997, Using geochemistry to interpret porcellanite stone axe production in Ireland. *Journal of Archaeological Science* 24, 757–763.

Mercer, R., 1980, *Hambledon Hill: a Neolithic Landscape*. Edinburgh: Edinburgh University Press.

Mercer, R., 1999, The origins of warfare in the British Isles. In J. Carman and A. Harding (eds), *Ancient Warfare*, 143–156. Stroud: Sutton Publishing.

Miller, R., McEwen, E. and Bergman, C., 1986, Experimental approaches to Near Eastern archery. *World Archaeology* 18, 178–195.

Moore, D. G., 2004, Hostilities in early Neolithic Ireland: trouble with the new neighbours – the evidence from Ballyharry, County Antrim. In A. Gibson and A. Sheridan (eds), *From Sickles to Circles: Britain and Ireland at the Time of Stonehenge*, 142–154. Stroud: Tempus.

Odell, G. H., 1988, Addressing prehistoric hunting practices through stone tool analysis. *American Anthropologist* 90, 335–356.

Odell, G. H. and Cowan, F., 1986, Experiments with spears and arrows on animal targets. *Journal of Field Archaeology* 13, 195–212.

Owen Smith, M. S., 1981, *High Velocity Missile Wounds*. London: Edward Arnold.

Patten Report Recommendations 69 and 70 Relating to Public Order Equipment, 2004, Belfast: The Northern Ireland Office in association with the Association of Chief Police Officers.

Piggott, S., 1962, *The West Kennet Long Barrow: Excavations 1955–56*. London: HMSO.

Pope, S. T., 1918, A study of bows and arrows. *American Archaeology and Ethnology* 13, 329–414.

Pryor, F., 1976, A Neolithic multiple burial from Fengate, Peterborough. *Antiquity* 50, 232–233.

Quatrehomme, G. and İşcan, M. Y., 1999, Characteristics of gunshot wounds in the skull. *Journal of Forensic Sciences* 44, 568–576.

Saville, A., 1990, *Hazleton North: the Excavation of a Neolithic Long Cairn of the Cotswold Severn Group*. London: English Heritage.

Schulting, R. and Wysocki, M., 2005, 'In this tumulus were found cleft skulls…': an assessment of the evidence for cranial trauma in the British Neolithic'. *Proceedings of the Prehistoric Society* 71, 107–138.

Shea, J., 2001, Experimental tests of Middle Palaeolithic spear points using a calibrated crossbow. *Journal of Archaeological Science* 28, 807–816.

Smith, R. A., 1927, Flint arrow-heads in Britain. *Archaeologia* 76, 81–106.

Smith, M. J., Brickley, M. B. and Leach, S., 2007, Experimental evidence for lithic projectile injuries: improving identification of an under-recognised phenomenon. *Journal of Archaeological Science* 34, 540–553.

Smith, O. C., Pope, E. J. and Symes, S. A., 2003, Look until you see: identification of trauma in skeletal material. In D. Wolfe Steadman (ed.), *Case Studies in Forensic Anthropology*, 138–154. New Jersey: Prentice Hall.

Spindler, K., 1994, *The Man in the Ice*. London: Weidenfeld and Nicholson.

Taylor, K. J., 1996, The rough and the smooth: axe polishers of the Middle Neolithic. In T. Pollard and A. Morrison (eds), *The Early Prehistory of Scotland*, 225–236. Glasgow: Edinburgh University Press.

Thorpe, I. J. N., 2006, Fighting and feuding in Neolithic and Bronze Age Britain and Ireland. In T. Otto, H. Thrane and H. Vandkilde (eds), *Warfare in Archaeological and Social Anthropological Perspective*, 141–166. Denmark: Aarhus University Press & Jutland Archaeological Society.

Thurnam, J., 1857, On a cromlech-tumulus called Lugbury near Littleton Drew. *Wiltshire Archaeological and Natural History Magazine* 3, 164–177.

Topping, P., 2004, The South Downs flint mines: towards an ethnography of prehistoric flint extraction. In J. Cotton and D. Field (eds), *Towards a New Stone Age – Aspects of the Neolithic in South-East England*, 177–190. York: Council for British Archaeology (Research Report 137).

Tyler, A., 1976, *Neolithic Flint Axes from the Cotswold Hills*. Oxford: British Archaeological Reports (British Series 25).

Whittle, A., 1991, Waylands Smithy, Oxfordshire: excavations at the Neolithic tomb in 1962–63 by R. J. C. Atkinson and S. Piggott. *Proceedings of the Prehistoric Society* 57, 61–101.

Woodward, A., 2000, *British Barrows – a Matter of Life and Death*. Stroud: Tempus.

Wysocki, M. and Whittle, A., 2000, Diversity, lifestyles and rites: new biological and archaeological evidence from British earlier Neolithic mortuary assemblages. *Antiquity* 74, 591–601.

Chapter 14

Prehistoric extraction: further suggestions from ethnography

Peter Topping

INTRODUCTION

The mines, interesting as they were, have revealed nothing new or original (Holleyman 1937, 250)

Prehistoric mining is frequently characterized as a purely functional activity, and clearly in some instances this was true. However, the question becomes clouded at extraction sites where surface deposits or outcrops make extraction unnecessary. This is illustrated at the flint mines at Grime's Graves, Norfolk, England, where the post-abandonment use of surface-collected nodules supplemented by the small-scale recycling of flint from pre-existing chipping floors occurred during the later Middle Bronze Age (Longworth *et al.* 1991, 30). Groups do not readily dig for raw materials if they do not need to. The picture is further complicated at sites where non-functional assemblages have been recovered, including faunal and human skeletal material.

In addition, clear evidence of settlement at mines in the UK is rare, suggesting that many were 'special' places in the cultural landscape, only exploited on a temporary or seasonal basis – something which site location, working conditions and weather patterns may have deeply influenced. On the South Downs this can be seen at the mines at Cissbury, Church Hill, Blackpatch, and Harrow Hill (all in West Sussex, England), which lie in isolation between the Rivers Arun and Adur on an area of chalk downland which is devoid of any other contemporary monument (cf. Kinnes 1992, 167, fig. 1A,11; Oswald *et al.* 2001, 117–148). In this area the distribution of ground axeheads is almost exclusively limited to the lower-lying coastal plain or the chalkland talus, reinforcing the separation of settlement and domestic activities from the South Downs mine locations (Figure 14.1).

To date most research has focused upon the technological aspects of pre-industrial mining, an approach which has failed to address the social context of extraction, despite a number of writers previously recognizing this shortcoming (cf., for example, Barber *et al.* 1999; Edmonds 1990; Gero 1991; Ingold 2000; Torrence 2001).

To explore this issue a collection of ethnographic case studies drawn from North America and Australia have been analysed to identify what Lewis-Williams and Pearce (2005, 9) have recently attempted to characterize as 'the universal foundations of [cultural] diversity'. Much of the North American ethnographic data has been presented in some detail previously so will not be reproduced here (cf. Topping 2004; 2005). In summary, however, these data record rituals underpinning extraction and reduction sequences followed by specialized artefact use and circulation. The ethnography also details the ritualization of many seemingly 'domestic' activities.

Several recurrent themes emerge from the ethnography:

1. many mines were considered 'special' places in the cultural landscape;
2. procurement strategies could be ritualized;
3. many groups had craft specialists;
4. exclusive procedures for reduction and knapping existed;
5. 'special' artefacts were crafted for ceremonial use and kinship building, some dispersed through long-distance trade;
6. gender issues; and
7. linkages between the knapper, the knapper's products, and the worldview of the community.

Much of this cultural evidence creates a self-perpetuating, cyclical social system; the procurement, reduction, and curation phases ultimately lead back to further procurement as artefact renewal stimulates social renewal. The use of 'special' artefacts underpins processes of legitimization, kinship, and clan building, and wider social control. Amongst Aboriginal

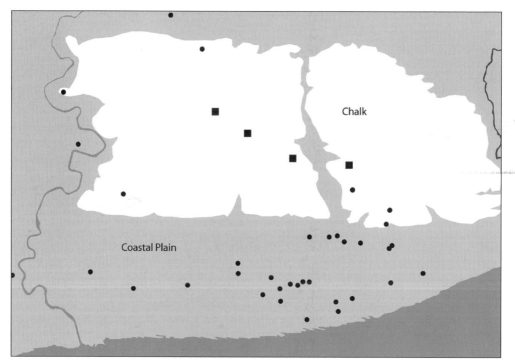

Figure 14.1. The location of ground flint axeheads and extraction sites around Worthing in Sussex. Despite the fact that four major flint mine complexes (squares) are located on the chalk downland, most of the finds of ground axeheads (dots) have been from the low-lying coastal plain (© Dave Field).

Australians restrictions or taboos exist at extraction sites (e.g. Flood 1995, 271–273; 1997, 34–35). Here the quarries and finished artefacts of mined stone are imbued with powerful social values through a direct association between the raw material and Ancestral Beings from the Dreaming (Flood 1997, 114; Taçon 2004, 31). Mine location and raw material choice are often driven by these associations, particularly in the selective acquisition of bright or colourful stones or minerals which are considered to be the fossilized body parts of powerful Ancestral Beings. The resulting crafted artefacts are believed to have an embedded 'ancestral potency' (Brumm 2004, 147).

Access to certain Australian Aboriginal quarries is restricted by age and gender, and conduct at these quarries is designed to provide protection from these powerfully charged locations. Important quarries might be visited from distances of between 500km [311 miles] (Taçon 2004, 34) and 1000km [621 miles] (Brumm 2004, 153), illustrating the deep cultural value sedimented into ritualized long-distance journeys for mineral acquisition (Boivin 2004, 10).

AN INTERPRETIVE FRAMEWORK

The ethnographic data allow the development of an interpretive framework through the sequential ordering of events and their associated cultural material. This data matrix can then be compared with the archaeological record to inform the analysis of contextualized assemblages or built features from prehistoric extraction sites, *tentatively* suggesting underlying motives behind deposition (Table 14.1)

Using this framework as a basis for analysis, it is possible to review the excavation data from the South Downs flint mines to broadly characterize exploitation in the earlier Neolithic period. This can then be contrasted with the evidence for later Neolithic mining at Grime's Graves to establish the degree of commonality in depositional patterning and temporal change within the mining process. As ever, the effects of taphonomic processes and excavation bias impose some limitations on interpretation.

Clearly, from the evidence of the ethnographic data and the potential archaeological correlates, certain features and deposits may have a multiplicity of uses and meanings, such as the deposition of animal remains which could be interpreted as pre- or post-extraction offerings. Many of these comprise articulated body parts or more rarely complete skeletons, such as the ox from the fill of Shaft 27 at Cissbury (Pull Archive, Worthing Museum and Art Gallery) or the dog skeleton from a gallery of Greenwell's Pit at Grime's Graves (Longworth and Varndell 1996, 23, 26, fig. 17). Similarly, the deposition of grouped antler picks may also illustrate pre- or post-extraction offerings or rites of renewal. The presence of human remains can also be seen to define differing foci; fragmentary body parts in shaft fills may have links to post-extraction offerings, whereas the rare complete inhumations may illustrate the sedimenting of ancestral associations and satisfying rites of renewal. As always, it is the precise context of the feature or deposit which can help to determine its original purpose.

The results presented in Tables 14.2 and 14.3, whilst allowing for an incomplete data set, do provide interesting trends. The presence of hearths at the bases of some shafts, or of charcoal deposits in galleries, occurs at 10.7 per cent of sites (3 of 28) in the earlier period (e.g. at Cissbury and Harrow Hill) but 34.2 per cent of sites (13 of 38) in the later period,

Ethnographic events	Ethnographic evidence	Possible archaeological correlates
(1) Purification rituals	Sweat lodges; hearths; pipe smoking; 'smudging' rituals [all adjacent to mines and quarries]	• Hearths at base of shafts and in shaft fills • Small charcoal deposits in galleries (e.g. Greenwell's Pit, Grime's Graves)
(2) Pre-extraction offerings	Tobacco; tobacco ties; avifaunal remains [all placed near extraction sites]	• Animal remains in placed or structured deposits in the mine workings • Pottery • Carved chalk objects
(3) Ritualised extraction	Various hand tools	• Antler picks, wedges and hammerstones left in mines • Caches of antler picks placed on chalk platforms • Chalk 'platforms' • Ox scapulae • Impact marks from ground stone axes • ? ground stone axes
(4) Post-extraction prayers and offerings	Tobacco; tobacco ties; avifaunal remains; graffiti and petroglyphs [all found in mine locales]	• Animal remains in placed or structured deposits in galleries and shaft fills • Caches of antler picks • Pottery • Carved chalk objects • Human remains • Graffiti
(5) Artefact production	Assorted hand tools at workshop locations; debitage	• Debitage in galleries and shafts • Chipping 'floors' on surface • Rough outs • Broken tools
(6) Ceremonial use of artefacts of mined raw material	Social events and rituals in various locations; artefact groupings (bundles) and ritual structures (altars, etc)	• Axes in structured deposits • Special groupings of artefacts • Axe hoards in various loci including non-mining sites
(7) Rites of renewal	Broken artefacts returned to mines and quarries, including broken blanks or preforms, offcuts / flakes and dust	• Broken axes • Pottery vessels/sherds • Broken/complete antler picks • Knapping debris in shaft fills • Human remains • Animal remains

Table 14.1. Ethnographic data for extraction strategies compared to the archaeological record from the Neolithic flint mines in England.

suggesting that fire, heat, light, and smoke may have played an increasingly important role in extraction. Using ethnography as a guide, the ritualized purification of miners and / or their tools at a hearth may have been an integral part of the extraction process, particularly as many hearths are not positioned to provide light or heat to the galleries. The small deposits of unidentified charcoal in many galleries in Greenwell's Pit and Pit 15 at Grime's Graves (Longworth and Varndell 1996, 12, 26–27, 55) may have been further evidence of ritualized purification by smoke. Ritualization was enhanced by accompanying paraphernalia, such as graffiti (Cissbury, Grime's Graves, and Harrow Hill), carved chalk objects (Blackpatch, Church Hill, Cissbury, Grime's Graves, and Harrow Hill) and the presence of chalk platforms and groups of antler picks, all suggesting a range of non-functional activities sedimented into the mining process. Carefully grouped artefacts or tools may represent ritualized extraction. The creation of sacred space is suggested by deposits ranging from animal remains, caches of axeheads, knapping debris, groups of antler tools, carved chalk objects, pottery, and grouped artefacts. Rare human burials are also recorded (see below).

Perhaps the most interesting trend is the prevalence of post-extraction deposits in the shafts and galleries at all of the mines. These range from artefacts to human and animal remains and clearly signify a continuing importance for many mines following the abandonment of extraction, which was periodically maintained through these staged deposits of assemblages.

Figure 14.2. Grime's Graves from the east (Photo taken 15 May 2004; © Pete Topping).

Site name	Assemblages in the mine workings	?Evidence for ritualised extraction	Post-extraction deposits in the galleries or shafts
EARLIER NEOLITHIC MINING			
Blackpatch Shaft 1	A; AX; C	AP; AX; CP; T; W	A; AX; D; T
Blackpatch Shaft 2	C	AP; D	AX
Blackpatch Shaft 3a	N/A	N/A	AX; D; T
Blackpatch Shaft 4	N/A	N/A	D;S
Blackpatch Shaft 5	C	AP; D	A; AX
Blackpatch Shaft 6			D
Blackpatch Shaft 7	C		A; AX; C; CH; D; IS; T
Blackpatch Shaft 8			AX; D; T
Church Hill Shaft 1			AP; AX; C; CH; D; IS; T; W
Church Hill Shaft 2	N/A	N/A	D
Church Hill Shaft 3	N/A	N/A	AX
Church Hill Shaft 4		AP; D; G; W	AP; AX; B; D; OS; W
Church Hill Shaft 5a		AP; D	A; AX; D; H; T
Church Hill Shaft 6		AP; OS; T; W	D; S; T
Church Hill Shaft 7		AP; OS; W	AP; AX; D; OS; W
Church Hill Pit A			AX; D; T
Church Hill Pit B			AX; D
Cissbury Shaft 18			D; T
Cissbury Shaft 23			D
Cissbury Shaft 24	T	W	A; AX; CH; D; OS; T; W
Cissbury Shaft 27	A; C; D; T	AP; W	A; AX; C; CH; D; OS; S; T
Cissbury 'Cave Pit'		AP; CP; G; H; W	
Cissbury Shaft VI			A; AX; C; S; T
Harrow Hill Pit 21	A; C; D	AP; CH; G; H; OS; W	A; AP; AX; C; CH; D; G; OS; T; W
Harrow Hill Shaft I		AP; W	AP; AX
Harrow Hill Shaft II		AP; W	A; AP; AX; D
Harrow Hill Shaft III		AP; CH; H; OS; W	AX; CH
Harrow Hill Shaft IV			AX

KEY: A = animal and bird remains; AP = antler pick; AX = axe(s); B = wooden bowl; BA = bone artefacts; BP = bone picks; C = carved chalk objects; CH = charcoal deposits; CP = chalk platform; D = debitage, chipping floors; G = graffiti; H = hearth(s); HS = hammer stones; I = impact marks from ground axes; IS = ?intrusive human remains; NH = nodule heap; OS = ox scapula shovels; P = Neolithic pottery; S = human skeletal remains; T = flint tools; W = antler wedges, hammers and tines; ? = contexts unclear.

Table 14.2. A tentative interpretation of the archaeological record from the earlier Neolithic flint mines in Sussex. (Information from Curwen and Curwen 1926; Holleyman 1937; the Pull Archive, Worthing Museum and Art Gallery).

Site name	Assemblages in the mine workings	?Evidence for ritualised extraction	Post-extraction deposits in the galleries or shafts
LATER NEOLITHIC MINING			
Grime's Graves Greenwell's Pit	A; AX; C; P	AP; CH; H; HS; I; W	AP; C; H; P; S
Grime's Graves Pit 1	A; C; P	AP; H; I	A; AP; AX; CH; D; H; P; S; T; W
Grime's Graves Pit 2	AX; C; P	AP; CP; G; H; I; T	AP; C; IS; H; P; T
Grime's Graves Beaver Pit	N/A	N/A	A; C; T
Grime's Graves Black Hole			C
Grime's Graves Pit 3 (III)		BP	D
Grime's Graves Pit 3A	D	AP; BA; HS	A; BA; NH; ?S
Grime's Graves Pit 4 (Peake)			D
Grime's Graves Pit 4 (IV)		BP	C
Grime's Graves Pit 5 (V)		BP	D
Grime's Graves Pit 6 (VI)			BP
Grime's Graves Pit 7 (VII)			H
Grime's Graves Pit 8		AP; BP	H
Grime's Graves Pit 9	N/A	AP; BP	?C; D; H
Grime's Graves Pit 10	N/A	AP; BP	?C; D; H
Grime's Graves Pit 11		AP; W	
Grime's Graves Pit 12		AP	A; AP; C; D; P
Grime's Graves Pit 13			
Grime's Graves Pit 14		AP; BP	A; AP; AX; C; CH; D; H; T
Grime's Graves Pit 15	?C	AP; CP; H	AP; ?C; D; H
Grime's Graves Pit 15A		AP; CH	N/A
Grime's Graves Pit 15B		AP; CH	N/A
Grime's Graves Pit 15C		AP; CH	N/A
Grime's Graves Pit 15D	BA; C; I	AP; CH; I; HS	N/A
Grime's Graves Pit 15E		AP; CH	N/A
Grime's Graves Pit 15F		AP	N/A
Grime's Graves Pit 15G		AP	N/A
Grime's Graves Pit 15H		AP	N/A
Grime's Graves Pit 15J		AP; CH	N/A
Grime's Graves Pit 15K		AP; CH	N/A
Grime's Graves 1971 Shaft	AX; C; D; P; T	AP; CP; H	D; H; P
Grime's Graves 1972 Shaft			P
Grime's Graves Shaft X			C; P
Grime's Graves Pit W			C
Grime's Graves Greenwell Shaft A	A	AP; W	
Grime's Graves Greenwell Shaft C & D	C; D; P	AP; CH; W	
Grime's Graves Greenwell Shaft E		AP; W	
Grime's Graves Pit east of Floor 4			A

Table 14.3. A tentative interpretation of the archaeological record from the later Neolithic flint mines in Norfolk. (Information from Clarke 1915; Longworth et al. 1991; Longworth and Varndell 1996).

Allowing for excavation bias, the data presented in Tables 14.2 and 14.3 could suggest that there was little significant difference temporally between activities which took place at the earlier Neolithic mines and those of the later period. Clearly the most common feature was the post-extraction commemoration of abandoned mines, signposting them in the cultural landscape through episodic deposition or staged events such as feasting. Such a range of activities has direct correlations with those encountered at causewayed enclosures, long barrows, and henges.

DISCUSSION

A detailed review of the archaeological record from the Neolithic flint mines in the UK suggests that many assemblages are not functional in relation to mining and cannot be linked directly to the extraction process *per se*, but rather form deposits – sometimes structured – which are zoned:

- human remains focus upon shafts and gallery entrances;
- pottery is primarily found in the shafts;
- carved chalk objects and graffiti generally occur near gallery entrances;
- hearths occur at the base or in the fill of shafts;
- flint and stone axeheads have been recovered from a range of contexts throughout the mines.

Much of this evidence clearly references access routes into the workings, signposting encoded messages recording the importance of place. An obvious example is the two

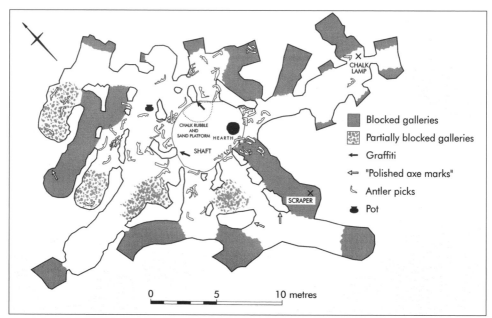

Figure 14.3. Grime's Graves 1914 excavations. Pit 2 plan of shaft, galleries and artefact deposition (based upon Clarke 1915, fig. 8; drawing © Trevor Pearson).

internally-decorated Grooved Ware bowls sitting upon a chalk platform located upon the floor of the 1971 Shaft at Grime's Graves (Mercer 1981, 24, fig. 11), carefully positioned at the subterranean entry point to the galleries. Similarly a grey flint axehead was found lying next to a carved chalk 'cup' at the entrance to Gallery 5 in Pit 2 at Grime's Graves – which was also one of the few galleries to feature ground axehead impact marks (cf. Figure 14.3; Clarke 1915, 85) – suggesting an enhanced significance to this gallery. Also in Pit 2 were two graffiti (Figure 14.4), the 'tally marks' and the 'sundial', which signposted the entrances to galleries 4 and 7, and gallery 6 respectively (Clarke 1915, 73–74).

The presence of flint and stone axeheads bears some consideration. Superficially, the discovery of axeheads might be expected if they were the primary mining tool. Certainly, in some European flint mines such as Rijckholt, near Maastricht in The Netherlands, this does appear to have been the case (Felder *et al.* 1998, 47–49). However, apart from the few scattered impact marks from ground axeheads surviving in certain galleries at Grime's Graves (possibly 6 galleries in Pit 1, 4 in Pit 2 [Figure 14.3]; cf. Clarke 1915, 43, 59, 73, 85), it is clear that the tool of preference was the antler pick, in association with tine wedges and hammers (Clutton-Brock 1984; Legge 1981). It therefore follows that the presence of rare ground axeheads or preforms (complete and broken), must have had an alternative *non-functional* role within the English mines. Considering the ethnography, such artefacts may represent the return of tools to their place of origin as a form of symbolic renewal. This would explain the more than 300 axehead roughouts recovered by various excavations at Grime's Graves or the cache of axeheads at Harrow Hill, where 33 'in various stages of manufacture' were discovered in Shaft III (Holleyman 1937, 239). One of these latter axeheads is of particular interest, the cutting edge was discovered 'just beneath the turf and

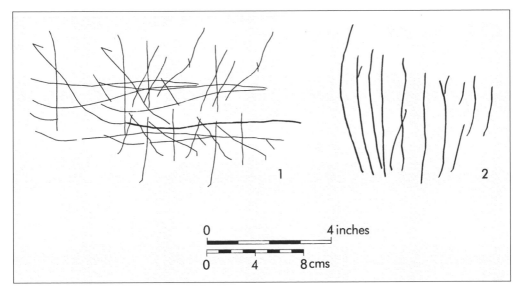

Figure 14.4: Grime's Graves Pit 2 graffiti. Key: 1 = the 'Tally Marks' located on the buttress between Galleries 4 and 7; 2 = the 'Sundial' located on the south side of the entrance to Gallery 6 (based upon Clarke 1915, figs 5 and 6; drawing © Trevor Pearson).

the butt end 8ft [2.4m] down [the shaft]' (Holleyman 1937, 242). The different provenances suggest that the uppermost fragment had remained in circulation longer, but had eventually been returned to the same mine as the first fragment – possibly their point of origin.

Rites of renewal could also underpin the presence of certain assemblages in various mines at Blackpatch where numerous deposits of knapping debris, cores, 'Cissbury' type axeheads, preforms, and scrapers were scattered throughout shaft fills and galleries. A similar situation was discovered at Church Hill, particularly in Shaft 6, where a sequence of knapping floors was found in the shaft fill, the third and final example nearly sealing the shaft. Various shafts and galleries at Cissbury produced parallel assemblages of debitage with complete and broken tools. At Harrow Hill Pit 21, a sequence of six 'nests' of flint flakes was recovered from the shaft fill, with others at the entrances to galleries I, II and V, the latter associated with a hearth, three axehead rough-outs, a broken axehead and a 'chopper' (Curwen and Curwen 1926, 132–133). Debitage in the shafts and galleries is unusual – so-called 'chipping floors' or knapping workshops are encountered regularly on the surface where major on-site reduction or tool production occurred. Knapping within the mines was clearly not on the same level as at the activity areas on the surface, it was more focused, on a smaller scale, and created by the crafting of only a few token implements destined for deposition in subterranean contexts.

Antler picks, wedges and hammers were the preferred extraction tools in the flint mines of England. Although many may appear to have been casually discarded in the mines, others clearly had been purposefully placed in particular contexts. At Grime's Graves in Pit 15, a chalk platform was discovered at the base of the shaft upon which had been placed seven antler picks, and which had a number of contentious carved chalk objects surrounding it (Longworth *et al.* 1991, 103–105); the 'Cave Pit' at Cissbury also featured a chalk platform with a number of antler tines lying upon it next to the 'cave', a unique subterranean hut-like structure built of chalk blocks (Park Harrison 1878, 421–422). Many antler picks lie adjacent to the hearths which feature so prominently on the base of many shafts, and suggest analogies with the purification of tools through ritualized exposure to smoke, an activity perhaps borne out by the numerous small charcoal deposits discovered in the galleries of Greenwell's Pit scattered amongst discarded antler picks (e.g. Longworth and Varndell 1996, 26–27). Although many of the antler picks were undoubtedly randomly discarded *in* the mines, the fact that so many remained below ground may also be significant. Ethnography records that at the Aboriginal ochre mine at Wilgie Mia taboos forbade the removal of extraction tools (Flood 1995, 273). The quantity and distribution of antler picks found in the excavations at Greenwell's Pit suggests that the miners must have had to literally crawl over a raft of discarded picks in some galleries. Over 570 picks were recovered from Greenwell's Pit, Pits 1 and 2, and the 1971 Shaft alone, which suggests an 'average' tally per pit of some 142.5 picks. If this number is multiplied by the number of earthwork shafts and pits (433), this would produce an estimate of 61,702 antler picks for the complex as a whole. This can only be viewed as a conservative estimate as undoubtedly many more extraction sites remain to be discovered beneath the coversands, as has been demonstrated in the West Field (Pits 8, 9, 10, 11 and 12) and the northern periphery (Pits 3, 4, 5, 6, 7, 13 and 14).

Avifaunal remains are only rarely found in flint mines. One example discovered in Greenwell's Pit was the skull of a phalarope, a shorebird, found positioned between a pair of antler picks with tines facing inwards, and an imported Cornish greenstone axehead placed at the base of the picks. Locating bird remains below ground could reference mythico-religious concepts relating to engendered sky and earth deities, creating a loaded metaphor for fertility and renewal. The additional presence of carved chalk phalli in Pit 15 and Greenwell's Pit may add weight to this suggestion, confirming the ethnographic observation that 'male spirits … are frequently understood to dwell within stone' (Boivin 2004, 5). Curiously, 'the skull of what appears to have been a mouse' was discovered with an antler pick in Gallery III of Pit 21 at Harrow Hill (Curwen and Curwen 1926, 115), hinting at other forms of symbolism in the mines (the fact that only the skull was discovered again suggests careful curation).

The discovery of the phalarope skull suggests that this species may have had a symbolic association with flint mining. Phalaropes are migratory with an arrival on the east coast of England from early March, peaking in mid-April (data from the British Trust for

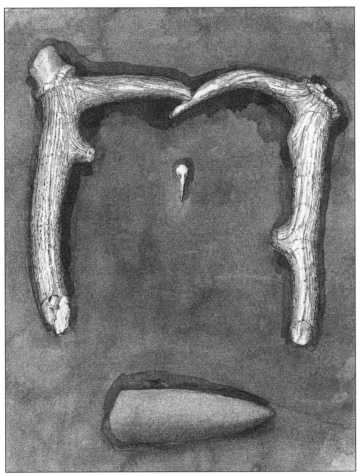

Figure 14.5: Greenwell's Pit, Grime's Graves. A reconstruction of the grouped antler picks, phalarope skull and Cornish greenstone axehead assemblage (© English Heritage; painting Judith Dobie)

Ornithology; http://blx1.bto.org/bt-dailyresults/results/cov5-05.html). Considering the difficulties of traversing slippery chalk surfaces and the short daylight hours in the autumn and winter months, the suggestion that flint mines were only used seasonally makes practical sense. Consequently, if seasonality was the norm, does the reverential treatment of the phalarope skull imply it had a special place in the iconography of the mines – did the appearance of this spring migrant trigger the annual mining operations at Grime's Graves? In addition, by implication of the fact that the phalarope is exclusively a coastal species, does this imply that the miners who exploited Grime's Graves were also coastal inhabitants who travelled across country to dig for flint in the Brecklands during the spring and summer months from their permanent winter camps?

The recovery of another 'possible' bird bone from Shaft 27 at Cissbury (Pull Archive, Worthing Museum and Art Gallery) may reinforce this symbolic association between mining and birds. The fact that long barrows have produced evidence of swan, crane, heron and geese – all migratory species – emphasizes the importance of avian seasonal indicators to Neolithic communities. These data parallel the use of medicine bundles by the Hidatsa in North America, which both focused upon the Big Bird ceremony associated with the spring migration of large raptors and corvids *and* provided the supernatural endorsement for flint knapping.

A further perspective on the multi-layered use of flint mines is provided by Barrow 12, a seemingly contemporary burial mound placed amongst the mines at Blackpatch (cf. Topping 2005, 67). The presence of burial mounds clearly centres an ancestral presence amongst the mines – alongside the less visible and equally rare shaft burials, such as the Shaft 27 inhumation from Cissbury. This skeleton of a *c.* 20-year-old female was discovered lying on her left side and facing into the mines, a position deliberately referencing the source of the flint. Chalk carvings were found nearby along with an unusual 'fossil like worm' that had curious phallic attributes. Although the exact cause of death is ambiguous, the pathology could be interpreted as a deliberate burial. Certainly a male burial from Shaft VI surrounded by chalk blocks and accompanied by grave goods demonstrates that formal burials did occur in the mines.

However, the treatment of human remains varied. Tindall's excavations at Cissbury discovered an assemblage comprising a human skull alongside that of a wild boar, two oxen, and the bones of a goat, ox and pig (Willett 1875, 341). Clearly this collection of both wild and domesticated animals juxtaposed with human remains created a specific cultural narrative.

Disarticulated body parts have been recorded in a few mines; an adult femur and child's mandible were recovered from the upper fills of Blackpatch Shaft 4; a single fibula from the base of Church Hill Shaft 6; a (possibly intrusive) juvenile female's lower limbs, mandible, vertebrae and rib cage in the middle layers of Grime's Graves Pit 2 associated with a mixed faunal assemblage (wild and domestic; Clarke 1915, 72, 79–80); and in Grime's Graves Pit 1 a skull was found wedged between chalk blocks and lying immediately above an ox bone midway up the shaft (Clarke 1915, 48–49, 69). Such body part use may have been linked to the wider excarnation continuum, illustrating similarities between the flint mines and the causewayed enclosures, long barrows, and henges.

The evidence of female skeletal material raises interesting questions about gender and the role of women in the mines, particularly as a second female skeleton was recorded near the base of Shaft H at Cissbury, although in this case found head down and near vertical, possibly representing an accident victim – or a sacrifice? The context of this skeleton suggests contemporaneity with the mining, and proximity could imply association. What slight evidence exists for the presence of children – the mandible from Blackpatch Shaft 4 – is ambiguous; does it demonstrate participation in the extraction process or a ritualized post-mortem deposit within the mines?

The fill of the shafts at many mines suggest episodic accumulation. At Shaft 27 at Cissbury, artefact assemblages represent at least 12 distinct depositional event horizons, changing significantly as the shaft was filled, the lower characterized by extraction and its abandonment followed by human burial, whereas the upper fills are associated with secondary activities relating to renewal and symbolic deposition (cf. Topping 2005, 70–79). This suggests that 'special' mines remained open following abandonment and became a focus for post-extraction events. The final deposit at Shaft 27 comprised three axehead roughouts placed on the backfilled Neolithic ground surface, a potent symbol of the mines' former location, now only marked by its spoil dump encircling the axeheads. An alternative final abandonment event occurred at Church Hill Shaft 5a, where a large fire was built over the sealed shaft, featuring burnt flint, debitage, an assemblage of tools and axeheads, all alongside the bones and teeth of an ox, suggesting feasting, renewal and dedication rituals.

The South Downs mines produced flint largely for axehead production. Interestingly, analysis of the depositional patterns of Neolithic axeheads from the coastal plain immediately south of the mines confirms that the majority were unused and carefully curated (cf. Gardiner 1990, 131; Holgate 1995, 157). Clearly here the source of the raw material was identified by the artefact type, which then followed a pre-determined trajectory and use-life.

Recent ethnography has also recorded how the form of an artefact can communicate both social identity and 'help establish homogeneity between individuals in different groups and hence facilitate the expansion of kinship networks' (Wiessner 1997, 159). An expansion of kinship networks may have resulted from the exploitation of the Neolithic flint mines, creating extended trade networks (e.g. Grime's Graves Cornish stone axehead and shorebird remains) to ensure the dissemination of both ideologies and worldviews while maintaining the symbolic currency of the 'special' artefacts crafted from mined flint which underpinned these concepts. Alliance building, kinship displays, renewal ceremonies, all influence the patterning of the archaeological record. Multi-layered meanings are framed by assemblage content and the context of deposition. However, caution is needed because symbolic meanings and social values can be obscured by an artefact's apparently 'functional' appearance or its seemingly random deposition in a 'functional' context.

Gould records that amongst the Australian Aborigines:

> *... quarries occur at or near sacred sites – that is, totemic 'dreaming' places. People who believe themselves to be descended patrilineally from the particular totemic being at one of these sites will make special trips to the quarry to secure the stone there. A man places a high value on stone from a site of his dreamtime totem. Stone like this is often transported over long distances (as much as 500km) and is given to distant kinsmen of the same totemic patrilineage ... Because of his patrilineal relationship to the site, a man sees the stone as part of his own being ...* (Gould 1977, 164)

Trade to distant kin thus created linkages between people and place, maintaining the cultural identity of individuals (cf. Brumm 2004, 153).

Many Aboriginal quarries are used as a backdrop for important ceremonies. This may be paralleled on the South Downs where mines were not always located upon the better sources of flint (e.g. Harrow Hill and Blackpatch; cf. Barber *et al.* 1999, 73), suggesting that cultural importance rather than the quality of the raw material had been the most significant factor in choosing the site of these mines. The prominent location of many mines overlooking the surrounding landscape may have been deliberate to position them in a doubly liminal zone, carefully placed on the horizon between the earth and the sky, but also between the surface and the underworld. The apparent lack of domestic settlement at the mines reinforces the idea that they were 'special' places.

Why did certain extraction sites achieve this special place in the cultural landscape? The fact that mines were dug into the earth – often mythologized as a deity – may have given mining a deep cultural resonance if miners believed they were entering the body of a supernatural entity. As Bates has observed:

> [i]n all traditional cultures, there were sacred places which ... existed in the material world but which had extraordinary significance as entry points to another world. They were literally and metaphorically doorways into the spirit realm. (Bates 2003, 57)

The miners operated in a dimension where the possibilities of an interface with the spiritworld must have appeared stronger. The dangers of mining – both physical and metaphysical – would have heightened the social value of mined materials which became charged with otherworldly associations, becoming as Bradley (2000, 85–90) has suggested 'pieces of places', embedded with a deeper symbolism than more easily obtained materials. This is most graphically illustrated by the restricted range of raw materials used for stone axehead production throughout the Neolithic period, particularly from exposed quarry sites such as the near vertical faces of Top Buttress on Pike O'Stickle. It was the degree of difficulty sedimented into procuring *recognizable* types of stone that both visibly labelled the context of the raw material and thus created its social value. Identifiable varieties of stone sedimented biographies into an artefact, which in turn allowed it to transmit cultural narratives to the community.

The artefact-rich record recovered from many UK mines, suggests that *ad hoc* extraction did not always take place. To ignore the potential role of ritualized mining may miss the social context of both extraction and its outcomes. Many mines and quarries clearly played an important part in providing culturally-valuable raw materials literally from the psychological interface between the living communities and the mythically-charged fabric of their contemporary worldview. The resulting carefully crafted and curated artefacts became metonymic 'tools' to mediate between communities, their gods and ancestors, underpinning social control and stimulating world renewal.

ACNOWLEDGEMENTS

The author would like to thank Martyn Barber, Dave Field, Dave McOmish and Gill Varndell for many useful discussions about the nature of Neolithic mining; Dave Field for the use of Figure 14.1; Trevor Pearson for drafting Figures 14.3 and 14.4; and Dave McOmish and Dave Field for reading and commenting upon the draft text. Alan Saville deserves thanks for encouraging the production of this chapter when the author had not expected to write anything further on flint mines. Any errors remain the responsibility of the author.

BIBLIOGRAPHY

Barber, M., Field, D. and Topping, P., 1999, *The Neolithic Flint Mines of England*. Swindon: Royal Commission on the Historical Monuments of England/English Heritage.

Bates, B., 2003, *The Real Middle-Earth: Magic and Mystery in the Dark Ages*. London: Pan Books.

Boivin, N., 2004, From veneration to exploitation: human engagement with the mineral world. In N. Boivin and M. A. Owoc (eds), *Soils, Stones and Symbols: Cultural Perceptions of the Mineral World*, 1–29. London: UCL Press.

Bradley, R., 2000, *An Archaeology of Natural Places*. London: Routledge.

Brumm, A., 2004, An axe to grind: symbolic considerations of stone axe use in ancient Australia. In N. Boivin and M. A. Owoc (eds), *Soils, Stones and Symbols: Cultural Perceptions of the Mineral World*,143–163. London: UCL Press.

Clarke, W. G. (ed.), 1915, *Report on the Excavations at Grime's Graves, Weeting, Norfolk, March-May 1914*. London: Prehistoric Society of East Anglia.

Clutton-Brock, J., 1984, *Excavations at Grimes Graves, Norfolk 1972–1976, Fascicule 1: Neolithic Antler Picks from Grimes Graves, Norfolk, and Durrington Walls, Wiltshire: a Biometrical Analysis*. London: British Museum Publications.

Curwen, E. and Curwen, E. C., 1926, Harrow Hill flint-mine excavation, 1924–5. *Sussex Archaeological Collections* 67, 101–138.

Edmonds, M., 1990, Description, understanding, and the chaîne opératoire. *Archaeological Review from Cambridge* 9(1), 55–70.

Felder, P. J., Rademakers, P. C. M. and de Grooth, M. E. Th. (eds), 1998, *Excavations of Prehistoric Flint Mines at Rijckholt-St. Geertruid (Limburg, The Netherlands)*. Bonn: Habelt (Deutsche Gesellschaft für Ur- und Frühgeschichte: Archäologische Berichte 12).

Flood, J., 1995, *Archaeology of the Dreamtime* (Revised Edition). London: Harper Collins.

Flood, J., 1997, *Rock Art of the Dreamtime*. London: Harper Collins.

Gardiner, J. P., 1990, Flint procurement and Neolithic axe production on the South Downs: a re-assessment. *Oxford Journal of Archaeology* 9(2), 119–140.

Gero, J. M., 1991, Genderlithics: women's roles in stone tool production. In J. M. Gero and M. W. Conkey (eds), *Engendering Archaeology: Women and Prehistory*, 163–193. Oxford: Blackwell.

Gould, R. A., 1977, Ethno-archaeology; or, where do models come from? A closer look at Australian Aboriginal lithic technology. In R. V. S. Wright (ed.), *Stone Tools as Cultural Markers: Change, Evolution and Complexity*, 162–168. Canberra: Australian Institute of Aboriginal Studies/New York: Humanities Press Inc.

Holgate, R., 1995, Neolithic flint mining in Britain. *Archaeologia Polona* 33, 133–161.

Holleyman, G., 1937, Harrow Hill excavations, 1936. *Sussex Archaeological Collections* 78, 230–251.

Ingold, T., 2000, *The Perception of the Environment: Essays on Livelihood, Dwelling and Skill*. London: Routledge.

Kinnes, I., 1992, *Non-Megalithic Long Barrows and Allied Structures in the British Neolithic*. London: British Museum (Occasional Paper 52).

Legge, A. J., 1981, The agricultural economy. In R. J. Mercer, *Grimes Graves, Norfolk: Excavations 1971–72, Vol. I*, 79–103. London: HMSO (Department of the Environment, Archaeological Reports No. 11).

Lewis-Williams, D. and Pearce, D., 2005, *Inside the Neolithic Mind*. London: Thames and Hudson.

Longworth, I., Herne, A., Varndell, G., and Needham, S., 1991, *Excavations at Grimes Graves, Norfolk 1972–1976, Fascicule 3: Shaft X: Bronze Age Flint, Chalk and Metal Working*. London: British Museum Press.

Longworth, I. and Varndell, G., 1996, *Excavations at Grimes Graves, Norfolk 1972–1976, Fascicule 5: Mining in the Deeper Mines*. London: British Museum Press.

Mercer, R. J., 1981, *Grimes Graves, Norfolk: Excavations 1971–72, Vol. I*. London: HMSO (Department of the Environment, Archaeological Reports No. 11).

Oswald, A., Dyer, C. and Barber, M., 2001, *The Creation of Monuments: Neolithic Causewayed Enclosures in the British Isles*. Swindon: English Heritage.

Park Harrison, J., 1878, Additional discoveries at Cissbury. *Journal of the Royal Anthropological Institute* 7, 412–433.

Taçon, P. S. C., 2004, Ochre, clay, stone and art: the symbolic importance of minerals as life-force among aboriginal peoples of northern and central Australia. In N. Boivin and M. A. Owoc (eds), *Soils, Stones and Symbols: Cultural Perceptions of the Mineral World*, 31–42. London: UCL Press.

Topping, P., 2004, The South Downs flint mines: towards an ethnography of prehistoric flint extraction. In J. Cotton and D. Field (eds), *Towards a New Stone Age: Aspects of the Neolithic in South-East England*, 177–190. York: Council for British Archaeology (Research Report 137).

Topping, P., 2005, Shaft 27 revisited: an ethnography of Neolithic flint extraction. In P. Topping and M. Lynott (eds), *The Cultural Landscape of Prehistoric Mines*, 63–93. Oxford: Oxbow Books.

Torrence, R., 2001, Hunter-gatherer technology: macro- and microscale approaches. In C. Panter-Brick, R. H. Layton and P. Rowley-Conwy (eds), *Hunter-Gatherers: An Interdisciplinary Perspective*, 73–98. Cambridge: Cambridge University Press.

Wiessner, P., 1997, Seeking guidelines through an evolutionary approach: style revisited among the !Kung San (ju/'Hoansi) of the 1990s. In C. Barton and G. Clark (eds), *Rediscovering Darwin: Evolutionary Theory and Archaeological Explanation*, 157–176. Arlington, MA: American Anthropological Association (Archaeological Papers 7).

Willett, E. H., 1875, On flint workings at Cissbury, Sussex. *Archaeologia* 45, 337–348.

Chapter 15

'Shiny and colourful': raw material selection and the production of edge tools in Late Neolithic Makriyalos, Greece

Christina Tsoraki

A study of technology is not complete without some knowledge of the properties of the raw materials utilized, and also, if possible, an inventory and similar knowledge of those which were not utilized.
(Goodman 1944, 416)

INTRODUCTION

Analysis of ground stone assemblages in the prehistoric Aegean has focused mainly on technomorphological and typological issues without exploring the character of this technological scheme in detail. Regarding the production of ground stone tools Perlès (1992, 134) has argued that it 'seems to have tended towards the most efficient balance between means employed, labour time and functional purpose'. Thus 'time-saving procedures' (Perlès 1992, 131, table 5) would be selected. Moreover, she argues that with a few exceptions lithic tools have a 'predominantly utilitarian character ... used for common, everyday needs' (Perlès 1992, 143) and contrast with fine ware and other rare types of artefacts such as ornaments that carried a 'social' meaning (Perlès 1992, 144). Thus, of the three exchange systems she envisaged for the Greek Neolithic, ground stone tools should be attributed to that for utilitarian products, 'mainly economic in purpose ... free from symbolic connotations' (Perlès 1992, 149). Hence, a rigid distinction is drawn between functionality and symbolic character.

These suggestions have been made for the Greek Neolithic as a whole, but to date, have not been explored in a more contextualized manner and at the scale of the single site. Analysis of the ground stone assemblage from the Late Neolithic site at Makriyalos in northern Greece could help test these suggestions and investigate in depth the character of tool production and use within one single settlement. The large size of the assemblage (*c.* 8800 artefacts) and the rich contextual evidence allow in-depth exploration of technological practices and choices exercised during the Late Neolithic period in Greece.

The location of the Makriyalos settlement in a diverse geological area gave access to a wide range of rock types as indicated by the rather large number of raw materials employed in the ground stone assemblage (*c.* 25 rock types). The question this geological diversity and availability raises is to what extent the use of different raw materials was selective and to what extent the reasoning behind this selectivity can be addressed. Thus one of the issues to be explored here is the relationship between raw materials and different tool categories. The physical properties of rock types used will be characterized in order to establish their suitability for tool production. This type of analysis could allow us to establish whether the choices exercised relate primarily to the utilitarian properties of rocks selected or perhaps reflect preferences of a non-practical character. This chapter will concentrate on the edge tool category (axeheads, adze-blades, chisels) which will be contrasted with grinding/abrasive tools, the largest tool category in the assemblage.

THE SITE AND THE ASSEMBLAGE

The Neolithic site of Makriyalos represents one of the largest flat-extended settlements in Macedonia, Greece (Kotsakis 1999; Pappa and Besios 1999a) (Figure 15.1). The estimated size of the settlement is *c.* 50 hectares while the excavated area spreads over six hectares.

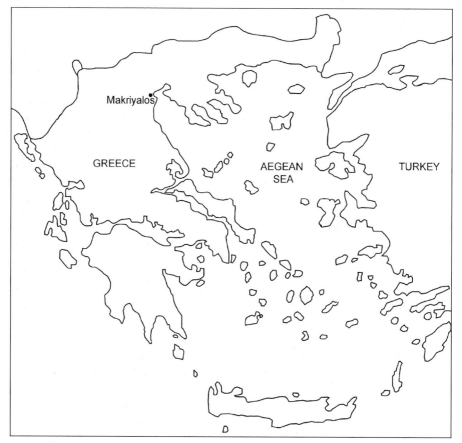

Figure 15.1. Map of Greece showing the location of Late Neolithic Makriyalos.

Two phases of Late Neolithic occupation have been identified (Makriyalos I and II), dated to the late sixth and fifth millennia BC (Pappa and Besios 1999b, 177–180). The architectural elements that came to light include two ditches enclosing the settlement of the first phase, a third ditch within this enclosure, habitation structures in the form of pits attributed to both phases, and also rectilinear buildings from Makriyalos II (Pappa and Besios 1999a). The ground stone assemblage consists of 8842 artefacts in total which have been attributed to seven main categories: edge tools (21%), grinding / abrasive tools (59%), percussive tools (2%), perforators (1%), multiple-use tools (3%), ornaments (1%) and miscellaneous (2%). Artefacts that survive in a fragmentary state and could not be attributed to a specific tool category have been recorded as 'indeterminate' (11%) (Table 15.1). For the sake of brevity the edge tool assemblage from both phases will be treated as a whole.

Selecting rocks, making tools: patterns of raw material selection

Within the ground stone assemblage all three general rock categories – igneous, metamorphic and sedimentary – occur (Table 15.1), but metamorphic and sedimentary rocks more frequently (39% and 35% respectively) than igneous (17%). In total 25 rock types have been identified, seventeen of which appear within the edge tool category, but rock types are not distributed evenly among the different tool categories. Within the edge tool assemblage, mainly metamorphic (44%) and igneous rocks (44%) are attested, while specimens attributed to the sedimentary group are rare (1%). A very different pattern emerges, however, when the grinding/abrasive tool category is considered: sedimentary rocks predominate (56%), followed by metamorphic rocks (35%), while igneous rocks appear very rarely (4%) (Figure 15.2). The selective use of raw materials for the production of specific tool types can be further demonstrated when the edge tool assemblage is broken down into more precise rock categories (Table 15.2). There is a clear preference for serpentinite, which is used for 36% of the 1893 edge tools, but represents only 10% of the total ground stone assemblage; almost 80% of the serpentinite artefacts unearthed during the excavation are edge tools. Dolerite is the second most common rock type used for edge tools (11%), while basalt (6%) and generally fine grained varieties of igneous rocks (together 13%) are also frequent.

More interesting patterns of raw material selection emerge when the edge tool category is broken down into axeheads, adze-blades and chisels (Table 15.2). In the case of axeheads, although serpentinite is most frequent (25%), there is a strong preference for igneous rocks (59%), and in particular for coarser-grained varieties (gabbro, diorite, dolerite), which are encountered two or three times as frequently as in adze-blades. Within the adze-blade category, the preference for serpentinite is stronger (41%), but dolerite (8%) occurs quite frequently and fine-grained igneous basalt and andesite (14%) are attested more frequently than in axeheads or chisels. In the chisel assemblage, the selection of serpentinite is most marked (67%) and metamorphic rocks as a group make up 82%, while igneous rocks are employed relatively infrequently (13%).

The evident selection of specific rock categories for specific tool types (coarser grained igneous rocks for axeheads, fine grained igneous rocks for adze-blades, serpentinite for chisels) is, *inter alia*, of considerable typological interest. The classification of edge tools following this tripartite system (based on the working edge profile and the relationship of

OBJECT CATEGORY

GEOLOGICAL CATEGORY		INDETERMINATE	EDGE TOOLS	PERCUSSIVE TOOLS	PERFORATORS	GRINDING/ ABRASIVE TOOLS	MISCELLANEOUS	MULTIPLE-USE TOOLS	ORNAMENTS	TOTAL
Sedimentary	Count	156	19	6	4	2917	9	6	3	3120
	% within Object Category	16.3%	1.0%	3.9%	9.5%	56.1%	5.1%	2.0%	2.4%	35.3%
Metamorphic	Count	264	836	50	36	1825	107	194	105	3417
	% within Object Category	27.5%	44.2%	32.3%	85.7%	35.1%	60.1%	66.2%	84.0%	38.6%
Igneous	Count	401	824	13	1	198	33	32	1	1503
	% within Object Category	41.8%	43.5%	8.4%	2.4%	3.8%	18.5%	10.9%	.8%	17.0%
Quartz	Count	30	0	64	0	122	5	53	3	277
	% within Object Category	3.1%	.0%	41.3%	.0%	2.3%	2.8%	18.1%	2.4%	3.1%
Fossilised material	Count	0	0	1	0	2	0	0	0	3
	% within Object Category	.0%	.0%	.6%	.0%	.0%	.0%	.0%	.0%	.0%
Talc	Count	0	0	20	0	0	0	0	0	20
	% within Object Category	.0%	.0%	12.9%	.0%	.0%	.0%	.0%	.0%	.2%
Indeterminate	Count	108	214	1	1	133	24	8	13	502
	% within Object Category	11.3%	11.3%	.6%	2.4%	2.6%	13.5%	2.7%	10.4%	5.7%
Total	Count	959	1893	155	42	5197	178	293	125	8842
	% within Object Category	100.0%	100.0%	100.0%	100.0%	100.0%	100.0%	100.0%	100.0%	100.0%
	% of Total	10.8%	21.4%	1.8%	.5%	58.8%	2.0%	3.3%	1.4%	100.0%

Table 15.1. Cross-tabulation showing the relationship between geological category and object category.

ROCK TYPE		TOOL CATEGORY				TOTAL
		EDGE-INDETERM-INATE	EDGE-AXE	EDGE-ADZE	EDGE-CHISEl	
Indeterminate	Count	116	13	80	5	214
	% within Tool Cat	12.0%	12.7%	11.2%	4.7%	11.3%
Well cemented sandstone	Count	6	0	11	0	17
	% within Tool Cat	.6%	.0%	1.5%	.0%	.9%
Dolomite	Count	1	0	0	0	1
	% within Tool Cat	.1%	.0%	.0%	.0%	.1%
Flint	Count	0	0	1	0	1
	% within Tool Cat	.0%	.0%	.1%	.0%	.1%
Serpentinite	Count	300	25	290	71	686
	% within Tool Cat	30.9%	24.5%	40.6%	67.0%	36.2%
Schist	Count	15	1	17	8	41
	% within Tool Cat	1.5%	1.0%	2.4%	7.5%	2.2%
Gneiss	Count	0	0	1	0	1
	% within Tool Cat	.0%	.0%	.1%	.0%	.1%
Marble	Count	3	0	3	1	7
	% within Tool Cat	.3%	.0%	.4%	.9%	.4%
Slate	Count	1	0	0	0	1
	% within Tool Cat	.1%	.0%	.0%	.0%	.1%
Granulite	Count	0	0	1	0	1
	% within Tool Cat	.0%	.0%	.1%	.0%	.1%
Indeterminate Metamorphic	Count	55	3	34	7	99
	% within Tool Cat	5.7%	2.9%	4.8%	6.6%	5.2%
Granite	Count	0	0	1	0	1
	% within Tool Cat	.0%	.0%	.1%	.0%	.1%
Gabbro	Count	29	9	20	1	59
	% within Tool Cat	3.0%	8.8%	2.8%	.9%	3.1%
Granodiorite	Count	1	0	0	0	1
	% within Tool Cat	.1%	.0%	.0%	.0%	.1%
Diorite	Count	41	7	21	2	71
	% within Tool Cat	4.2%	6.9%	2.9%	1.9%	3.8%
Dolerite	Count	138	17	58	2	215
	% within Tool Cat	14.2%	16.7%	8.1%	1.9%	11.4%
Basalt	Count	54	6	52	3	115
	% within Tool Cat	5.6%	5.9%	7.3%	2.8%	6.1%
Andesite	Count	50	2	25	2	79
	% within Tool Cat	5.2%	2.0%	3.5%	1.9%	4.2%
Andesite-Basalt	Count	34	0	22	0	56
	% within Tool Cat	3.5%	.0%	3.1%	.0%	3.0%
Lydite	Count	0	0	1	0	1
	% within Tool Cat	.0%	.0%	.1%	.0%	.1%
Indeterminate Igneous	Count	126	19	77	4	226
	% within Tool Cat	13.0%	18.6%	10.8%	3.8%	11.9%
Total	Count	970	102	715	106	1893
	% of Total	51.2%	5.4%	37.8%	5.6%	100.0%

Table 15.2. Cross-tabulation showing the relationship between specific rock types and edge tools.

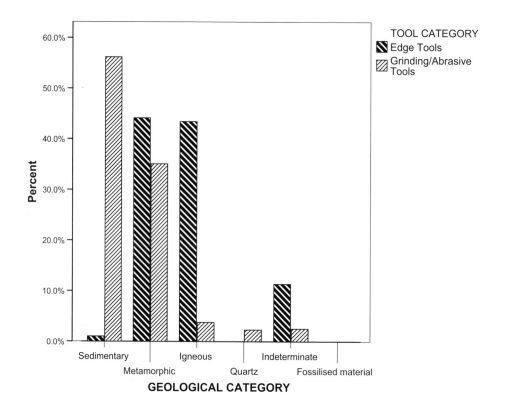

Figure 15.2. Bar chart indicating the percentage of rock categories within edge and grinding/abrasive tools.

the working edge to the haft), and its applicability in archaeological assemblages, has been questioned extensively (e.g. Heider 1967; Moundrea-Agrafioti 1981; Moundrea-Agrafioti 1996; Semenov 1985). This typological classification seems to have carried some real meaning in the everyday life of the people of Late Neolithic Makriyalos, however, since they chose different types of rocks for the production of each of these tool types. Moreover, the predominance of serpentinite in the chisel category is interesting in regard to the argument of Moundrea-Agrafioti (1996, 104) that there is no raw material standardization for chisels as they represent reworked axeheads and adze-blades. Traces of similar resharpening and sawing are found on some of the Makriyalos tools, but igneous rocks, although well represented in axeheads and adze-blades at Makriyalos, are used only infrequently in chisel manufacture. Even if some chisels do represent reworked axeheads and adze-blades, therefore, it is clear that serpentinite was actively selected for chisels.

Why were specific raw materials selected for the production of certain tool types? One way to approach this question is to consider the physical properties of the different rocks used and their suitability for tool production. This may clarify whether the choices made relate primarily to the utilitarian properties of rocks or to non-utilitarian characteristics.

Assessing raw material properties and variability

Although the Makriyalos edge tool assemblage includes a great number of raw materials, consideration should also – ideally – be given to which of the raw materials available locally have not been used in edge tool manufacture. This requires a very good understanding of the raw materials available in the area around Makriyalos. According to geological maps produced by the Greek Institute of Geology and Mineral Exploration (IGME) (sheets for Katerini, Kolindros, Platy, Alexandreia, Kontariotissa-Litochoro), Makriyalos and the surrounding area are characterized mainly by alluvial deposits created by streams that carry material from various parts of Mt Olympus and the Pieria Mountains. It is unclear, however, which of the different rock categories are found within these alluvial deposits. Nodules found on the site suggest that both primary outcrops and secondary deposits were used to manufacture tools. Despite this, the precise locations of these raw material sources are not known. Thus, at present, raw material selection can only be addressed in relation to the raw materials within the ground stone assemblage.

The metamorphic rocks attested in the Makriyalos assemblage mainly exhibit foliation (gneiss, schist and slate), although non-foliated marble has been widely used as well. Their grain size can vary from fine to coarse. Serpentinite, the most common metamorphic rock used for edge tools, is a metamorphosed ultramafic rock where the ferromagnesian silicate minerals of olivine and pyroxene have been altered to serpentine minerals (Blatt and Tracy 1996, 367; Press and Siever 1986, 437). Its structure can vary from slightly to markedly schistose, while the grain size can vary from fine to coarse (Blatt and Tracy 1996, 367; Jones 2000, 212; Pellant 2000, 194). The metamorphic rock types used for edge tool manufacture are mainly fine- to medium-grained, while both foliated and non-foliated varieties are present.

The second geological category attested in the assemblage is igneous rocks, among which can be distinguished two broad categories: coarse- (phaneritic rocks) and fine-grained (aphanites). The first category is comprised of the plutonic rocks granite, gabbro, diorite, pyroxenite and granodiorite. The fine-grained varieties are represented by the volcanic rocks basalt and andesite, the texture of which can often be holocrystalline. In a few cases these rocks exhibit a porphyritic texture in which larger crystals (phenocrysts) are set in a finer grained matrix (Blatt and Tracy 1996, 518). The most common rock type is dolerite, a medium-grained variety of basaltic composition and holocrystalline texture (Jones 2000, 180). Igneous rocks are characterized by interlocking crystals set in a compact matrix with no banding or foliation. All of these rocks, with the exception of pyroxenite, are mainly attested in the edge tool category.

Sedimentary rocks represent the third geological category within the assemblage. The rock types encountered are fine- to coarse-grained sandstone with poorly cemented grains, limestone, flint, dolomite and fine- to medium-grained sandstone with well sorted and well cemented grains. The latter three categories are employed in edge tool manufacture.

The different rock categories exhibit very distinctive textural features and thus present great variability in their physical properties. One of the raw material properties encountered in many lithic studies is hardness measured against the Mohs scale (e.g. Moundrea-Agrafioti 1981; Stroulia 2003). The Mohs scale refers to the classification of 'the relative abrasiveness of minerals', tested by scratching (Attewell and Farmer 1976, 8–9; cf. Brown 1981, 98; Goodman 1944, 417). As most rocks consist of a number of minerals with different properties, however, and only a few (such as flint and obsidian) represent monomineralic rocks, this hardness test does not seem to be adequate. It should be noted that the hardness of a rock does not depend only on its mineral components, but mainly on 'the strength of the matrix bonding the grains or crystals in the stone' (Dickson 1981, 27; cf. Brown 1981, 97). Moreover, the choice of a relevant testing method should relate to processes directly involved in tool production. Thus, a hardness test that measures raw material behaviour under specific operational procedures, e.g. scratching, does not indicate satisfactorily response to operations employed in tool manufacture and use (Dickson 1981, 27; Goodman 1944, 418).

Goodman (1944) and Dickson (1981) have suggested toughness as a property that could prove very useful when studying raw materials employed in edge tool manufacture and use, for instance the reaction of rocks to percussion flaking and pecking/hammering and use in percussive tasks. Following experimental work and highway engineering research, Dickson (1981, 27–31) concluded that fine-grained rock types are more durable to crushing than coarse-grained rocks. His experimental work has shown that fine-grained raw materials with holocrystalline or hypocrystalline texture, with small elongated crystals that do not follow a specific orientation, such as basaltic rocks, are best suited for the production of edge tools (Dickson 1981, 28).

Another potentially useful property is tensile strength, as has been illustrated in the study of the Neolithic axehead trade in Britain (Bradley *et al.* 1992). As Attewell and Farmer (1976, 186) have argued, it is very difficult to create a rigid strength classification system for rocks, as strength and other properties of raw materials are largely affected by other parameters such as their composition, structure, texture, weathering, porosity and density. A general and indicative classification system may be formed, however, grading rock types from very weak (5–20MPa) to very strong (160–320MPa) (Table 15.3). Igneous rocks and metamorphic rocks can exhibit the highest levels of strength while sedimentary rocks, due to their formation processes, are graded lower.

STRENGTH CLASSIFICATION SYSTEM	VALUE RANGE (MPA)	ROCK TYPES
Very weak	5–20	Weathered and weakly–compacted sedimentary rocks
Weak	20–40	Weakly-cemented sedimentary rocks; schists
Medium	40–80	Competent sedimentary rocks; some low density coarse grained rocks
Strong	80–160	Competent igneous, metamorphic rocks and some fine grained sandstones
Very Strong	160–320	Quartzites; dense fine-grained igneous rocks

Table 15.3. Strength Classification System (values are given in megapascal (MPa); after Attewell and Farmer 1976, 186).

At this stage of research, time and cost have not permitted the author to conduct similar tests for the Makriyalos edge tool assemblage, but an indication of strength measurements for the relevant rocks can be obtained from published sources (e.g. Lama and Vutukuri 1978). Values have not been found for serpentinite, however, probably because this rock type has not been used in engineering work and thus has not been tested. Moreover, as noted in a number of archaeological reports, the hardness of serpentinite specimens varies from soft to quite hard and has been graded from 3 to 6.5 on the Mohs scale (e.g. Moundrea-Agrafioti 1981; Perlès 2001; Stroulia 2003). This may be related to the great variation that serpentinite specimens can exhibit in texture, as exemplified in the Makriyalos and other Neolithic assemblages (e.g. Alisoy 2002). This variability and lack of consensus regarding the hardness of serpentinite makes the characterization of serpentinite difficult and calls for an in-depth analysis of the properties of this raw material that has been extensively used in edge tool manufacture.

DISCUSSION: CHOOSING MEANINGFUL MATERIALS, MAKING POWERFUL TOOLS

The selection of raw materials

Although a wide variety of rock types was exploited at Makriyalos, certain categories of rocks, primarily serpentinite and igneous rocks, were clearly selected for fashioning edge tools. Igneous rocks, and in particular fine-grained varieties such as basalt, represent materials with crystals tightly held and thus are considered to be particularly tough. The density and toughness of these raw materials suggest that an ability to withstand the effects of great percussive force was a desired characteristic of edge tools and, in this respect, it could be argued that the selection of igneous rocks was functionally driven.

If we assume that different tasks were performed by axeheads and adze-blades, then an interesting pattern emerges in the rock types selected. Thus, axes have been traditionally regarded as chopping/percussive tools (Adams 2002, 166), employed quite often in tree felling. In that respect the use of rock types reacting well to impact force would be expected. The people from Makriyalos, however, seem to have favoured for their axeheads coarser-grained varieties which, due to the larger crystals set in their matrix, are less likely to withstand impact force as effectively as the fine-grained alternatives. Yet the latter category and in particular basalt, which represent the toughest rocks within the Makriyalos assemblage, are preferentially used with adze-blades which could have been employed in lighter woodworking tasks. This implies that the choice of raw materials cannot be explained merely in functional terms.

It has been argued quite extensively (e.g. Moundrea-Agrafioti 1981, 197–239; Perlès 2001, 232–236; Semenov 1985, 126–134) that axeheads and adze-blades could have been used in similar tasks indiscriminately and thus that specific functions cannot be attributed to either type. Edge tools as a group are used with direct or indirect percussion or pressure and have been associated mainly with woodworking tasks, ranging from tree felling to clearing shrubbery, but also with skin and bone working, while other uses such as digging and finer tasks such as trimming the end of bows (Blackwood 1950, 23; Edmonds 1995, 53; Perlès 2001, 232) cannot be excluded. This range of activities implies that materials able to withstand impact force would be desirable. Interestingly, however, the preferred raw material for these implements is serpentinite which, although presenting great variation in its properties, cannot be regarded as tougher than igneous rocks. Thus, its extensive use raises some questions.

The extensive use of serpentinite is a wider phenomenon documented in the whole of the Greek Neolithic (Moundrea-Agrafioti 1996, 104; Perlès 2001, 232). It has been suggested that the transformation of serpentinite into edge tools would require less time and effort due to its 'soft' character (Moundrea-Agrafioti 1981, 182; Stroulia 2003, 5), but this 'softness' would have an impact on the efficiency of the tool. Tougher materials than serpentinite would be better suited for many of the tasks listed above. Moreover, the schistocity evident in quite a few serpentinite edge tools from Makriyalos is parallel to the length of the tool, making it vulnerable to any impact force and thus limiting the tasks for which it could be employed (cf. Dickson 1981, 32).

The extensive use of serpentinite for chisels is also interesting because evidence of sawing on their margins and different episodes of resharpening show that effort and time were invested in their manufacture. This seems to contradict previous suggestions of the employment of 'time-saving procedures' (Perlès 1992, 131, table 5). Anyway, if the primary motive of the Neolithic inhabitants of Makriyalos was to acquire and use a material whose modification did not involve great effort or time investment, they could have chosen pebbles from nearby streams which with a modified edge (and thus minimal input) could have been equally efficient for tasks performed by chisels (cf. Adams 2002, 153).

Similarly, if the choice of raw materials related solely to their utilitarian properties, then it is difficult to explain why igneous rocks were not used more frequently for percussive tools as well (Table 15.1) but instead marble was repeatedly employed for such tasks. Yet, the holocrystalline texture of igneous rocks would be well suited for their use as percussive tools (Voytek 1990, 444). From a functional perspective, therefore, it is unclear why the people of Makriyalos did not use such tough materials for percussive tasks more frequently, but instead chose to use them preferentially with edge tools.

It is equally important to see the preferences exercised in relation to materials not selected for edge tool manufacture. As noted earlier, the sedimentary rock used for edge tool manufacture is mainly sandstone with very well-cemented grains. This raw material, which represents the most common material in the assemblage (29%), is very compact and tough and reacts well to impact force as indicated by the high frequency of pecking and repecking attested on the use faces of grinding slabs (cf. Dickson 1981, 28; for the use of sandstone axeheads see also Cooney and Mandal 1998; Elster 2003). Hence, its texture does not seem to preclude use for the production of edge tools. Yet, it has been used only rarely in the production of such implements at Makriyalos.

A similar situation is attested in the case of marble, the second most common material in the assemblage (19%). This material, though infrequent within the edge tool assemblage, appears to have been used extensively in percussive and grinding activities. Dixon has suggested that marble would be relatively easy worked into edge tools and could take high polish, but that marble axeheads would have been 'short-lived' (Dixon 2003, 140; for use of marble axeheads see also Elster 2003.). Marble could have been used, however, for lighter tasks performed by chisels and small sized adze-blades and serpentinite edge tools. Moreover, its use for small sized implements would be less time-consuming (in comparison to reworked axeheads and adze-blades) since an edge could be given easily to pebbles and cobbles that have the desired shape. Therefore, when considering arguments put forward for the selection of serpentinite due to its softness, the choice not to use marble cannot be explained in practical terms alone.

An artefact that deserves mention is one specimen made of flint. In the Greek Neolithic, in contrast to northern European Neolithic lithic traditions, flint edge tools seem to be scarce. Perlès has argued that during the Greek Early Neolithic no flint axeheads have been attested, while flint seems to have been used only in the absence of other appropriate raw materials (2001, 232–233). The rarity of flint edge tools is rather interesting as flint was used extensively for the production of chipped stone tools, while high-quality flint circulated over long distances in the Greek Neolithic from the Early Neolithic (Perlès 2001, 232). These circulation patterns seem to have expanded during the Late and Final Neolithic period (Moundrea-Agrafioti 1996, 103). In the case of Makriyalos the chipped stone assemblage comprises a variety of raw materials including high-quality flints such as 'honey' flints (Skourtopoulou 1999, 122–123).

Thus the question that arises is why flint has not been used more extensively in the production of edge tools in Makriyalos and in the Greek Neolithic in general. One issue relates to the physical properties of flint: though it is graded at 7 on the Mohs scale, its brittle character would make it vulnerable to impact force (Dickson 1981, 27; Perlès 2001, 233). Edge tools could have been employed, however, in other non-percussive tasks. Moreover, the extensive use of flint axeheads in northern European contexts indicates that the properties of flint in no way prevent its use for the production of edge tools. Another practical issue may have been the lack or limited availability of nodules of the required size for the production of edge tools, but the size of honey flint blades could reach and in a few cases exceed 100–120mm in length (e.g. Tringham 2003, 84), whereas the mean length of edge tools within the Makriyalos assemblage does not exceed 49.2mm. Moreover, the high quality of flaked flint artefacts shows that the Neolithic inhabitants of Greece possessed the required technical 'know-how', experience and craftsmanship to produce flint edge tools. Therefore, while the paucity of flint edge tools could relate primarily to practical reasons (properties, availability), it could also indicate a cultural choice to select particular raw materials for specific tool categories.

The surface treatment of edge tools

The selection of raw materials should be seen in relation to the surface treatment these raw materials received. When manufacturing techniques are considered, it is clear that polishing is the most frequently attested technique for the modification of all parts of edge tools (bit 96%; body 96%; margins 95%; butt 73%) and that it was applied to all rock categories. When the edge tool assemblage is broken down into the three general geological categories, however, evidence of polishing is more extensive in metamorphic and igneous than in sedimentary rocks. In sedimentary rocks, polishing does not seem to have been applied equally to all parts of the tool and the butt area has been modified more frequently by grinding, a technique that appears to have been used more often in this geological category than in the other two.

Different degrees of polishing are also attested within the assemblage (Table 15.4). Of all edge tools, excluding indeterminate cases, 43% exhibit a high level of polishing and

79% have been well or highly polished, but the degree of polishing varies considerably between rock categories. While 46% of metamorphic rocks and 39% of igneous rocks exhibit high polishing, only 12% of sedimentary rocks received a similar level of finishing. When specific rock types are considered, andesite has been highly polished most frequently (58%), while the majority of gabbro, serpentinite, andesite/basalt tools and the unique examples of granodiorite, gneiss, granulite and granite also occur within this category of polishing. Conversely, 50% of marble and 44% of sandstone products are not well polished, even though the few highly polished examples of sandstone edge tools, as well as polished surfaces created on other tool types (e.g. grinders and grinding slabs), testify that this type of sandstone could receive polishing.

Two interesting points can be made from the above results. First, there is a clear interest in creating smooth surfaces on *all* parts of an edge tool regardless of the raw material used. It has been argued elsewhere that grinding / polishing strengthens the edge and would reduce the friction on impact with wood (Dickson 1981: 32; Edmonds 1995: 51). Yet, in Makriyalos polishing extends to the whole tool surface and this cannot be explained by any functional reasons. In fact, a ground or polished surface near the butt is impractical as it would make the hafting process more difficult. Instead, the rough surface created during the pecking stage would be better suited for adjusting a tool firmly to its handle (Dickson 1981, 32; Semenov 1985, 69).

This implies that the creation of a smooth and often lustrous surface was a desirable trait in edge tools. Both grinding and polishing are time-consuming, strenuous activities that require persistence and 'some working knowledge' (Semenov 1985, 68). Yet, people chose

Geological Category		Degree Of Polish				Total
		Not Applicable	Not Well Polished	Well Polished	Highly Polished	
Sedimentary	Count	5	7	3	2	17
	% within GC	29.4%	41.2%	17.6%	11.8%	100.0%
Metamorphic	Count	18	138	264	364	784
	% within GC	2.3%	17.6%	33.7%	46.4%	100.0%
Igneous	Count	24	134	312	304	774
	% within GC	3.1%	17.3%	40.3%	39.3%	100.0%
Total	Count	47	279	579	670	1575
	% of Total	3.0%	17.7%	36.8%	42.5%	100.0%

Table 15.4. Cross-tabulation showing the relationship between geological category and the degree of polishing (excluding indeterminate cases) (GC=Geological Category). Definition of categories: Not Applicable: no polished surfaces; Not Well Polished: not very smooth surfaces; Well Polished: smooth surfaces with spots of sheen; Highly Polished: extremely smooth surfaces which reflect light.

to increase the time and effort spent in making tools to add a characteristic that does not seem to match the 'efficiently balanced' production argued for by Perlès (1992, 134).

It has been suggested that a high degree of polishing could reflect the non-functional character of tools (e.g. Edmonds 1995, 53; Sheridan *et al.* 1992, 398), but the Makriyalos edge tools represent tools that have been used on a regular basis to perform practical tasks. When the relationship is examined between degree of wear and degree of polishing, it is obvious that highly polished tools very frequently exhibit highly used or worn-out use surfaces and are by no means non-functional 'symbolic' tools. In fact, the number of tools with light wear is very low. Thus it is obvious that the Neolithic community of Makriyalos chose to invest additional time and labour in the production of their edge tools which at the same time gave them a more distinctive appearance (Edmonds 1995, 103). In this respect, the widely used dichotomy between 'utilitarian'/'functional' and 'symbolic'/'social' objects seems meaningless (cf. Edmonds 1995, 53; Karimali 2005, 200).

Polishing was evidently a very important stage in the *chaîne opératoire* for edge tools. The enhanced visual appearance of the rocks, the lustrous surface created, might have been regarded as an important, perhaps required, element in the production of a successful tool. This obvious concern with the appearance of edge tools may be linked with another physical property of rocks, their colour.

The colour properties of rocks

Colour is a physical property of raw materials that has not been discussed extensively in the context of lithic technology in Aegean archaeology. Yet, the colour properties of different raw materials have been discussed in relation to axehead making and exchange in other European Neolithic assemblages, suggesting that the visual appearance of axeheads may have been of great significance (e.g. Cooney 2002; Edmonds 1995). As has been argued elsewhere (Cooney 2002, 95; Edmonds 1995, 51), grinding and polishing not only create a smooth and shiny surface, but also enhance the colour properties of rocks.

The varied levels of polishing attested on different materials could be seen in relation to their colour properties. The colour scheme of serpentinite is the most diverse, ranging from light green to dark green, grey/green and black/green, but also the variability of different tones of greenish colour attested on the same artefact make this raw material look more spectacular. Regarding igneous rocks, Cooney (2002, 98) has suggested that the grinding / polishing process highlights the presence of naturally occurring 'streaks, speckles or spots' in these raw materials. Thus within the Makriyalos assemblage, the presence of feldspars in gabbro, diorite, granodiorite, dolerite and porphyritic andesite and basalt would be emphasized, creating an interesting contrast with the darker matrix of these rocks (Cooney 2002, 98) (Figure 15.3). In the case of basalt, there are examples with red veins (chromium) that are mainly highly polished or well polished, as are the visually distinctive gneiss and pink granite adze-blades. In essence a well polished surface allows the textural elements of the rocks to be emphasized and distinguished, acting as a mirror to internal properties not easily seen in unworked rocks.

This colour variability contrasts greatly with the relatively uniform colour of the sandstone and marble tools. Most of the sandstone specimens have a grey brown colour, while the marble specimens are white. It is tempting to suggest that the limited polishing of sandstone and marble tools is related to their uniform colour, thanks to which the end result of grinding / polishing would not be as striking as in the case of the igneous and serpentinite tools. As Taçon has argued, 'things that are bright and colourful are often especially potent' (2004, 31). Perhaps, therefore, the well-cemented sandstone and marble were not used extensively in edge tool production mainly due to aesthetic reasons and not for obvious practical ones.

The issue of colour properties has been discussed in relation to another category of ground stone technology, ornaments. As has been argued (Karali 1996, 165), bright colourful stones with interesting colour patterning (as well as colourful shells) were widely used for ornaments in the Aegean Neolithic. At Makriyalos, 58% of beads are made of serpentinite. If we accept that the selection of raw materials for bead making relates mainly to their colour properties, the clear selection of serpentinite for edge tools should be approached in similar terms.

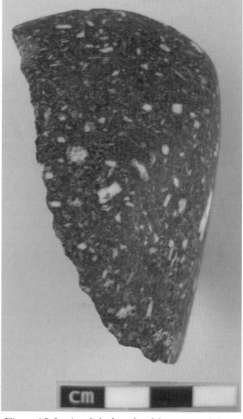

Figure 15.3. A polished axehead fragment exhibiting porphyritic texture (porphyritic andesite).

CONCLUSIONS

The analysis of the Makriyalos ground stone/edge tool assemblage has revealed clear preferences and selectivity patterns regarding the rock types used in tool production. An interesting aspect arising from the analysis is the possibility that the widely used and questioned typological scheme of axeheads, adze-blades, and chisels might have had a real significance to the people of Late Neolithic Makriyalos as indicated by the use of specific raw materials for the production of each of these tool types. The use of different rock types reflects choices, of which some may be explained in practical terms, but others do not seem necessarily related to function. Furthermore, the extensive use of polishing by enhancing both the colour properties and other distinctive textural features (e.g. porphyritic texture) of rocks indicates an interest in the visual appearance of these tools.

One of the wider issues raised by this analysis is the nature and effect of our analytical categories on our understanding of the past. A good example of this is the way in which rocks and minerals have been classified. Whilst in many cases they may seem to be straightforward, the raw materials categories employed in this analysis reflect understandings and concepts employed by modern geologists. This categorization is not the only way that the mineral world could be classified, however, and the different rock properties outlined here do not necessarily reflect a universal and diachronic understanding of how minerals and rocks might be perceived. Rocks could alternatively have been grouped and selected on the basis of their colour properties (colourful and versatile vs. lack of colour variation). Thus, it is important to acknowledge that our geological classifications are historically specific and culturally meaningful and alternative understandings and perceptions of rocks could and have existed (see also Boivin 2004 and other chapters in Boivin and Owoc 2004).

Rocks need to be considered as part of a wider landscape imbued with meaning and symbolism which formed the perceptions and understandings of the people of Makriyalos. Although the symbolic character of axeheads has been discussed in different contexts in European prehistory (cf. Edmonds 1995; Skeates 2002; Whittle 1995), within Aegean archaeology similar discussions are still very limited (cf. Moundrea-Agrafioti 1981: 182; Stroulia 2003, 24). Yet, as has been shown in the Makriyalos case study, these tools functioned at two levels; while covering everyday needs, they fulfilled a social function by acting as constant reminders of other elements of the landscape and the processes that brought them into being.

ACKNOWLEDGEMENTS

I am indebted to Manthos Besios and Maria Pappa for granting me permission to study the Makriyalos ground stone assemblage. I would also like to thank Mike Romano and Vassilis Roubos for offering valuable help with rock properties, and Mark Edmonds and Maria Pappa for providing comments on this chapter. I am particularly grateful to my thesis supervisor Paul Halstead for stimulating discussions and assistance with the editing of the text. This research was generously funded by the Greek Archaeological Committee (UK), the University of Sheffield and the Sheffield Centre for Aegean Archaeology.

BIBLIOGRAPHY

Adams, J. L., 2002, *Ground Stone Analysis: A Technological Approach*. Salt Lake City: The University of Utah Press.

Alisoy, H. A., 2002, Consumption of ground stone tools at Stavroupoli. In D. Grammenos and S. Kotsos (eds), *Sostikes anaskafes sto neolithiko oikismo Stavroupolis Thessalonikis*, 561–608. Thessaloniki: Arhaiologiko Institouto Voreias Elladas.

Attewell, P. B. and Farmer, I. W., 1976, *Principles of Engineering Geology*. London: Chapman and Hall.

Blackwood, B., 1950, *The Technology of a Modern Stone Age People in New Guinea*. Oxford: Pitt Rivers Museum, University of Oxford (Occasional Papers on Technology, 3).

Blatt, H. and Tracy, R. J., 1996, *Petrology. Igneous, Sedimentary and Metamorphic*. 2nd Edition. New York: W. H. Freeman.

Boivin, N., 2004, From veneration to exploitation. Human engagement with the mineral world. In N. Boivin and M. A. Owoc (eds), *Soils, Stones and Symbols. Cultural Perceptions of the Mineral World*, 1–29. London: UCL Press.

Boivin, N. and Owoc, M. A. (eds), 2004, *Soils, Stones and Symbols. Cultural Perceptions of the Mineral World*. London: UCL Press.

Bradley, R., Meredith, P., Smith, J. and Edmonds, M., 1992, Rock physics and the Neolithic axe trade in Great Britain. *Archaeometry* 34, 223–233.

Brown, E. T. (ed.), 1981, *Rock Characterization. Testing and Monitoring*. Oxford: Pergamon Press.

Cooney, G., 2002, So many shades of rock: colour symbolism and Irish stone axeheads. In A. Jones and G. MacGregor (eds), *Colouring the Past. The Significance of Colour in Archaeological Research*, 93–107. Oxford: Berg.

Cooney, G. and Mandal, S., 1998, *The Irish Stone Axe Project. Monograph I*. Dublin: Wordwell.

Dickson, F. P., 1981, *Australian Stone Hatchets. A Study in Design and Dynamics*. Sydney: Academic Press.

Dixon, J., 2003, Lithic petrology. In E. S. Elster and C. Renfrew (eds), *Prehistoric Sitagoi: Excavations in Northeast Greece, 1968–1970. Vol. 2. The Final Report*, 133–146. Los Angeles: Cotsen Institute of Archaeology, University of California. (Monumenta Archaeologica 20).

Edmonds, M., 1995, *Stone Tools and Society. Working Stone in Neolithic and Bronze Age Britain*. London: Batsford.

Elster, E. S., 2003, Grindstones, polished edge-tools and other stone artifacts. In E. S. Elster and C. Renfrew (eds), *Prehistoric Sitagoi: Excavations in Northeast Greece, 1968–1970. Vol. 2. The Final Report*, 175–195. Los Angeles: Cotsen Institute of Archaeology, University of California. (Monumenta Archaeologica 20).

Goodman, M. E., 1944, The physical properties of stone tool materials. *American Antiquity* 9, 415–433.

Heider, K. G., 1967, Archaeological assumptions and ethnographical facts: a cautionary tale from New Guinea. *Southwestern Journal of Anthropology* 23, 52–64.

Jones, A., 2000, *Rocks and Minerals*. London: HarperCollins.

Karali, L., 1996, Shell, bone and stone jewellery. In G. A. Papathanassopoulos (ed.), *Neolithic Culture in Greece*, 165–166. Athens: Nicholas P. Goulandris Foundation, Museum of Cycladic Art.

Karimali, E., 2005, Lithic technologies and use. In E. Blake and A. B. Knapp (eds), *The Archaeology of Mediterranean Prehistory*, 180–214. Oxford: Blackwell Publishing.

Kotsakis, K., 1999, What Tells can tell: social space and settlement in the Greek Neolithic. In P. Halstead (ed.), *Neolithic Society in Greece*, 66–76. Sheffield: Sheffield Academic Press (Sheffield Studies in Aegean Archaeology, 2).

Lama, R. D. and Vutukuri, V. S., 1978, *Handbook on Mechanical Properties of Rocks. Volume II: Testing Techniques and Results*. Clausthal, Germany: Trans Tech Publications.

Moundrea-Agrafioti, H. A., 1981, *La Thessalie du Sud-Est au néolithique: outillage lithique et osseux*. Thése de 3ème cycle, Université Paris X.

Moundrea-Agrafioti, H. A., 1996, Tools. In G. A. Papathanassopoulos (ed.), *Neolithic Culture in Greece*, 103–106. Athens: Nicholas P. Goulandris Foundation, Museum of Cycladic Art.

Pappa, M. and Besios, M., 1999a, The Makriyalos Project: rescue excavations at the Neolithic site of Makriyalos, Pieria, northern Greece. In P. Halstead (ed.), *Neolithic Society in Greece*, 128–135. Sheffield: Sheffield Academic Press (Sheffield Studies in Aegean Archaeology, 2).

Pappa, M. and Besios, M., 1999b, The Neolithic settlement at Makriyalos, northern Greece: preliminary report on the 1993–1995 excavations. *Journal of Field Archaeology* 26, 177–195.

Pellant, C., 2000, *Rocks and Minerals*. London: Dorling Kindersley.

Perlès, C., 1992, Systems of exchange and organization of production in Neolithic Greece. *Journal of Mediterranean Archaeology* 5, 115–164.

Perlès, C., 2001, *The Early Neolithic in Greece*. Cambridge: Cambridge University Press.

Press, F. and Siever, R., 1986, *Earth*. 4th edition. New York: W. H. Freeman.

Semenov, S. A., 1985 [orig. 1957], *Prehistoric Technology: An Experimental Study of the Oldest Tools and Artefacts from Traces of Manufacture and Wear*. Totowa, N.J.: Barnes & Noble.

Sheridan, A., Cooney, G. and Grogan, E., 1992, Stone axe studies in Ireland. *Proceedings of the Prehistoric Society* 58, 389–416.

Skeates, R., 2002, Axe aesthetics: stone axes and visual culture in prehistoric Malta. *Oxford Journal of Archaeology* 21(1), 13–22.

Skourtopoulou, K., 1999, The chipped stone from Makriyalos: a preliminary report. In P. Halstead (ed.), *Neolithic Society in Greece*, 121–127. Sheffield: Sheffield Academic Press. (Sheffield Studies in Aegean Archaeology, 2).

Stroulia, A., 2003, Ground stone celts from Franchtini Cave – a close look. *Hesperia* 72, 1–30.

Taçon, P. S. C., 2004, Ochre, clay, stone and art. The symbolic importance of minerals as life-force among Aboriginal peoples of northern and central Australia. In N. Boivin and M. A. Owoc (eds), *Soils, Stones and Symbols. Cultural Perceptions of the Mineral World*, 31–42. London: UCL Press.

Tringham, R., 2003, Flaked stone. In E. S. Elster and C. Renfrew (eds), *Prehistoric Sitagoi: Excavations in Northeast Greece, 1968–1970. Vol. 2. The Final Report*, 81–126. Los Angeles: Cotsen Institute of Archaeology, University of California. (Monumenta Archaeologica 20).

Voytek, B., 1990, The use of stone resources. In R. Tringham and D. Krstic (eds), *Selevac. A Neolithic Village in Yugoslavia*, 437–494. Los Angeles, Ca: UCLA (Monumenta Archaeologica 15).

Whittle, A., 1995, Gifts from the earth: symbolic dimensions of the use and production of Neolithic flint and stone axes. *Archaeologia Polona* 33, 247–259.

Chapter 16

Ideology and context within the European flint-mining tradition

Paul Wheeler

> '...*flint mines and quarry sites in terms of location and manner of exploitation highlight the desire to obtain stone in a particular way or from a particular place*' (Barber 2001, 23)

INTRODUCTION

Recent studies into the extraction of flint and stone in prehistory have seen a new philosophy regarding our attitudes to, and interpretations of, this subject. Much previous work focused on the morphology, technologies, and origins of artefacts and their associated quarries (e.g. Engelen 1980; Sieveking and Newcomer 1987; Weisgerber *et al.* 1980). Current research, however, seeks to re-evaluate data associated with depositional contexts in the flint mines and quarries of Britain and western Europe, with the aim of uncovering common practices and influences in the ideology behind flint mining and attitudes towards lithic raw materials. By seeking commonalities of depositional practice a number of issues and questions can be addressed, such as:

1) What common practices can we infer in the process of Neolithic flint mining?
2) What do these practices tell us about cross-cultural influences throughout Neolithic Europe?
3) Can anything be inferred about the beliefs of the miners and the relationship they had with the mines and with the raw material they extracted?

Analysis of these issues should not only further our understanding of cultural connections across Neolithic Europe, but also broaden our perspective on the attitudes of Neolithic societies towards flint itself, from its extraction and modification to its final deposition. In this chapter I shall address briefly each of the questions noted above. The geographical focus is the flint mines of south-eastern England and their chronologically contemporary counterparts in north-east France, Belgium, and The Netherlands (Figure 16.1).

COMMON PRACTICES WITHIN THE EARLY NEOLITHIC FLINT-MINING TRADITION ACROSS NORTH-WESTERN EUROPE

The first necessity of this study is to put the cross-regional analysis of flint mines into a relative chronological context. Previous studies have often compared mines which were in

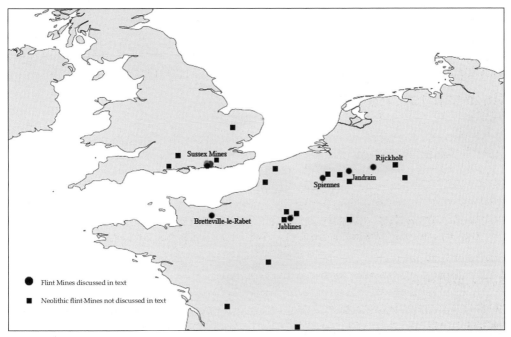

Figure 16.1. Location map of flint-mining sites in western Europe.

use a thousand years apart. Such a broad chronological span could be misleading when analysing the mines, especially when referring to common ideologies and structured depositional practices. Therefore, this study will deal only with sites that were in operation in the last few centuries of the fifth millennium cal BC and for the first half of the fourth millennium cal BC, as described below.

Blackpatch, Sussex, England

At least 100 shafts are known over an area of 1.5 hectares, and nine of the shafts have been excavated. The complex also consists of round barrows, chipping floors, and features which John Pull (the main excavator at Blackpatch) described as dwelling-hut sites (Pull 1932; Russell 2001, 24–84).

Cissbury, Sussex, England

The flint mines at Cissbury represent the largest complex of flint mines on the South Downs. Of the 270 known shafts, at last 20 shafts were excavated between 1873 and 1956 by various archaeologists including Colonel Augustus Lane Fox and John Pull. The shafts are associated with chipping floors and waste dumps, and round barrows are in close proximity. Networks of galleries were identified along with engravings on mine walls (Russell 2001, 170–192; Topping 2005, 63–93).

Church Hill, Sussex, England

Of the 26 shafts recorded, John Pull excavated six shafts and three lesser pits. The site also consists of a series of round barrows, waste dumps, and chipping floors. Within certain shafts, markings / signs were identified above the galleries (Barber *et al.* 1999; Russell 2001, 85–158).

Harrow Hill, Sussex, England

At Harrow Hill 160 pits have been plotted. Excavations by the Curwens began in 1924 and were continued by George Holleyman in 1936. A similar network of galleries to those at Cissbury has been identified. Linear, geometric graffiti have been identified among flint and chalk blocks within the mines (Curwen and Curwen 1926; Holleyman 1937).

Bretteville-le-Rabet, Normandy, France

Fifteen shafts have been excavated, identifying two seams of exploited flint. The site consists largely of bell pits with some short galleries and workshops in the top half of the shafts. Flint picks and antlers were used to extract the flint (Desloges 1986).

Jablines, Seine-et-Marne, France

The flint mines lie on a promontory of Le Haut Château, on the river Marne. Excavations took place between 1986 and 1990. Of the 766 shafts, 58 were excavated. Various forms of mine were identified, with the morphology of the mines dependent on the terrain (Bostyn and Lanchon 1992; 1995).

Jandrain-Jandrenouille, Brabant, Belgium

The mines of Jandrain-Jandrenouille lie on the edge of a plateau. Four shafts were excavated by Hubert in the 1970s, revealing vertical shafts with radiating galleries. Large quantities of waste flint picks were found in the backfill. Ceramic finds associate the Jandrain-Jandrenouille site with the Michelsberg culture (Hubert 1974; Weisgerber *et al.* 1980, 429–431).

Petit-Spiennes and Camp-à-Cayaux, Hainault, Belgium

Spiennes is the largest Neolithic flint mine in Europe. It lies on a promontory, 6km south of Mons and covers an area of 100 hectares. Excavations have shown the shafts form an irregular network. At Camp-à-Cayaux there could be up to 20,000 shafts, whilst at Petit-Spiennes there are approximately 5000 shafts in a 14 hectare area. Various excavations have unveiled a complex network of deep shafts with an extensive system of galleries (Hubert 1978; 1980; Weisgerber *et al.* 1980, 414–421.).

Rijckholt-St. Geertruid, Limburg, Netherlands

The extensive mining complex at Rijckholt consists of a maximum of 5000 shafts, which were in use over a period of approximately 1300 years. Extensive excavations of the site took place between 1964 and 1973 by the Prehistoric Flint Mines Working Group (Bosch 1979; Felder 1981; Felder *et al.* 1998; de Grooth 1998).

The sites above have been selected for analysis as they contain the largest pool of evidence of excavated and recorded material within the chronological time-scale identified. Although far more flint-mining sites are known within the study region stated and within the dates identified, the excavated material from them is limited. Figure 16.2 shows the relative chronology of these Early Neolithic (4500–3000 cal BC) flint-mining sites in western Europe, based on the latest and earliest calibrated dates recorded for each site under study. Overall the mines were in operation at approximately the same time, the data indicating a common exploitation period around 3800 cal BC.

In order to determine common cultural and ideological similarities within the Neolithic flint-mining communities, each of the mining sites will be considered with the aim of identifying similar or uniform practices within the mining traditions. It is necessary, however, to understand the influence of the environmental context in which this analysis rests, as the location and geology of each individual site will affect the mining process and aspects of its morphological and technological development. Once environmental and geological influences on the variation within the flint-mining traditions are understood, it will be possible to evaluate the similarities that remain and determine their cultural and ideological significance.

A methodology has therefore been constructed which identifies the different processes involved in flint mining. Each process is analysed to establish the variation that takes place throughout the mines in Europe (Table 16.1). This methodology is designed to determine why certain choices were made and to try to understand the reasoning behind the methods used. Ultimately, cultural or environmental determining factors are identified as the main cause of variation. Where the environmental or geological condition within each process

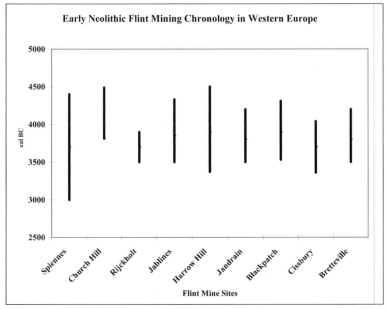

Figure 16.2. A schematic chronology for Early Neolithic flint-mining in western Europe.

MINING PROCESSES	VARIATIONS WITH EACH MINING PROCESS	DETERMINATION
Location and topography of the mines	• Plateau edges • Overlooking water • Distances from settlement areas	Environmental
Morphological structure of the mine	• Shafts and galleries • Open quarries • Bell pits • Small pits	Environmental
Positioning and quantity of mines	• Regular/Irregular spacing • Dispersed/Nucleated/Clustered positioning	Environmental
Flint seam exploited	• First seams • Specific seam • All seams	Cultural
Tools used to dig shafts	• Antlers • Flint picks • Bone tools • Wooden tools	Environmental
Mechanism of extraction	• Digging under seam and let gravity release the block/nodule. • Digging around chalk fissures until nodule is freed	Environmental
Mechanism of the removal of chalk and flint	• All chalk and flint removed to surface • Dispersed around empty galleries	Cultural
The process of backfilling the mine	• Mine left open – natural infill • Backfilled immediately in one go • Staged and purposeful backfilling	Cultural
Process of abandonment	• Abandoned due to collapse • Mining completed in quarry/shaft • Unknown abandonment	Environmental/ Cultural
Position of chipping and working floors	• In the mouths of filled shafts • Around the mouth of shafts • Scattered around mining complex	Cultural
Structure and contents of working floors	• Large/Small quantity of flint waste • Hearths and domestic debris • No domestic debris	Cultural
Tools constructed and manner of completion	• Axeheads • Blades • Other flint tools • Roughouts	Cultural

Table 16.1. Mining processes at European flint-mines.

cannot be the explanation for variation it remains to hypothesize upon socio-cultural and economic reasons for differences in mines. Thus the methodology identifies that mining processes such as the location, morphology, positioning of the mines, tools used, and the method of extraction are superficial differences largely dependent on environmental conditions.

For example, the structure of the mines at Rijckholt varies from those in West Sussex. Although both shaft galleries and small pits occur at both localities, the size and depths of each are very different. This is largely as a result of the prevailing geological conditions. At Rijckholt the chalk is generally poorly fractured, coarse and very soft. The bedrock is covered by 7m of loose gravels and loess overburden (Mortimore 1981). The site is also peppered with unstable solution channels, all of which subsequently affect the size, structure, and nature of exploitation of the mining complex. By contrast, the chalk of the Sussex Downs is more stable and lies closer to the surface. The Sussex mines do not seem to be affected by the problem of solution pipes. Thus, it might be suggested, different sets of engineering problems needed to be overcome in order to successfully proceed with the extraction process. The nature of the chalk influenced the process of extraction, including the tools used. Flint picks were the necessary tool of extraction at Rijckholt, whereas antler picks were more commonly used in the exploitation of flint at the Sussex mines.

Thus some mining processes appear to be choices made by necessity and not associated with any cultural stigma or preference. Other variations in mining practice are explored below with the aim of identifying how these might manifest cultural choices.

THE CHOICE OF FLINT SEAM EXPLOITED

At each site, the miners had to make decisions about which flint seams would be exploited. The choice of flint seam to be exploited would theoretically be governed by choosing the highest quality flint or maximizing the quantities exploited through the process of mining. However, the evidence from the mines suggests a quite different scenario – that the particular flint seam (or seams) exploited by Neolithic miners is a culturally determined factor.

Mining at Rijckholt and the majority of the Sussex mines by-passed the first easily exploitable seams and utilized specific bands of flint lower down (Curwen and Curwen 1926; Felder *et al.* 1998, 39; Pull 1932, 25). At Spiennes the miners often exploited the lowest safely accessible seams, reaching depths of up to 16m (Hubert 1978). At Jablines and Jandrain-Janrenouille, although first and second seams were exploited, the required flint continued to be difficult to access and mines often reached depths of 5m and 6m respectively (Bostyn and Lanchon 1992, 58–87; Hubert 1974).

The miners throughout this period were frequently bypassing the more easily accessible flint in the first or second seams they encountered and were deliberately exploiting the deeper seams. This suggests that exploiting the maximum quantity of flint was not the determining factor regarding the choice of seams extracted. Similarly, quality was not always paramount, as at Blackpatch where the high-quality uppermost seam was not utilized for flint extraction (Pull 1932, 25). With the exception of Bretteville-le-Rabet, the common cultural practice of exploiting certain specific seams, often the lowest safely accessible bands of flint, occurs amongst the remaining sites.

As with some stone axehead procurement sites, perhaps it was the difficulty of obtaining the raw material that created the social values embedded within the objects being manufactured (Topping 2005, 83–84).

TOOLS MANUFACTURED AND THE MANNER OF THEIR COMPLETION

The mouths of backfilled mine shafts were used as working-floors in all the sites except Jandrain-Jandrenouille and Spiennes. At these two sites and others, the edges of the shafts were used as chipping floors. Analysis of the waste debitage indicates evidence for the primary and secondary stages of de-cortication most commonly associated with axehead manufacture. Blade manufacture also takes place during this period along with other flint artefacts, but in much smaller quantities.

The main product manufactured at all of the mine sites in this study seems to be the trapezoidal axehead. The process of manufacture is almost always the same. The raw flint is chipped to form roughouts (Bostyn and Lanchon 1992, 136–139; Desloges 1986; Russell 2001, 45–48), which are transported to a secondary site for final finishing and polishing (Collet *et al.* 1971; Desloges 1986; Pull 1932, 112–114). This process is also identified at the chronologically contemporary stone axehead 'factories' of Great Langdale, Cumbria (Bradley and Edmonds 1993, 37–38) and to a certain extent at the dolerite A factories at Seledin, France (Le Roux 1971).

Although these similarities could be said to reflect fundamental common-sense solutions to the organization and demands of the industrial process involved, it is noteworthy that each site under analysis embodies such a set of common practices.

If almost all the sites are involved with the production of the same tools and in a similar way then perhaps, as Topping (1997) has suggested, they operate within a system of widespread cultural stigmas and taboos on how to mine flint and create axeheads.

THE PROCESS OF BACKFILLING A MINE

Attention has been paid in the description of numerous mining sites to the backfilling of the shafts. Within this cultural process the evidence shows that empty disused galleries are commonly used to disperse already excavated chalk rubble (Bostyn *et al.* 1992, 58–87; Desloges 1986; Felder *et al.* 1998, 39; Hubert 1974; Russell 2001, 27–34). There are purely economical and time and labour reasons for such a process, but the practice occurs throughout the mines of Europe.

Associated with this practice, we find evidence that certain galleries, usually those between two separate shafts, were left open; perhaps deliberately left rubble-free as emergency exits, thus ensuring access to the surface in case of a collapse. The mines at Rijckholt, Jandrain-Jandrenouille, Jablines, and potentially at Bretteville–la-Rabet, Church Hill, and Cissbury, all show evidence for this (Bostyn and Lanchon 1992; Desloges 1986; Felder *et al.* 1998, 22; Hubert 1974; Russell 2001).

Subsequent episodes of the backfilling of shafts not only show systematic, episodic accumulation, but also deliberate deposition within the shafts. Episodic shaft infilling is recorded at all the sites under study. Various episodes of deliberate and natural infilling appear to take place, illustrating the obscure importance of the backfill event (Bostyn and Lanchon 1992, 58–87; Desloges 1986; Felder *et al.* 1998, 22–27; Hubert 1974; Russell 2001, 87–91). A functional interpretation would expect backfilling to take place immediately and haphazardly in order to fill a dangerous and deep hole and to dispose of unwanted soil and extraction waste around the periphery of the shaft (Sieveking 1979). However, the evidence from certain shafts throughout the mines considered here indicates structured episodes of backfilling took place, in between periods of natural silting, often culminating with the mouths of the shaft being used as knapping floors.

Topping's recent work using ethnographic records hypothesizes formal structured deposition within the backfill of shafts. Using Shaft 27 at Cissbury as an example, he suggests that the first episodes of deposition within the shaft were associated with cleansing rituals and offerings, subsequent deposits were associated with the process of extraction, and later episodes of deposition were associated with tool production and rites of renewal (Topping 2005). This is an interesting concept, which raises the question as to whether such ideologies and beliefs potentially associated with depositional practices in the Cissbury mines could be extended to, and recognized at, the other mines of western Europe? To investigate this, certain depositional episodes from the sites within the study are highlighted briefly below.

At Church Hill good-quality tools were found throughout the galleries of Shaft 6, giving the impression the mines were abandoned in a hurry or that the tools were purposefully deposited. Within the fills of Shafts 1 and 4 were finished and unfinished tools, along with flakes and carved chalk objects (Russell 2001, 87–103).

Between the fills of Shaft 2 at Harrow Hill, deposits of axeheads, bones, and nests of flakes were identified. In Shaft 3, the two parts of a broken axehead were found at opposite ends of the shaft (Holleyman 1937, 239–242). Pull (1932, 37–40) recognized the artificial infilling of Shaft 1 at Blackpatch, identifying episodes of burning, along with deposits of bones and tools in varying stages of manufacture throughout the layers of backfill, one of which was described as an occupation layer.

The potential structured depositional nature of these finds mirrors those of Shaft 27 at Cissbury and thus similar theoretical explanations regarding the nature of the backfill event can be hypothesized.

At the Continental mines there are, for example, deposits of unused picks and roughout axeheads in Shaft 2 at Jandrain-Jandrenouille, along with quantities of flint picks throughout the backfill (Hubert 1974, 15). Similar phenomena were recognized at Bretteville-le-Rabet, where deposits of unused tools were also found within the shafts. Further evidence from the pits suggests tools were deposited at the base of exploited seams (Desloges 1986, 95). Hoards of picks were identified at Rijckholt deposited in the galleries and structured skull deposits have also been recorded (Felder *et al.* 1998, 25; Sieveking 1979). Such deposits could be interpreted as offerings, potentially associated with rites of renewal.

The large numbers of roughout axeheads found throughout the mine shafts at Jablines, Rijckholt, and Spiennes (Bostyn and Lanchon 1992; Felder *et al.* 1998; Verheyleweghen 1966), add to suppositions about the potential symbolic nature of the mines and the deliberate deposition of certain artefacts.

All these deposits highlight the importance and symbolic significance of material culture and its relative associations within a mine. Perhaps they point to episodes of liminality, with flint and chalk viewed as living entities within the miner's cosmos. Within this liminal framework deposits of unused picks could represent purity within a polluted mine, in which human beings had disturbed its natural order.

Further symbolic practices associated with flint mining can be recognized through the analysis of human remains deposited in the mines at Rijckholt. A skull with no mandible was deposited at the end of one of the galleries, in a shallow pit (de Grooth 1998). The gallery was later backfilled with chalk, except around the area of the skull (Bosch 1979; De Grooth 1998). Very similar practices have been identified at Spiennes, where buried skulls without mandibles occurred in deposits associated with a specially protected part (Verheyleweghen 1966).

The human remains identified in the Sussex mines do not indicate identical practices in southern Britain. At Blackpatch the disarticulated remains of an adult femur and human jaw bone from a young person were identified within Shaft 4, and at Cissbury the full skeleton of an adult woman was found at the entrance to a gallery in Shaft 27 (Russell 2001, 178–184). These individuals appear to have either been killed in the process of mining or to have been buried within the mine. This could well reflect the symbolic and structured nature of deposition associated with flint mining.

These common practices show that, across Europe, cultural ideas as well as the physical processes of mining technology and techniques were being transferred; perhaps the ideology and beliefs integrated with such activities and process were held in common as well. The integration of these strands of evidence helps us begin to visualize commonalities within the European flint-mining tradition and enables us to explore the nature of contact between these different communities and the common ideological bond that may lie between them.

BELIEFS AND ATTITUDES TOWARDS STONE

What can be hypothesized about the common ideologies as regard flint mining and the procurement of stone? This chapter has shown the importance given to the backfilling of mines and the subsequent placement of particular deposits in shaft infills. Perhaps these episodes and deposits could be linked to ethnographic and ancient myths associated with the ritual of mining and the regeneration of stone. Various rituals and rites have been recorded that were performed to ensure the continued productivity of mines and quarries (Desloges 1986; Eliade1956; Topping 2005, 85–90). The practice of depositing unused picks and roughout axeheads could, for example, have been symbolically analogous to planting a seed for the growth of a new crop.

It has also been suggested that the choice of flint to be exploited at many flint mines was related to the degree of difficulty in its procurement. This theme is echoed amongst stone axehead 'factories'. The porcellanite axehead quarry of Rathlin Island, off the north-east coast of Ireland, could only be accessed by sea and it was often the most isolated outcrops of suitable rock which were exploited at Langdale in the English Lake District and at Seledin in Brittany (Bradley and Edmonds 1993, 41; Le Roux 1971). Such attitudes towards the procurement of the raw material emphasize the social value of the axehead within the Early Neolithic cultures of western Europe.

Further common practices are the almost universal dominance of axehead manufacture at these early fourth millennium BC sites, and the subsequent method and process of manufacture of the axeheads. As at the stone quarries, axeheads are the primary product of manufacture at the flint mines, and the practice of creating the roughouts at the mine before being transported to a secondary location for finishing is also the same as at the stone quarries. Perhaps it is in the association with axeheads that the true symbolic significance of the quarry and mining sites lay. The axehead is self-evidently a common motif and artefact throughout the Early Neolithic (Barber 2001). Whether on account of their aesthetic beauty, the distances travelled by way of exchange, or the variety and affiliation of the deposits from which they derived, axeheads were objects associated with highly charged symbolism (Whittle 1995).

As the place where an axehead was created, its birthplace so to speak, the mine or quarry would probably also have been steeped in symbolism. The stone bedrock could have been perceived as the mother of the axehead; this is where the life cycle of the axehead began. The archaeological record contains a great deal of information about the deposition of axeheads in their final resting places and many archaeologists have identified this deposition as symbolic practice. Deposition in pits and ditches could be synonymous with concepts associated with the ending of life's journey and the eventual returning to the earth. The evidence from the flint mines shows the importance placed upon episodes of backfilling and the significance of structured depositional events, thus adding weight to the symbolic significance that is also placed upon sites associated with the genesis of axeheads.

Naturally, such a hypothetical interpretation for the ideologies associated with flint mining must be treated very cautiously. Other objects were manufactured at the mines; axeheads were not the sole product from extracted flint. Would the blades, flakes, scrapers, arrowheads, etc., made from mined flint also have distinctive connotations? In the Later Neolithic axeheads were not the primary product at flint mine and quarry sites, where blades, knives, and other artefacts dominated, as at Grand Pressigny in France and Grime's Graves in England (Cordier 1956; Saville 1981). Structured depositions arguably appear to still take place at these later sites, even though the axehead itself no longer holds the same importance. Perhaps the Later Neolithic sees a new ideology evolving as a variant of the old?

To explore the possibilities of such ideologies, further investigation of the association of lithic raw materials and axeheads in non-mine contexts, such as causewayed enclosures, is required. Martyn Barber (2001, 25) has previously highlighted the presence of flint nodules in ceremonial monuments, perhaps thus representing the symbolic importance of the raw material. Also the identification of those intermediary locations at which the finishing of roughouts and the polishing of axeheads took place would permit a fuller understanding of the axehead lifecycle, and presumably such places would similarly be part of the same cultural ideology associated with the mines and quarries.

CONCLUSION

The evidence collated to date implies that mine and quarry sites across western Europe not only share common morphological characteristics but are also involved in common cultural practices. Many of the differences between the mines are superficial and can largely be explained by environmental circumstances. Beyond this is a level of similarity that extends beyond technological demands. The various broad similarities identified across Europe and within flint-mining and stone-quarrying traditions show that in essence Early Neolithic communities seem to share not only a technical awareness but also an ideological consciousness regarding the extraction of stone. It is this action of extracting stone from the earth for the creation of axeheads which appears to be integral to this early western Neolithic common ideology.

If similar mining practices and perhaps associated ideologies apply contemporaneously along the Sussex Downs and on the Continent, is it possible to identify further common practices and ideologies embodied within other cross-channel Early Neolithic activities and monuments? Using the flint-mining traditions across Europe, this chapter has begun to explore not only the tangible evidence for cross-channel contact within this period, but has endeavoured to understand and suggest elements of a common ideology between western European Neolithic communities.

BIBLIOGRAPHY

Barber, M., 2001, Flint mines in the early Neolithic and beyond. Raw material sources and later prehistory in southern England. In A. T. Smith and A. Brooks (eds), *Holy Ground: Theoretical Issues Relating to the Landscape and Material Culture of Ritual Space. Papers from a Session held at the Theoretical Archaeology Group Conference, Cardiff 1999*, 21–26. Oxford: British Archaeological Reports (International Series S956).

Barber, M., Field, D. and Topping, P., 1999, *The Neolithic Flint Mines of England*. Swindon: English Heritage.

Bosch, P. W., 1979, A Neolithic flint mine. *Scientific American* 240(6), 126–132.

Bostyn, F. and Lanchon, Y. (eds), 1992, *Jablines: Le Haut Château (Seine-et-Marne). Une minière de silex au Néolithique*. Paris: Editions de la Maison des Sciences de l'Homme (Documents d'Archéologie Française 35).

Bostyn, F. and Lanchon, Y., 1995, The Neolithic flint mine at *Jablines, 'le Haut Château' (Seine-et-Marne)*. *Archaeologia Polona* 33, 297–310.

Bradley, R. and Edmonds, M., 1993, *Interpreting the Axe Trade: Production and Exchange in Neolithic Britain*. Cambridge: Cambridge University Press.

Collet, H., Deramaix, I., Sartieaux, P. and Vander Linden, M., 1997, Fouille préventive de puits d'extraction de silex à Petit-Spiennes (Hainaut). *Notae Praehistoricae* 17, 203–212.

Cordier, G., 1956, Le vrai visage du Grand-Pressigny. In *Congrès de la Société Préhistorique Française, XVe Session Poitiers-Angouleme*, 416–445. Paris: Société Préhistorique Française.

Curwen, E. and Curwen, E. C., 1926, Harrow Hill flint mine excavation 1924–5. *Sussex Archaeological Collections* 67, 103–138.

Desloges, J., 1986, Fouilles de mines à silex sur le site néolithique de Bretteville-le-Rabet (Calvados). *Revue Archéologique de l'Ouest* (suppl. n°1), 73–101. (Actes du Xe colloque interrégional sur le Néolithique, Caen, 1983).

Eliade, M., 1956, *Forgerons et Alchimistes*. Paris: Flammarion.

Engelen, F. H. G. (ed.), 1981, *Third International Symposium on Flint, 24–27 Mei 1979 – Maastricht*. Maastricht: Nederlandse Geologische Vereniging (*Staringia* 6).

Felder, P. J., 1981, Prehistoric flint mining at Ryckholt- St. Geertruid (Netherlands) and Grimes Graves (England). In F. H. G. Engelen (ed.), *Third International Symposium on Flint, 24–27 Mei 1979 – Maastricht*, 57–62. Maastricht: Nederlandse Geologische Vereniging (*Staringia* 6).

Felder, P. J., Rademakers, P. C. M. and de Grooth, M. E. Th. (eds.), 1998, *Excavations of Prehistoric Flint Mines at Rijckholt-St.Geertruid (Limburg, The Netherlands)*. Bonn. Deutschen Gesellschaft für Ur- und Frühgeschichte (Archäologische Berichte 12).

de Grooth, M. E. Th., 1998, The flint mines at Rijckholt-Sint Geertruid and their socio-economic interpretation. In M. Edmonds and C. Richards (eds), *Understanding the Neolithic of North-Western Europe*, 351–369. Glasgow: Cruithne Press.

Holleyman, G., 1937, Harrow Hill excavations, 1936. *Sussex Archaeological Collections* 78, 230–251.

Hubert, F., 1974, Minières néolithiques à Jandrain-Jandrenouille en Brabant. *Archaeologica Belgica* 167, 5–45.

Hubert, F., 1978, Une minière néolithique à silex au Camp-à-Cayaux de Spiennes. *Archaeologica Belgica* 210, 5–44.

Hubert, F., 1980, Zum Silexbergbau von Spiennes (B1). In G. Weisgerber, R. Slotta and J. Weiner (eds.), *5000 Jahre Feuersteinbergbau. Die Suche nach dem Stahl der Steinzeit*, 124–139. Bochum: Deutschen Bergbau-Museum.

Le Roux, C. T., 1971, A stone axe-factory in Brittany. *Antiquity* 45, 283–288.

Mortimore, R. N., 1981, The engineering domains and classification of chalk in relation to Neolithic flint mining with special reference to Grime's Graves England and Rijckholt-St. Geertruid Holland. In F. H.G Engelen (ed.), *Third International Symposium on Flint, 24–27 Mei 1979 – Maastricht*, 30–35. Maastricht: Nederlandse Geologische Vereniging (*Staringia* 6).

Pull, J. H., 1932, *The Flint Miners of Blackpatch*. London: Williams and Norgate.

Russell, M. (ed.), 2001, *Rough Quarries, Rocks and Hills: John Pull and the Neolithic Flint Mines of Sussex*. Oxford: Oxbow Books.

Saville, A. 1981, *Grimes Graves, Norfolk. Excavations 1971–1972. Vol 2: The Flint Assemblage*. London: HSMO

Sieveking, G. de G., 1979, Grimes Graves and prehistoric European flint mining. In H. Crawford (ed.), *Subterranean Britain: Aspects of Underground Archaeology*, 1–43. London: John Baker.

Sieveking, G. de G. and Newcomer, M. N. (eds), 1987, *The Human Uses of Flint and Chert. Proceedings of the Fourth International Flint Symposium held at Brighton Polytechnic 10–15 April 1983*. Cambridge: Cambridge University Press.

Topping, P. 1997, Structured deposition, symbolism and the English flint mines. In R. Schild and Z. Sulgostowska (eds), *Man and Flint: Proceedings of the VIIth International Flint Symposium, Warszawa – Ostrowiec Swietokrzyski, September 1995*, 127–132. Warszawa: Institute of Archaeology and Ethnography, Polish Academy of Sciences.

Topping, P. 2005, Shaft 27 revisited: an ethnography of Neolithic flint extraction. In P. Topping and M. Lynott (eds), *The Cultural Landscape of Neolithic Mines*, 63–93. Oxford: Oxbow Books.

Verheyleweghen, J. 1966, Le néolithique minier belge: son origine et ses relations culturelles. *Palaeohistoria* 12, 529–557.

Weisgerber G., Slotta R. and Weiner J. (eds), 1980, *5000 Jahre Feuersteinbergbau. Die Suche nach dem Stahl der Steinzeit*. Bochum: Deutschen Bergbau-Museum.

Whittle, A., 1995, Gifts from the earth: symbolic dimensions of the use and production of Neolithic flint and stone axes. *Archaeologia Polona* 33, 247–259.